S0-BIO-344

VB6 UML
Design and Development

Jake Sturm

Wrox Press Ltd. ®

VB6 UML
Design and Development

© 1999 Wrox Press

All rights reserved. No part of this book may be reproduced, stored in a retrieval system or transmitted in any form or by any means, without the prior written permission of the publisher, except in the case of brief quotations embodied in critical articles or reviews.

The author and publisher have made every effort in the preparation of this book to ensure the accuracy of the information. However, the information contained in this book is sold without warranty, either express or implied. Neither the authors, Wrox Press nor its dealers or distributors will be held liable for any damages caused or alleged to be caused either directly or indirectly by this book.

wrox

Published by Wrox Press Ltd,
Arden House, 1102 Warwick Road, Acocks Green, Birmingham B27 6BH, UK.
Printed in Canada
3 4 5 6 7 8 9 TRI 00 99

ISBN 1-861002-51-3

Trademark Acknowledgements

Wrox has endeavored to provide trademark information about all the companies and products mentioned in this book by the appropriate use of capitals. However, Wrox cannot guarantee the accuracy of this information.

Credits

Author
Jake Sturm

Additional Material
Russell Freeman
Alex Homer
Dave Sussman
Donald Xie

Managing Editor
Dominic Shakeshaft

Editors
Craig A. Berry
Kate Hall
Susan Holmes

Technical Reviewers
Matt Bortniker
Henri Cesbron
Robert Chang
Stephen Danielson

Technical Reviewers
Robin Dewson
Hope Hatfield
Robann Mateja
Frederick T. Rossmark Jr.
Marc H. Simpkin
Mike Sussman
Gwen Sturm
Rob Vieira
Sakhr Youness

Design/Layout
Noel Donnelly

Cover
Andrew Guillaume
Concept by Third Wave
Photo by Unique Photography

Index
Catherine Alexander

About the Author

Jake Sturm has extensive programming experience, throughout all levels of software development. He has been involved in every aspect of Visual Basic application development, from simple executables to complicated Client Server applications and a host of Active-X controls. Jake has expanded his programming from simply using VB for an entire project, to include the full range of Microsoft BackOffice products such as SQL server, IIS, and MTS. He has also worked extensively with VBA in both Microsoft Office and ASP pages.

Jake has always viewed programming and project management as a creative process, no different from an artist creating a sculpture or painting. Visual Basic, combined with Microsoft's Back Office products, allows the developer to create a masterpiece.

Presently, Jake is working for Microsoft Corporation as a Consultant.

He lives in New Jersey with Gwen, his life and business partner, her two beautiful daughters, Jill and Lynzie, his son, Will, who is a computer genius, and their four psychotic cats.

Dedication

To my wife, Gwen, whose support and endless hours of work on this book have made this book possible. To our four children, Jill, Lynzie, Will and Maya, who have waited patiently for this book to be finished so that we could spend time with them again. To my mother, Estelle, who has always believed in me and helped me get to this point.

Acknowlegements

The creation of a book is a team effort. The author is in the center, developing and laying out the ideas for the book. The author works out a rough image of the text, while an entire team stands behind him refining, polishing and perfecting it. The most important member of my team was my wife, Gwen, who has been at my side every minute that I have been writing this book. She has worked with me, editing text and creating drawings, often into the wee hours of the morning. I admire and appreciate her dedication.

The entire staff at Wrox Press has also been phenomenal. They have worked countless hours to shape and mold this book into its current format. I would like to acknowledge some of the people there, in particular: $(Dom)^2$, Craig and Susan. I especially want to thank Dominic Shakeshaft, my original and primary contact for this book, who has spent many late hours pulling this together. I would also like to thank Craig Berry for his detailed review of the code, his patience, and for his suggestions for improving the code.

Finally, I would like to thank, you, the reader, for purchasing this book. I hope this book provides you with a great deal of information, and answers to questions that you have been searching everywhere for. I also hope that this book empowers you to use Visual Basic to make Enterprise projects in a clear, simple way.

Table of Contents

Chapter 5: Class Diagrams   133

Get ADO
connection

[Successful]

Set Recordset
cursor location

Set Recordset
source

Set Recordset
connection

Introduction

Congratulations! By choosing this book you have realized, or are about to realize, that you need to employ some form of design methodology to help you design your applications. This is a conclusion that is realized by surprisingly few Visual Basic developers – and it's time the VB developer community got the message.

Visual Basic is to blame here. VB has always been a very easy language to develop in - perhaps too easy. Until VB5 and 6, Visual Basic was perceived as a tool for quickly prototyping and testing applications, and as such was never really used for any serious development. Times change though - VB has grown up It's now quite possible and even preferable to develop Enterprise solutions primarily in VB, as it is still so easy to use. Unfortunately, many developers still think that they can dive straight into coding their n-tier applications, and consequently run into all sort of problems. I've got a hat-full of anecdotes of developers having to rewrite huge sections of code because they didn't design and manage the project properly.

UML, or the Unified Modeling Language, is the solution to these problems. It provides a comprehensive system for designing object-oriented applications in a logical, structured manner. Through the use of a series of diagrams, you can gradually refine your design until you are left with your objects and their properties, methods and events. It's an iterative process, so that you may continually revisit your analysis to create the most effective design. It also helps you to discover common patterns in the application's structure, which allow you to code the implementation in a more efficient and practical manner.

This book isn't just about using UML to design your applications though. It's also about how to turn all the analysis and wonderful diagrams that you have created into Visual Basic code.

In this respect, we're going to be following the design and implementation of an involved DNA project throughout the book. We'll start at the project's beginning, follow it right through the design stage, and finally implement that design in VB. By the end of the book, we'll have done a lot more than designing a VB project - we'll have built a fully working application. More than this even: we'll have created a DNA framework, from which you will be able to take our basic design and implementation and extend it to your own projects.

UML should be an essential part of any application design and the sooner Visual Basic developers come to realize this, the less time and effort will be wasted in ineffectual design.

What's Covered in This Book

VB6 UML: Design and Development will take you through the building of a DNA application, from the initial design decisions through to its implementation using MTS, RDS and ADO. At each step, we'll examine how we can employ UML analysis to develop and improve our design.

In Chapter 1, we'll see an overview of the main UML diagrams and learn why we should be using UML in our project design. We'll also see how well UML and VB tie together.

In Chapter 2, we'll cover some basic aspects of Project Management and take our first look at the Northwind project we're going to be developing throughout the book. We'll also learn how frameworks and patterns can help to improve our design and reduce coding effort.

In Chapter 3, we'll start the design process in earnest. We'll interview some of the main actors in the Northwind company and develop our first UML diagrams. This initial use case analysis will form the basis for the majority of the following analysis and design. At the end of this chapter, we'll have a good idea of the principle objects that we're going to be developing.

In Chapter 4, we'll move on from our initial use case analysis and begin to create interaction diagrams that allow us to not only determine the methods our objects need, but also help us to see common patterns between the objects. Discovering patterns is a powerful technique that allows us to reduce the amount of coding that we need to write.

In Chapter 5, we'll refine our design down yet further and begin to construct a picture of the classes that will form our objects. We'll think about how our classes will interact and what properties they will need.

In Chapter 6, we'll go back to the use case and design a prototype user interface. Through this prototype and additional meetings with user we can see how to design effective and efficient GUIs.

In Chapter 7, we'll take a breather, assess what we've achieved so far, and look ahead to how we will begin to design the VB implementation of our project. This chapter marks a change in focus from the user requirements design analysis to the framework design analysis - how we will use technologies such as DNA, RDS and MTS in our application.

In Chapter 8, we'll take a break from design and explore the technologies and frameworks that we're going to be implementing. We'll get a brief introduction to DNA, ADO, RDS and class hierarchies. We'll then see how these frameworks tie in with the design we've created so far.

In Chapter 9, we'll see how the frameworks collide with the UML design in the form of activity diagrams.

By Chapter 10, we're ready to start coding. Before we dive into the main project implementation, though, we're going to build a test project to test out some the technologies and design we've developed so far. We'll encounter some of the unique problems that arise when developing a DNA application, and how best to resolve them. We'll learn that our current design doesn't scale very well and that we'll need to modify it to include MTS.

Chapter 11 takes off from Chapter 10 by giving a quick overview of MTS and then we begin the coding in earnest. By the end of this chapter, we'll have a full implemented server component.

Chapters 12 and 13, cover all the details of implementing client-side components for the server component. We'll see how we the design we've developed allows us to re-use a lot of our code across components.

In Chapter 14, we'll construct the GUI that we prototyped earlier in the book and see how our design requires very little code on the user interface to function.

Finally, in Chapter 15, we'll take a quick look at Unit Testing and Quality Control and learn some methods of testing and debugging our components.

What You Need to Use This Book

This book requires Visual Basic 6.0 (preferably the Enterprise Edition). You should also have Windows NT Option Pack installed so that you have MTS and IIS (or PWS for 9x platforms). Although you can run the project without either of the above.

I haven't used any modeling software such as Visual Modeler or Rational Rose but feel free to use them or any other software you have to follow along with me.

Conventions Used

I've used a number of different styles of text and layout in the book to help differentiate between different kinds of information. Here are some of the styles I've used and an explanation of what they mean:

> **These boxes hold important, not-to-be forgotten, mission-critical details which are directly relevant to the surrounding text.**

Background information, asides and references appear in text like this.

❑ **Important Words** are in a bold font
❑ Words that appear on the screen, such as menu options, are in a similar font to the one used on screen, for example, the <u>F</u>ile menu
❑ Keys that you press on the keyboard, like *Ctrl* and *Enter*, are in italics
❑ All filenames, function names and other code snippets are in this style: DblTxtBx

Code that is new or important is presented like this:

```
Private Sub Customer_OnAdd()

  MsgBox "The AddToDatabase method has been invoked."

End Sub
```

Whereas code that we've seen before or has little to do with the matter being discussed, looks like this:

```
Private Sub Customer_OnAdd()

  MsgBox "The AddToDatabase method has been invoked."

End Sub
```

Source Code

All the projects that are given in this book can be downloaded from Wrox's web sites at:

```
http://www.wrox.com/
http://www.wrox.co.uk/
```

Tell Us What You Think

This is my first book and I hope that you'll find it useful and enjoyable. You are the one that counts and I would really appreciate your views and comments on this book. You can contact me either by email (feedback@wrox.com) or via the Wrox web site.

Get ADO
connection

[Successful]

Set Recordset
cursor location

Set Recordset
source

Set Recordset
connection

Introducing the Unified Modeling Language

Many people have a rather vague idea about what **UML**, or the **Unified Modeling Language**, actually is and how and why it's used. This is especially problematic in Visual Basic because it is so easy to dive straight into the IDE and produce a lot of code very quickly. This is one of Visual Basic's best and worst points.

Visual Basic is great in that you can knock up a project with relatively little effort, especially if you use any of the myriad of wizards that Microsoft have so helpfully provided. There is a flip side though. Because we can code VB relatively easily, there's a tendency not to think about project design beforehand, but rather to do the design 'as we go along'... which is just a gentle way of admitting that no design work is going into the project at all. VB programmers can get away with this on small experimental applications, but when they move into more ambitious programs - and most particularly, into multi-tier application development - then it's a serious professional error to rely on such an ad hoc design approach.

Designing even a two-tier client/server application is scary enough though. This is when we really should begin to think about using UML. UML, as you will see throughout the book, provides an object-oriented method by which you, and others in your development team, can create a design for an effective, efficient application.

In this chapter we will cover:

- ❑ A definition of UML and why we would want to use it
- ❑ A brief introduction to some of the core UML diagrams we'll be using
- ❑ An overview of the whole UML design process

❑   How UML diagrams gradually define the project we're designing
❑   How Visual Basic and UML work together
❑   The approach that I'll be using in this book

From now on I will refer to the Unified Modeling Language as UML.

What UML Is (and what it is not)

As the programming community began to see that object-oriented programming (OOP) solved many of the problems of medium to large project development, it also became clear that there had to be some efficient, effective, uniform method of designing object-oriented projects.

UML is a set of standard models used to design an object-oriented project.

However, while UML does provide a mechanism that helps us to design object-oriented projects, it offers little in the way of help when it comes to coding the project.

UML does not describe the implementation of these models.

So there you have it: UML is a set of standard models to design object-oriented projects - but it is *not* a description of how to actually implement those models. We will be exploring the full meaning of this definition of UML throughout the book - but it's not a bad place to start.

Before we go any further, you might be considering this question: is UML the only set of standard models to help with OO programming? A brief history of UML will answer this inquiry, and also offer you an idea of the impressive credentials that UML has behind it as a practical tool.

A Brief History of UML

Over the past two decades, several modeling methodologies and languages have emerged, each having its own strength and weakness. The prominent methods have been:

❑   The Booch method
❑   Object Modeling Technique (OMT)
❑   Object-Oriented Software Engineering (OOSE)
❑   Coad-Yourdon and Fusion

In 1994, the three principal authors of Booch, (Grady Booch), OMT (James Rumbaugh) and OOSE (Ivor Jacobson) started the process of merging the three methods to form a Unified Modeling Language.

The Unified Modeling Language has since been developed by a consortium of companies led by Rational Software Corporation. In November 1997, UML 1.1 was certified as an industry standard by the **Object Management Group (OMG)**.

Members of the OMG include almost all of the major software companies, including Microsoft, IBM, Computer Associates, Oracle, Sun, and Compaq. Such a strong industry alliance ensures that the UML is well accepted and implemented in the computer industry. Currently, many modeling tools such as Rational's *Rational Rose* support the UML.

What Exactly is a Model?

Let's dig a little deeper now about what UML actually is... so far, we've established that UML is a set of standard models that we use to design object-oriented programming projects. But what do we mean by a *model*, and what, accordingly, does that mean a *modeling language* is?

A **model** is a description of the problem we are set to solve. It simplifies the reality by capturing a subset of entities and relationships in the problem domain.

> *A problem domain describes not only a particular problem but also the conditions under which the problem occurs. It's therefore a description of a problem and the relevant context of that problem.*

A model shows us what the problem is and how we are going to tackle it. We may use diagrams, text, or any other agreed form of communication to present the model.

> **Models visualize the system we are about to build.**

A **modeling language**, therefore, is a language for describing models. Modeling languages generally use diagrams to represent various entities and their relationships within the model.

UML was created to fulfill these tasks:

- ❑ To represent all parts of a project being built with object-oriented techniques
- ❑ To establish a way to connect ideas, concepts and general design techniques with the creation of object-oriented code
- ❑ To create a model that can be understood by humans and also by computers - so that a computer can generate a major portion of the application automatically

UML accomplishes these tasks by having a series of different models. Each model represents a different view of the project. Some models are built from others, so there is a logical sequence in which the models are built.

Why Use UML?

Before we actually overview some of the details of UML and why it's so powerful, it's worth taking a moment to put everything we've discussed so far in context: why use UML?

I mentioned earlier that without employing a decent design method such as UML, most VB programmers will only really be able to develop programs in an ad hoc manner. This will, more often than not, lead to badly thought through programs and, ultimately, a lot of unsuccessful VB applications. We therefore need to use UML because it's a key to successful project design and development for us.

Many developers quickly feel overwhelmed when they try to build Enterprise level Visual Basic projects. These projects are difficult and complex. They not only require knowledge of how to program several different types of Visual Basic components, but also how to make these components work with server products, such as Microsoft Transaction Server (MTS), SQL Server (or other databases) and Internet Information Server (IIS).

As this book will show you, UML modeling is the key to being able to successfully build an advanced VB project - such as an Enterprise project. You will see how UML models help us to understand our user's requirements, then transform these requirements into a realistic project design, and finally help turn that design into the most efficient Visual Basic code possible... with the least amount of effort. These models will also cut down on overall costs and development time.

While UML is an essential tool for creating Visual Basic projects, it is only a part of a larger puzzle. In addition to understanding UML, a Visual Basic developer must:

❑ Understand the features of Visual Basic, and how these features integrate with server products
❑ Know how to apply these VB features to the design of the project
❑ Know how to turn their design into Visual Basic code

When we first try to put all of these pieces together in a Visual Basic project, we can easily get lost in the maze of components, programming techniques, and constraints of the system. From our very first steps into the world of UML, I will show you how UML models can create order out of this chaos. If you want to learn how to build Visual Basic Enterprise solutions in a rational, sane way, with a high probability of success, then this book is for you.

UML: The Key to Success

You may well be beginning to form a vague idea of how UML can help with our projects, but you may also be wondering how other areas of project management tie in with using UML.

There is a remarkably strong connection between UML and project management - please consider these three points:

❑ A successful object-oriented Visual Basic project is built on a foundation of good project management
❑ The foundation of good project management is thoroughly designing your project
❑ The foundation for good object-oriented design is UML

We shall discuss the concept of project management in detail in the next chapter. However, I wish to emphasize at this point that ultimately *a successful VB project depends on using UML*.

This is a visual representation of a simple fact: an understanding of UML provides the foundations for developing a well-designed and well-managed Visual Basic project.

The Project Development Process

Although UML is the key to developing a project, it does not necessarily help in defining the actual process that we will be following. As you will see, project development is a circuitous, iterative process. It can essentially be divided into the following phases:

- ❑   Requirements Analysis
- ❑   Analysis
- ❑   Design
- ❑   Implementation - Coding and Testing

The analysis and design phases, especially, involve the use of UML diagrams.

A Whirlwind Tour of UML

To get you familiar with some of the diagrams and terms we'll be using throughout the book, I am going to take you on a whirlwind tour of UML. While this will be just a quick overview of UML, it should provide an initial insight into how UML can help us. By presenting this overview now, I will also be able to offer you an early glimpse of the larger UML picture.

> *In case you're wondering, we'll be learning more about the full details of UML diagrams and exactly what those details mean from Chapter 3 onwards. For now, enjoy the whirlwind tour so you can see how all the parts of UML fit together to form a cogent design method for VB programmers.*

The building blocks of UML are things and relationships:

- ❑   **Things** in UML describe conceptual and physical elements in the application domain
- ❑   **Relationships** connect things together

These two elements are brought together in UML **diagrams** to help us visualize things and their relationships in a well-structured format.

UML Diagrams

There are quite a few UML diagrams that you can use when designing your application, and you can pick and choose those which will be of most use to you. However, there is a basic core set of diagrams that you will almost certainly use. This core set of diagrams includes:

❑ Use Case Models
❑ Interaction Diagrams
❑ Class Diagrams
❑ Activity Diagrams

We'll now run through these types of diagram at whirlwind pace - I'll explain how you can methodically go about creating your own diagrams later on in the book, when we come to build a real-world project. You'll notice, as we run through them, that some diagram types have sub-types themselves (such as collaboration and sequence diagrams). This may be your first clue as to the richness and diversity of UML as an analytical design tool.

> **Notice that as we progress through this sequence of UML diagrams, we will also be progressing towards an ever more focused and clearly defined idea of the project we are designing and planning to develop. This is one of the fundamental points of the UML approach.**

Use Case Models

This is the first step on our journey towards a clear definition of the project we are designing with UML. We go straight to the people who will use the system we're building. The **use case** model translates the user's needs into an easy to understand model. The user may be an individual or an external system and is known as an **actor**. So in a nutshell, the use case model is a representation of how the system, or part of the system, works from the actor's point of view.

Use case models can be built from interviews with the user, and are the first step in converting the user's needs and requirements into a useful model.

> *Use cases are more like a model than a diagram because they describe the system, or parts of the system, with words rather than with pictures.*

Use cases are detailed enough to include all of the information on the project, but simple enough for even the most technically challenged user to understand. Use cases can also be associated with **business rules**, which explain special rules, related to the use case.

Let's take an example. In an order entry application, the use cases could include descriptions of various sub-parts of the system. These sub-parts, that together could make up the whole system, could be such things such as Taking an Order, Creating a New Customer, etc. For the use case Create New Customer, there could be a verbal description of the process of creating a new customer that looked as follows:

USE CASE: CREATE NEW CUSTOMER

Overview
The main purpose of this use case is to create a new Customer

Primary Actor
Sales Representative

Secondary Actor
None

Starting Point
The use case starts when the actor makes a request to create a new Customer

End Point
The actor's request to create a Customer is either completed or cancelled

Flow of Events
The actor is prompted to enter information that defines the Customer, such as Name, Address, etc. The actor will then enter the information on the Customer.

The actor can choose to save the information or cancel the operation. If the actor decides to save the information the new Customer is created in the system, and the list of Customers is updated.

Alternative Flow of Events
The actor attempts to add a Customer that already exists. The system will notify the user and cancel the create operation.

Measurable Result
A Customer is added to the system

Business Rules
Customer
Customer Fields
Restrict Customer Create

Use Case Extensions
None

Without getting too heavily involved right now in the details of this use case, what we're seeing here is a verbal description of what happens when someone using the program we want to design needs to create a new customer. Actors are identified (sales representatives). Start and end points located (in this case, a sales representative asking to create a new customer, and successfully having created a new customer), and a flow of events are drawn up to explain how the system can get from the start point to the end point. Further to this, some alternative sequences are mentioned (perhaps the user decides they don't want to add a customer half way through the process), measurable results are defined, and some business rules are created.

One of these business rules is called **Restrict Customer Create**. This business rule has been added to the design of this project to ensure that nobody will be able to create a customer who already exists on the system. This **Restrict Customer Create** business rule might be written as follows:

BUSINESS RULE: RESTRICT CUSTOMER CREATE

Overview
This rule is for when a Customer is added to the system

Business Rule Type
Requirement

Business Rule
Each Customer must have a unique CustomerID

Each Customer should only be listed once in the system

Derived Business Rules
None

This definition simply describes the business rule itself and what type of rule it is, and then states the conditions of the rule being defined. Business rules are highly contextual to the actual business environment in which the program is being written, but this is a good way to present them clearly and professionally.

Depending on the size of the system we're working on, we may actually need to create quite a few of these use case statements and business rules before we have captured the key aspects of the system we're designing. It's crucial, however, that we draw up these statements from the people who will be using the system, and the people who want to see the system in place. It's the first step in our design process.

That's all we need to know about use cases for now - but you'll see a much more in-depth discussion and tutorial of them in Chapter 3.

Interaction Diagrams

Interaction diagrams are the next step of the UML design process. Interaction diagrams concentrate on showing how objects or things in the system interact with each other to give a dynamic view of the system. There are two basic types of interaction diagram:

❑ **sequence** diagrams
❑ **collaboration** diagrams

Essentially these both model the same information, except that sequence diagrams emphasize time ordering whereas collaboration diagrams show spatial or structural organization. We'll take a quick look at both of these now, and pick up on sequence diagrams later on in Chapter 4.

For the most part, you choose to create either collaboration diagrams or sequence diagrams. While we will discuss both types in this whirlwind tour of UML, we will primarily be using sequence diagrams throughout this book.

Sequence Diagrams

This type of diagram can be used to convert the written use case models that we saw in the previous section into a clearer visual model. This visual model will show how the objects associated with a particular use case communicate with each other and with users over time. Sequence diagrams are very general. For example, they may show that some Object 1 passes a message to some other Object 2, and that Object 2 then performs some operation within itself and finally returns the message back:

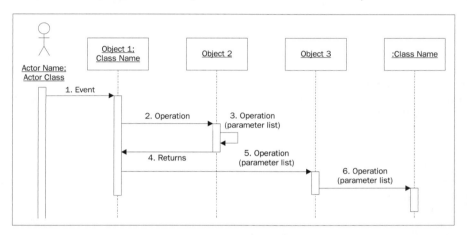

The internal workings of Object 1 that led to the creation of the message, and the internal workings of Object 2 that led to the return message, are not shown in sequence diagrams. (Details of the inner workings of the objects are represented in another type of diagram called an activity diagram - which we'll see in a later phase of the UML design process.)

Sequence diagrams map out every possible sequence of events that can be performed within each use case, including correct and incorrect paths. The correct paths in the sequence diagrams can be used to design the GUI of the project as they show what the user will need to do to interact with the application. Incorrect sequences will later be used to map out errors and how to handle these errors.

Sequence diagrams also show what public methods and properties our components must have. You can compare the sequence diagrams for one or more components and attempt to find patterns that exist that can be used to simplify the coding of the components.

Collaboration Diagrams

Collaboration diagrams are also built from the use cases - but that this time the emphasis is on the spatial distribution of the objects involved. This is not to say that there are no temporal elements in collaboration diagrams, since the sequence of events is mapped using numbers:

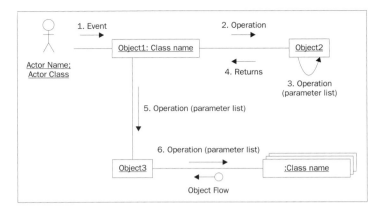

Personally, I often find this type of diagram quite confusing in comparison with the equivalent sequence diagrams. This particular collaboration diagram presents the *same* situation as the sequence diagram we just looked at - Object 1 and Object 2 have exactly the same relationships as before. However, it should be said that there are times when collaboration diagrams can make good sense - especially if we find that we want to emphasize a set of objects themselves rather than any sequence of events between them.

We're still not finished yet though - the final stage in the overall UML design process is to move on to our class diagrams.

Class Diagrams

A class diagram is a simple static picture of a class; as such, it will include all of the public and private methods and properties of that class. Class diagrams are, of course, built from use cases and sequence diagrams that we've been developing throughout the UML design process.

Here's a sample class diagram:

This sample class diagram is simply a schematic layout of the relevant information that we would need to go away and create the objects we've developed in our UML design process straight into the VB programming environment.

Naturally, for a larger project we would probably need to derive many such class diagrams in order to complete the design of all the objects involved in our system.

We'll see class diagrams in much more detail in Chapter 5.

Using class diagrams and software products, such as HOW from Riverton Software, we can automatically generate code for our applications. In this book I will not use any UML software products however: my aims here are to teach you what's really happening from the ground up. Once you understand the underlying concepts, the decision is yours whether you choose to use a package such as HOW, or write all your own code directly.

Activity Diagrams

Activity diagrams take the information available from the collaboration and sequence diagrams that we've just looked at, and present that information in a more detailed fashion. The purpose of activity diagrams is now to show the inner workings for a particular object.

> **As you may have noticed, we are gradually moving towards more and more detail about our project design as we proceed through the different UML diagrams.**

Activity diagrams can map out a method or property showing what that method or property has to do in a step-by-step manner. Activity diagrams will look very similar to mapping out a method or property using pseudo-code. This detailed map can then be used to explore the best method of coding a method or property, check for missing or unnecessary sections, and as a guide to writing the code. Here is a sample activity diagram:

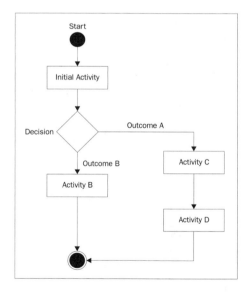

This activity diagram simply specifies what Activity is to be initiated at a certain Decision point, depending on the outcome of that Decision. This is a step-by-step definition of certain situations that pertain to the project we are designing and about to develop in VB, and is a considerable way forward in our journey towards defining a project and preparing it for development and implementation.

Other Diagrams

The diagrams we've looked at so far (use cases-sequence-activity-class diagrams) form the essential parts of UML that we need to build a Visual Basic project, and so we will be focusing on them in greater detail throughout the text. There are, however, other models that I won't be discussing in great detail, and I mention them now for sake of completeness for the interested reader. These other diagrams include:

- ❑ **Statechart Diagrams**: A model of the different possible states of a system's objects
- ❑ **Component Diagrams**: A model showing how different objects will be combined to make a component
- ❑ **Deployment Diagrams**: A model showing how each component will be placed on various hardware
- ❑ **Object Diagrams**: A simplified collaboration diagram.

Now that we've defined the core diagrams that are involved with designing a project with UML, we can draw our first conclusions about how these diagrams can be put to together.

The UML Process

We can view the use case diagrams as defining the project from the outside. This definition will place certain limitations on the system, and will affect our choices about how the system will be built.

So far, however, I've suggested that there's a completely straight progression from one type of diagram to the next - that we can move from use cases to sequence diagrams to class diagrams to activity diagrams to VB. While these different UML diagrams most certainly do move us towards an ever more focussed definition of our project design, in reality we can't always travel in a straight sequence. Project design is often a more iterative process than this.

A rather more realistic sequence for the UML process is presented in the following diagram:

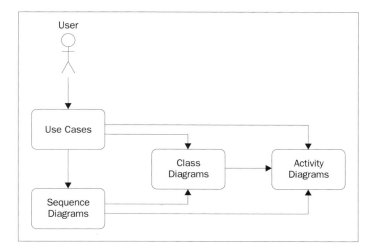

I think it's a good idea to take this on board as soon as possible: common sense tells us that sometimes our later thoughts on some sequence diagrams, for instance, may affect our earlier thoughts on how we built our activity diagrams - and so on.

We should also recognize that this picture needs to take into account the constraints and rules of the other tools we are using to build this project - such as the programming language and technology that will be used to implement the project itself. While the private methods and properties of our classes, as well as the series of steps our code will follow (as shown in our activity diagrams) are all internal to our system, how our system will work from the inside is determined by the choices that we make when building our system. These external factors must also therefore be taken into account:

- ❏   The programming language we are going to use
- ❏   The operating system our project will work with
- ❏   What server components, such as MTS, our system must use
- ❏   What technologies, such as ADO, our system must use

Using information on how each of these choices affects our system, we will be able to define the different parts of our activity diagrams and complete the methods and properties of our classes.

The user's requirements and the business requirements will create the use case documents. These use cases will mold the project design from the outside. The programming language, operating system, server components and technologies will mold the project from the inside. These two forces meet at the activity diagram, where both external and internal forces shape the methods and properties of each class.

These factors can all be viewed as follows:

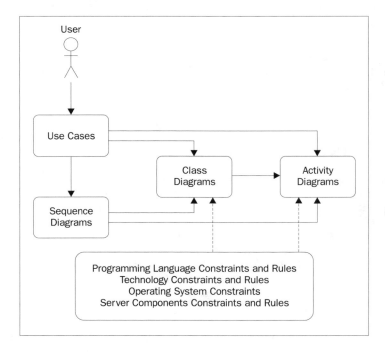

VB and UML

The UML models and diagrams are powerful tools that we can use to build complex projects. Unfortunately, translating theory into reality sometimes is not so easy. UML was designed for languages that are completely object-oriented, and for users who are well versed in the theoretical aspects of software engineering.

Visual Basic approaches OOP from a slightly different approach from languages such as C++. Visual Basic users tend to be less interested in theory and more interested in application. Our presentation of UML will be geared to both the Visual Basic language and application development. To accomplish this, we will keep the explanations of UML simple and show how to apply each model to building a VB project. We will occasionally bend the models a little bit, but in the end, we will have a method that is specifically geared towards Visual Basic. Before we can move on there are two important questions that need to be answered:

- ❑ Does the Visual Basic programming language possess enough object-oriented features to be used with an object-oriented modeling language such as UML?
- ❑ Do Visual Basic Projects require good management practices such as modeling the project with UML?

Is Visual Basic an Object-Oriented Language?

The object-oriented programmer sees a software system as a set of objects that interact with each other.

> **An object is an abstraction of an entity in a problem domain. As in the real world, objects are related to each other and they also communicate with each other.**

Whether Visual Basic can be considered an object-oriented language is a rather controversial topic. I will give you several arguments, which I hope will convince you that Visual Basic is object-oriented enough to make OOP projects, and that these projects can best be built using UML.

Technically speaking, an object-oriented language must include inheritance. As Visual Basic does not include inheritance, by this definition it is not object-oriented. Is this the end of the discussion? For some people it is, but I don't feel the discussion should end there.

Inheritance is a powerful tool that allows us to build many similar objects from one base class. For example, I can create a Dog, Cat and Rat object from a common Animal class. The Animal class will have properties such as Height, Weight, Color and methods such as Walk, Sleep, and Run. This relationship is called an *is a* relationship. A Dog *is an* Animal. A Cat *is an* Animal. Unfortunately, in VB we cannot make one base class (such as Animal) and use the identical class to create a Dog, Rat and Cat object.

However, we can get around Visual Basic's lack of inheritance by using object hierarchies. The lack of inheritance in the Visual Basic language does not prevent us from making objects that have an *is a* relationship, it is just more difficult to do so. Inheritance can have some problems, such as when an existing method or property in a base class has to be changed. Inheritance is often misused and is not the solution to every problem. While it would be nice to have inheritance in Visual Basic, it does not prevent us from making object-oriented components.

To demonstrate this let us focus on what these components are supposed to do, rather than the methods we use to build our object-oriented components. An object-oriented language must be able to build components that have the following properties:

- ❑ The component performs a specific task properly, efficiently and reliably
- ❑ The component is robust enough to work even under stressful or unexpected circumstances
- ❑ The component is maintainable and reusable
- ❑ The component can be built within budget, in a manner that is efficient and allows on-time delivery
- ❑ The component is completely self-contained (we can change the component without affecting the system the component is in)
- ❑ The component can perform different functions depending on how it is being used

Visual Basic components designed with UML models, and working under an Enterprise system that includes MTS, can be built with every one of those properties. I'm not going to say we will do this in the same manner as we would in a C++ program - I'll admit that sometimes we do have to get really creative to get VB components to do these things. Yet a properly designed VB component can do everything a component built from a true object-oriented language can do.

Because VB components can fulfill the requirements of an object-oriented component, I will treat Visual Basic as if it were an object-oriented language. You can form your own opinion. Hopefully, I have not offended you by saying that Visual Basic is object-oriented.

> *If you would like to learn more about objects and OOP, then I recommend you read "Beginning Visual Basic 6 Objects", (Wrox Press) for an introduction to object-oriented programming, and "Professional Visual Basic 6 Business Objects", also published by Wrox Press, for a more advanced discussion on using objects with VB6 in a business environment.*

Do Visual Basic Projects Really Need UML?

Having presented my case for VB being sufficiently object-oriented to use UML, I will return to a key question: do VB programmers really need UML? I keep coming back to this question - because it's so important. I've already criticized the ad hoc design methods of many programmers, and stressed how essential it is to have a decent design approach behind all your projects. UML is perfect for that.

But now consider the following:

> **Project management is the most essential part of a successful Visual Basic project.**

Regardless of the language used, most software projects are failures. A quick look at the statistics shows that one-third of all corporate software projects are cancelled before completion, and five out of six completed projects are unable to deliver the desired features. It doesn't have to be this way. This entire book focuses on showing you a coherent, clear way to manage an object-oriented Visual Basic project using UML. If you follow the methods outlined in this book, you can almost guarantee the success of your projects.

My Approach

My approach in this book is different from what you'll find in most other UML books. I want this book to be a tool that will teach you UML and also help you to able to program an Enterprise level Visual Basic project. Therefore, the goals of this book are as follows:

❑ To explain each of the essential UML diagrams and show you how to build them yourself
❑ To teach you how to use these UML diagrams to design an Enterprise level Visual Basic application
❑ To show you how to convert a UML design into Visual Basic code

To attain my second and third goals, my book will use UML diagrams to design a three-tier Visual Basic 6 project.

> **A three-tier project is divided into a client component, a server component, and a database. If you're not familiar with these elements, don't worry - we'll see a lot more about these later in the book.**

This project can be used, with minor modification, in many of the Enterprise Projects you may build. From Chapter 3 onwards, we shall be working our way through the complexities of building this type of real-world application. Together, we shall deal with the same questions, problems, and difficulties that you are likely to encounter when making your own applications. At every step of the way, I will demonstrate how UML will help us find the answers, solve our problems, and remove the complexities and difficulties of this project.

Almost every chapter will introduce and explain another piece of the Enterprise puzzle, and show just how UML can help you put that piece into its appropriate place. In the next chapter, I will lay the foundation you need to understand the book's project by giving you grounding in good project management and good Visual Basic programming techniques.

As you may have a limited amount of experience with the wide range of BackOffice products and Visual Basic programming techniques needed to build this project, I will also show you everything you need to know about programming a three-tier Visual Basic project - from RDS (Remote Data Services) to ADO (ActiveX Data Objects) and MTS (Microsoft Transaction Server).

A Real-World Project

The Visual Basic project that we're going to build will be an Order Entry project. We will go through each stage, as it would happen on a real project. As UML models are needed to build our Order Entry application, these models will be defined in detail and then used.

> **The final model we build can be used as the building block for any three-tier Visual Basic application.**

This book follows the normal progression of a project. Each step of the way our UML models will be guiding us and helping us build our project. We'll begin to examine this project (and how to manage it) straight away in the next chapter.

Summary

This chapter has been designed really just to familiarize you with some of the what and why of UML. Hopefully, it should now seem less like a vague concept and more like a sensible practical methodology that you are looking forward to seeing implemented in the design of a three-tier Visual Basic project.

So far we've seen:

- ❑ Exactly what UML is
- ❑ How UML helps us to design our projects from an OOP approach
- ❑ An introductory look at some of the core UML diagrams
- ❑ The UML Process in overview
- ❑ The approach that I'll be taking in this book

As we progress through this book we will consider each aspect of UML in more detail as we see it in action as our project develops.

Now that we've taken an initial glimpse at UML and some of what it can offer us, we will move on to taking a closer look at the project that we're going to be developing throughout the book, and some basic elements of project management.

Project Design and Management

Visual Basic's ability to create a wide range of powerful, efficient applications has made it one of the most commonly used programming languages. Unfortunately, its relative ease of use has often resulted in programmers neglecting one of the most important parts of project management: the formal design phase. While skipping a formal design phase might save some time at the beginning of the project, it will prove costly later on.

How costly? In the best-case scenario, a great deal of time will be needed toward the end of the project, during the maintenance and upgrade phases. In the worst-case scenario, a lack of planning will result in a complete failure of the project. Companies are still creating applications without a formal design phase, believing that they are cutting back on the overall time of the project. In reality, this will always result in a short-term gain and a long-term loss.

UML is ultimately about creating successful projects. Before we approach the details and application of UML (from Chapter 3 onwards), it seems appropriate to consider the other techniques and practices that are allied with UML, and that we will see through the pages of this book.

The key to any successful project is design and management, so we'll be looking at the following subjects in this chapter, all of which are allied in principle to the UML approach:

- ❑ Designing a Project
- ❑ Creating Standards
- ❑ Frameworks and our Northwind project
- ❑ Patterns - making future projects easier
- ❑ The Project Development Lifecycle
- ❑ The Enterprise Application Model
- ❑ Techniques for Project Management
- ❑ Part 1: Project Design
- ❑ Part 2: Project Implementation

Designing a Project

When we're designing any project, we must have a general plan to guide that design process. Imagine you were an architect designing a ranch-style house. As an architect you have a wide range of freedom with regard to how you design the ranch house. Yet, there are certain design limitations and various rules or standards that must be followed. You cannot, for example, put the bedrooms on the second floor, because a ranch house has no second floor; nor are you likely to have the front door leading directly into the master bedroom. You will also have patterns which are common to many houses. The design of the ranch house will be built upon established **standards**, an existing **framework**, and some established **patterns**.

A framework is a skeleton for the design. It provides merely the bare bones, but it does give the architect a guide to work off. This framework will be built out of different components, such as the entrance hallway, the master bedroom, the living room, etc. Each of these components will be built from a well-defined pattern. An example of a pattern for an entrance hallway for a house could be:

> *The front door leads into the entrance hallway. The hallway will have a coat closet and will lead into the living room.*

The architect creates a design using components made from patterns, and places these components in their appropriate places within an established framework. The framework, components and patterns come from years of experience, testing and experimentation to find the best possible elements to design a house:

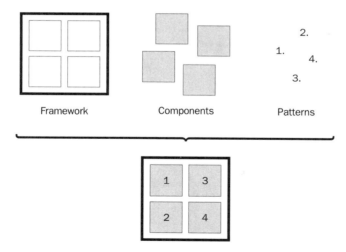

Just as an architect has a framework and patterns, software developers also have frameworks that tell them where to place their components, and patterns that describe how these components should be designed and built. We are now going to consider exactly what standards, frameworks and patterns are in relation to our Visual Basic project.

Standards

Before a single line of code is written, we must create a set of standards. Standards fall into the following categories:

Documentation Standards

Prior to creating UML documents, we must have a set of standards explaining how these diagrams will be drawn, where they will be stored, and what procedures will be used to access and edit them. It is pointless to have someone working on detailed UML design documents if these documents simply get filed away and forgotten. Making sure that there is a **repository** to hold all of the documents, prior to creating any of them, ensures that nothing will get lost or forgotten. Repositories also prevent two team members from doing the same or conflicting work. The repository will allow any member of the development team to have access to the documents, and this makes it easier for them to implement the design.

Coding Standards

Coding standards will help you transform your UML diagrams into a set of uniformly coded components that become the working application. Coding standards allow a component to be passed from one team member to another for additional coding work, quality control, or assembly without the second developer having to spend hours trying to understand the code. Each programmer will have his or her own artistic style, which will influence their style of coding, but their style should not violate any of the team standards. While some developers may view this as restricting, developers have to understand that they are working on a team. As a team member you have to develop techniques of coding that allow the entire team to work effectively and efficiently.

These will include the naming conventions used in your code, commenting of code, use of enumerated types and constants, global constants, and any other methods of coding that will be done by all of the developers.

Choosing the Right UML Tools

The tool that your team is using to create UML diagrams should also be part of your standards. When choosing a UML tool, make sure that it is one that can be understood by the most junior developer. An extremely sophisticated tool that can make every possible UML diagram, but can only be used and understood by a few members of your team is a useless tool. Every team member has to be part of the project. Having UML diagrams that cannot be understood by all of your developers excludes some developers from contributing to the design process as well as making it nearly impossible for them to know how to build the components within the project. Standard tools are Visual Modeler, which comes with the Enterprise edition of Visual Studio, HOW from Riverton software, and Rational Rose from Rational software.

Frameworks

Frameworks should be chosen before the final code is written for a project and before the creation of UML diagrams that are dependent upon the internal workings of the system.

> **Frameworks provide skeletal designs that can be built upon to create an organized system where many components work together.**

A project design must work in accordance with these frameworks. As a large portion of the design is based on these frameworks, the designer should thoroughly test them before actually committing to their use and designing the project with them. Frameworks fall into one of the following two categories:

General Frameworks

These can be applied to whole projects and determine where components must be located and what tasks each component must perform. In addition to these general frameworks, there are also smaller component frameworks that come from some of the components that we use to build our project.

Component Frameworks

These components will be a fundamental part of our system and have rules associated with their use.

We can define a component framework like this:

> **A component framework is a smaller framework that is derived from some of the components used to build our project. These components will be a fundamental part of our system, and have rules associated with their use.**
>
> **These rules must affect the way we design one or more other components of our project to classify them as a framework.**

As this is my own definition, I will discuss it in more detail. Both the ADO and MTS can be considered frameworks by this definition, so we will use them as examples:

- ❑ ADO can be used as a component of a project to give other components in the project the ability to communicate with a data store
- ❑ MTS can be used to manage server component transactions and to manage the creation and destruction of these server components

ADO and MTS both have numerous rules that must be followed if they are to work properly. These rules will place constraints on the design of the components. They will shape the way nearly every component of the system is designed.

Like any component in an object-oriented project, a component framework will perform a whole set of operations for us without us worrying about how these are done. This is encapsulation. I'm using the phrase *component framework* because these components are more than just a simple piece that we plug into our system. The frame of a house, which is also a component of the house, will determine the shape and structure of the entire house. The components that our project is built on, the ones that will define and shape the internal structure of our project, such as ADO or MTS, are the components that I will refer to as frameworks. From this point onward, I will simply refer to these as frameworks of our system instead of calling them component frameworks.

Choosing Frameworks

The choice of a framework should be made very carefully, as it can shape the inner workings of our project. Programming technology is new and evolving every day. Just because the literature says a framework can solve a certain set of problems, that doesn't necessarily mean it really can. Unless we actually test the framework ourself and prove that it works under the set of conditions that we require it to, we cannot be sure that it really works.

During the design phase, the majority of any quality control resources should involve the testing of various frameworks and patterns. Having blind faith that something will work is not only foolish, but could cost millions of dollars and months of time. I am saying this from personal experience.

> *One company spent over a year developing a middleware solution that completely depended on a non-Microsoft DLL working under MTS. The first time the developers actually checked to see if this DLL really worked under MTS was when the project was completed. The DLL functioned fine as long as five or less users were accessing the component. When more users tried to use the component, everything froze and came to a grinding halt. As this was supposed to be an Intranet solution used by hundreds of users at the same time, this certainly was not a workable solution. Four months of additional work resulted in a rewriting of the project that finally allowed multiple users.*
>
> *This company was fortunate as they were able to salvage most of the original work, but this mistake could easily have resulted in starting from the very beginning. If this company had spent two days writing a small test application to load test the DLL during the design phase, this problem would have been detected and several months of work would have been saved.*

I could tell you many other stories where entire projects were built based on a framework or technology that simply would not work for a project, and was only discovered during the final phase of the project. Remember that the majority of the frameworks are new and have only been tested in a limited number of environments.

Make sure that the framework is appropriate for your project:

- ❑ The framework must do what your project requires
- ❑ The framework must work in the environment you need
- ❑ The framework must work as you expect it to

Patterns

Patterns are becoming the hottest new idea in OOP. There is good reason for this. A pattern can provide us with a basic blueprint that we can use to design our project.

> **A pattern is a common solution to a common design problem within a project.**

Patterns can allow us to build our components in an assembly line manner. Patterns help a project stay within time deadlines, keep costs down and significantly reduce the amount of coding that needs to be done. Without a pattern telling us how to build our components, we will find ourselves asking questions such as, "*Will we build our customer object for the client as a single class or do we build it as a class hierarchy from one, two or perhaps three classes?*" Having a well-defined pattern, which shows exactly how we should build a component, provides us with the answers to questions like these.

I see patterns being classified as either general or specific.

General Patterns

These apply to a general system and have nothing to do with choices of operating systems, programming languages, or technologies. An example of this would be a general pattern for making an Order Entry application. Every Order Entry application will have certain features regardless of what you use to build it. This type of pattern is useful because it can guide you in a general design of your project. We won't be concerning ourselves with general patterns in this book, because I want us to drill right down to some in-depth UML analysis and build from zero up.

Specific Patterns

These can be used to build a particular component of a system, and they are dependent upon the system that we're using. For example, if I were building a three-tier project, I might need to build dozens of client components. It would be really helpful if I could find a pattern to build this type of component. I could then reuse this pattern over and over again, to design and build all of my client components.

UML diagrams will not only provide us with the patterns that exist within our project's components, but also show us how to code these objects. If we are fortunate, there will already be a coding solution for the patterns we find in our UML diagrams. If there isn't already a pattern, we will need to create activity diagrams in order to map out the coding solution.

Unfortunately, you see very little discussion of patterns in the Visual Basic literature, so there are very few patterns for Visual Basic components. Visual Basic has only recently moved toward being object-oriented, and I believe that many developers are still trying to write OO programs using non-OOP techniques. As the Visual Basic community moves more toward using OOP techniques, I think they will also be jumping onto the pattern bandwagon.

Finding Your Own Patterns

Patterns that show how a component will actually perform its required task are not so obvious and are rarely already defined. For example, the three-tier framework dictates that there will be client components with certain properties, but how we actually make this client component have these properties is completely up to us.

There are many resources that can guide us in finding these patterns, but for the most part we will end up designing the patterns for the individual components ourselves. This is especially true because many of the frameworks are so new that there are often very few, if any, patterns created for the framework's components. In addition, since these frameworks are new, they usually have not been thoroughly tested either.

This means that before we use any framework we will first have to create our own patterns and thoroughly test them. While this may sound difficult, it really is not.

Throughout this book I will show you that these patterns can be found quite easily if we design our components with UML models. The patterns we will use to design our project will be based on object-oriented principles, good coding techniques, and sound project management.

Why Are Patterns So Useful?

Project design really comes from two sides: the inside and the outside. The outside is based on our user requirements, and the inside is based on the programming language, technologies, and server components that we choose.

If we are using the same internal system for all of our projects, then once we've designed and built the internal components for the first time, we can reuse them for all of our projects based on this internal system. By the same reasoning, once we've designed and coded our Enterprise patterns, in order to build future Enterprise projects, we only need to be concerned with the user requirements and building the external part of our project; the patterns will provide everything else.

If we take all of these patterns and put them together, we can build what can be considered our own Visual Basic 6 Enterprise framework. This framework will have a set of rules that must be followed, and will shape how we build the rest of our project, i.e. the external part built from the user requirements (and use cases).

> *Creating entire frameworks to build a particular type of project is perhaps one of the most efficient ways of building projects. Many companies and third-party software vendors are working late hours trying to make frameworks like this for Visual Basic 6 Enterprise projects.*

We can think of this as building prefabricated houses. Every prefabricated house is built from a similar structure, a basic framework that will underlie every house. This doesn't mean that the houses will all look identical. Once we move beyond the basic framework, each house will have certain things added to make it unique: landscaping, color arrangement, bathroom fixtures, carpeting, etc. While the framework of each house is identical, we can place different things within this framework to make completely different houses.

When it comes to our Visual Basic projects, the idea is to make "prefabricated" projects. We make our basic framework and then, based on the users' requirements and the needs of the particular project, we will add the features to make the application unique.

Building the framework is usually the most difficult part of a project. From design to implementation, it can take six months to a year. However, once these frameworks have been established, we don't have to worry about things like making connections to databases. As long as we follow the rules of our Visual Basic Enterprise framework, the framework will handle all of these things. We only need to be concerned with adding features that are required by our project.

The Northwind Project

To demonstrate how to determine standards, frameworks, and patterns for a particular project I am going to introduce the project that will form the practical examples examined in this book.

IES Incorporated

IES Inc. is a development company. They have been contacted by the Northwind Company to build an Order Entry application for them. In addition to Order Entry, this project will also provide reports for management.

The Northwind Company

The Northwind Company has, until recently, been very small: it has not really required a very sophisticated system to do this. They are now expanding, and they are going to need a larger, more sophisticated system.

The Initial Meeting

An initial meeting between IES Inc. and the managers of Northwind has taken place. Their current system is a non-networked order entry application. This application only allows one order entry clerk to enter information. The application generates a few limited reports. Paper copies of all orders are printed and sent to the shipping department, and another copy to an administrative assistant for filing. As the order is filled, items that were shipped are crossed off the sheet. At the end of each working day, these sheets are used to enter all of the items that have been shipped that day into the system. Orders that are out of stocked items will be filed in a folder at the shipping department. They will remain there until the product is restocked. This system cannot be upgraded for multiple users, and has no ability to be used for an Internet environment. Northwind is expanding, and expecting to add at least five new order entry clerks that will need access to an order entry application. Also, to increase business, Northwind want to begin selling their products over their Internet.

Northwind's Requirements

After some discussion, the main requirements for the Northwind project were found to be as follows:

- ❑ The system needs to function over an Internet and a local intranet.
- ❑ The main order entry application will be a Visual Basic executable program, connected to a middle tier server component that will communicate with the database and perform various functions.
- ❑ There will also be an intranet application that will allow Northwind managers to access reports on sales.
- ❑ Northwind requires the ability to track every order, and generate reports on the status of every order.
- ❑ The application will also be accessible to shipping, so that information on items shipped can be entered immediately.
- ❑ There is a planned e-commerce web site for selling the products over the web. The system should be designed with this in mind.
- ❑ The bulk of these applications should be built from the same reusable components.

Choosing the Frameworks

Let's examine the basic requirements that Northwind have stipulated and see which technologies, and thus which component frameworks, would be best suited for the process. By the time we've completed the finished the project, we'll have created a general framework for the Order Entry part of this application.

Internet/Intranet

This requirement can be achieved by having a client that does not have a continuous connection to the database. This means that state has to be stored on the client, and the server components have to be stateless.

Data Access

The choices for data access with Visual Basic include DAO, ODBC Direct, RDO, and ADO. Let's consider the candidate technologies in turn, weighing up the pros and cons to make a decision on which technologies we'll use for the Northwind project.

❑   **DAO (Data Access Objects)** has been around for several years now, but works poorly with remote data sources. Although DAO allows us to connect and disconnect from a data store as many times as we like, it does not support disconnected recordsets.

Disconnected recordsets are well suited to Internet requirements (we discuss these technologies in much more detail in Chapter 8).

❑   If we were using DAO, and we wanted to update our data store regularly, we would really want to establish continuous connection to our data store. But a continuous connection to the data store will not work for us – given the details stipulated in the previous Internet/intranet requirements. DAO is therefore not suitable for this particular project.

❑   **ODBC Direct** requires a continuous connection in the same way that DAO would have done; so ODBC Direct will not work for our project.

❑   **RDO (Remote Data Objects)** is a thin layer on top of ODBC, and inherits from ODBC the ability to create client cursors - which allows for disconnected recordsets. While RDO will work for our project, its use is limited to relational databases using ODBC. As we are not sure what type of database Northwind is going to upgrade to, the choice of RDO will limit the choices of the new database to relational databases with ODBC drivers.

❑   **ADO (ActiveX Data Objects)** is the primary method of database connection that Microsoft is currently supporting, and it's the technology that Microsoft is focusing a great deal of development upon. ADO has a wide range of features that allow you to get extensive information from disconnected recordsets, including the ability to reconcile inconsistencies in the data. ADO has a rich set of features specifically designed for building a project that maintains state on the client and has no state on the server. ADO also offers an object model that's fairly simple to use and can work with both relational and non-relational databases. Using ADO will allow the user to upgrade to a very wide range of databases. Overall, ADO would be a better choice than RDO for this project. ADO is therefore our chosen method for database connection in this project.

Another technology we have chosen is **Remote Data Services (RDS)**. RDS does offer some potential advantages over other methods of connecting to remote objects, such as **DCOM**. DCOM relies on the operating system to handle security, and this requires a great deal of work setting up the components. DCOM also has some security issues when running through a proxy server that assigns IP addresses to the internal computers. RDS places the burden of security on the component, which eliminates the difficulties of setting the component up for use on both the client and server. This is a great advantage, and makes RDS a better choice than DCOM for this project.

The Programming Language

We have made the decision to use Visual Basic for all of our components. Is this the best choice for making this type of project? We could use other programming languages to make this project, or even to make parts of this project. Since one of the requirements of our system is to use a Windows-based operating system, our choices include Visual Basic, Visual C++, Java, and a few other languages.

When it comes to building the GUI, Visual Basic offers a clear advantage over C++ and Java. The choice of Visual Basic, rather than another GUI building programming language, would probably be based on the following factors:

❑   What language the developers are familiar with
❑   How well supported the language is
❑   How easy it is to find information on building projects with the language

❑   How efficiently the components built with the language work
❑   How well the components can perform the tasks required by the system

Visual Basic is a very popular programming language. Let's say the developers are familiar with Visual Basic. With this being the case, Visual Basic can easily fulfill every requirement listed above. Visual Basic has a rich set of features that allows one to build powerful applications.

While Visual Basic is a great choice for the GUI, what about the rest of the application? Both C++ and Java can build powerful components, but they both require a longer time to develop. Java does not offer any major performance gains over a Visual Basic project. As this system will be Windows based on the client and server, there is no need for Java's ability to work on multiple platforms. Java offers no major advantage over Visual Basic, and will take longer to build - so we will eliminate it as an option for this project, especially if the developers are not familiar with the language.

C++ might produce faster components, but is speed an important factor for our project? There will be at most a few dozen Order Entry Clerks, so the internal system will never be too heavily stressed. As for the future Internet applications, the few milliseconds gained by using C++ will make little difference in the response time of the Northwind web site. In a site with tens of thousands of users per day, we may want to get into a discussion of the benefits gained by programming in C++. In a site that is likely to get a few hundred to perhaps a few thousand hits per day, a Visual Basic component, running under MTS, can handle the stress.

Three-tier Framework

The three-tier framework we discuss in this chapter can be considered to be a general blueprint mapping of where our components must be located and what tasks each component should perform. The three-tier framework will define where your components go and what tasks they must perform. A three-tier project has the data in one location, the database-related functionality in another location, and the user interface and non-database related functionality in a third place:

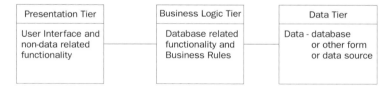

Each of these three pieces has a well-defined location and set of tasks they must perform. The general framework is more concerned with defining what different parts of the system will do, and where they will do it, rather than how they will do it.

A three-tiered architecture is the primary framework we will be working with. This framework will actually have several other frameworks within it, such as the ADO framework, and the Microsoft Transaction Server (MTS) framework.

Working with these Frameworks

Having a basic understanding of these frameworks is only the first step towards being able to determine how to use these frameworks in our project. These frameworks are all fairly new, and they sometimes do not work as they are supposed to. Even when they work as advertised, they may not work for our particular project. The information we gather is just the starting point. Once we understand the technology, we must figure out how to make it work for our project.

Often there are many ways we can build a component using a framework. Some solutions will work very well for our system, and others will not work at all. For example, where is the best place to put the middle-tier component? Do we put it on its own server, or do we put it on the same server as the database? Either choice can result in a drastically different overall performance of our entire system.

> **Here is a fundamental truth for every Visual Basic programmer involved with this kind of development.**
>
> **There is no one solution that will work for every three-tier project.**
>
> **Each project will have its own arrangement of components using frameworks in a way that results in the best performance for the system. And every business problem has its own unique rules that will affect how best to build a three-tier solution for it.**
>
> **Working through a test project is the best way to find the most suitable techniques for using a framework in your project.**

A test project will help us find the most efficient way to use a framework for a given project. Based on our tests and the information we gather, we can create an accurate technology model (a model of all the technology, such as the ADO or MTS that will be used within the system). This technology model, combined with the UML models, can help us create the most efficient solution for the project's design.

Patterns Used in the Project

While preparing the example for this book, I wanted to use a good object-oriented pattern for the client side of our three-tier project using Visual Basic. I wanted to create a client example that had the following features:

- ❑ It should be an example that you, the reader, could use in real projects and could solve some of your current programming needs.
- ❑ It should be reusable in many different types of projects.
- ❑ It should be built from a pattern, so that you can build similar client components from this pattern with very little modification.
- ❑ It should provide data controls (such as a grid control or a textbox) since Visual Basic is primarily a GUI language and it's important to link the GUI to the client objects.
- ❑ It should provide information through standard properties.
- ❑ It should be built from code that is fairly simple.

Using UML patterns that we'll design through the first half of this book, we'll be able to carry on through and use our UML diagrams to build a Visual Basic **code template** for the client components.

We'll be coding these components in the second half of the book, and our Visual Basic code template will be used to build most of the client components. You'll see, as we progress from design to development, that these code templates allow us to build many similar components from one template quickly and efficiently. Entire portions of our project can be created from a few code templates.

The Project Development Lifecycle

It may initially seem to odd to describe a project as having a lifecycle. Indeed, if you haven't seen a project developed with any formal plan then it may not seem appropriate to you. However, once we employ a more structured approach to project development, a clear set of stages does emerge.

The basic stages of a project could be divided up like this:

- ❏ Initial development of the project
- ❏ Requirements Development
- ❏ Architecture
- ❏ Design and Quality Control
- ❏ Stage 1 detailed design, implementation, testing and release
- ❏ Stage 2 detailed design, implementation, testing and release
- ❏ …
- ❏ Stage N detailed design, implementation, testing and release
- ❏ Final Release

As you should be able to see, the process is **iterative** and **incremental**. It's iterative in that we revisit several stages again and again; and it's incremental since with each iteration we advance the project slightly. You'll see how this approach can lead to obvious benefits and help reduce errors and bugs shortly.

The Enterprise Application Model

Microsoft has defined an **Enterprise Application Model** as a model for developing Enterprise level projects. An Enterprise Application Model consists of the following sub-models:

- ❏ **User Model**: This model shows the user requirements, and how these requirements will affect the design of the project.
- ❏ **Business Model**: This model shows the business requirements of building the project. Included in this model is the cost of the project, the time it will take to build the project, the platforms the project must support, the cost savings, the profit to be earned through this project, and so on.
- ❏ **The Development Model**: This model consists of two components. One component is concerned with the development of the process model, and details issues such as planning, deliverables, and scheduling. The second component covers the roles of the team members and concentrates on the management of teams.
- ❏ **Physical Model**: A model showing all of the hardware components of the system and how they fit in with the other models.
- ❏ **Logical Model**: A model of the components of the system and the rules that will govern these components.
- ❏ **Technology Model**: A model providing all of the information required to make the choices on the technology used for the system. A technology model may include an analysis of DAO, ADO and RDO to determine what is the best method for connecting to the database.

Although we won't be explicitly following the Enterprise Application Model, I've introduced it here because it is related to the way I've structured this book. So let me explain how each sub-model of the Enterprise Application Model is realized in this book.

The User Model

The primary component of our User Model will be Use Cases. The user interviews and sequence diagrams can also be included within the User Model.

The Business Model and the Development Model

We have covered some of the Business Model and the Development Model in this chapter. We will not go into any more detail about how you actually model costs, make a schedule, and other issues related to this topic. These topics are covered in project management books, and do not have any major impacts on our diagrams. The platforms that we will be using do impact our diagrams, but the choice of platforms is usually a preset requirement, so this will not require any more discussion.

The Physical Model

The Physical Model will have a major impact on our project. We'll be discussing this later on in the book, when we make a physical UML diagram to model the computers in our system, and the components on those computers.

The Logical Model

The Logical Model can be built out of two UML diagrams: the Class diagrams that will model the components, and the Business Rules that will define the rules governing these components. We'll be developing Class diagrams and Business Rules as we progress through the UML process.

The Technology Model

The last model in the list is the Technology Model. This model, like the Business and Developmental models, does not actually fit into any UML model. But it's important that we do model the technology of our system when we build our use cases, as the technology will have a major impact on our activity and class diagrams.

The Technology Model should cover the following:

- ❏ A list of the different types of technology that can be used for this project
- ❏ The advantages and disadvantages of each of the technologies
- ❏ A detailed description of the technology
- ❏ Rules associated with using this technology

As I mentioned previously, we'll be going through many of these phases throughout the book. However, I won't refer directly to this model again: we'll be concentrating on the UML Process itself, as that's the focus of this book. But if you meet the Enterprise Application Model again in your travels, you'll at least know how it links into what we're doing in this book.

Project Management

Following the methods of good project management has become critical for successful projects. This is especially true for Visual Basic, now that it is evolving into an object-oriented language. Projects that get bogged down in the later stages, that require long periods of debugging, and that miss deadlines are usually the result of poor project management, and are not failures of Visual Basic.

Proper project management is essential. However, this book is more concerned with UML, and as a result, you may find that we either skip or barely touch on some of the concepts outlined below. Nevertheless, you should apply them with the utmost vigilance in your VB projects.

We will divide project management into two major parts:

- ❑ Project Design
- ❑ Project Implementation

The rest of this chapter will drill down to a detailed discussion on Project Design and Project Implementation from the perspective of good project management. Here is a precise map of the topics we'll cover in the rest of this chapter:

- ❑ **Part 1: Project Design**
  - ❑ Documentation of Specifications Prior to Writing Code
    - ❑ Documentation Leads to Project Direction
    - ❑ Documentation is the Basis of the Review Process
    - ❑ Documentation Can Save Time and Money
  - ❑ A Graphical User Interface (GUI) Prototype
  - ❑ Documentation of Risks
    - ❑ Categorizing Risks
    - ❑ Risk Assessment
    - ❑ Personnel Issues
  - ❑ Maintaining a Library
    - ❑ Libraries Provide Clarification
    - ❑ A Library Acts as a Safeguard

- ❑ **Part 2: Project Implementation**
  - ❑ Building the Project Incrementally and with Components
    - ❑ Simpler Project Management
    - ❑ Keeping Users Happy
    - ❑ Time and Money Savings
    - ❑ Development Flexibility
  - ❑ Testing Frequently and Documenting All Bugs and Changes
    - ❑ Error Management
    - ❑ Error Location
  - ❑ Careful Design of all Components
    - ❑ Ill-Contained Components Lead to Delicate Projects
    - ❑ The Registry Must Be Kept Tidy

Part 1: Project Design

Good project design comprises four main parts, which we will now discuss:

- ❑   Documentation of Specifications Prior to Writing Code
- ❑   Building a Graphical User Interface (GUI) Prototype
- ❑   Documentation of Risks
- ❑   Maintaining a Library

These are all undertakings that will continue as the project develops, particularly as this is most commonly an iterative process. However, these tasks can be distinguished from actual project implementation considerations, since they should be started prior to any code being written.

Documentation of Specifications Prior to Writing Code

Although it isn't always an achievable goal, we should aim to complete all documentation for each stage of a project before the first line of code is written. This documentation includes models, specification documents, and user documents.

Documentation Leads to Project Direction

Documentation of project specifications will result in an agreed and specific direction for the project. Once the users' requirements are completely described in specification and design documents, the users can sign off on these documents. These documents then act as a contract that locks the users and developers into one particular set of specifications. Changes can only be made when both parties agree to sign off on it.

If documentation is not undertaken, the design of the project will be more fluid, allowing the users to add or remove items from the project throughout the project's lifetime. Although this may initially seem beneficial, it can result in *feature creep*, where the users, project managers, and every other person involved in the project keep adding features. This may persist up to the point where the project is nearly complete, and at that point the addition of more features can result in the dramatic rewriting major sections of the application. Obviously, this would not be good - so we must document early to avoid feature creep.

Documentation is the Basis of the Review Process

Once a document of the project specifications has been produced, it can act as the basis of a specification review process. A select group of users, who represent the typical users of the system, can be given time to review all of the project's specifications and the entire design at the beginning of the project prior to the developers writing code.

Thus, if the application is doing something it is not supposed to do, or not doing something it should, the user should be able to catch this mistake. Showing users documentation and prototypes, as discussed below, should allow any changes to the requirements to be found before the application is actually built. Without a design document, features that are missing, improperly functioning or unnecessary are not likely to be discovered until the first releases.

Documentation Can Save Time and Money

Using documentation both to provide project direction and for the review process will help to prevent code being rewritten once an application is partially built.

Fixing any errors found during a review of the design document (and user interface prototypes) requires simply rewriting the design document and making the necessary changes to the project's models. In the worse case scenario, this will result in only throwing away a few days or weeks of design work as opposed to much, much more application development time.

To correct mistakes found once the application is partially built requires the code to be re-written or thrown away and replaced by the correct code. This usually takes a great deal of time and consequently money. Planning and design allow you to find problems early on when they are easy to fix. Poor or insufficient planning results in mistakes being caught or not caught later (anywhere from the beginning of coding to after the final release) when they are difficult and expensive to fix.

If major corrections are made to a project when the application is partially built, the project should be completely re-tested to ensure that the new changes are both working correctly and have been properly implemented. Unfortunately, the changes usually result in a missed deadline and the project may be released without thorough re-testing. The end result is an application that will almost certainly have serious bugs.

> **The earlier an error is caught the easier it is to fix. The further along a project is the harder and more expensive in time and money it will be to make a change.**

A Graphical User Interface (GUI) Prototype

Visual Basic makes it simple to build a GUI prototype. This prototype can simulate the functionality of the final application and can be used as a reference for building the real GUI.

The GUI prototype can be used to review the interface requirements. When the users work with the prototype, they can ensure that the interface is easy to use and can determine whether the application is really doing everything they require. A review of a GUI prototype combined with a review of the design documentation allows the user to inspect the application design via two different techniques, one visual and one written. Using two methods helps to eliminate the possibility of missing a mistake and results in a design that is exactly what the users need.

If this review process has not taken place, the interface may need to be completely redesigned once the application is complete. If the project is written correctly, which for most projects means components, this may only result in a minor revision of the GUI and small changes within the code. However, if the project is not compartmentalized, then it is likely that this could result in major re-coding.

Documentation of Risks

Risks are anything that can negatively affect the project. They include problems with design, personnel, technology, etc. Any technology or programming technique that has not previously been used by the development team should be considered a risk.

Just because the documentation says something should work, that does not mean that it will!

These technologies and techniques can be tested with small test applications during the design phase to ensure that everything will work prior to the code being written. Just as design documentation and prototypes help to make sure that the project will work **externally**, small test applications can be used to check that the project will work **internally** prior to actually building the project. We shall therefore consider the following project management techniques for dealing with risks:

- ❑ Categorizing Risks
- ❑ Risk Assessment
- ❑ Personnel Issues

Categorizing Risks

Any changes in specifications, especially when made late in the project's development, can be a major risk factor to every aspect of the project. Changes made after the coding begins can be assessed by how greatly they will affect the project, how major the changes will be, and how they will affect the overall ability to complete the project on time. Changes can be categorized as follows:

- ❑ Easy to implement, large benefit
- ❑ Hard to implement, large benefit
- ❑ Easy to implement, small benefit
- ❑ Hard to implement, small benefit

As a guideline, changes falling into the first category should almost always be made. Those in the second category should only be made after careful consideration and research. Those falling into the third depend upon the nature of the change, and can be implemented after some consideration. The last category should almost never be implemented.

A risk document can contain sections for each risk. Each section lists what is being done to reduce or eliminate the risk, and an estimate of the financial and time effects of the risk. Each solution can be documented, including the effects of each solution on project costs and project schedule. There should also be a section to note the date when the risk is eliminated.

Risk Assessment

A risk document allows both the development team and the users to review each and every identified risk. Allowing all of the developers to place possible risks into the risks document makes certain that those who are writing the code are most likely to see the problems and take appropriate measures.

Users and the developers requesting a change to the project should sign off any change that will have a major effect on the project. Doing this will usually result in any unnecessary changes being dropped as no one wants to sign off on something non-critical that will force a major delay of the project. This will also force users to carefully consider all requirements. If the risk of adding new features is not evaluated, the changes may take a long time to implement or may prevent the project from ever being completed.

When risks are not written down, they tend to be ignored, overlooked, or forgotten. In addition, if there is no system for managing risks then there is no standard way for handling them - and solutions become haphazard. Without risk assessment and prior testing of a new technology, the discovery that the technology will not work for a project usually occurs during final testing of the completed product. This can result in the entire project being redesigned and rewritten, with a resultant loss of a great deal of work and money.

Personnel Issues

Personnel shortage issues should also be addressed in the risk document. Evaluating the risks from personnel shortages and compensating for them, by adjusting schedules and workloads so that no one is overburdened, will not only help keep the project running smoothly, but also reduce the risk of losing developers. If personnel shortages are not addressed, unrealistic demands may be made on the developers. This in turn leads to poor morale and often the churning out of code without careful design.

Maintaining a Library

A library allows everything to be clearly documented. As the project evolves through the design phase, each change is documented and can later be retrieved for review. During the implementation phase, each version of the project will also be saved in the library. The key benefits of maintaining a library are therefore as follows:

- ❑ Libraries Provide Clarification
- ❑ A Library Acts as a Safeguard

Libraries Provide Clarification

The library acts as a record of everything that happens to a project throughout its lifetime. People involved in the development of a complex project may only be working on one specific area of that project. If at some time someone needs to find out why certain features were added or removed, users and developers can review how and why these changes occurred. As long as the users and developers sign everything off and all risks are documented, any changes that were made can be shown to have been approved by everyone, and the risks accepted by all.

A Library Acts as a Safeguard

Saving a record of every version allows us to follow a project through its development, and more importantly, it allows us return to an earlier version of the source code if a serious problem is found in the latest revision. If developers do not submit the code to a library prior to making a code change, and that change causes the project to completely fail, then the developers will have no easy way to get back to the earlier working version of the code. The only possible way back is to go through the code and try to find all the changes that were made. If the changes are not documented within the code, these changes may be difficult or impossible to find, and we risk facing a complete failure of a project.

A library records all aspects of a project. If one of the original developers leaves the company, their knowledge of the project does not leave with them. It is still in the library. This information can be used during revisions or on future projects to determine the best techniques and methods for creating this type of project. Without a library, all information on the project is sitting within the heads of the people working on the project or in scattered documents.

Part 2: Project Implementation

Now that we have discussed the issues that lead to good project design, it is time to think about the issues of project implementation. The main elements of good project implementation that we will discuss are:

- ❏ Building the Project Incrementally and with Components
- ❏ Testing Frequently and Documenting Bugs
- ❏ Careful Design of all Components

Build the Project Incrementally and with Components

Building a project in increments means that the application is built in several stages. Each stage implements another piece of the application, and each stage is complete when that part of the application is functioning.

> **This means that each stage ends with the application working, fully tested, and capable of performing a certain part of the complete project.**

The key to building incrementally is building the project from separate, well-defined components. These components are like bricks that can be used to build our project. If one component fails or does not perform properly, only that component needs to be replaced; the rest of the project is unaffected.

Each stage will go through a full cycle of building the components required for the stage using detailed design documents, testing the components, and testing the entire project as each component is added. The different stages do not have to follow one after another. Different stages can be occurring at the same time by different developers.

Building applications in increments does take extra work up front because the project will have to be carefully planned and designed. However, building an application incrementally offers many advantages:

- ❏ Simpler Project Management
- ❏ Keeping Users Happy
- ❏ Time and Money Savings
- ❏ Development Flexibility

Simpler Project Management

A large and complex project is broken down into many smaller projects. Smaller projects are easier to manage and, as long as the project is object-oriented, easier to adjust to changes in technology. If a change in technology forces a change in the application, an object-oriented project will usually only require one or two components to be changed.

When a project does not produce any functioning components until the final phases of the application, it is difficult to determine how much is being accomplished and difficult to monitor what stage the project has reached. Often the only way to estimate the progress of the project is to ask the opinion of developers. Team managers will rely on statements such as, "We are 80% of the way done with this particular module". Unfortunately this number is not based on any measurable test of completeness, and can therefore result in missed deadlines. Incremental development, on the other hand, allows project managers to at least monitor how many components have been completed.

Smaller incremental projects will also benefit the developers. Short-term accomplishments are easier to envision and to meet. They help to keep developers focused on the completion of a set of features within a small amount of time, instead of something way off in the future. Human beings work best when they have very clear, identifiable goals and a reasonable time to accomplish tasks. Churning out code for long periods of time, without actually producing anything workable, becomes very tedious. More importantly, completing a task one or two years down the road is very difficult to work toward.

Keeping Users Happy

Large projects take considerable time to complete. Users will become nervous and impatient if they do not see a working application for a long period of time. By developing the project incrementally, the developers will be able to show the users a working application at the end of each stage. When developing projects over a long period of time, users will feel more secure when parts of the application are actually functioning.

The initial stages of a project could complete the most critical parts of the application. When these parts are finished, the application can be given to the user. As later stages are completed, the user can be given upgrades, which contain more functionality. This means that a user could have a partially working application that performs all of the essential functionality of the project within a short time as opposed to having to wait a long time for the finished product.

Time and Money Savings

As with other project management techniques, building incrementally will allow errors and changes to be dealt with as soon as possible. Any such errors in design or code will be discovered at the end of each stage, rather than at the completion of the project. Problems can also be discovered when an individual component is completed and tested in its own right.

> **Remember, the earlier a problem is found, the easier it is to fix.**

When a project is not developed as a set of incremental components, the application can only be tested as a whole. If there are problems at this final stage, they will take much longer to track down and fix than if they were identified within a specific component.

Even when developing a project with components, however, there can be serious problems if you do not build the project in increments. If a component functions perfectly on its own, it may still produce errors when placed within the project. Until each component is tested separately and within the project, we cannot say it is complete.

Development Flexibility

If the application is going to be used in many different environments, building a project with components means that these components can be reused in these different environments. Without skillful project development, it may be necessary to build completely different applications for each environment. This requires a great deal of extra time and money, and results in building several applications with identical functionality.

Testing Frequently and Documenting All Bugs and Changes

Developing the project in increments using components will allow project teams to test each component separately as it is completed, and also to test the entire project as each component is added.

Testing and debugging go hand in hand. Both should be performed in a careful, planned manner that not only gives the highest probability of finding problems, but also of finding where the problems are occurring. Carefully designed charts and procedures should be created for testing and debugging.

If any changes are made to the project, everything should be re-tested. Carefully document, inside and outside of the code, all of the bugs that were found, when they were found, who fixed them, and how and when they were fixed. A haphazard method of debugging, i.e. just stepping through the code and making random changes to suspect areas, is like driving a bulldozer through your code.

We will now discuss the following project management issues that are relevant when the team are testing and debugging code:

- ❑ Error Management
- ❑ Error Location

Error Management

Documentation ensures that bugs are actually fixed. Placing documentation within the code allows you to see where changes are made in case the changes result in further problems. One way of doing this is to place module and function level headers in the project code which detail the description, the parameters passed, the parameters returned (or changed), and a local revision history of the changes made to each function.

> *Without this documentation, developers are left with no way of tracking which repairs were made, or any way to change the repairs should they create further problems.*

A testing phase that is not coherent and clear can result in errors being missed by the developer and found later by the user. I acknowledge that even with the best testing and design, a few bugs may still get through: but a poor testing phase will result in a complete infestation rather than one or two small bugs.

Documentation will also allow the project team to review every error once the project is complete - which can help prevent them from being made again in future projects.

Error Location

Testing a component by itself outside of the entire project can identify bugs located within that component. In this way, we can limit the possible bug sources to the component itself (private methods and properties), which makes them easier to track down.

Once the component is found to be bug free, any bugs found when the component is placed within the entire project are probably related to how the component communicates to the rest of the project (public properties and methods). This allows both the public and private methods and properties to be fully tested.

Testing an application only when it is complete or after several components have been put together, makes it very difficult to find which component is causing the problem. The loss in time is enormous, but more importantly, the project manager may have to ask his developers to spend many frustrating days tracking the problem down.

Failure to test the entire project after each change or addition can result in bugs hiding in unsuspecting places. Always remember that making any changes to an application may affect parts of the project we would not expect to be affected by the change.

Careful Design of all Components

We've seen the benefits of using components to build a project in a more efficient, effective manner. Components can be easily tested, upgraded, and changed with only a minor impact on schedule and costs. Yet one has to ask, "Just how does one build a Visual Basic application out of components?" The answer is by building your project from objects.

Visual Basic objects (which include your own classes, textboxes, ADO, etc.) can be considered as individual components. These objects can be put together to build larger objects, such as forms and ActiveX Controls, which will then be assembled into the final project. Using object-oriented programming in Visual Basic is therefore the best way to create projects using components. In other words, building projects incrementally using components, and the whole OOP strategy, go hand-in-hand.

> *Visual Basic programmers must finally break away from the pre-Visual Basic 4, 32-bit applications which were, in their best implementations, modular but still monolithic procedural applications. While Visual Basic's syntax may still be Basic style, its projects and coding can be object-oriented.*

The following considerations will arise from any careful approach to component design:

❑   Ill-Contained Components Lead to Delicate Projects
❑   The Registry Must be Kept Tidy

Ill-Contained Components Lead to Delicate Projects

If any component is not well contained, the entire project becomes a stack of cards. Everything is dependent upon everything else, and bad containment results in the creation of spaghetti code.

Making one change may result in many parts of the application being affected in an unpredictable manner. Poorly designed objects cannot be pulled out of the project and tested by themselves. The result is that making a code change could require the project team to test everything in the project - just to see if something else has been affected. And if something else does break, another change is necessary... and the whole process soon becomes unmanageable.

Testing becomes a complex tangle of trying to debug an entire project at once and tracing back and forth through thousands of lines of code. Not a great situation for any project to be in.

The Registry Must be Kept Tidy

One less obvious problem with poorly built objects is the amount of work required to change our own Visual Basic objects (such as an ActiveX DLL). This is down to Visual Basic's handling of COM on our behalf.

When we compile a Visual Basic ActiveX project, it assigns several unique numbers called GUIDs (Globally Unique Identifiers) to the component; these are stored in the system registry. If the component is further developed with changes to its public interface, then subsequent compilations of these projects will result in new GUIDs being assigned. Any computer that registered the original version will have to have that registry information updated, often manually, using the `regsvr32` program.

When we build a component and distribute it, we are making a promise that we will never, ever change its interface at any time. We may add methods and properties (which fits perfectly with building our project in increments), but changes to the existing interface must never happen. Breaking this promise means we have to pay the price, i.e. a whole lot of cleaning up.

The only way to prevent this from happening is for the project manager to insist upon the project team carefully planning their objects to ensure that they are building them correctly from the first release.

> *It is true that we should be able to leave the old registry entries in the registry without causing any harm. In my experience, though, I have found that this can cause your component not to run properly; so I would always clean up dead entries.*

Summary

Using the techniques outlined in this chapter, project managers will be able to guide their teams towards preventing cost and time overruns, poor morale, poor code, and projects that do not do what they are supposed to do. These basic techniques provide security, giving the users and developers a clear, safe way of managing a project on time and within budget.

In this chapter we covered:

- ❑ What is involved in designing a project
- ❑ Why it's necessary to use standards
- ❑ How frameworks restricted our project development
- ❑ How patterns can make future projects easier to develop
- ❑ The Project Development Lifecycle
- ❑ How the Enterprise Application Model applies to this book
- ❑ Plenty of project management techniques:
- ❑ Part 1: Project Design
- ❑ Part 2: Project Implementation

Now that we have an understanding of basic project management practices, we are all set to start our actual design work in UML. The first step is to determine the project requirements, so that's what we'll look at in the next chapter, as we conduct some interviews and build some use cases.

```
          │
          ▼
    ┌─────────────┐
    │   Get ADO   │
    │ connection  │
    └─────────────┘
          │
          ▼
          ◇──────────
         ╱ ╲
        ╱   ╲
        ╲   ╱
         ╲ ╱
          ◇
          │
 [Successful]
          │
          ▼
    ┌─────────────┐
    │Set Recordset│
    │cursor location│
    └─────────────┘
          │
          │
          ▼
    ┌─────────────┐
    │Set Recordset│
    │   source    │
    └─────────────┘
          │
          │
          ▼
    ┌─────────────┐
    │Set Recordset│
    │ connection  │
    └─────────────┘
          │
          │
          ▼
```

Requirements Development

3

Before we can design a project, we must first find out exactly what our project is supposed to do when it's finished. Of course, it's also just as important to know what the project is *not* supposed to do when we're through. So here's a clear rule: for projects we're working on that have users, we should center our external design upon the requirements of those users.

It's possible to determine the requirements of the project by interviewing the users and finding out how they are going to use the system, what their needs are, and how they expect the system to work. There will be different types of users, of course, and we should meet with at least one representative - preferably more - from every user type.

In the language of UML, a type of user is called an **actor,** and a written model of the way that the actor uses different parts of the system is called a **use case**.

This chapter concentrates on the UML model that is most likely to be the starting point of any project: the use case. Here's how we'll explore use cases in this chapter:

- ❑ We start with a clear explanation of the possible relationships that can exist between objects. This concept of relationships between objects is fundamental to a full understanding of use cases.
- ❑ We then examine how to identify the potential users of a project, and the best way to determine the requirements of these users. We learn how to convert this information into a use case. Along the way, I'll present some examples of creating use cases that are relevant to our project.
- ❑ Once we've established our use cases we can go on to consider how they are related to one another and to the users of the system. This information is represented in a use case diagram.
- ❑ Finally, I'll demonstrate how we can identify some of the project's objects from our use cases.

This chapter will therefore provide a clear step-by-step guide to creating use cases, use case diagrams, and identifying the user-determined objects of the system.

Before we start looking at actors and use cases, however, we need to understand those relationships between objects that I mentioned a moment ago.

Relationships

Objects are things. **A relationship** is a connection among things. In the real world, we have relationships that connect things together. For instance, an employee works for a company. The relationship between the employee and the company is **works for**. A car has an engine, a steering wheel, and four wheels. The relationship between the car and its engine is a ...**has a**... relationship.

> In object-oriented modeling, we are interested in three types of relationships. They are **dependency, association**, and **generalization**.

Let's run through these different types of relationship now.

Dependency

A **dependency** relationship indicates that one object **knows another**. Changes to the latter object (the known object) affect the former object (the knowing object). In Visual Basic, adding a reference to a component to a project establishes a dependency. That is, the project depends on the component.

Dependency is usually a one-way relationship. The fact that a project depends on a component does not necessarily mean that the component depends on the project.

In UML, a dependency is represented by a dashed directed line from the *dependent* object to the *depended* object. The diagram below shows a dependency relationship between a Visual Basic project and the ActiveX Data Object (ADO) library:

In the above dependency, any changes made to the ActiveX Data Object also change the project. If the project is originally built using ADO 1.5 and it is now using ADO 2.0, you might need to change a certain portion of code so that it will take advantage of new features offered by ADO 2.0. When we distribute the project, the ADO 2.0 library must be distributed.

Association

An **association** indicates that an **object's state depends on another object**. To understand the state of the dependent object, we must understand its relationship with the object it depends upon. For instance, let's say it's a fact that someone called David works for Wrox Press; but, if we didn't actually know anything about what David did for a living, we would need to know whom David **works for** before we could understand what David does when he's working. David's state depends on another object: the company he works for.

An association usually connects two objects, and in that case we say that it is a **binary association**. A less common type of association is an **n-ary association**, where more than two objects are connected.

In UML, an association is represented by a solid line connecting two or more objects, as illustrated here:

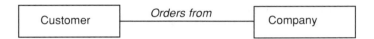

> *You can also add an arrow indicating the direction of the association, if you think it makes the diagram clearer. You'll notice that the accompanying text "Order from" in the diagram above makes the direction of the relationship fairly clear however.*

It is often desirable to know how many instances of a class are allowed in an association. For instance, an order can have one or more order lines. The allowed or required number of instances is called the **multiplicity** of the association. In UML, a multiplicity of exactly one is shown as 1, and a multiplicity of one or more is shown as 1..*. This representation is illustrated below:

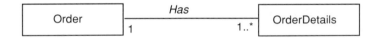

This figure says that for each Order, there must be one or more OrderDetails lines. If your company has decided that you can create an order without any order line, this multiplicity becomes zero or more, represented as 0..*. You may also specify other multiplicity condition such as zero (0), zero or one (0..1), or m to n (m..n).

A normal association between two classes represents a peer-to-peer relationship. That is, both classes are of equal importance. However, classes are sometimes related to each other in a way that one class is a part of another class. Therefore, they form a whole/part relationship. For instance, an order line is a part of an order.

Two special cases of associations, namely **aggregation** and **composite aggregation**, are used to model such relationships. Let's take a look at aggregation and composite aggregation now.

Aggregation

An **aggregation** is represented in UML as an association with a diamond attached to the "whole" class. An Order/Customer relationship is illustrated here:

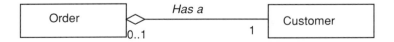

This diagram specifies that an Order must have a Customer, hence the multiplicity of 1 on the Customer end. The zero or one multiplicity (0..1) of the Order class, on the other hand, specifies that a Customer can exist without any order attached to it. Although a Customer is a part of an order, its life does not depend on the Order. If an Order is deleted, the Customer record may still remain in your system.

In other instances, the life span of a **Part** object in a Whole/Part relationship depends on the **Whole** object. For example, when a car is destroyed, its steering wheel will also be destroyed. Of course, you may argue that we may be able to reuse the steering wheel; I personally would not keep my steering wheel though. This type of relationship is called a composite aggregation.

Composite Aggregation

A perfect example of a **composite aggregation** is the Order/Line association we used earlier. When an Order is deleted, all OrderDetails lines are gone with it. A composite aggregation is represented in UML as an aggregation with a solid diamond:

We can show the relationships among the Order class, the OrderDetails class, and the Customer class in one diagram:

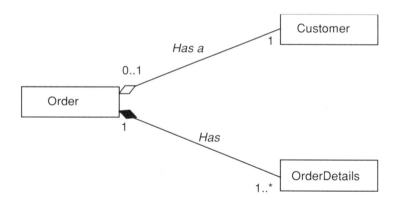

This diagram simply merges the two previous diagrams we've been developing into a more concise visual statement about the relationship between our Order class and the Customer and OrderDetails class.

Generalization

A **generalization** is a relationship between a general class and a specific type of it. For instance, a Customer class may represent all our customers while a GoodCustomer class may represent customers who have good credit records. In this case, the GoodCustomer class is said to be a specialization of the generic customer class.

A generalization represents an **is-a-kind-of** relationship. That is, a good customer is a kind of customer.

In UML, a generalization is represented as a solid line with a triangle pointing to the generic class, as shown below:

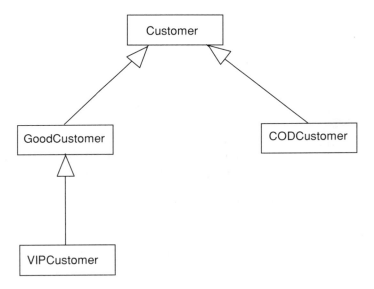

In this diagram, the GoodCustomer class represents customers with good credit record. The CODCustomer class represents customers who must pay when the goods are delivered (Cash On Delivery). They are both special kinds of the generic customer class. The VIPCustomer class further represents all good customers who spend $10,000 or more every month.

> One of the most notable shortcomings of Visual Basic 6 is the lack of inheritance implementation. There is no way to model generalization in Visual Basic. For this reason, we will not discuss generalization further in this book.

We will now move on to consider actors and use cases in more detail.

Actors

Actors do not necessarily have to be people. They can also be other external systems calling your system. The **system** includes all of the components within our project. These components communicate with each other by passing messages back and forth. In the case of an n-tier framework, the system is composed of everything that makes up the client, business and data tiers.

> **Actors are not part of the system. Actors are external to your system. They are something that must interact with the system.**

An actor can be a person, such as an order entry clerk. For instance, if our application were using an online credit card checking system that was external to your project, this would be an example of another system that could be considered an actor.

An actor can:

- ❑ Get information from the system
- ❑ Put information into the system
- ❑ Both of the above

Identifying Actors

An initial interview with someone in management can give us an overview of the system and the people involved with the system. From this interview it should be possible to generate a list of possible actors. After talking with these people, we might find that certain people actually play several different roles and are actually several different actors. On the other hand, we might find that several users may only be one actor. Defining an actor is not always easy.

> **Remember that actors do not represent every single person using the system. Actors represent a particular type of person that interacts with the system.**

For example, in the order entry application, our actors would include user types such as the order entry clerk, the manager, the person who is in charge of products, etc.

We must also be careful not to get too specific with our actors. For example, we could have two people taking orders, one by phone and another who is taking orders through the mail. In this case, we would *not* make two roles for this if the two people were interacting with the system in the same way. As far as the system is concerned, if they both are entering orders the same way, then they are the same actor.

The following list of questions can help us to identify actors:

- ❑ Who will be interested in this particular task?
- ❑ Who will this task benefit?
- ❑ Where is the system going to be used and who will be the people located there?

❑ Who will put the information into the system?
❑ Who will use this information?
❑ Who will edit and delete this information?

We can ask these questions, and other related ones, during our interviews with users of the system we're designing and developing.

UML Representation of Actors

In UML, actors are represented by a stick figure, as shown below:

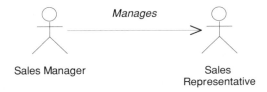

The directed line in the above figure represents a unidirectional association between the Sales Manager actor and the Sales Representative actor. That is, a Sales Manager manages sales representatives. Most UML tools allow you to enter specifications of actors so that you can document everything related to the actors.

Now we can represent actors, classes and relationships, let's move straight on to some interviews so we can begin to put into action what we've learned so far.

Interviewing Users

Once we have a list of potential actors for our system, we will want to interview at least one person from each group.

When interviewing a user, here are some of the key questions you want answered:

❑ What roles does the user play and what does the user do in each of these roles?
❑ Does the user play more than one role in the system?
❑ Does the user create, edit, delete, or save any information in the system?
❑ What type of information does the user require to perform their task?
❑ What are possible things that the user can do that are incorrect tasks?

These questions are not necessarily questions that you are going to ask the user directly. Instead, these are questions that should be answered by the end of the interview – but that you may want to broach indirectly. The best way I have found to do this is to work around the questions, leading the conversation towards the topics themselves. Why? Because your interviewees may clam up if you ask them directly... or even worse, they may give you idealized answers based more on what they think should happen rather than what actually does happen!

Our list of potential actors include the Sales Representative, the Sales Manager, the Vice President of Sales and the Inside Sales Coordinator. Over the next few pages we will be interviewing these users and recording their requirements in use cases.

What follows is an interview with Valerie, Northwind's order entry clerk, who has been entering orders in the application that Northwind wants to replace. She will be describing what she does with the current system. Externally, the new system will perform similar tasks, though it may do it in a very different way. Internally, the new application will be completely different, which is why the old application is being replaced instead of being rewritten.

Interview with the Sales Representative

Interviewer: Valerie, why don't you start by telling me what you're currently doing and how you do it?

Valerie: Basically I'm an Order Entry Clerk - so I enter the new orders. We've got a computer system, which is supposed to make things easier. It's like a database that I can get information from and add things to. Everything I need should be in the database. A customer calls in with an order and I take their details. Then I take their order – which tells us how many of our products they want.

Interviewer: So could you tell me what customer details you need and why?

Valerie: Well, first I need their company name and address so that I can tell whether they're a new or an old customer. We have a list of customers to check from. Each customer has an ID number but I'm not allowed to change that. We have different customers with the same name so that's why we need their address. Also, if we have a new customer call in, I need to set up a new account for them. At this point I also check that the details on our list are correct - maybe the customer's moved.

Interviewer: OK, so what do you do next?

Valerie: Well, then I just take the details of their order, what they want from our catalog and how much. The products are stored in the database too. I confirm these details and the computer works out how much it's all going to cost and then I make sure the customer is happy with the price. Of course, I can't give them a deal or anything, but sometimes they haven't realized how much their order is going to come to. So anyway once the order is taken, I save it to the database and wait for the next one.

Interviewer: Right, so could you tell me how the customer receives his goods?

Valerie: Oh yes, sorry, I have to do that too. From another list I select a suitable shipper depending on the company's address, and add the cost of shipping to the cost of their goods and then check if the price is OK.

Interviewer: So adding new customers is one of your responsibilities. Could you tell me how you go about setting up an account for a new customer?

Valerie: Yes, that is one of my responsibilities. I'm supposed to be adding new customers or changing a customer's details. To check if a customer is new, I have to search through our list. If the customer is new I take the customer's company name and address, and add it to our list on the database. The computer then generates the customer ID. Also, a customer may call up and say that their address has changed, and so one of my responsibilities will be changing the customer's address. I have to get the customer information from the database and modify it. All this can take some time because we have a lot of of customers. What I would really like is an easier way to check customers – like if I just typed in the company name and it knew if the customer existed or not. Or even if it gave me a list of customers with that name straight away rather than me having to find it myself.

Interviewer: Are there any possible errors that can occur while you are doing this?

Valerie: Yeah, if someone else is changing a customer record, I won't be able to modify it until they are done. One thing that is really annoying is that each field can only be a certain length, but the program will allow you to type in as many letters as you want. If you type too much, the program will just chop off the extra letters.

Interviewer: How long can the fields be?

Valerie: Umm, here. I've written it down. The company name can be 40 letters; the contact name, 30 letters; the contact title, 30; the address, 60; city, 15; region, 15; postal code, 10; country, 15; and the phone and fax, 24 digits. I have to remember these.

Interviewer: Do you have any other responsibilities besides taking orders? Can you edit orders or change orders or do things like that?

Valerie: No, I can't change an order. Once I've entered an order, if there's an error in the order, the Sales Manager has to take care of it and he is responsible for modifying the orders.

Interviewer: Can you tell me about the products?

Valerie: No, I don't have anything to do with them, the inside sales person handles that.

Interviewer: Does any one else handle orders?

Valerie: Yeah, sometimes when we are shorthanded or really busy, the Sales Manager will step in and take orders.

Interviewer: Can you think of anything else that you like or dislike about your current system?

Valerie: Well we have a lot of products, and different products clearly belong to different categories. Sometimes it takes me a long time to find the right product because they are all in one long list. I could find each product much more easily if they were split up into the different categories.

Interviewer: Thank you for your time.

Making Sense of Interviews

This interview allowed us to gather a lot of information, which we can pick through to get a general overview of what tasks Valerie performs. Once we've done this, we can return and ask more specific questions to fill in the missing pieces. As with most of the parts of project design, ascertaining the user's requirements can be an iterative process.

Once we have gone back and spoken to Valerie about any aspects of the interview that were confusing, we can create a summary of the interview so that the information is much clearer and broken down into tasks that we believe represent her requirements for the **new** system.

> **The summary for each task will form the basis of a use case.**

Our summary of her interview is as follows.

Summary of the Interview

This describes the actions that Valerie performs already (hence Valerie is that Actor). Any aspects of these tasks that will be altered should also be included. One aspect that she is unhappy with is the long list of products that she has to search through. Therefore, we have added a new stage where she can select the product category before she chooses the actual product.

The Actor Creates an Order

- ❑ The actor receives the phone call from a customer
- ❑ The actor is asked by the customer to place an order
- ❑ The actor retrieves the name and address from the customer
- ❑ The actor enters the name in the system
- ❑ The actor checks whether the customer's personal information is correct
- ❑ If the information is correct, the actor requests the order information
- ❑ The actor retrieves the product names and quantities from the customer
- ❑ The actor selects a product category
- ❑ The actor selects the products
- ❑ The actor types a quantity for each product
- ❑ The actor selects a shipper
- ❑ The actor confirms with the customer that all the information is correct
- ❑ The actor completes the Order Details
- ❑ The actor saves the order to the database

The Actor Modifies Customer Information

- ❑ The actor retrieves a customer record
- ❑ The actor makes a request to modify the customer information if the customer information is incorrect
- ❑ The actor changes the customer information so that it is correct
- ❑ The actor confirms the new information with the customer
- ❑ The actor saves the new customer information

The Actor Creates a New Customer

Here we address another problem that Valerie experiences. In the new system she will be able to jump directly to the appropriate customer by typing in the company name. If this company name does not already exist, the system will create a customer ID and allow the relevant information to be entered.

❑   The actor makes a request to create a new customer or the actor can type in the name and the system will automatically allow her to add a new customer (if there are no existing customers with this name)

❑   The actor enters the information on the customer

❑   The actor verifies that the customer information is correct

❑   The actor saves the new customer information

Other Information

❑   A customer consists of the following fields and field sizes:

❑   Company Name: 40 characters
Contact Name: 30 characters
Contact Title: 30 characters
Address: 60 characters
City: 15 characters
Region: 15 characters
Postal Code: 10 characters
Country: 15 characters
Phone: 24 characters
Fax: 24 characters

❑   The system assigns the customer and order IDs

❑   Customer and order IDs can not be edited

The Use Case

A use case tells us all about how the actor uses the system, and so it should be written from the actor's perspective. The second thing to notice is that the above summaries could have been written down during the interview. In other words, we can begin to build our use case while interviewing the user.

When the interview is complete, the user can look over the use case and verify that all of the information is complete and correct. Use cases and the use case diagrams are not only the starting point for all of our other UML diagrams, they are also a very easy to understand, user-friendly way of mapping out the system's requirements. Use case diagrams, which are diagrams showing the relationships between use cases and actors, provide something that any user should be able to understand and be able to use to verify if the information is correct.

Use Case Criteria

The structure of all our use cases should be very clear:

> **Every use case must have a starting point, an ending point (which includes canceling the task), and a measurable result.**

From the interview summary we've conducted, we can see that there are several use cases here. The use cases we can create from this interview are:

- ❑ Create an Order
- ❑ Modify a Customer
- ❑ Create a New Customer

Although Valerie talked about modifying orders, the manager performs this task, so I haven't included it here. These three tasks all have a beginning, an end and a measurable outcome, so they all classify as use cases.

Note that Create a New Customer and Modify a Customer are tasks that are actually performed as part of Create an Order. When one use case is part of another, we say that *one use case uses the other use case*. In our analysis, Create an Order <<uses>> Create a New Customer and Modify a Customer. In this system, a customer cannot exist unless they have placed an order, so these two subtasks will always be part of Create an Order.

How to Build a Use Case

Once we've determined what our use cases are, we need to build them. There are many ways of building use cases. Many references just have a single block of text that contains all the information. I feel it is better to break the use case into separate sections so that you can be sure that all of the required sections are properly filled in. Sections also make it easier to read and find information in the use case. Our use cases will consist of the following sections:

- ❑ **Name**: a useful name for each use case
- ❑ **Overview:** The purpose of the use case
- ❑ **Primary Actor:** The main actor that will perform the use case
- ❑ **Secondary Actors:** Additional actors that will perform the use case
- ❑ **Starting Point:** The first action to be performed in the use case
- ❑ **Ending Point:** The last action to be performed in the use case
- ❑ **Measurable Result:** The final measurable result of the use case
- ❑ **Flow of Events:** A complete description of everything that occurs from the start to the end of the use case
- ❑ **Alternative Flow of Events:** Any event that could occur that is not along the normal flow of events. These will include all error conditions
- ❑ **Use Case Extensions:** Occasionally a use case can be broken into several smaller use cases. There will be a main use case that uses several other use cases. This section lists all of the use cases that the use case uses
- ❑ **Outstanding Issues:** Any issues relating to the use case that have not yet been resolved

Trying It Out – Building Use Cases

Let's now create our first use case based on the summary we created above. We could use a UML tool such as HOW from Riverton, a drawing program such as SmartDraw, or in fact any program that allows us to work with graphics. HOW not only allows us make our use cases, but can also generate Visual Basic code. SmartDraw can only make our diagrams. Use a tool that suits your needs.

It's important that you actually do these examples, as these diagrams can appear deceptively simple until you start trying to create them yourself!

The UML does not specify the format and the style of documentation. In general, companies establish their own documentation standard and methods to extract relevant information from interview notes. Let's review the interview with our Sales Representative, Valerie, in detail now, to see how we can actually generate a use case document from our notes.

Remember now, there are three use cases associated with our Sales Representative:

- ❑ Create an Order
- ❑ Modify a Customer
- ❑ Create a New Customer

The order in which we create these use cases is discretionary. For illustrative purposes, we will begin with the Create a New Customer use case, and I'll go through the creation of that use case with you step-by-step, so you'll know exactly what's going on.

Once you're more familiar with how to draw up use cases like this, we'll run through the Modify a Customer and Create an Order use cases more briskly. So let's begin with a detailed study of how to create our first use case.

Use Case: Create a New Customer - A Step-By-Step Guide

We will now develop the use case for Create New Customer. This use case meets all the criteria for a use case, but don't forget that it's actually used by the use case Order Entry. The Sales Representative would never be adding a new customer unless a new customer had called in to place an order!

So let's run through the creation of the Create New Customer use case. We should first of all ensure that our use case has a clear and explanatory *Name*. For this task, Create New Customer is very clear and seems the most appropriate name:

Name: Create a Customer

If we now follow the instructions in the "How to Build a use case" section, above, we can see that the next thing to do is create an *Overview* or summary of the purpose of the use case. This is clearly to generate a new customer to list in the database. Therefore we have:

Overview: The main purpose of the use case is to create a new customer.

Next, we need to consider the *Primary* and *Secondary Actors* associated with this system. This is not necessarily as simple as it might at first seem. For this use case our primary actor is the Sales Representative, and there are no secondary actors. Let's carry on building these sections then:

Primary Actor: Sales Representative
Secondary Actor: None

> **You may be wondering why the Sales Manager isn't listed as a Secondary Actor, as Valerie did say that the Sales Manager sometimes steps in and enters orders.**
>
> **The point here is that entering an order does not make the Sales Manager qualify as a Secondary Actor, because when the Sales Manager steps in and enters an order, they are now performing the task of a Sales Representative. The Sales Manager is therefore acting as a Primary Actor. This is probably one of the most confusing parts of use cases.**

Actors represent roles that different people step into when interacting with the system. Anyone can step into that role regardless of what their actual title is. Whether it is the person whose job title is Sales Manager, or the person whose job title is Sales Representative, both of them are performing the Sales Representative task when they enter orders into the system. There is no secondary actor here. New customers are only added to the system during the entry of a new order, which is only done by the actor called Sales Representative.

Now we turn to the use case criteria of *Starting Point*, *Ending Point*, and *Measurable Result*. The use case clearly starts when the actor requests to make a new customer and ends when the customer has been added or when the request is cancelled. Therefore, if successful, the Measurable Result must be that a customer has been added.

Starting point: This use case starts when the actor makes a request to create a new customer

Ending point: The actor's request to create a customer is either completed or canceled

Measurable result: A customer is added to the system

Next, we come to the meat of the use case: the *Flow of Events*. There are two use case flows. The first describes what happens if everything goes to plan. The second, the alternative flow of events, describes what happens when difficulties unforeseen by the actor arise or if mistakes are made. Let us first consider the flow of events. The actor has already requested to create a new customer. Then:

- ❑ The actor is prompted to enter information that defines the customer, such as name, address, contact, etc.
- ❑ The actor can choose to save the information or to cancel the operation.
- ❑ If the actor decides to save the information the new customer is created in the system, and the list of customers that was presented earlier is updated.

Now for the alternative flow of events:

❑ The actor attempts to add a customer that already exists. The system will notify the user and cancel the operation.

❑ The actor enters an improper value for one of the fields. The system will not allow the update until a proper value for the field is entered.

The last two sections are the *Use Case Extensions* and *Outstanding Issues*. It is not sensible to break down this particular use case into smaller use cases, and there are no unresolved points - so this part is simply:

Use case extensions: None
Outstanding issues: None

We are now in a position to put all of this information together and to build out Create New Customer use case as shown here:

USE CASE: CREATE NEW CUSTOMER

Overview

The main purpose of this use case is to create a new customer

Primary Actor

Sales Representative

Secondary Actor

None

Starting point

This use case starts when the actor requests to create a new customer.

Ending Point

The actor's request to create a customer is either completed or canceled.

Measurable Result

A customer is added to the system.

<u>**Flow of Events**</u>

The actor is prompted to enter information that defines the customer, such as name, address, contact, etc. The actor can choose to save the information or to cancel the operation. If the actor decides to save the information the new customer is created in the system, and the list of customers that was presented earlier is updated.

<u>**Alternative Flow of Events**</u>

The actor attempts to add a customer that already exists. The system will notify the user and cancel the operation. The actor enters an improper value for one of the fields. The system will not allow the update until a proper value for the field is entered.

<u>**Use Case Extensions**</u>

None

<u>**Outstanding Issues**</u>

None

In this example, we rewrote the interview summary in the flow of events. We could, however, have just copied our summary exactly as it was and placed it in the flow of events. Either way is correct. Use a format that works best for you, your group, and your users.

Use Case: Modify a Customer

Looking back at our interview with Valerie the Sales Representative, and the summary we drew up called "The Actor Modifies Customer Information", we can translate the information from that summary into a use case just as we did for Create New Customer. We can consider each of the sections that make up a use case individually. We can then put all the information together to form the final use case. The Modify a Customer use case now looks as follows:

<u>**USE CASE: MODIFY A CUSTOMER**</u>

<u>**Overview**</u>

The purpose of this use case is to modify customer information.

Primary Actor

Sales Representative

Secondary Actor

None

Starting Point

The actor must have displayed a list of customers.

Ending Point

The modification is either completed or canceled.

Measurable Result

A customer's record is updated.

Flow of Events

This use case begins when the actor requests to review an existing customer and the system presents the information, as well as a list of products that the customer has purchased. The actor makes a request to edit the customer. The actor can edit all the information except the list of products. This list of products is updated when a customer places a customer order for a product. The actor can either save the changes and return to the list of customers or can return to the list of customers without any changes being saved. If the actor chooses to save the changes, the edited customer information is saved and the list of customers is updated.

Alternative Flow of Events

An improper value for one of the fields is entered. The system will not allow the update until it is corrected. Another actor is using the customer record and the customer record is locked.

Use Case Extensions

None

> **Outstanding Issues**
>
> None

Use Case: Create an Order

Our next use case that results from our interview with the Sales Representative Valerie is Create an Order. This use case is created in exactly the same way as the previous two. Here is the finished article:

> **USE CASE: CREATE AN ORDER**
>
> **Overview**
>
> The main purpose of this use case is to create a new product order for a customer
>
> **Primary actor**
>
> Sales representative
>
> **Secondary Actor**
>
> None
>
> **Starting Point**
>
> The actor requests to make a new order.
>
> **Ending Point**
>
> The order is either created or canceled.
>
> **Measurable Result**
>
> An order is created.

Flow of Events

The actor received the phone call from a customer. The actor is asked by the customer to place an order. The actor opens up the order entry form. The actor retrieves the name and address from the customer. The actor enters the name in the system. The actor confirms that the customer's personal information is correct. If the information is correct, the actor requests the order information. If the customer information is incorrect the actor updates the customer information. The actor selects a product category. The actor selects the products. The actor types a quantity for each product. The actor selects a shipper. The actor confirms with the customer that all the information is correct. The actor completes the order details. The actor saves to the database.

Alternative Flow of Events

None

Use Case Extensions

None

Outstanding Issues

None

Interview with the Sales Manager

I will now present the transcript of an interview with the Sales Manager. Afterwards, we repeat the process of extracting the relevant information from the interview and then creating the necessary use cases.

Interviewer: Could you start by telling me about your responsibilities and how you perform your duties?

Sales Manager: Yes, well actually I have quite a lot of responsibility. I have two main duties: deleting customers and editing orders. With deleting customers I have to check the customer's credit record, and if they are a bad customer I just delete them. Editing an order is pretty self-explanatory.

Interviewer: OK, let's take deleting a customer and expand on that. Are there specific criteria that determine whether a customer should be deleted - or is it left entirely to your judgement?

Sales Manager: Well, I have to check the credit history, billing history and their current balance. Information from all three will determine whether I delete them. Obviously I can't delete a customer if he has debts or is waiting for an order to be processed. Sometimes it isn't a clear-cut case. Then I hand it on to the Vice President of Sales

Interviewer: Is there any other reason why you might delete a customer?

Sales Manager: No.

Interviewer: So let's move to editing an order. Could you give me more details on that?

Sales Manager: Well it's very straightforward. If a customer rings in to change his order, or the Order Entry Clerk makes a mistake when entering the order, I need to make the changes. In fact I waste most of my time sorting out other people's mistakes. OK, so I get the order from the database and edit it by changing the products or quantity, and then save it again. Sometimes the customer changes his mind completely and cancels his order; then I have to delete the whole thing.

Interviewer: So another of your duties is deleting an order?

Sales Manager: That's what I said, and sometimes the Vice President of Sales does this too. Obviously I can't delete an order if shipping is in progress. The same is true for editing the order. Sometimes customers ring in and want to be removed from the system entirely. Then I have to delete the customer. And another thing, at the end of the day I have to print out the reports from the reports menu.

Interviewer: Thank you for your time.

Summary of Interview with the Sales Manager

As you can see, interviewing people isn't always easy. At the end of an interview like this, you might not feel confident that the Sales Manager has given you all the relevant information. Initially the Sales Manager told us that he only had two main tasks, but as the interview progressed it became clear that his job was more involved. Clearly, once you've made the uses cases, it's necessary to show them to the actor so that they can be reviewed and appropriate changes made. The summaries of the tasks are as follows.

Actor Deletes Customers

- ❑ The actor selects a customer
- ❑ The actor reviews the customer's credit history, billing history and current balance
- ❑ The actor deletes the customer if the customer is in poor standing or has requested to be removed from the system
- ❑ The actor cannot delete the customer if the customer has outstanding orders or unpaid debts

In a real application, it is likely that the customer would be marked as inactive instead of actually being deleted.

Actor Deletes Orders

- ❏ The actor selects an order
- ❏ The actor deletes order
- ❏ The actor cannot delete an order once shipping is in progress

Actor Modifies an Order

- ❏ The actor selects an order
- ❏ The actor clicks Edit button
- ❏ The actor changes either products or quantity
- ❏ The actor cannot edit an order once shipping is in progress
- ❏ The actor saves new order

Other Information

- ❏ The actor prints daily reports from a reports menu

Immediately after we interviewed the Sales Manager, we had a chat with the Vice President of Sales to confirm his role in the tasks mentioned by the Sales Manager. The Vice President of Sales clarified the situation. Among his duties are deleting a customer and deleting an order, but he does not share any other duties with the Sales Manager.

Use Case: Delete Customer

In exactly the same way that we made use cases for the Sales Representative, we can create uses cases for the Sales Manager. The only difference here is that we have a *Secondary Actor*. Although the Vice President of Sales does share some of the same tasks as the Sales Manager he should not be considered to be the same actor. The reason is straightforward. Because the Vice President does not perform all the tasks that a Sales Manager can, it is not possible for him to step into the role of the Sales Manager. The three use cases associated with the Sales Manager would be as follows:

USE CASE: DELETE CUSTOMER

Overview

The purpose of this use case is to remove customer information.

Primary Actor

Sales Manager

Secondary Actor

Vice President of Sales

Starting Point

The actor must have displayed a list of customers.

Ending Point

The customer is either deleted or the delete is canceled by the system.

Measurable result

A customer is deleted.

Flow of Events

This use case is started when the actor requests to review an existing customer. The actor then requests to delete the customer information.

If there are outstanding unfilled customer orders or debts for the customer the actor will be advised of this by the application and the delete will not be allowed. If there are no outstanding orders or debts the actor is prompted to accept or cancel the operation. If the actor accepts the operation, the customer is deleted from the system and the customer list is updated.

Alternative Flow of Events

The actor tries to cancel a customer who has an outstanding order or debt. The customer delete will be canceled.

Use Case Extensions

None

Outstanding Issues

None

Use Case: Delete Order

USE CASE: DELETE ORDER

Overview

The purpose of this use case is to remove an order

Primary Actor

Sales Manager

Secondary Actor

Vice President of Sales

Starting Point

The actor displays the list of orders

Ending Point

The order is either deleted or the delete is canceled by the system.

Measurable Result

An order is deleted.

Flow of Events

This use case is started when the actor requests an order listing. The actor then requests to delete an order. If shipping is in progress the actor will be advised of this by the application and delete will not be allowed. If shipping has not started the actor is prompted to accept or cancel the operation. If the actor accepts the operation the order is deleted from the system.

Alternative Flow of Events

The actor tries to delete an order that is being shipped. The order delete will be canceled.

<u>Use Case Extensions</u>

None

<u>Outstanding Issues</u>

None

Use Case: Modify Order

<u>**USE CASE: MODIFY ORDER**</u>

<u>Overview</u>

The purpose of this use case is to modify an order

<u>Primary Actor</u>

Sales Manager

<u>Secondary Actor</u>

None

<u>Starting Point</u>

The actor displays the list of orders

<u>Ending Point</u>

The order is either modified or the edit is cancelled by the system

<u>Measurable Result</u>

An order is edited

Flow of Events

This use case is started when the actor requests to display the order listing. The actor then requests to modify an order or cancel the operation. If shipping is in progress, the actor will be advised of this by the application and the edit will not be allowed. If shipping has not started the actor can edit the products and quantities.

Alternative Flow of Events

The actor tries to modify an order that is being shipped. The order edit will be canceled.

Use Case Extensions

None

Outstanding Issues

None

If you had any difficulties understanding how any of these use cases were put together, you need to go back to the step-by-step guide. Follow through the Create a New Customer example that I presented, bearing in mind the use case that you are interested in. All use cases are created in the same way.

Summary of Interview with the Inside Sales Coordinator

I'm sure that by now you're getting the hang of interviewing the actors of the system and extracting the relevant information from them. So here I will just present the summaries resulting from an interview with the Inside Sales Coordinator. As you can see, the Inside Sales Coordinator has six distinct tasks. He is responsible for entering information about new products and changing information about and deleting existing products. He will also now be responsible for creating, modifying and deleting categories.

Actor Creates New Product

❑ The actor requests to create a new product
❑ The actor enters new products information
❑ The actor saves product information

Actor Modifies Product Information

❑ The actor requests a product
❑ The actor requests to modify product
❑ The actor changes fields
❑ The actor saves record

Actor Deletes Product Information

- ❑ The actor requests a product
- ❑ The actor deletes product

Actor Creates New Category

- ❑ The actor requests to create a new category
- ❑ The actor enters new category information
- ❑ The actor saves category information

Actor Modifies Category Information

- ❑ The actor requests a category
- ❑ The actor requests to modify category
- ❑ The actor changes fields
- ❑ The actor saves record

Actor Deletes Category Information

- ❑ The actor requests a category
- ❑ The actor deletes category

To save a lot of space, I've just included these summaries for the Inside Sales Coordinator. As you can see, there are six use cases associated with the Inside Sales Coordinator - I leave it up to you to develop these and see if you're comfortable now with building your own use cases.

That's our round of interviewing done, and our use cases drawn up (if you haven't drawn up the Inside Sales Coordinator use cases, don't worry: there's plenty for us to be getting on with). We can now convert these use cases into use case diagrams, which are a useful visual presentation of the information we've gathered so far. These diagrams also allow us to draw together information across several use cases. Let's move on.

Use Case Diagrams

A use case diagram offers a static view of the relationships between different use cases and actors. A use case is represented in UML as an oval, as shown below:

Modify a Customer

In UML, every use case (such as the one presented here diagrammatically by the oval) must have at least one actor. (So if we find ourselves with a use case that isn't associated with any known actor, we'd better go back and see whether we've actually gone wrong in our analysis somewhere!)

This level of abstraction, where we can represent use cases diagrammatically with these ovals, allows us to present a larger view of the system as we understand it so far: the actors in our system, and their interaction with the use cases we've been developing, can all be represented in a clear diagram. This is a useful step forward in our definition of the system we're defining.

In the following section, therefore, we'll build a use case diagram as we investigate our system requirements. We'll achieve this by employing the use cases we've just made.

Creating a Use Case Diagram - A Step-By-Step Guide

The Sales Representative

We have a detailed description of the Create New Customer use case and we can use it as the starting point for our project's use case diagrams. Since this use case has an actor, the Sales Representative, we need to place her in the diagram. To do this, we simply add an *Actor* to the diagram. We do need to give the *Actor* a name, of course; a reasonable name in this case is *Sales Representative*:

Sales
Representative

Preferably, we should also enter a description of the actor. Most modeling applications provide additional documentation tools for such purpose. For instance, when you double-click on an actor in the use case diagram in Rational Rose, you can enter a description for it:

This description will then be displayed when you select the Sales Representative actor:

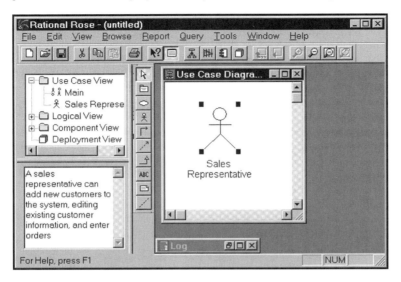

You can then carry on to add all known actors to the diagram. For now, we will move on to add a use case to the diagram.

> **If you don't have a copy of Rational Rose, it is not a problem. Rational Rose, and other such tools, just make life easier for you... but there's nothing stopping you from drawing these diagrams in any graphics package you have available, or even drawing them on paper!**
>
> **For the purposes of this book, I am teaching you how to think with UML and how to use UML analysis to design and develop successful VB applications. Use the tool that suits you – it's the analysis that really counts, not the means by which you create these diagrams.**

You start to add a use case by placing an oval to the diagram, and then giving it a name. Here is how things look in Rational Rose at this point:

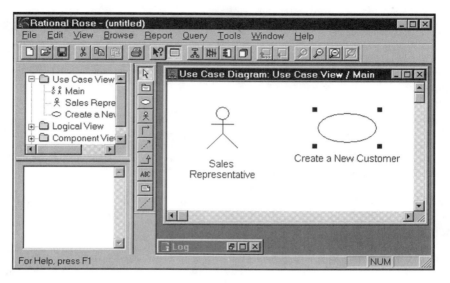

You may also enter a description of the use case, just like we did with the actor. Since we've already created a use case specification for the Create New Customer use case, we can simply use that same description. If you feel that the whole specification is too long, you can enter a short paragraph or two and place a reference to the full specification document. In Rational Rose, this description may also be shown in an information box:

Now Actors and use cases are not isolated entities in the system. They are associated with each other. We can therefore draw a line connecting an actor and a use case, like this:

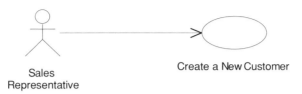

The above diagram clearly illustrates the relationship between an actor and a use case: a Sales Representative can create a new customer.

We can now add the Modify a Customer use case to our diagram. First create a new oval representing the use case, and assign it a name. Then we can enter a brief description for it. Finally, we draw a line connecting the Sales Representative actor to this new use case.

Our use case diagram should now look like this:

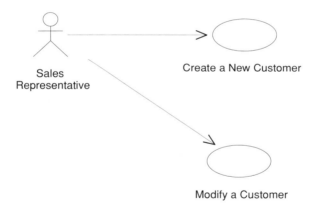

Now we can follow the same steps we just ran through for the Create a New Customer and the Modify a Customer use cases, to add the Create an Order use case to our diagram. As usual, we should at least give it a name and a brief description. Our use case diagram now details three use cases and one actor, and it looks like this:

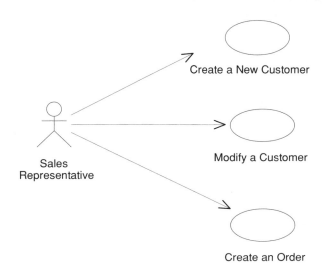

Use Cases Stereotypes

As I just mentioned, the actor and uses cases are not isolated entities. They are connected to one another. If you think about it, we're bound to find that there often exist relationships between use cases. Let's take a look at the Create an Order use case and ask ourselves this question: what happens if the order is raised for a new customer? Will the system allow for entering an order for a customer who has not had an account with your company? If so, what information must be entered into the system? If not, what should the Sales Representative do?

The <<uses>> StereoType

Assume that the Northwind Company requires that every customer must have an account. A reasonable solution is to ask the Sales Representative to create a new customer record before entering the order. The Create an Order use case thus uses the Create a New Customer use case. Since we have already developed a Create a New Customer use case, we should be able to use it to model this situation. In which case, we say that the Create an Order use case *uses* the Create a New Customer use case.

UML models this type of relationship with the <<uses>> stereotype. We can now enhance the previous diagram to show the <<uses>> stereotype among use cases:

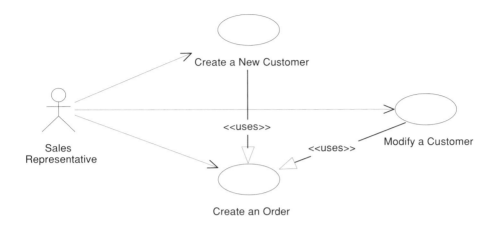

The fact that one use case uses the functionality provided by another is represented with a directed line from the *client* use case to the *base* use case, as in the above figure. The relationship between these two use cases is marked with the stereotype name <<uses>>.

> *In our diagram, the Create a New Customer use case is the client use case, and the Create an Order use case is the base use case.*

So now we've modeled the situation where an order is placed for a new customer. But now let me ask you this: are all orders the same? For instance, what happens if a VIP customer requests an order to be delivered *immediately* using the fastest shipping method? The Northwind Company would probably want to make sure that a VIP customer like this gets their products as soon as possible. My point here is that although we've modeled the ordering situation, we haven't reflected in our diagram that different ordering situations may occur - such the VIP fast order situation.

One possible solution would be to use a flag to indicate that the order being created had to be done extra-fast for our VIP customer. This is a good solution if the only difference between a standard order and a VIP order is speed. But using a flag like this would become a bit harder to model if there were further significant differences between two different types of order.

For example, let's suppose for a moment that the Northwind Company had some more rules about VIP orders:

The Sales Representative must check if that customer has purchased a minimum of $10,000 worth of products per month in the past 12 months.

If the customer does not meet the criteria, they will be charged a special handling fee.

The Sales Representative must also check whether there is sufficient inventory on hand to cover the order and the availability of the shipping company.

If these VIP rules really did exist at Northwind, we would obviously be looking at a different ordering situation from the standard one we've drawn up in our use case diagram above. We would need a way to adapt our initial use case diagram to reflect the different VIP order situation.

The VIP rules I've just shown you are **not** *a part of the Northwind project we're developing through this book (if you take a look at the interviews and use cases, you'll see they were not mentioned). However, I will now run you through exactly what we would do if we were indeed faced with these different situations based around one of our use cases.*

The <<extends>> Stereotype

As we just found out, creating an expedient VIP order would be quite different from creating a normal order. Since these are two significantly different situations, they would deserve two different use cases. The first step would be to recognize this fact, and create a new use case to detail these VIP expedient orders.

Once we had created this new use case, we could then say that our new use case (for VIP orders) **extends** the functionality of the original Create an Order use case.

We could then model this kind of use case relationship with the **<<extends>>** stereotype in UML. If a use case is a variation of another use case, it is said to *extend* the original use case. In this example, the Creating an Expedient Order *extends* the normal Create an Order use case, as shown below:

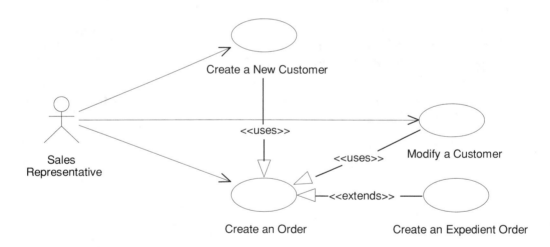

As with the <<uses>> stereotype, the directed line and the <<extends>> stereotype indicates the relationship between the Create an Order and Create an Expedient Order use cases.

> *This example of an expedient VIP order was given only to illustrate the <<extends>> stereotype.*
> *If we examine the use cases of the Sales representative, we can see that this example is not*
> *applicable to our system.*

Let's return now to where we left off before we started considering all those VIP rules. So far, we've built the use case diagram for the Sales Representative; we can now go on to consider the other actors in our system.

The Sales Manager

Next we'll consider the Sales Manager. The Sales Manager is associated with three use cases:

- ❑ Delete a Customer
- ❑ Modify an Order
- ❑ Delete an Order

We can also now begin to identify the relationship between these two actors:

- ❑ The Sales Manager
- ❑ The Sales Representative

Right now, we know that Sales Managers *manage* Sales Representatives. At this stage, we're not actually sure whether this relationship is relevant to our system, but we should capture the fact anyway. And if the relationship later turns out to be unimportant, we can always remove it from the diagram.

Let's add a direct relationship between the two actors, and update our use case diagram to reflect the three use cases that the Sales Manager is associated with:

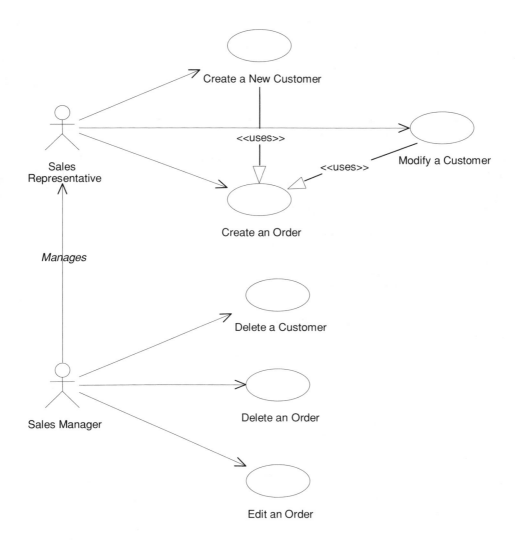

Our use case diagram now has two actors and six use cases. The diagram's getting a little crowded. You may want to put your graphics talent into good use to arrange the elements in the diagram to make it look good to your customer. Just remember that the most important task right now is to capture the functionality of the system, so don't waste too much time on beautifying it. After all, by default, good programmers are poor artists.

The Inside Sales Coordinator

We now turn our attention to the Inside Sales Coordinator. As we did earlier, let's start by adding Inside Sales Coordinator actor and his six associated use cases to the diagram. Then connect these elements with an association, as follows:

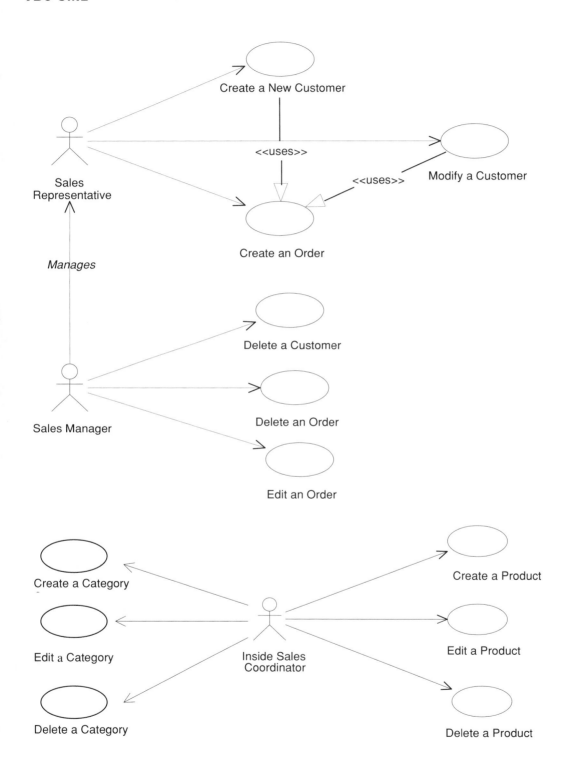

With the addition of these use cases, the first version of our use case diagram is completed. As you can see, we have captured a set of functions the system must perform. Here are some of the advantages of using these diagrams so far:

- ❑ Having to draw up diagrams has forced us to be quite explicit about what we've learned from our interviews and use case analysis
- ❑ We've drawn together a lot of related information and managed to represent some complex relationships therein (if you look at the interviews themselves, it isn't that easy to follow what's going on in the system)
- ❑ Our client can understand what we've been analyzing without having to learn a foreign language in order to communicate with us
- ❑ We're gradually defining a Visual Basic system that we're going to be able to successfully develop

We've come a long way already: these diagrams have helped us to define the system we're building, and to present some clear analysis of what we know about the system thus far.

Reviewing Use Case Models

Once we've built all our use cases, refined them, edited them and brought them to a point where we feel they accurately represent the information gathered from our interviews, we must turn them over again to the people who are going to use the system we're developing. The beauty of a use case is that it is simple enough for just about any user to understand. After a careful review of the use cases by the users, they can offer corrections and suggestions. Once these corrections have been made, the users should perform a further review.

> **It's important to realize that these use cases simply show what the user would do with the system under development. We have not really explored the following question: "Is this what the user really wants to do?"**
>
> **Once our use cases are complete, we should review them with the user, and be ready to discuss any recommended changes to the way the task is performed.**

Here's a simple but beautiful truth: it's much easier to update use cases than it is to change a completed project. While building and reviewing our use cases may itself appear time consuming, our entire project will be built from these use cases. Getting them right will mean that our project will be right. Leaving errors in our use cases will mean our project will have errors and will have to be redone - probably somewhere toward the end of development, when it's expensive to make these changes.

There should also be a detailed review of our use cases from a developer's point of view; for instance, what is the best system to implement these tasks? For this book, we will assume that this has already been done, and a DNA Visual Basic application has been chosen as the best way to implement the system. But we'll come back to discuss technological specifications again during our design process.

We've Made Our Use Cases; What Next?

Once we've made our use cases, they become a key part in the next stage of our analysis. As you may remember from the UML overview in Chapter 1, the next stage in the UML process is to identify the components of the system we're developing. We need to define what these components are, how they interact with each other, and also how they communicate with our system users.

However, if we think about this for a moment, the use cases can only deal with those components that the actors (users) are interacting with. Nothing else can really come out of our interviews but this type of information. Since the user usually does not interact with any objects that are working behind the scenes, such as the server objects, these invisible objects will not generally be a part of our use cases.

> Use cases primarily identify client-side objects: these are objects that the users interact with, such as the Customer object or the Order object.

So how will we ever design a system from a set of use cases if our users don't know a lot about what's really going on behind the scenes? The truth of the matter is that the **framework** that our project uses will also provide a number of those invisible, behind-the-scenes objects that the user may never know about. In this book, for example, we'll be using a three-tier framework, and several component frameworks, such as the ADO, RDS and MTS.

> Our UML design will therefore take account of use cases and also system framework considerations. Part of our skill will be to bring these two concerns together, as we shall see through this book.

Don't worry if you're new to the idea of frameworks and technologies such as ADO and MTS: we'll be exploring these topics in a lot more detail in later chapters. You might also want to check back to our discussion of frameworks, ADO and MTS from Chapter 2.

Let's now bring our analysis back to what we've drawn up so far - which is our set of use cases. These use cases will allow us to progress to the next stage in the UML process: identifying the visible objects that our user interviewees were able to talk about.

Identifying Objects from the Use Cases

The rules for identifying objects from our use cases are as follows:

- ❑ Objects are things: usually nouns, but sometimes they can be expressed as verbs.
- ❑ Objects contain some type of information (Visual Basic properties); that is, they have state.
- ❑ Objects have some type of behavior (Visual Basic methods); i.e. they do something.
- ❑ Any component that contains something that has already been identified as an object is also an object. For example: a car component contains tire and engine objects, so a car is also an object.

You may be wondering about the first rule: how can a verb be a thing? Looking at this sentence: "The customer orders..." the verb orders can be considered a thing, as the sum of all things that the customer orders will become an order. An order contains information such as the products purchased, their prices, etc. An order has behavior; it can be updated, created, deleted, saved, and reviewed. An order has properties, such as the total amount, customer name, etc. Orders also contain products, which are another type of object. Looking at the verb orders, we can see that we should actually rephrase our description to say: "The customer will have an order...." Order is now a noun. Be careful when you look at the descriptions of your systems. Sometimes things expressed as verbs can be rewritten as a noun and meet the requirements of being an object.

Identifying objects: a step by step guide

Let's start to identify objects in the domain by analyzing each use case. First up, take a look at the Create a New Customer use case for the Sales Representative, and highlight all the nouns:

- ❑ The **Sales Representative** requests to create a new **customer**
- ❑ The **Sales Representative** must enter the **name**, **address**, and **contact** information of the **customer**
- ❑ The **Sales Representative** saves the **customer**
- ❑ The **Sales Representative** does not save the **customer**
- ❑ The **system** confirms that the new **customer** is saved

Next, we must consider each noun in turn to see whether it is an object...

Noun: Sales Representative

Is a Sales Representative an object? Of course Valerie is an object. But is Valerie, as a Sales Representative, relevant to the system we're developing? It appears that Valerie plays no part in the operations we have identified. That is, she only interacts with the system as an actor.

In this case, there is no black and white rule that we can apply to decide whether an actor should be modeled as an object in the system.

If we think about this a little further, we can imagine that at some point, Northwind might use the system to record all Sales Representatives in the system. For instance, when a Sales Representative logs on, the system might need to verify that Sales Representative's identity before accepting their requests. If that were the case, we would need to model a Sales Representative as an object in the system.

However, in the use cases we've drawn up, Sales Representatives are only ever actors, and are not themselves recognized within the system. We will therefore not model Sales Representatives as an object in our system, because we have not identified such a need.

Noun: Customer

Is a customer an object? Yes, they are. But is this object relevant to the system? Absolutely! The system will maintain a list of customers and all customers can order products.

Is the name of a customer an object? Yes, it is. Is this object relevant to the system? It surely is. Do we need to model it as an object? It depends. If a name is just a character string that represents the customer's business name, defining it as an object does not seem to be necessary, since we could simply use a built-in string type.

Is the address of a customer an object? Again the answer is yes, and it is certainly relevant to the system. Do we need to model it as an object? We are not sure about this yet. If we only need a string of characters, we do not want to create an object for it.

However, what if we need to extract parts of the address later on? For instance, if the Northwind Company decided to launch a marketing campaign targeting customers in a particular area, it might need to extract the postcode from the address. Attempting to extract such information from a flat string could be tricky. If, on the other hand, we had modeled the address as an object that had a street number, a string name, a city name, a state name, and a postcode, we could easily obtain that postcode from a customer record.

We can use our imagination and experience to make a decision here. The result is rather academic. Let us just say that since this is not clear at the moment, we will not model the customer address as an object. We can always come back to change it.

> **Remember that object-oriented analysis and design process is an iterative process, and it's unlikely that we will get everything right in the first attempt.**

To save us from repeating the same argument again, let's also assume that we will not model the customer contact as an object.

In fact, regardless of whether or not we model the various customer details as objects, there is one thing that we can decide right now: these things are all properties of customers. (In Visual Basic, we will make them properties of the Customer class when we design classes later on.)

Noun: System

Finally, after several cups of coffee and heated debate, we reach the last noun. Is the system an object? Yes it is, but it represents the whole system, not a part of it:

> The **system** confirms that the new customer is saved.

Since the system is not going to be self-aware, most likely, this reference to the system is not in itself relevant to the system itself. Therefore, we will not model it as an object in the application domain.

> *As we progress through our design and development, we'll come to see that it isn't going to be the system that accepts or rejects the requests from the user. It is most likely that an object representing a system function will handle the request in question.*

We've now completed our analysis for this particular use case - Create a New Customer. We've identified one object: `Customer`. Document it!

Equally importantly, we must not forget the questions we've asked and assumptions we have made during this analysis procedure. Questions such as whether the customer address should be an object itself remain unresolved, and must be addressed sooner or later. We should document these questions thoroughly.

We won't analyze the rest of use cases in the same detail right now because I've just stepped through the fundamental process, and the logic for the other use cases would be the same. You would be bored to death if I repeat this eight times. But let me stress this point: the efforts we make to create a good design of the system will save us from countless frustrating days when we have to change our code to meet the ever-changing requirements. It's worth getting it right first time around.

By my reckoning, if we've looked through all the remaining use cases for the Sales Manager and the Inside Sales Coordinator, and performed the noun-object-relevance criteria that we used above, we would end up with the following list of (highlighted) nouns that also qualify as objects in our system:

- ❑ The actor retrieves the **product** names and quantities from the **customer**.
- ❑ The actor completes the **order details**.
- ❑ The actor saves the **order** to the database.
- ❑ The actor selects a **shipper**.
- ❑ The actor prints daily **reports** from a reports menu.
- ❑ The actor selects a product **category**.

We therefore have the following components:

- ❑ Customers
- ❑ Products
- ❑ Orders
- ❑ Order Details
- ❑ Shippers
- ❑ Reports
- ❑ Categories

It may take some time to identify the objects or components of a system. However, the important thing is that we have managed to identify all the visible objects in the problem domain. We have laid a solid foundation on which we will be able to move forward.

Why Identify Objects from Uses Cases?

For the project we are building in this book, we're going to use the Northwind database. You might argue that since we already have a database (Northwind.mdb), why don't we just create objects based on the existing tables? We could, after all, design our objects by creating properties for each field - and design a set of methods that would manage the tables.

While it is indeed important that our objects have properties that represent the structure of the data in the database, and that the methods do not violate the database's integrity, our objects will have a lot more to do than merely maintain a database. We will have client objects that are providing information to the users, objects that have nothing to do with the database (you could create a component to manage fonts for printed reports), and finally we will be dividing our objects across tiers (more on that later). In addition, we will need methods to handle communication between two different objects - which is not something we can easily see from the database structure.

> Starting with a database structure and working backward cannot create all of our objects efficiently or accurately. It is also quite possible, of course, that there may not yet be a database at this early point in the development of the system!

Our components should initially be designed from use cases that center on how the users will use the system. This design can later be expanded to include the effects of frameworks, for instance. My point, here, is that when our objects are based on the needs of the user, it becomes a much simpler task to build applications based on these objects that will satisfy all of the user's needs.

This is Just the Beginning

Design is not a linear process. We do not sit down with the users, perform a perfect set of interviews and make every use case from these interviews. We can't then go on to create the remaining UML diagrams and complete the project in a serial manner. In reality we perform the interviews, review the interviews, and begin to turn them into use cases. These use cases will reveal additional information that we will need to get from the user. As we look at the use cases, we may find some of them need to be expanded into several use cases, and have dependencies that we had not considered. We will go back, perform more interviews, rebuild our use cases and then reevaluate everything again. Once we feel everything is complete we move on to the next stage of the project. Later in the project, we will probably find we are still missing pieces of information. Once again we may have to build additional use cases. Throughout the project, the idea of what our components should be, and how they should be built, will undergo many revisions as we refine our UML diagrams. Welcome to the iterative world of design - and remember the cataclysms that await VB programmers who try to survive without UML!

Summary

In this chapter, we've a taken an in-depth look at use cases and use case diagrams. They are the first key UML models that we encounter when we create a project. These models are used to determine the system requirements from the user's point of view. We should be able to identify many of the project's objects from these use case models.

We have taken the first steps into the project that we will build as we progress through this book. We have interviewed members of the Northwind Company sales team, and condensed a profuse amount of information into a clear and concise set of use case models. We then drew up a use case diagram, and finally identified the visible objects that users could relate to in this project.

In the next chapter, we will convert our written use cases into sequence and collaboration diagrams, which will give us a more refined visual model of the events that occur between actors and components in the system, and between the different components themselves within the system.

Get ADO
connection

[Successful]

Set Recordset
cursor location

Set Recordset
source

Set Recordset
connection

Interaction Diagrams

Now that we've learned how to build use cases and use case diagrams, it's time to move on to the next stage of our project design: **interaction diagrams**. By developing our interaction diagrams, we will continue moving towards a more detailed definition of our system design through the UML process.

There are two types of interaction diagram:

❑ Sequence diagrams
❑ Collaboration diagrams

Sequence and collaboration diagrams present the same information in different forms, and may be used interchangeably. Each diagram offers its own advantages, and the type of diagram that the you choose will depend on your own particular preference, and the particular details of your project.

The use cases and associated diagrams that we developed in the previous chapter have allowed us to identify the system's components and how these objects communicate with the actors and each other. Using this information, we can now represent the interactions between these components, and between objects and actors in interaction diagrams.

Although the two types of interaction diagram essentially display the same information, sequence diagrams, as the name suggests, tend to concentrate on the temporal element, while collaboration diagrams emphasize the spatial element of interactions.

Once our interaction diagrams are complete, they will help us find any patterns that exist within our system, help build our user interfaces, and provide the information needed to carry the system design on further. But before we get ahead of ourselves, let's find out more about sequence and collaboration diagrams.

What is an Interaction Diagram?

An interaction diagram represents an interaction pictorially. It includes any actors, objects or components that are involved in the interaction, and also displays any messages that are passed between them.

Interaction diagrams allow us to look at each of our components from the outside. In these diagrams, our components are black boxes that perform certain functions. Other components or actors send requests in the form of a message to a component, and the component responds by performing some function.

> *For example, the message could be a request to update a record, and the response could be updating the record in the database and then sending a return message to say that the update was successful.*

Interaction diagrams are an excellent way to start us thinking about the public methods of our objects. These public methods represent the **responsibilities** of our objects; that is, what they can do for other objects in the system - or actors outside of the system. Of course, we've already seen that our components are initially designed from interviews and use cases: they tend to center on how the users will use the system. But we can expand upon this user-centric design later on, once we're established along our design track. At that stage, we will also include the design effects of frameworks and system constraints, for instance.

When our objects are based on the user's needs, it becomes a simple task to build applications out of these objects. The design of the external part of the project is driven by the user requirements, and will therefore have a high probability of meeting these requirements.

Of course, there are many other requirements, such as the system working efficiently, or getting the right information showing in the right place... but these considerations should all be based on internal requirements.

> **Internal requirements will extend our design once we've understood the system in terms of the external user's requirements.**

Interaction diagrams are a tool for us to describe our system with far greater definition than we have so far seen. Our interaction diagrams will very much rely upon our earlier use case analysis, but they will take that analysis much further. So let's move straight on and consider: if we can use sequence or collaboration diagrams, which one is best?

Sequence or Collaboration: Which is Best?

Since sequence and collaboration diagrams can theoretically model the same information, how do we choose the one that is best for our application?

Sequence and interaction diagrams are usually constructed from different UML models - and therefore focus on different aspects of design. As we are about to find out, the question we really need to ask is "Do we want to base our project design on the user's point of view?"

Sequence diagrams are built from use cases. Since use cases represent the client side of the application, sequence diagrams will be heavily focused on the client side of the application. Once all use cases have been converted into sequence diagrams, it's possible to expand these sequence diagrams to include server side components. This makes building sequence diagrams a two-step process:

❑ Convert the use cases into sequence diagrams
❑ Expand these diagrams to include the components invisible to the user

Collaboration diagrams, on the other hand, are usually built from an entirely different modeling technique that uses **CRC cards**, although they can be built from use cases.

> **CRC stands for Class, Responsibility and Collaboration. The CRC card technique of designing a project focuses on the components in the system instead of the user requirements. While we will use the CRC diagrams as a tool to help us build activity diagrams, it is really a completely different approach to designing your project from using use cases.**

I will include a brief discussion of collaboration diagrams, as it is possible to produce them from use cases - and they are a commonly used part of the standard.

I will not go into a discussion of making CRC cards and converting them into collaboration diagrams, however, as I feel the use case approach is more appropriate for a Visual Basic project. The heart of a Visual Basic project is still the user interface, and this interface should be based on the user's requirements, not just the components the user employs.

Sequence Diagrams

Sequence diagrams represent interactions. They show how messages are passed over time between components and from actors to components of the system. These messages will define the public methods of the components.

We have two choices when it comes to sequence diagrams:

❑ Represent all the possible events that can occur for a use case within a single sequence diagram.
❑ Build one sequence diagram for each possible event in a use case.

We could, for example, build a sequence diagram that just shows communication between the actor and the customer object when creating a customer. We could also build another diagram that shows the communication between all of the objects, including the actor, the customer component, the server component and the database component.

Sequence diagrams are models of the system: they can be used to visualize the communication within the system, thus to help the developer arrive at the best design of the system.

Sequence Diagrams: A Primer

In this section, we're going to build a generic sequence diagram. I'll be using an example scenario that is *not* associated with our Northwind project, because right now I just want to teach you what each part of the diagram represents and how these parts fit together. Once we've looked at these fundamentals of sequence diagrams, we'll return to our Northwind project and start building the relevant sequence diagrams.

Starting Points

As I've already mentioned, the starting point for our sequence diagram should be a use case. As you will recall from the previous chapter, we can identify from a use case the objects and components that are required for a particular interaction.

We can usually start by assuming that our interaction will need an actor and some objects. We can therefore draw up this elementary situation as shown here:

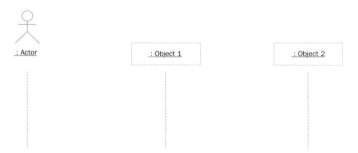

Timelines and Lifetimes

A `dashed vertical` line in the previous diagram extends from the actor and from each object. This line is a *timeline*, where time starts at the top of the diagram and ends at the bottom. This line indicates the lifetime of the actor and objects. In this example the actor and objects are aligned horizontally and their timelines are of the same length. This means that for the interaction modeled here, the objects exist simultaneously and for the same duration.

Object Lifetimes – Creating and Destroying Objects

In a sequence diagram most of the objects will persist for the entire duration of the interaction, but this not a necessity. It is obviously possible for objects to be created and destroyed, and this needs to be represented in a sequence diagram; it's actually quite easy to represent this, as you can see in the following diagram:

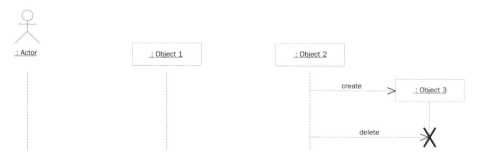

Object 2 creates Object 3, which then exists until it's destroyed by Object 2 again. This is shown first with the word create over the arrow leading out of Object 2's timeline, and then by the word delete over the arrow with a cross at the end of Object 3's timeline.

Actor and Object Messages

In the previous diagram, we cannot really think that Object 2 spontaneously created Object 3. It would have been responding to a message from one of the other objects. We show messages between the actor and the various objects with arrows connecting the timelines. The order in which these messages occur is represented by where they occur on the timelines: the higher up they are, the earlier they occur. Hence the *sequence of events* is shown in this diagram:

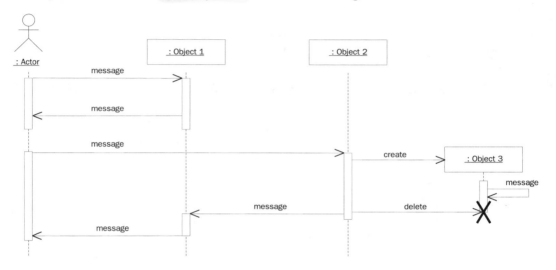

We can see here that the interaction commences when the actor sends a message to Object 1. Object 1 then returns a message to the actor, which then talks to Object 2. As a result Object 3 is created - and so it continues… the interaction shown here finally ends when Object 1 sends a message to the actor.

Reflexive Messages

In the sequence diagram we've just looked at, you'll see that Object 3 sends a message to itself. This is known as a reflexive message, and is represented by an arrow that loops back on itself. Reflexive messages can represent situations where an object needs to communicate within itself – something we'll find arising later on.

Focus of Control

You may also have noticed the long thin boxes that are present along the time lines in our last sequence diagram. These represent the *focus of control*. This is the period of time that an object/actor is responsible for an action. This may be direct control or indirect control resulting from a sub-procedure.

> *Although these focus of control boxes may be useful, it's worth noticing that the sequence of events occurring during an interaction is adequately represented without them.*

Sequence Diagrams and Timed Events

Sequence diagrams can also have comments placed beside the messages - indicating the length of time each message should take. We can also make our arrows indicate whether the message is sent asynchronously (the message is sent and the sender continues doing tasks) or synchronously (the message is sent and the sender waits for a response before continuing). How might this be useful? We could use this notation in our diagrams to show allowable times for the middle tier object to connect to the database.

For the purposes of this book, we don't really need this extra information in our sequence diagrams. I direct the interested reader towards *'Instant UML'* also by Wrox Press, for a broader treatment of the UML notation at large.

Right now, that's all we need to know about sequence diagrams to start creating our own diagrams for our Northwind project. Don't worry - I'll take you through the diagrams step-by-step.

Building A Sequence Diagram - A Step-By-Step Guide

You're about to see that we can build a sequence diagram by methodically running through the details of the use cases that we've previously prepared, and asking ourselves all the time how we can present what we know about the system within a sequence model. We'll start by creating a sequence diagram from our Create New Customer use case.

Create New Customer Sequence

We are going to put a lot of effort into making the Create New Customer sequence diagram. This will be our first proper sequence diagram, so we're going to take things slowly and build it up step-by-step. Once we understand how this particular sequence diagram is created, we can step things up a bit and move more swiftly through the remaining diagrams.

Create New Customer: Sequence Diagram Objects

Before we start to build a diagram, we need to review our use case specification. We need to know what objects are involved in the use case so that we can add them to the sequence diagram.

In the Create New Customer use case we have only one object: Customer. So let's add Customer to the sequence diagram. The way in which a sequence diagram is created varies among different modeling tools. I will assume you have found a tool that suits you.

First, add a new object to the diagram. It should look something like this:

Note the colon before the class name Customer. The colon indicates that this is an instance, or object, of the class.

> Objects interact with each other; classes do not. If you are unclear about this distinction, you might want to read an object-oriented tutorial to get the hang of this. For the moment, it's enough to know that we instantiate objects from classes, which are essentially the blueprints for our objects. If you want to learn more about this, I refer you to "Beginning VB Objects" also published by Wrox Press.

Only objects participate in sequence diagrams. The timeline descends from the object box and, as I mentioned earlier, represents the time the object exists, and will also indicate the order of interactions among objects in the diagram.

Create New Customer: Sequence Diagram Actors

Just as with use case diagrams, sequence diagrams should also show the actors involved. If we take a look at our use case we'll find that we only have one actor:

Primary Actor: Sales Representative
Secondary Actor: None

Let's add the Sales Representative actor to our sequence diagram:

In the same way as for the Customer object, an instance of the Sales Representative actor, indicated by the colon preceding the actor's name, is placed in our diagram. It also has a time line attached to it.

Create New Customer: Sequence Diagram Starting Point

A sequence diagram has a starting point that corresponds to the starting point in the use case. If you cast your mind back you will remember this:

Starting Point: This use case starts when the actor makes a request to create a new customer.

Now there is a problem here: what object does the actor make the request to? It seems quite obvious that the Customer object is the target. But how does an actor interact with an object? Through an *interface*, of course.

An interface may be a form with input fields mapped to the Customer object, or an ActiveX Control hosted in a web browser. Either way, we know that there is an interface between the actor and the Customer object. We should add it to the diagram and place it in between the actor and the object, like this:

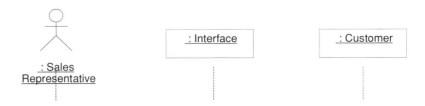

Create New Customer: Sequence Diagram Messages

We will now use a directed line from the instance of the Sales Representative actor to the Interface object to represent a message sent from the actor to the object. We should also give this message a name or a description to specify its task:

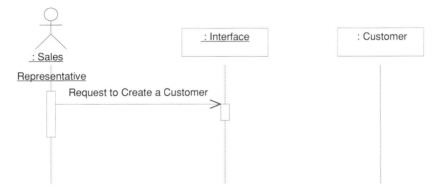

Now we can see that a Sales Representative can send a "Request to Create a Customer" message to the Interface object. Remember, the tall, thin rectangles are called the focus of controls. They show the period of time during which an object is performing an action. The top of the rectangle indicates the start of the action, and the bottom is its completion.

Create New Customer: Sequence Diagram Flow of Events

Next: what should the Interface object do when it receives the request message? We need to look back at the use case again, this time at the flow of events:

Flow of Events: The actor is prompted to enter information that defines the customer, such as Name, Address, Contact, etc. The actor can choose to save the information or to cancel the operation. If the actor decides to save the information the new customer is created in the system, and the list of customers that was presented earlier is updated.

Let's break this up into individual steps. First of all:

❑ The actor is prompted to enter information that defines the Customer, such as Name, Address, Contact, etc.

Clear enough? Not exactly. How is the actor prompted? It may be that the Interface displays relevant fields so that the actor can enter data into those fields. Ok, let's assume that this is the case; but how does the Interface know that it should display those fields? It may simply display such fields when it receives the request. Or it may pass the request to the Customer object to ask for permission and further instructions. Let us assume, again, that the latter approach is the one we want. So we'll add another message to the sequence diagram:

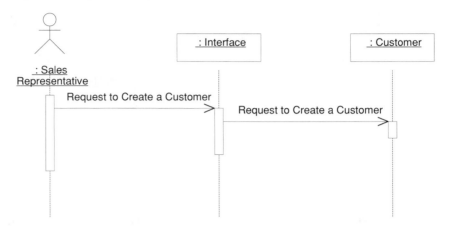

By now you're probably wondering why we don't have a more detailed description of events in the use case. The answer? The use case specification is adequate for its purpose because it provides enough information to specify the user's needs and to allow them to review it. Our Sales Representative Valerie really doesn't care how the customer entry form figures out what it should do when she clicks on the Add Customer button, for example. As long as Valerie gets to enter the new customer information, she is happy.

> *So we know that our use case specification is too limited for direct translation into a sequence diagram. If it were anything otherwise there would be little point in having both models. So what do we do? In general, we should talk to our customer or review the requirement document in order to find out exactly what should be done. For instance, do we need to put some kind of verification or authorization process in this case? We would also update our use case specification to include the further information. This is another example of iterative analysis and design process at work.*

What should the Customer object do when it receives the request to create a new customer? Again, the use case doesn't say anything about that. This is understandable, since the question is really about the internal message handling - and the use case only identifies the external behavior of the system. We'll leave this issue for later stage: when we understand a bit more about the system. As we will discover later, there are other UML diagrams that consider these interactions in more detail.

For now, just add a message to the sequence diagram indicating that the Customer object accepts the request, like this:

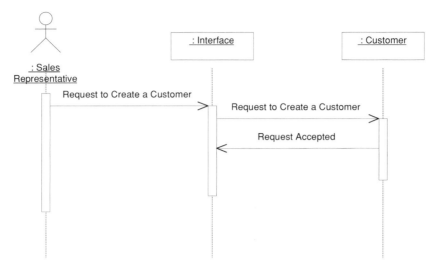

The Interface object will simply display the fields so that the Sales Representative can enter customer data. The use case specification states that:

❑   The actor will then enter the information on the customer

We need to add yet another message to our sequence diagram – one that represents the action when the Sales Representative enters customer data:

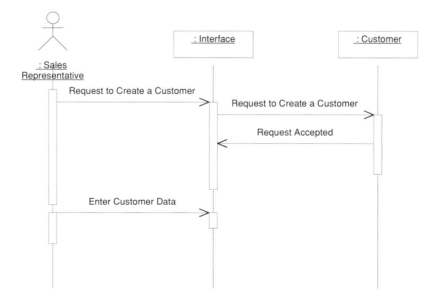

The Interface object does not need to communicate to the Customer object while the Sales Representative is entering the data. When Valerie, the Sales Representative, has finished however, she would tell the Interface object to save the data as stated in the use case:

❑ The actor can choose to save the information …

We must therefore add the message Save Customer Data to our sequence diagram:

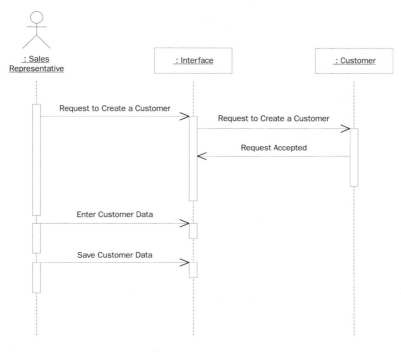

Create New Customer: Sequence Diagram Branches

The use case also specifies that:

The actor can choose … to cancel the operation.

This means that we need to add a new message to the diagram indicating this possible cancel event. Here we need to indicate that the Sales Representative *either* saves the information *or* cancels the request. We will need to use **branches** to represent this either-or situation. The mutually exclusive conditions are given in brackets before the message:

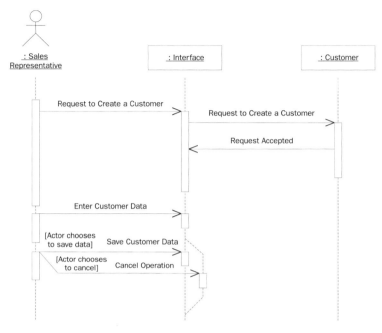

You can see that the timeline of the Interface has been split into two at this point:

Either: the [Actor chooses to save data]
Or: the [Actor chooses to cancel]

As the interaction progresses only one of these timelines will be followed, depending on the decision of the Sales Representative to either save or cancel.

The use case then says that:

❑   If the actor decides to save the information, the new Customer is created in the system

Obviously, the Interface object will need to send a message to the Customer object indicating that it should save the customer data:

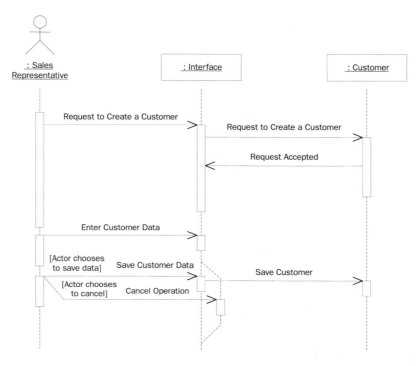

How does the Customer object save the new Customer? Usually this is done by writing the Customer data to a database. We do not care how this can be achieved, but we do need to show this process in the diagram. We should add a new object, DB Business Logic, to our sequence diagram:

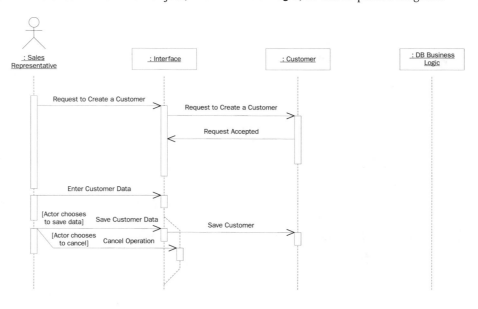

The name of the new object is not important at this stage, as long as it shows what the object is. We can then let the **Customer** object send a message to the **DB Business Logic** object to save the customer record, like this:

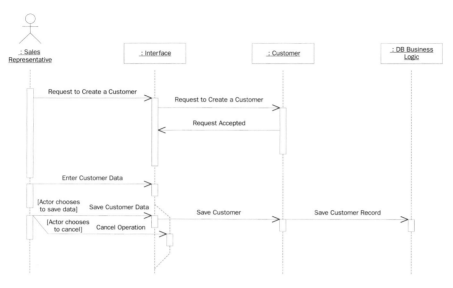

The use case specifies that something in particular happens after the customer record is saved in the database:

❏ A list of Customers that was presented earlier is updated.

Again, the use case doesn't say how the **Customer** list is updated, so we'll just assume that this is done when the **DB Business Logic** sends back a confirmation that the **Customer** record is saved:

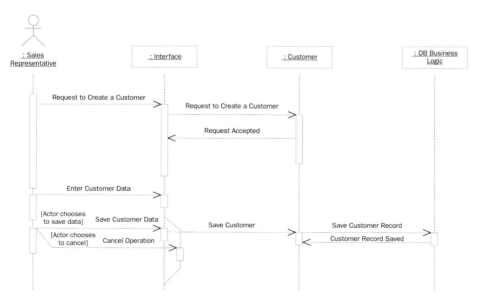

The Customer object may then send a confirmation back to the Interface object:

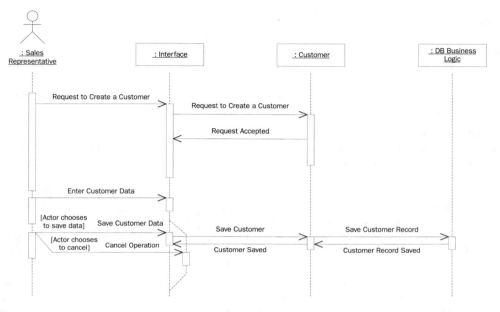

The Interface object will update the Customer list by sending an Update Customer List message to itself. We'll model the behavior of an object sending a message to itself with a directed line starting and ending at itself, as shown in the following sequence diagram:

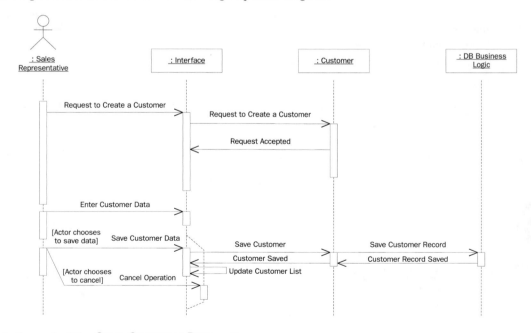

That is the end of the Save Customer Data action.

Create New Customer: Sequence Diagram Alternative Flows

If we look at the use case specification again now, we'll see that there's a set of alternative flows of events:

Alternative Flow of Events

❑ The actor attempts to add a customer that already exists. The system will notify the user and cancel the operation.

❑ The actor enters an improper value for one of the fields. The system will not allow the update until a proper value for the field is entered.

Alternative Flow #1

Let's look at the first of these alternative flows. The question is: which object is responsible for finding out whether or not a Customer already exists in the system: the Customer object or the DB Business Logic object?

> **Remember, from Chapter 2, that we are using a disconnected recordset. All of the customers will already be within the customer object. Finding out whether a customer exists will not therefore require communication with the database.**

Let's say that when the system tries to save a Customer record, it first checks to see whether this is an existing customer. If this is an existing customer, it will send back an error indicating this condition. How it checks for the existence of a customer is not important at this stage. We do need, however, to indicate in our sequence diagram that there is a possible error if there is already an existing customer. We can do this by letting the Customer object return an error message to the Interface.

This is another situation where branching occurs. The Customer object **either** proceeds to save the information **or** it informs the interface that it isn't possible because the customer already exists. Let's develop our sequence diagram accordingly:

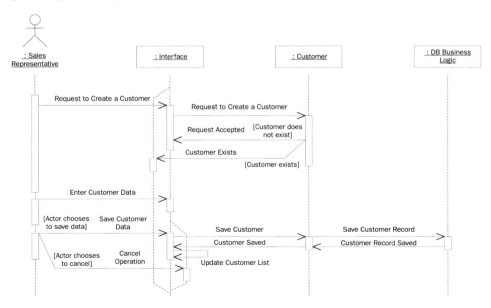

Alternative Flow #2

The second Alternative Flow of Event is:

❑ The actor enters an improper value for one of the fields. The system will not allow the update until a proper value for the field is entered.

We will not show this in our sequence diagram because it specifies the internal behavior of the Interface object. This problem should be tackled when we have more details.

Create New Customer: Sequence Diagram Ending Point

The Ending Point of the use case is that:

Ending Point: The actor's request to create a customer is either completed or canceled.

This requires no more messages and concludes this diagram. So that's it - we have successfully created the Create New Customer sequence diagram by methodically going through the stages outlined by the use cases and asking ourselves how we can represent that information in a sequence model.

In this example, we have had a good look at the creation of a sequence diagram from the corresponding use case. We can go ahead and create sequence diagrams for the rest of use cases. I will not explain every step or message again, only those that are significantly different from what we have covered here.

Modify Customer Sequence Diagram

With our Create a New Customer sequence diagram done, the Modify Customer sequence is an easier task. The only difference worth mentioning is that the **Starting Point** of this use case specifies a pre-condition:

❑ The actor must have displayed a list of customers.

However, this precondition does not specify any action required. Therefore no message is created from it. Compare now the Create New Customer sequence we just created with this finished Modify Customer sequence diagram:

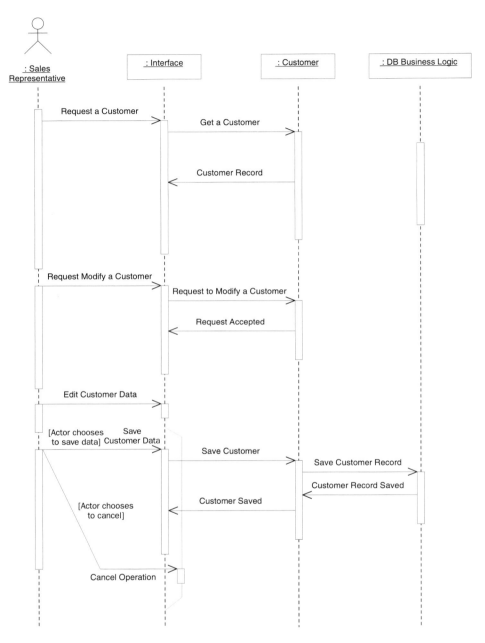

You'll undoubtedly notice that both sequences have a lot in common. Keep watching this space, and let's move on to the next sequence.

Delete Customer Sequence Diagram

Once again, the Delete Customer diagram is fairly straightforward. Nothing new is introduced here. Remember to create this diagram in the same way as the Create New Customer. Just follow the Delete Customer use case through and build up the sequence diagram step-by-step. Here is my finished sequence diagram:

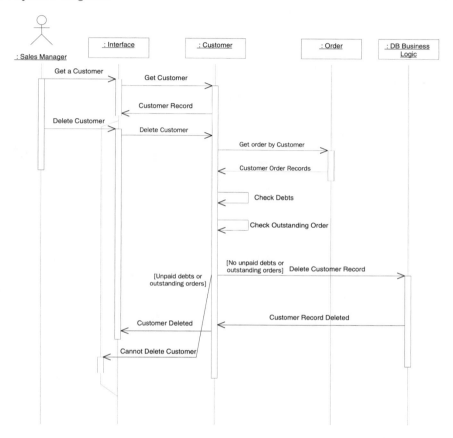

Notice here that the customer can only be deleted if they have no unpaid debts and no outstanding orders. Therefore, it's necessary for the Customer object to check this out. Our Customer object does this by obtaining the order information for the particular customer from the Order object. The appropriate checks are then made by the Customer object – represented in the diagram by those arrows that double back on themselves.

If there are no unpaid debts or outstanding orders then the Customer object will send a Delete Record message to the DB Business Logic object. If, however, there *are* unpaid debts or outstanding orders, the Customer will not attempt to delete the record; instead, it will send back an error message to the Interface object.

In this sequence diagram, I have chosen not to show the cancel operation. This is because I wanted to show you that it not essential to include the whole of the use case within a sequence diagram. It's quite legitimate to model only part of a use case, if that best suits your needs.

Order Sequence Diagrams

We have covered all the diagrams for the Sales Representative. By now, you're probably getting quite proficient at creating sequence diagrams, so I'm going to present just the Modify Order and Delete Order diagrams here. You can work through them with the use cases from chapter 3.

Modify Order

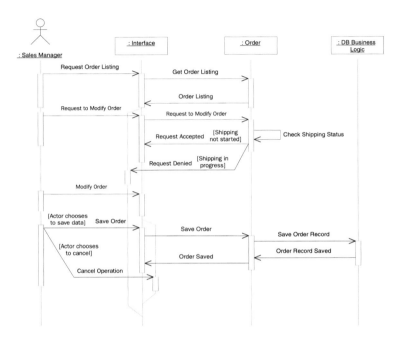

Delete Order

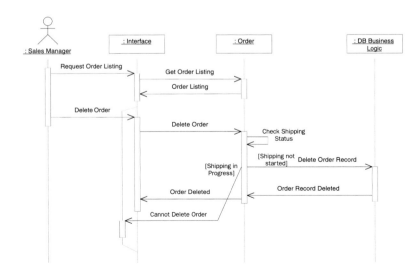

So now you're probably thinking: OK I understand how to build these sequence diagrams and they look pretty good. But why should I bother? What do they give me? To answer these questions, I need to present a few more diagrams. Not only will they give you more practice if you work through them, but they will reveal something very useful. Let me present these next diagrams, and I will be in a great position to answer this question.

Product Sequence Diagrams

Here I present the use cases for the three Product interactions and then their sequence diagrams that are Create New Product, Modify Product, and Delete Product. Working through these diagrams will help to enforce the ideas we have covered so far.

Create New Product - Use Case

USE CASE: CREATE NEW PRODUCT

Overview

The purpose of this use case is to create a new product

Primary Actor

Inside Sales Coordinator

Secondary Actor

None

Starting Point

The actor requests to add a new product

Ending Point

The product is created or the operation is cancelled.

Measurable Result

A new product is created.

Flow of Events

This use case is started when the actor requests to add a new product. The system will always accept the request and prompt the actor with a new product entry form. The actor can then enter the product data. Once the edit is completed, the actor can request to save the product. The actor can request to cancel the operation before the product is saved

Alternative Flow of Events

The actor tries to create a product that already exists. The save operation will be cancelled and the system will provide an error message indicating the cause of failure.

Use Case Extensions

None

Outstanding issues

None

Create New Product - Sequence Diagram

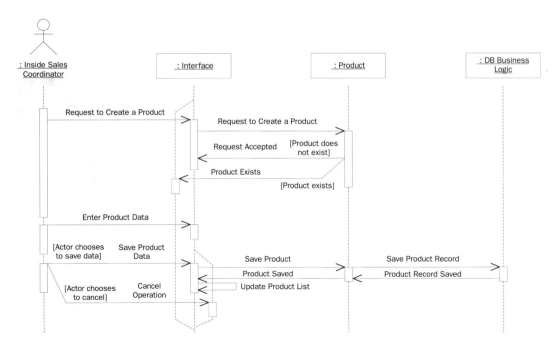

Modify Product - Use Case

USE CASE: MODIFY PRODUCT

Overview

The purpose of this use case is to modify an existing product

Primary Actor

Inside Sales Coordinator

Secondary Actor

None

Starting Point

The actor requests to modify a new product

Ending Point

The product is modified or the operation is cancelled.

Measurable Result

A new product is created.

Flow of Events

This use case is started when the actor requests to modify a product. The system presents the actor with the product's data. The actor can then request to delete the product. The actor can request to cancel the operation before the product is deleted.

Alternative Flow of Events

If the requested product does not exist, the system will return an error.

Use Case Extensions

None

Outstanding Issues

None

Modify Product - Sequence Diagram

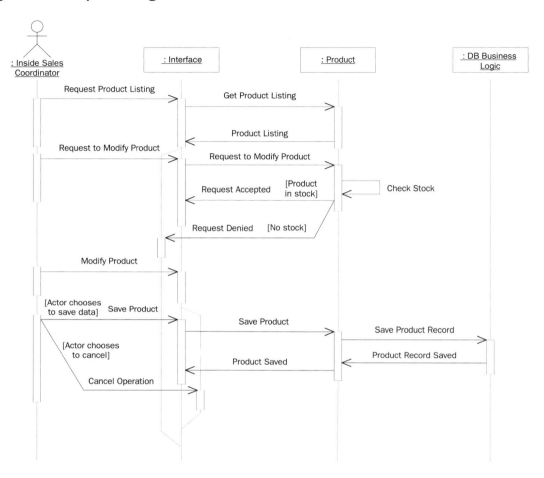

Delete Product - Use Case

USE CASE: DELETE PRODUCT

Overview

The purpose of this use case is to delete an existing product

Primary Actor

Inside Sales Coordinator

Secondary Actor

None

Starting Point

The actor requests to delete a new product

Ending Point

The product is deleted or the operation is cancelled.

Measurable Result

A product is deleted.

Flow of Events

This use case is started when the actor requests to see a product. The system will always accept the request and present the actor with the product's data. The actor then requests to delete the product or cancel the request.

Alternative Flow of Events

If the requested product does not exist, the system will return an error. If there is still some of the product in stock, the system will return an error.

Use Case Extensions

None

Outstanding Issues

None

Delete Product - Sequence Diagram

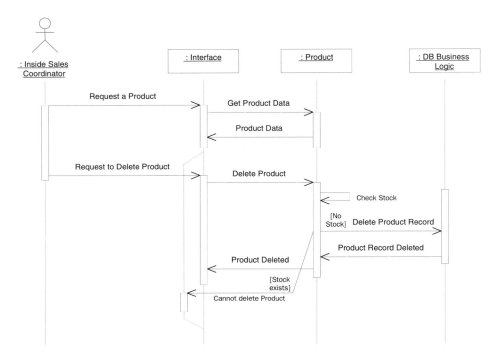

Why Use Sequence Diagrams?

So now it is time to ask: What have these sequence diagrams given us? As you've seen, the sequence diagrams serve the purpose of clearly identifying the sequence of events in our application. As I shall show later in the book, this will help us make better Visual Basic forms and ActiveX components.

Sequence diagrams also convert the verbal use case into a picture that maps all of the messages. A picture is always simpler to understand, and this will make it easier for us when we come making class and activity diagrams.

When we are creating our sequence diagrams we often discover that the use cases have not answered all the questions we need answering. Making sequence diagrams highlights these shortcomings and provides a mechanism for iterative design.

Sequence diagrams can also show us the order of events a user goes through when interacting with the user interface. This can be very useful when making the GUI. This is an important point - and I devote whole chapters to designing the GUI later in the book.

Another great reason for creating sequence diagrams is that they can help us identify patterns. Let's explore this idea in light of our sequence diagram analysis.

Finding Patterns in our Sequence Diagrams

We've looked briefly at patterns in Chapter 2, but it's now time to start applying what we learned in that early chapter to the development of our Northwind project that's been taking place in all these sequence diagrams.

Please go back and take a look at the Create New Customer sequence diagram. Now look at the Create New Product sequence in conjunction with Create New Customer diagram. It is easy to see that these diagrams are similar. In fact, they are practically identical.

Now take a look at the Delete Customer, Delete Order and Delete Product sequence diagrams. A pattern is emerging here as well. The same is also true of the Modify Customer, Modify Order and Modify Product diagrams.

If we were to look at the properties of these Customer, Order and Product components, they would all seem very different. A sequence diagram, though, only looks at the messages being passed back and forth, which means that it only looks at the **object's public methods**. When we view these three objects' methods, we see that they are all very similar. We can also see that the DB Business Logic component works in an identical manner for all three objects. What does it mean when things have the same methods but different properties?

To answer this question, let's step back for a moment and use *cars* for our next example. Each car is an object with its own set of properties, but every car shares the same underlying functionality.

It might be worth just stopping and thinking about this for a moment. Every car has a unique set of properties that helps us to identify them: color, shape, type of wheels, manufacturer, etc. Yet, even though cars have different properties, they all perform pretty much the same activities: accelerating, braking, turning corners, indicating at junctions, etc. Although every car has a different set of properties that makes it unique, they all function in largely the same manner. We do not have to find a whole new way of making a car each time we want to make a new, unique car. We can use the same technique to build a car whether it is going to be red or metallic silver, four seats or two. Since the way every car works is essentially the same, we only need one way to build an infinite number of unique cars. The way a car is put together (wheels, steering wheel, lights, dashboard...) is a pattern. It is because of this pattern that we can use the same technique to build an infinite number of unique cars (just look down your street).

Components work in the same way. Even though they may have different properties, they can still work in exactly the same way. If we know how to design or build one of these objects, we know how to build all of them. Once we figure out how to build my Customer object, we will also know how to build Order and Product components, too. By building similar sequence diagrams from our Modify and Delete use cases, we have found that these tasks are also alike for our Customer, Order and Product components.

How Can We Take Advantage of Patterns?

Let's take this one step further and try to see how this will affect our Northwind project. If Visual Basic had true inheritance, this certainly would be a place we could use it. We could build one base class that had all of our methods (remember, the methods are the same for all our objects). We could then inherit this class into our Customer, Order and Product objects. We would then have the same methods within each of our classes but would only have coded these methods once (in the base class). Unfortunately, we don't have inheritance in Visual Basic so let us snap back to the real world and find a way to take advantage of this pattern in Visual Basic.

Interfaces

There's a lot of confusion about Visual Basic interfaces. A Visual Basic interface is a class with methods and properties with no code. Another Visual Basic class can then implement this interface. The class that implements an interface will get all of the methods and properties that are in the interface. These interfaces allow you to have one standard set of methods and properties for a group of similar components.

For example, I could create an `Animal` interface that has a `Move` and a `Sleep` method. I could then implement this interface into a `Rabbit` component. I would then have to write the code to make the `Rabbit` object move or sleep the correct way for a rabbit when these methods are called. I could also make a `Cat` component that implemented the `Animal` interface, and write the appropriate code for that object. If I had an object built from the `Animal` interface, I could call the `Move` method and that object would respond in the way that was appropriate; that is, the rabbit would jump and the cat would walk. This is a form of **polymorphism**.

While this form of polymorphism could be useful in our current example (since we do want all of our components to have the same methods), it will not offer us any advantage in actually coding our components. Remember: an interface has no code within it, the classes that implement the interface must write all of the code for the methods and properties in the interface. We are looking for a solution where we can write code once, and reuse it for all of our components. Interfaces will not provide this type of solution.

While interfaces could apply here, they will greatly complicate the code and offer only a small improvement in our coding solution. It is for this reason we will not discuss them any further.

Object Hierarchies

The other option is to use an object hierarchy to build our objects. The hierarchy would look something like this:

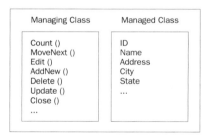

The hierarchy here is between the Managing Class and the Managed Class.

On the bottom of this hierarchy is a class that could contain the properties of the object (the Managed Class). As all of these objects have different properties, this class will be completely different for each of our objects.

Next up in the hierarchy, is a class that will manage the Bottom class, which we will call the Managing Class. This class will contain all of our client side methods, such as `Move to the Next Customer`, `Add a New Product`, `Count Customers`, `Update Products`, etc.

When considering this hierarchy, we discover one amazing fact: the Managing Class would be 99% identical for every one of our objects! This is really something - a few hours of work talking to our users, converting this information into use cases and sequence diagrams, has helped us find a pattern within our system. Once we have the Top class coded, we can then build all of the rest of our client side objects by simply making the Bottom classes - which is a relatively easy task.

The Managing Class performs the same basic tasks for all of these objects.

We can see that our client components will have many methods that will be the same for all the components. Using Visual Basic, we can build one of these client components, such as the Customer component, and use it as a code template to build the other client components – such as the Order component, the Product component, etc. When we look at the sequence diagrams for different components and find patterns like this, we can turn these patterns into code templates. The relationship between patterns and code templates is very similar to the relationship between a component and a class. We will discuss this in a later chapter – it's going to be an important part of our project design.

Without this ability to identify patterns, we would have been making these components separately... almost certainly we have saved time and development funds by identifying patterns.

> **The time spent using UML has already paid off.**

How Detailed Should Sequence Diagrams Be?

As I've stated previously, UML is a fairly open standard. Exactly how you implement the UML is entirely up to you. You need to find a technique that works best for you. This applies as much to sequence diagrams as any other stage of the UML process. The amount of detail you include in these diagrams will depend upon their intended purpose.

For example, the diagrams we've just created are quite detailed. This was because I wanted to give you a thorough grounding in building sequence diagrams.

Let's pull out from these diagrams, and take look at some of them in less detail. Below are the three less-detailed sequence diagrams for Modify Customer, Modify Product, and Modify Order:

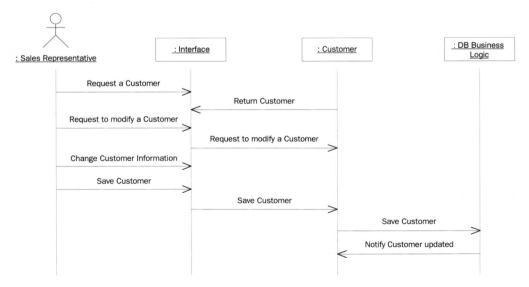

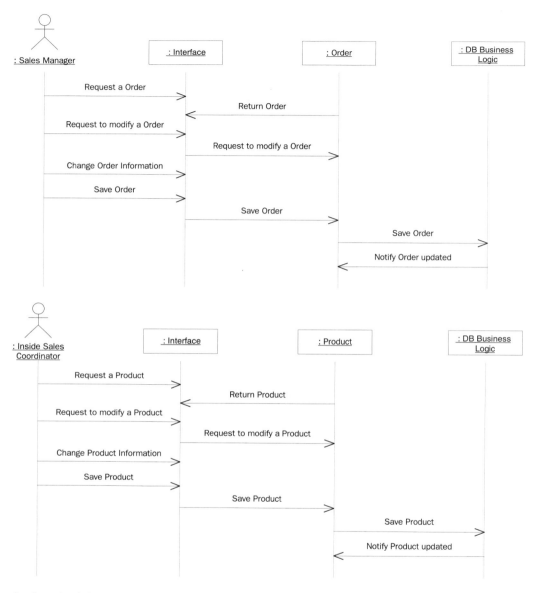

Clearly they don't have as much information on them as those we created earlier. However, on inspection, some common patterns become evident between them.

UML is a tool that is supposed to simplify our project design, not cloud the issue. It makes sense, then, to include only as much detail as we need. We might not get this balance right first time, but after review and iteration we should find these diagrams are a great help.

From now on, the sequence diagrams we encounter through the book will be just detailed enough to suit our purposes.

Collaboration Diagrams

As our use cases become more complicated and we refine our sequence diagrams, it's quite likely that it will become difficult for us to keep track of all the objects in the interaction. Collaboration diagrams, which model an interaction among objects rather than the sequence of events, present a view of the system from a different angle.

> **Collaboration diagrams emphasize the nature of the object interaction, rather than the timing of the interaction.**

Collaboration diagrams do show how messages pass back and forth between objects, and between the objects and the primary actor, however - just like a sequence diagram. A collaboration diagram can still represent an entire use case, or a portion of a use case.

Collaboration Diagrams: A Primer

Much as we've just done for our sequence diagrams, we'll now build a collaboration diagram step-by-step. This collaboration diagram will represent the same interaction as the sequence diagram we built; I'll run through each part of collaboration diagram and explain how they all fit together.

As before, the starting point for this diagram is a use case. The first thing we need to do is identify the actor and the objects. The actor is again represented as a stick figure, and each object is represented as a square with the object name - Object1, Object2 and Object3. We then place them on the diagram as shown.

You will note that the actor and objects are no longer positioned horizontally, and that Object 3 is drawn even though it does not exist at the beginning of the interaction.

> *This is because a collaboration diagram concentrates on the structural organization of the objects rather than the timing of the messages throughout the interaction.*

Lines are then drawn between the actor and objects that interact with one another, representing the links between them.

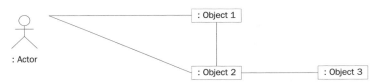

Arrows show messages being passed back and forth. Up to now, there is no reference to time, so we need to number the messages in the order they will occur. Note that a reflexive message is represented by a loop. This diagram shows the same information as the generic sequence diagram. If you look at them together you can see how they emphasize different aspects of the same interaction.

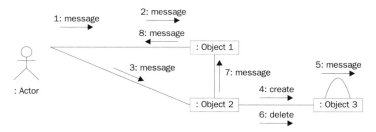

Building Collaboration Diagrams - A Step-By-Step Guide

Now we have a generic idea of how a collaboration diagram works, let's create a collaboration diagram for the same use case for which we originally made a sequence diagram in step-by-step fashion: the Create New Customer collaboration.

Create New Customer Collaboration

It's now time for us to build a proper collaboration diagram. We're going to start by building the Create New Customer collaboration diagram. Just as we did for the Create New Customer sequence diagram, we're going to build up the collaboration diagram gradually. I will provide an explanation as each new building block is added.

Create New Customer: Collaboration Diagram Actors

The first thing we need to do is identify the actors and objects that participate in this interaction. For this information, we must turn to the Create New Customer use case. The actors can be extracted directly from the use case. The objects must be obtained from the use case, using the rules given in the previous chapter. We find that the actor is the Sales Representative and we need an Interface object, a Customer object, and a DB Database Logic object. We need to add these to our diagram as shown below:

You'll have noticed the first difference between the collaboration diagram and the sequence diagram: the collaboration diagram does not show objects with timelines. This is because the timing is no longer a crucial part of the diagram. When we show messages passing among the objects, we simply use a number to indicate the event in the sequence.

Create New Customer: Collaboration Starting Point

The use case starts when a Sales Representative requests to create a new customer through the Interface object. First, add a line representing the link between the actor and the Interface object to the diagram. This indicates that the two objects are related:

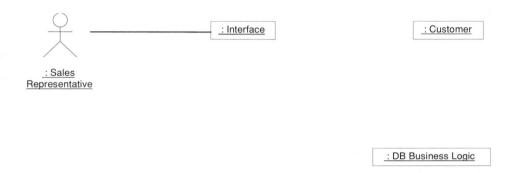

Create New Customer: Collaboration Event Flow

Next, add a directed line from the actor to the Interface object. Since this is the first message in the diagram, we assign it number one:

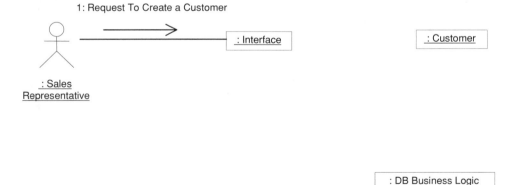

The Interface object then sends a **Request to Create a Customer** message to the Customer object. Again, we need to draw a link between these two objects and a directed line from the sending object to the target object:

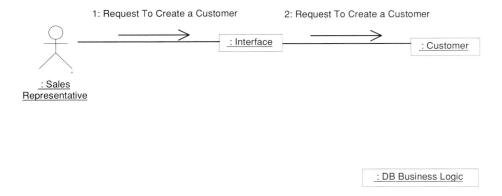

When the Customer object receives the request, it sends a **Request Accepted** message back to the Interface object. This time, we direct the message from the Customer object to the Interface object:

The Sales Representative can then enter the customer data to the Interface object. This is our fourth message:

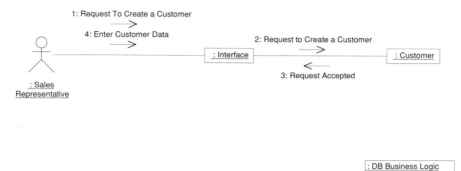

When she is done, the Sales Representative can send another message to the Interface object, indicating that they wish to save the customer data. This is our fifth message in the diagram:

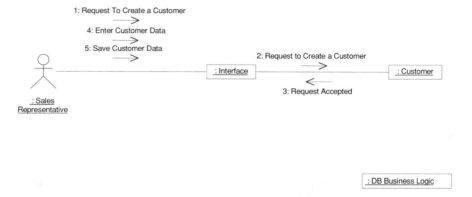

Now the Interface object will pass the request, along with the data, to the Customer object. This is message number six:

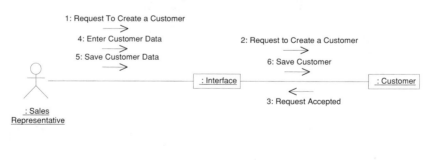

Now the Customer object can send back two messages. The first is a Save Customer Record message that indicates the success of the request operation. The second is a Customer Exists message indicating that the save operation failed.

Because the consequent events are different based on the returned message, we'll analyze the success scenario first, and then move on to the fail scenario that occurs if the customer already exists.

Flow #1: Customer Created - Success

The Customer object will send the message Save Customer Record to the DB Business Logic object. As usual, we should create a link between the two objects before adding the message to the diagram:

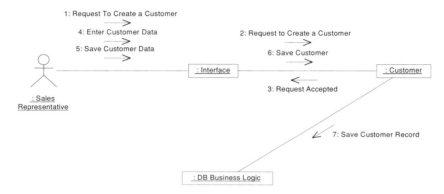

Note that we reorganized the objects so that the diagram fits in the page. With a Modeling tool, this should be as easy as dragging the object box and dropping it to a suitable place.

When the Customer object receives the success message, it sends a Customer Saved message to the Interface object. These are messages eight and nine:

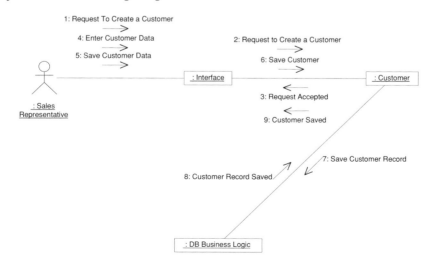

The Interface object now needs to send a message to itself to update the customer listing. We model this by creating a link from the Interface object back to itself. We then add a directed line representing the Update Customer Listing message:

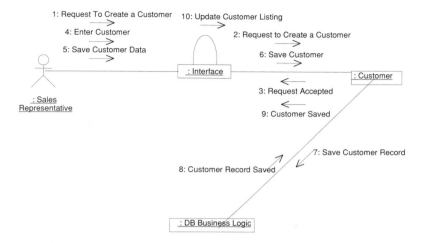

Where the arrow points to is not important, nor is the placement of the link, above or below the object box. This completes the flow of messages for the successful creation of the customer record.

Flow #2: Customer Already Exists - Failure

Now let's deal with the second scenario when the customer already exists in the system. This flow is a failure: we can't create a new customer if that customer already exists in the system. The Customer object sends a Customer Exists message to the Interface object, and it becomes message number eleven.

You could argue that it should be number seven, since it is really an alternative message to the Customer Record Saved message. It does not really matter though, as the timing of the events is not important in the collaboration diagram.

You might think that this is a strange thing to say. If the numbering of the messages is not important, why do we bother to number them at all? Well, we want to display as much information on a diagram as possible, but not at the expense of the diagram's primary purpose. In this case, the collaboration diagram is supposed to help us to understand the organization of the objects for a particular interaction. If we were to split the objects into two parts to ensure that the numbering was consistent, it would defeat the object of the diagram.

One way to circumvent this problem would be to make two diagrams, one for each scenario. That is precisely what we are going to do. That is one of the beauties of UML: its fluidity.

> **We are not constrained to model the entire use case in a single diagram. We may choose the most appropriate way for our particular problem.**

So we need to revert to the diagram where only the first six messages were displayed. It is shown here, with the addition of the message from the Customer object telling the Interface object that the customer already exists (message number 7):

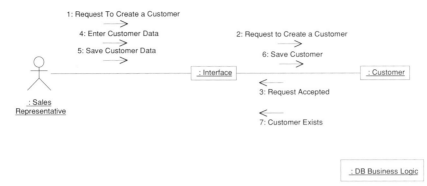

The last event of the Create New Customer use case is when the Sales Representative cancels the operation to the diagram. This will involve a message being sent to the Interface object. It's obvious that this will add nothing new to the structural organization of our objects. We therefore do not include this diagram.

That concludes our first collaboration diagram. It might seem intimidating when you look at the end result if we hadn't built it ourselves. However, as you should have realized by now, there is really no magic in building such a diagram.

Modify Customer Collaboration Diagram

To reinforce the concepts that we have covered here, I will show you the complete Modify a Customer collaboration diagram here:

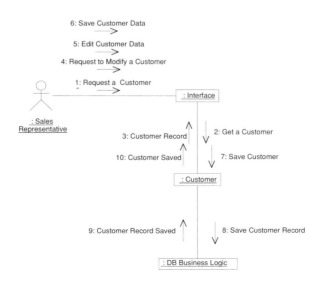

Note that the placement of objects and messages is not consistent with the previous diagram. I did this just to demonstrate that we can have a different configuration of drawing diagrams. However, when you apply this to real world projects, you should define a consistent presentation for your diagrams and stick to it.

Why Use Collaboration Diagrams?

Just like the sequence diagrams, collaboration diagrams also show us what methods our objects will need and what patterns exist within our system. For example, from the collaboration diagrams, we can see that the customer component must have a method to add a new customer, return a new customer, and to update the customer. We can also obtain patterns from collaboration diagrams. These will be patterns for the organization of our objects.

I don't want to dwell on collaboration diagrams for too much longer now, as we won't be pursuing them any further in our Northwind project. I've shown you enough to get a feel for what they're about, and whether you'd like to research them further for yourself.

Summary

Collaboration and sequence diagrams provide a bridge between our text based use cases and our pictorial UML diagrams. Either one of these diagrams can be used to show the dynamic behavior of your system. Every use case should be represented by either a sequence diagram or a collaboration diagram. It's important to find a method that works for your project and your team. Take some time out and try to build some additional sequence diagrams and collaboration diagrams.

Using these UML diagrams, we can find patterns that we can use to simplify coding our Visual Basic applications. Finally, these diagrams place our use cases within our frameworks, determine whether our use cases are complete enough to perform all of the system's required tasks, and see if everything can work together.

The eagle eyed among you will have noticed that we have not built the **Create an Order** sequence diagram. This is because one of the other uses of sequence diagrams is to help build the GUI. These diagrams allow us to maintain form control and build forms based on how a user does a task. We shall make and use the **Create an Order** sequence diagram in Chapter 6, where we explore this idea of creating a GUI prototype from a sequence diagram.

In the next chapter, we turn our attention to another UML model: the class diagram. This will take us to the next stage of the UML Process for our Northwind project.

```
                    ┌──────────────┐
                    │   Get ADO    │
                    │  connection  │
                    └──────────────┘
                           │
                           ▼
                          ◇
                         ◇ ◇ ───────────────
                          ◇
                           │
          [Successful]     │
                           ▼
                    ┌──────────────┐
                    │ Set Recordset│
                    │cursor location│
                    └──────────────┘
                           │
                           │
                           ▼
                    ┌──────────────┐
                    │ Set Recordset│
                    │    source    │
                    └──────────────┘
                           │
                           │
                           ▼
                    ┌──────────────┐
                    │ Set Recordset│
                    │  connection  │
                    └──────────────┘
                           │
                           ▼
```

5

Class Diagrams

We have now spent quite a lot of time with UML in the early design stages of our project. We've examined the user requirements, and what objects we'll need to fulfill those user requirements. It's now time for us to delve a little deeper, and turn our attention to system design. To do this I will need to introduce to you a new UML model, the **class diagram**.

Let's just consider for a moment what we've achieved so far:

❑ In Chapter 1, we overviewed the whole UML Process and saw how we would gradually refine our UML design to be increasingly more detailed, until the point where we should be ready to translate our UML into Visual Basic code

❑ In Chapter 2, we considered good project management, and made some decisions about the technologies we'll be using for our Northwind project.

❑ In Chapter 3, where we developed use cases, we identified a list of objects in our application domain

❑ In Chapter 4, we created our sequence diagrams, and specified how actors and objects interact with each other. This level of analysis supplied enough information for some comprehensive discussion between our customer, the Northwind company, and ourselves, the development team.

Typically, we shall have several meetings with our customer on the functionality and the external behaviors of the system. During those meetings, we should reach agreement on how the system works from the user's point of view. That is, we should have presented enough information for our customer to judge the usefulness of the system in relation to their business requirement.

It's very likely that such meetings would expose some of the shortcomings of the initial requirements. The customer might, for instance, find that the flow of operations does not match their business procedures. They could also discover some of the implicit requirements of the system. For example, our analysis tells us that a Sales Representative will find a product by first selecting a category and then selecting a product from a list of products that belong to that category. This means that someone in the Northwind company must be able to create, edit, and delete the product categories. But this would lead to a whole new set of use cases concerning the maintenance of product categories. We may have to go through several such iterations to further polish our system analysis.

Once we've understood the system well enough, however, we should move on to the system design. We will need to analyze the internal working of our system. In the object-oriented analysis and design paradigm, this means that we must start to create a hierarchy of classes that make up the backbone of the system.

So this brings us to our next UML model, the **class diagram**. From our use cases and sequence diagrams, we can create **classes** that will provide the infrastructure of the Northwind ordering system. So, let's move right on to the next stage of the UML Process and take a look at these class diagrams.

What is a Class Diagram?

In the previous chapters, we use the term **object** to describe the entities in the system. An object may be a product, or it may be an order. Objects of the same type have the same properties and behaviors. For instance, every product will have a Product ID. Products and their Product ID can be added to the system, and these Product ID's can also be changed during the life of the Product as a part of the system. We model such properties and behaviors into classes.

In UML, a **class** is the description of a set of objects with the same attributes, operations and relationships. Each object is an instance of a particular class. For example, we do not say that we order a book, we say we order the "Visual Basic 6 UML Design and Development" book. Here, `Book` may be a class, and the VB6 UML book is then an instance of `Book`.

> **Classes do not interact with each other. We create instances of particular classes to instantiate objects. It is our objects that interact with each other.**

A class diagram shows a collection of these classes and how they are related to one another. It offers a simple static view of the classes of a system. Class diagrams show the `Public` and `Private` methods and properties of our classes. The number of class diagrams required to model a system will depend on its size and complexity.

In a class diagram, a class is represented in its most simple form as a box with the class name within it, as shown here:

```
ClassName
```

As it stands, however, this is not very useful. We need some additional information about the class. We display this information by dividing the class diagram into three sections:

- ❑ The top section contains the name of the class
- ❑ The middle section contains the properties of the class
- ❑ The lower section contains the methods of the class

A typical class diagram looks something like this:

```
+--------------------------------+
|                                |
|          Class Name            |
|                                |
+--------------------------------+
| + Public Property Name         |
| # Friend Property Name         |
| - Private Property Name        |
+--------------------------------+
| + Public Method Name           |
| # Friend Method Name           |
| - Private Method Name          |
+--------------------------------+
```

We place a symbol next to each of these properties and methods to indicate its level of visibility. The plus signs + indicate `Public` properties and methods, while the negative signs − indicate `Private` properties and methods. We use the hash sign # to indicate `Friend` properties and methods.

> **Friend** properties are properties that can only be seen by other modules within the component.
>
> A component using another component cannot see any **Friend** properties within the component it's using.

Class Types

Classes can be broken into four different categories, depending on what type of object we intend these classes to become. These four categories of class are:

- ❑ Business Entity Objects
- ❑ Business Service Objects
- ❑ System Entity Objects
- ❑ System Service Objects

Business Entity Objects

Business Entity Objects usually represent *persistent* information that is to be stored somewhere, primarily in a database. For example, we might have a table in our database called Customers and we might have a client class also called Customers. Properties associated with a Business Entity Object will mostly represent fields from the database, such as CustomerID.

> *However, it is possible to have a Business Entity object that is non-persistent. Non-persistent information could include calculated fields in the order entry, which would not be stored in the database.*

Business Entity Objects generally contain very few methods, and consist mostly or completely of properties.

Business Service Objects

Business Service Objects do not represent *persistent* information. They perform business functions. Most commonly, Business Service objects manage other objects. For example, a Customer managing class could have methods to Move to the Next Customer, Find Customer, Delete Customer, etc.

Business Service objects generally contain very few properties, and consist mostly or completely of methods.

System Entity Objects

System Entity Objects usually represent information that is stored *persistently* and that *relates to the system*. These objects are usually internal to the system performing tasks that do not relate to the database information. An example of this would be an object handling the user's preferences, such as properties of the GUI. This information could be stored in the registry on the client machine.

System Service Objects

System Service Objects handle *non-persistent* information that *relates to the system*. An example of this would be an object that handled the verifying and charging of a customer's credit card.

> **We will only build Business type objects in our project, since we're focusing on the information in the database for our Northwind application. A more complete application, however, would require all four types of objects, and UML diagrams could be used to build all of them.**

Identifying Classes

We can extract a collection of classes from the list of objects that we identified in the previous chapters. At the end of Chapter 3, we had the following object list:

- ❑ Customers
- ❑ Products
- ❑ Orders
- ❑ Order Details
- ❑ Reports
- ❑ Shippers
- ❑ Categories

Clearly in a book like this, we will not have time to take an in-depth look at every single object in our project. For example, we have not considered the Shipper or Supplier objects in detail. Similarly, although we have not previously examined the Employees object in previous chapters, it should be clear that we will need one for our full application. After all, we have many different types of employee: the Sales Representative, Sales Manager etc. These objects will be included in our class diagrams. You can make these other objects if you feel you need some more practice at the UML models we've looked at so far.

In Chapter 4, where we developed our sequence diagrams, we added two more objects. The first of these was the Interface object, which was the visual interface of the system. The second object we introduced was the DB Business Logic object, which enabled other objects to communicate with the underlying database.

As we will see later, we can break each of those two objects into a collection of smaller objects. For now, though, we will treat them as single objects that provide a set of functions for other objects. How they actually work internally is not relevant at this stage.

The first stage of building a class diagram is to display all the classes, as shown here:

This class diagram incorporates lots of different classes, and will eventually show how these classes are related to one another; it will also, when we have finished our analysis, display the properties and methods for each of these classes. There's a lot to do then, at this stage of the UML process - so let's get started by learning about the different types of associations that may exist between classes.

Associations Between Classes

Associations between classes generally fall into three categories:

- ❑ Ordinary associations
- ❑ Inheritance
- ❑ Aggregation

Ordinary Associations

Ordinary associations are relationships between two classes where one class does not require the other class to exist. Each class has equal responsibility in the relationship. Ordinary associations are represented by a line connecting the classes:

Inheritance

An **inheritance** relationship exists when one class object is a specialized version of another class object. Inheritance relationships are represented with a line with a triangle in it:

Aggregation

There are two types of aggregation:

- ❑ Composite aggregation
- ❑ Simple aggregation

A **composite aggregation** is a relationship between two classes where one class cannot exist without the other class. This is usually a *one-way* relationship.

The Order Details class requires the Orders Class. An Order Detail cannot exist without an Order, but an Order can probably exist without an Order Detail. A filled in diamond in the line connecting the classes represents a composite aggregation:

A **simple aggregation** is a more general type of relationship where one of the classes simply has more responsibility than the other class. A diamond that is not filled on the line connecting the classes represents a simple aggregation:

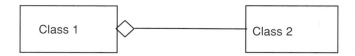

Class hierarchies can be represented as composite aggregations, since the each class in the hierarchy is dependent on the class above it. In Visual Basic we will deal primarily with composite classes.

When building our class diagrams, we look through our use cases and sequence diagrams to find the properties, methods and relationships between classes. Normally, we should find these properties from our uses cases, and the methods from our sequence diagrams.

Deriving Class Properties

To understand where we get our properties from in a class diagram, we need to take a step back and see what else our use cases have to offer. Use cases have already been very useful. They've defined our user requirements and helped us to create our interaction diagrams. But there's yet more information lurking within them. The question is: How do we extract this information? The answer is with **Business Rules**.

> *Strictly speaking Business Rules are not part of the UML standard. They do, however, complement UML by helping us get the most out of our UML models. Before we can use Business Rules to our advantage we need to find out a bit about them.*

Business Rules

Generally speaking, Business Rules are any rules that place restrictions on a use case, or have an effect on the outcome of a use case. There are five types of Business Rules:

- ❑ Requirement rules
- ❑ Definition rules
- ❑ Factual rules
- ❑ Constraint rules
- ❑ Derivation rules

Requirement Business Rules

This is the most general type of Business Rule. The Requirement can represent any part of the system's operation or any business policy that needs to be taken into consideration when designing the system. Requirements are generally phrased in pure business language, and usually can be broken down into smaller rules.

Example: "Customers are billed on the last day of the month." This rule would be derived from several other rules, such as: "customer's bills include new charges and unpaid balances, calculation of customer's unpaid balance, calculation of unpaid charges, etc."

Definition Business Rules

A Definition defines a **business term** found in a use case. A business term usually refers to a piece of information that's stored (usually in a database) or displayed (such as a calculated value). Business terms usually become classes.

Format: The <business term> has a(n) <attribute>

Example: The customer has a customer billing address where the customer prefers all billing correspondence to be sent. It can be different from the shipping address.
In this example the "customer" is the business term and the "customer billing address" is the attribute.

Factual Business Rules

A Fact relates one business term to another business term. Facts are often relationships, attributes, or generalizations between two business terms.

Format: Every (Each) <business term> <relationship to> <another business term>

Example: "Every ordered item is a product" or "Every customer has a billing address."

Constraint Business Rules

This is a Constraint on the behavior of the system. Any rule that only allows a certain range of values can be considered a constraint. When Constraint Business Rules are applied to terms whose values are inputted by the user, these values are usually checked with and **If** statement. Errors are a result of Constraint Business Rules and code must be written to follow an alternative flow that results from this violation. There should be at least one Constraint Business Rule for every Alternative Flow.

Format: <business term> must <constraint>

Example: "A customer's state must be one of the 50 states" or "The state name must be two letters".

Derivation Business Rules

A Derivation represents any information that is derived from other information in the system. Derivation Business Rules will result in a block of code that performs a task, such as calculating the sales tax. Often Derivations become separate functions or sub-procedures.

Format: <derived item> <rules for derivation>

Example: Net Pay is calculated by subtracting deductions from Gross Pay.

> **Definition and Fact Business Rules can be used to determine the properties of our objects, and which objects contain other objects, i.e. object hierarchies.**

Implementing Business Rules

The Constraint, Fact and Derivation Business Rules are essential elements for converting UML diagrams into a Visual Basic application.

Using Business Rules with our use cases will greatly simplify coding. It's important to make sure that all of the Fact, Constraint and Derivation Business Rules are implemented in our code.

> *The easiest way to do this is to put a comment into the code with the name of the Business Rule that the code is based on. We can later do a search on the code for every one of these rules; if we do not find a reference to the Business Rule in our comments, then we know we forgot to implement a rule.*

Since we are now creating class diagrams, we can associate the Business Rules with the properties and methods of our classes. In this way, we will know exactly what rules apply to each class and where they should be placed. A significant portion of the code we will need to write for our objects will be defined by these rules.

The Business Rules will determine the correct values for the properties, what properties an object will have, and methods of deriving the information needed by the class.

> **Alternative flows will show us how to handle errors.**

The methods of our components, and how our components communicate with the rest of the system, will be determined by sequence and/or collaboration diagrams. Hopefully, you're beginning to see how UML diagrams can be used to carefully map out how we will build our objects and how we will write our code. So let's get straight on now and develop some Business Rules for our Create New Customer use case.

The Business Rules for Create New Customer

Let's take another look at the Create New Customer use case that we developed in Chapter 2, and build some Business Rules from it.

Each component in our system should have a Definition Business Rule that defines it. From this Definition Business Rule, we can get the properties of the object that will be an instance of this component.

Our first port of call, therefore, is a Definition Rule. We need to find out exactly what constitutes a customer. Because this is the first Business Rule that we've encountered, I am going to show you what it looks like and then explain each section individually.

<u>Business Rule: Customer</u>

<u>Overview</u>

This is a definition of a Customer

<u>Rule Type</u>

Definition

<u>Rule</u>

A customer has the following information associated with it:

CustomerID

Region

CompanyName

ContactTitle

ContactName

Address

City

PostalCode

Country

Phone

Fax

Required

Yes

Default Values

None

Associated Business Rules

Customer Fields

Customer in the System

Customer Can Place Orders

Let's go through each of these sections in turn, now, and follow the analysis through so that we are quite clear about how we built this Business Rule.

The Overview and Rule Type Sections

These sections should be fairly self-explanatory. The only thing to say is that the **Overview** should be concise and accurate. We should be able to see at a glance exactly what this Business Rule is about.

The Rule Section

We now move to the main section, the **Rule** section itself. Remember that this type of rule defines a business term and takes the form:

The <business term> has a(n) <attribute>

We are interested in the information associated with a Customer. So let's think back to the interview and the use case we created from it. We know that when a Customer telephones in, the Sales Representative asks for their Name, Address, City and other pertinent details. Therefore a Customer has these attributes (as listed in Customer Business Rule):

Rule

A customer has the following information associated with it:

Region
CompanyName
ContactTitle
ContactName
Address
City

PostalCode
Country
Phone
Fax

We also know that each Customer has a unique identifying name, the CustomerID, so we've also included that in our **Rule** section:

Rule

A customer has the following information associated with it:

> CustomerID
> Region
> Company Name
> etc.

If we refer back to the information that the Customer is asked for by the Sales Representative, we'll notice that we've already covered most of the elements in this Customer Business rule.

The Required Section

The next section of our Customer Business Rule, the **Required** section, defines whether the Customer is a necessary field within that database - clearly it is, but there is no default value for the Customer. Therefore, in our Business Rule, we have:

Required

Yes

It's worth noticing, by the way, that the **Required** section only features in the definition type of Business Rule.

The Associated Business Rules Section

Finally, we need to consider any other **Associated Rules** of the Customer. Running through the details I've presented in our Customer Business Rule, we know that each element of the customer's address and details, which we have listed above, will also need defining - this is accomplished with the Customer Fields rule:

Associated Business Rules

Customer Fields

We also know that Customers have orders associated with them. Entering these orders is, after all, the primary purpose of the Sales Representative. This is represented in our **Associated Rules** by the Customer Can Place Orders rule:

<u>Associated Business Rules</u>

Customer Fields
Customer Can Place Orders

Finally, one other thing we know is that there are certain restrictions for the Customer. For example, we will only allow a Customer's details to be added to the system if they don't already exist in the sytem. This is represented in our **Associated Rules** by the Customer in System rule.

Why Use Business Rules?

What we have learned already from this one Business Rule? Well, we know that our Customer object will have a number of properties: CompanyName, ContactName etc. We don't yet know enough about these properties, of course, but that extra information will come with extra Business Rules. We also know that there will be an Order object associated with the Customer object (we've just inserted the rule Customer can Place Orders).

Now you might be thinking to yourself: "I already knew we needed an Order object. I didn't need a Business Rule to tell me what I already know." To some extent, that is true. We could get this information directly from the interview. However, Business Rules provide a logical way of extracting such information. Without these rules we are much more likely to miss something important. As we encounter different type of Business Rules that serve different purposes, you will come to realize just how useful they are.

Creating the Associated Business Rules

So now we should take a look at the Associated Rules that we've listed in our Customer Business Rule. These rules were:

- ❑ Customer Fields
- ❑ Customer in the System
- ❑ Customer Can Place Orders

Let's take the Customer Fields rule first. We know, from our earlier analysis, that there is a restriction placed on each of the customer fields regarding its format. Therefore, our rule should be a Constraint Rule. By considering all of the customer fields in turn, we would arrive at a Business Rule that looked something like this:

<u>Business Rule: Customer Fields</u>

<u>Overview</u>

These are the conditions for the fields associated with a Customer.

Rule Type

Constraint

Rule

CustomerID will be a unique five character string based on the customer name.

Region will be a State or Province up to 15 characters.

CompanyName will be a string less than 40 characters.

ContactTitle will be a string less than 30 Characters long, acceptable values are:

Accounting manager

Assistant Sales Agent

Marketing Assistant

Order Administrator

Owner

Owner/Marketing Assistant

Sales Agent

Sales Associate

Sales Manager

Sales Representative

ContactName will be a string less than 30 characters.

Address will be a string less than 60 characters.

City will be a string less than 15 characters.

PostalCode will be a string less than 10 characters

Country will be a string less than 15 characters

Phone will be a string less than 24 characters.

Fax will be a string less than 24 characters.

Associated Business Rules

None.

This Customer Fields Business Rule might look good, but it has some problems. It's actually made up of several smaller Business Rules! There should actually be a Definition Business Rule for each field giving details of that field.

> *While this may seem like a lot of work for very little gain, looking at the Northwind database you will discover that Customers are companies, not people! We need to be rather careful, and Definition rules will help us to focus on anomalies like this.*

The identifying field for a Customer is CompanyName. Having a Definition Business Rule for CompanyName will make it easy for everyone to understand this. Once all the smaller Business Rules are created, we'll then be able to refer to them in our (rewritten) Customer Fields Business Rule, and make Customer Fields itself a Requirement Business Rule rather than a Constraint rule. Our Customer Fields Business Rule then looks like this:

Business Rule: Customer Fields

Overview

These are the conditions for the fields associated with a Customer.

Rule Type

Requirement

Rule

The fields associated with a customer will be constrained as described by the rules listed in the Associated Business Rules section.

Associated Business Rules

Customer CustomerID

Customer Region

Customer CompanyName

Customer ContactTitle

Customer ContactName

Customer Address

Customer City

Customer PostalCode

Customer Country

Customer Phone

Customer Fax

These **Associated Business Rules** would all be of the same form. This allows us to focus on the process itself for the purposes of this book – so I'd like to show you just one of these for the moment, the Customer Customer ID Business Rule:

Business Rule: Customer CustomerID

Overview

The Business rule defines the CustomerID attribute of a Customer.

Rule Type

Definition

Rule

A Customer has a unique CustomerID

Required

Yes

Default Values

None

Valid Values

A five character string based on the Customer name

Attribute Class

Customer

Associated Business Rules

None

As you can see – nothing very surprising here: we've simply created a Definition Business Rule that defines the valid values of the Customer name. The key point about this Rule is how it fits together with our **Customer Fields** rule of course.

Once again, we've seen here that creating UML diagrams is an iterative process. We began with our initial ideas, refined them, expanded them, and corrected them. We've taken our original **Customer Fields** *Business Rule, thought about things, and developed a new set of Business Rules from it.*

We'll now examine the other two rules associated with our original **Customer** Definition Business Rule

❑   Customers in System
❑   Customer Can Place Orders

Here are the Business Rules that I derived for these rules:

Business Rule: Customers in System

Overview

This Business Rule limits the number of times a customer can be listed in the system.

Rule Type

Constraint

Rule

Each customer must only be listed in the system once

Class

Customer

Associated Business Rules

None

This Business Rule is quite simple; but as I mentioned earlier, we need to ensure that code is written to implement it – it could be catastrophic to underestimate how important this rule would be to our system!

We now look at the Customer Can Place Orders rule, and its associated Orders Relationship rule:

Business Rule:Customer Can Place Orders

Overview

The relationship between a customer and an order.

Rule type

Fact

Rule

A customer can place an order

Associated Business Rules

Orders Relationship

Business Rule: Orders relationship

Overview

This Business Rule shows the relationship between a customer and an order

Rule Type

Fact

Rule

Every customer has at least one Order that is in progress, complete or canceled.

Associated Business Rules

None

The Orders relationship provides us with something new. It does not give us an attribute of the Customer object, but it does intimate how the Order and Customer objects are related.

Looking at the rule: Every Customer has at least one Order that is either in progress, complete or cancelled, this means that without an order the Customer would not exist:

The Order *has* a Customer

The Class Diagram for Customer

OK – all this information has taken us further than we might think. Putting everything together that we now know about the Customer object, part of our class diagram will certainly look as follows:

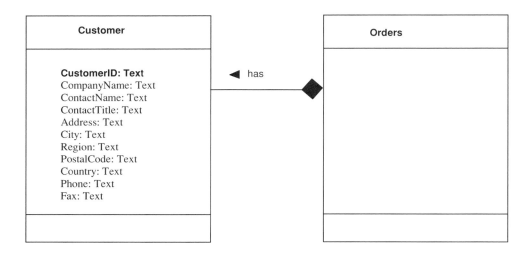

So we can see how useful Business Rules can be. They help us to extract the properties of our objects in a logical and consistent manner. They also help us to identify the associations between our classes.

There are many Business Rules associated with the use cases and our objects. You should try to create those that are the most appropriate to your project. This is not always straightforward and, as with so many aspects of project design, this will be an iterative process.

The Northwind System Class Diagram

The next logical step in creating our class diagrams should be to derive the methods.

Deriving these methods will lead naturally to a discussion of class hierarchies. For the moment, I'd like us to concentrate on our class diagrams. So let's put together everything that we've learned so far, and create a class diagram for everything we know about the system up to this point.

If we apply the same analysis that we used to derive our Customer class diagram, to then derive a class diagram for the whole system, we should find ourselves having arrived at a diagram rather like this:

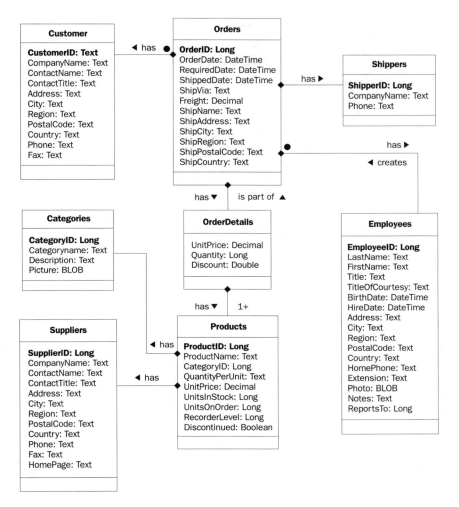

In this, our system class diagram, we've have a very detailed explanation of the relationships between all of the classes in our system as we understand it so far.

We've posited all the objects we've been talking about, identified their relevant properties, and drawn appropriate associations between them. Let's explore this diagram in a little more detail now though: you're bound to have seen some new features in this diagram that we haven't talked about yet.

Roles: 'Has' and 'Is A Part Of'

You will notice that there are tags next to the associations in our system class diagram, above. These tags are called **roles**, and we can have roles for *both* classes in an association. These roles provide more information about the association between the two classes involved. Let's take a careful look at a few of our roles...

Take a look at the roles between the OrderDetails class and Orders class. The arrow pointing from the Order class to the OrderDetails class says: **has** which means that the Order object will have an Order Details object associated with it. The arrow pointing from the Order Details object to the Order object says: **is part of** showing that the OrderDetails is part of the Order. This is a **composite aggregation**, which is represented by the filled in diamond attached to the Orders Class.

Cardinality

When we're using an association we can display the **cardinality** between the classes. Cardinality shows how many of one class is associated with another class. Cardinality can have the following values:

- ❏ One class is associated with zero or more of the other classes. This is the **default** and is not specified (so there's nothing to add to the diagram).
- ❏ One class is associated with one or more of the other classes. This is represented by a **1+**.
- ❏ One class is associated with either zero or one of the other classes. This is represented by an **open circle**.
- ❏ One class is associated with exactly one of the other classes. This is represented by a **closed circle**.

There are other cardinal symbols, but these are the most common.

The Products/Orders Association

Looking at the relationship between Products and Order Details we see that the 1+ means there is anywhere from one to many Product objects associated with an OrderDetails object.

The Orders/Employees Association

The tag has shows us that the Order object has an Employee object associated with it. The tag pointing in the other direction shows that the Employee *creates* an Order.

Now take a look at the association between the Orders object and the Employees object. We can see that there is a filled in circle next to the Orders object. This means that the Orders object is associated with exactly one Employees object. There is nothing next to the Employees object, however. This means that the default cardinality is in place here, and that the Employee object is associated with none or more Order objects.

The Orders/Customer Association

This association is quite similar to the previous one. We have put a has pointing from the Order to the Customer, showing that an Order object has a Customer object associated with it. We could also put another role pointing the other way and call it *places* to show that a Customer places an Order. The Orders object has a filled in circle next to it and is associated with exactly on Customer object, while the default cardinality applies to the Customer object.

Summary of the Northwind System Class Diagram

In our system class diagram, we've made a very detailed diagram showing the relationships between all of the classes in our system as we understand it so far. Try to make a diagram like this yourself. Include the roles we have talked about so far, and add the roles we have left out.

> A class diagram is a very powerful tool, giving us deep insight into the relationships between the classes in our system.

Remember, however, that class diagrams are built from *all the other* UML diagrams that we've created previously. As we continue using UML diagrams to design our system, we'll be adding more information into our system class diagram.

Deriving Class Methods

As I mentioned earlier, before we drew up our system class diagram, we need to find the methods for each of the objects that we've identified so far in the system. I also mentioned that to do this, we would need to return to our sequence diagrams from Chapter 4. So that's just what we'll do now.

In a sequence diagram, one object interacts with another by sending it a message. For instance, in the Create New Customer sequence diagram, the Interface object can send a Save Customer message to the Customer object. From that detail, it becomes fairly clear that we're going to need a SaveCustomer() method. The question is, which class should provide this method, the Interface or the Customer?

> There's no hard and fast rule for deciding this. One great technique we can use here though, is to let the class with the *most knowledge* about a particular task handle that task.

So for the SaveCustomer() task, which class knows most about the customer? It has to be the Customer class! Now I'll grant that this particular example wasn't very difficult. Sometimes, we will find it harder to make this type of decision in more complicated situations, but it's always a useful technique to apply.

> *As you may have guessed, deriving class methods is no small topic. It requires good understanding of object-oriented analysis and design. You will also need to understand Design Patterns. An excellent book on that subject is 'Design Patterns – Elements of Reusable Object-Oriented Software' by Erich Gamma, et al. (Addison-Wesley).*

In this chapter, we'll be using one of the common approaches for deriving class methods from interaction diagrams. This approach runs as follows:

> If an object sends a message to another object, we will implement a method in the destination class. We can then let the originating object call this method in the destination object.

For example, the Customer class should implement a SaveCustomer() method, and an Interface object should then send the Save Customer message to a Customer object by calling its SaveCustomer() method.

Now that we've established some of the theory behind deriving class methods, it's time to put this into practice.

Customer Class Methods

We'll now focus on one class, the Customer Class. First we will review the information we already have on the Customer object, and then we'll add more information and UML diagrams.

In Chapter 3, we created three use cases for the Customer object:

❑ Create New Customer
❑ Modify Customer
❑ Delete Customer

In Chapter 4, we went on to convert these use cases into the following sequence diagrams. Let's see what each of these diagrams can tell us about class methods. Here's our Create New Customer sequence diagram:

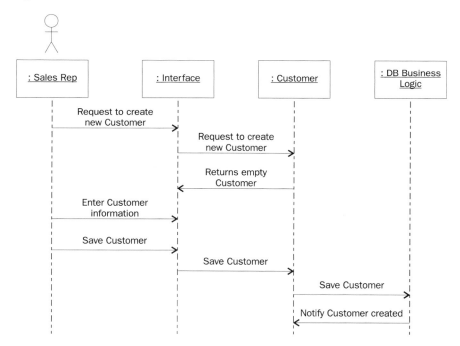

From this diagram, we can see that the Customer object must be able to take a request to Add a New Customer, be able to Return (a New) Customer, and Save (a New) Customer.

You'll notice that I'm presenting less-detailed versions of our sequence diagrams. If you remember back to Chapter 4, we discussed how it's useful to be able to increase and decrease the detail in these diagrams to suit our needs. This less-detailed view will suit our needs for deriving class methods.

Now here's our sequence diagram for **Modify Customer**:

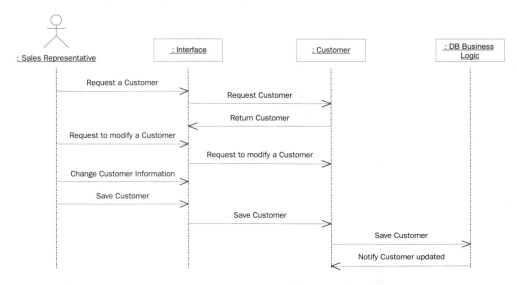

From this sequence diagram, we see that our Customer object must be able to take a Request (for an) Existing Customer, be able to return an Existing Customer, take a Request to Edit a Customer, and take a Request to Save a Customer. Returning an existing Customer means we also have to be able to move through Customer records and retrieve a customer by their ID or name.

Now let's take a look at our Delete Customer sequence diagram:

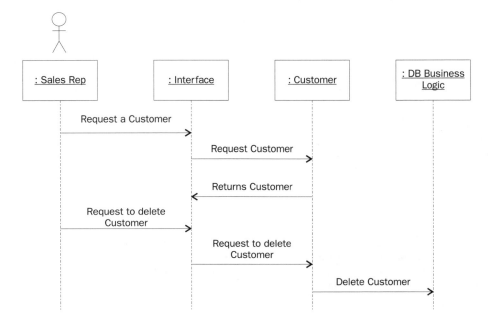

This sequence diagram shows that our Customer object must also Delete a Customer.

We can now map all of these responsibilities of our Customer object to methods for the Customer object. Here's a table that presents the information we've just gathered from our sequence diagrams:

Task	Method
Add a New Customer	AddNew
Return a New Customer	AddNew
Save a New Customer	Save
Request an Existing Customer	Move Previous, Move Next, Move First, Move Last, Move Item (because we need the ability to select a customer)
Delete a Customer	Delete
Edit a Customer	Edit
Save Edit	Save

Now we've derived these methods, we're ready to add them to the Customer class diagram that we started earlier - we've established the properties for this class diagram, so let's go ahead now and add the methods:

```
                    Customer

        CustomerID: Text
        CompanyName: Text
        ContactName: Text
        ContactTitle: Text
        Address: Text
        City: Text
        Region: Text
        PostalCode: Text
        Country: Text
        Phone: Text
        Fax: Text

        AddNew()
        Save()
        MovePrevious()
        MoveNext()
        MoveFirst()
        MoveLast()
        MoveItem()
        Delete()
        Edit()
        Save()
```

When we previously looked at the sequence diagrams for our components, we noticed that most of these components required these same methods. Since these methods were the same for several components, we showed that they formed a **pattern**. To demonstrate this pattern, we'll now look at the methods of the Product class, create our Product class diagram, and see what emerges.

Product Class Methods

Once again, we are going to look at the sequence diagrams for Create New Product, Modify Product and Delete Product. This time we will only concentrate on the methods that the Product object has in common with the Customer object.

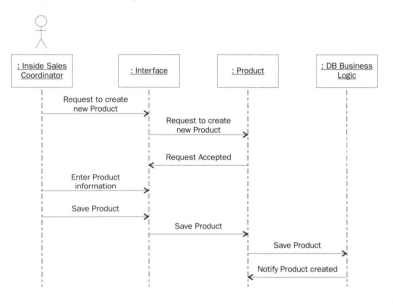

From the Create New Product diagram we can see that it will require an Add New Product and a Save Product method.

Let's now take a look at the Modify Product sequence diagram:

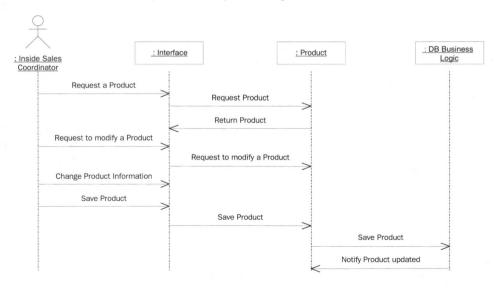

From this sequence diagram, we see that our Product object must be able to take a Request for an Existing Product, be able to return data on an Existing Product, Edit an Existing Product, and Save a Product.

Finally, let's looking at the Delete Product sequence diagram:

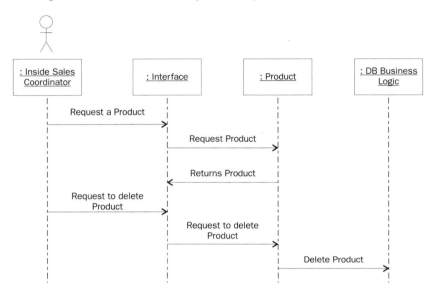

From this diagram, we find that we also require a Delete Product method.

From this brief look at the Product sequence diagrams, we can see that the Product object will possess many of the same methods as the Customer object. Here's a table of the methods we've derived for the Product sequence:

Task	Method
Add a New Product	AddNew
Return a New Product	AddNew
Save a New Product	Save
Request an Existing Product	Move Previous, Move Next, Move First, Move Last, Move Item (because we need the ability to select a Product)
Delete a Product	Delete
Edit a Product	Edit
Save Edit	Save

Now we've derived these methods, we're ready to add them to the Product class diagram. We didn't develop the Product class diagram step-by-step earlier, but we did draw up a version of it in our Northwind system class diagram. Here's the final Product class diagram:

Product
ProductID: Long ProductName: Text CategoryID: Long QuantityPerUnit: Text UnitPrice: Decimal UnitsInStock: Long UnitsOnOrder: Long RecorderLevel: Long Discontinued: Boolean
AddNew() Save() MovePrevious() MoveNext() MoveFirst() MoveLast() MoveItem() Delete() Edit() Save()

Now we've completed our Customer and Product class diagrams, we'll be able to compare them both and analyze the pattern between them that's emerging.

A Pattern: Customer and Product Class Diagrams

Take a look at both the Customer and Product class diagrams we've created. It's quite clear that they have different properties but share the *same methods*. Obviously, there's a pattern here - but how can we best take advantage of this? To answer that question, we need to return to an earlier topic: class hierarchies.

Class Hierarchies and Patterns

As we did previously, we can break up our objects into a two-class hierarchy based on the pattern that we've just identified. The following diagram shows how we're going to build our Customer/Product objects from a class hierarchy:

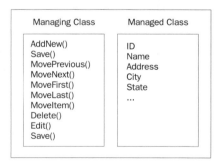

As you can see, we've simply put all of the common methods between our Customer and Product objects into the Managing Class.

The Managing Class for the Product component will be nearly identical to the component we'll develop for the Customer component. This will be true for many of our components. The different components will share some common methods in the Managing Class, but the properties in the Managed Class will be different for each component (such as Customer and Product, for instance).

> **Using class diagrams, we have managed to precisely define the pattern that's been emerging from our sequence diagrams, and create a documented class coding strategy for when we come to develop our actual project.**

Summary

We've covered a lot of ground in this chapter. Not only have we introduced class diagrams, but we've also turned our attention to Business Rules and the emergent patterns that we noticed in our sequence diagrams some time ago. By developing our class diagrams like this, we've managed to take our design of the Northwind project a lot further, defining classes and strategies to take advantage of patterns. This will have real benefits when we come to develop our Visual Basic project.

So here's what we've covered in this chapter:

- ❑ What constitutes a class
- ❑ Class diagrams and how to create them in UML
- ❑ Associations between classes
- ❑ Deriving class properties
- ❑ Deriving class methods
- ❑ Creating Business Rules
- ❑ The relationship between sequence and class diagrams
- ❑ Using patterns in our design analysis

Class diagrams can be considered as the natural progression from our use case and sequence diagram models. They are the next stage of the UML Process. In this chapter, we were able to use the information from use cases and sequence diagrams to help us create the class model diagrams.

Our UML diagrams (use case, sequence and class diagrams) have helped us to get a great deal of information about our Customer and Product components. From the information we've gathered so far from the UML Process, we'll be able to move on now to actually prototype a GUI (graphical user interface) for our system in the next chapter.

6

Prototyping the GUI

In Chapters 3 and 4 we learnt about use cases and sequence diagrams. These UML models help us to understand the user requirements, to visualize the sequence of events that occurs during an interaction, and to find patterns common to these interactions. Another important role that these models serve is to help us to build a graphical user interface.

Once our use cases and sequence diagrams are complete, we have sufficient information to make a general GUI prototype. By creating a GUI prototype, which can be shown to the user before the final release of the application, we can make sure that it fulfills all of the user's requirements.

In this chapter we will:

❑ See what problems arise when the GUI is not based on the users' needs
❑ See how our UML diagrams can help us create a more logical, user friendly design
❑ Implement this design to build a better GUI prototype for our Order Entry application

I won't show you how to actually build the prototype in this chapter, as there is little implementation we can actually perform behind the scenes at this point. In Chapter 14, we'll build the final GUI design.

Form Control

UML use cases and sequence diagrams will allow us to follow one of the most important standards of Visual Basic, **maintaining form control**. Form control should be used to keep the tasks the user has to perform as simple as possible.

I'm sure you've seen applications where there is a multitude of forms to complete a single task and the poor user has to constantly jump back and forth from one form to another in order to complete a single task.

Those sort of applications usually come about when the developers have designed the forms around a database rather than what the user actually has to do. For example, a project designed around a database that has a Customer, Employee and Order table would have forms to maintain each of these tables. If a user wanted to update a customer while entering an order, they would have to leave the Order Entry form and go to the Customer form. Once the customer had been entered into the system, the user would then have to return to the Order Entry form and refresh that form.

Clearly, this is an overly complex, labor-intensive process. There must be a better solution.

And of course, there is a better solution. It is only common sense that the forms should be based on the roles the system's users perform and what each of these roles entails. Use cases can provide us with the actors, which represent the different roles, and also a description of what each of the actors does in that particular role. Sequence diagrams provide a picture of how each of these tasks is performed and the order of events.

It's for this reason that we will build our GUI prototype based on the actors we have created and the tasks that they perform. In this way we will produce task-oriented forms.

> By a task, I mean a series of events as described by one or more use cases. It's possible that one task will contain several other smaller tasks. For example, we know that **Order Entry** contains the **Add** and **Modify Customer** tasks.

Order Entry GUI

To see how a use case and sequence diagram can help us to prototype a GUI, we will first build the sequence diagram for Entering an Order from the use cases of Chapter 3. Since this diagram is going to be used to build a GUI prototype, we only want to see how the user interacts with the client side objects.

Building the Order Entry Sequence Diagram

We know that the first thing the actor (in this case the Sales Representative) will have to do is make a request to the retrieve the record for a customer who has just phoned in to place an order. This request will be made to the Customer object via the Interface object. There is, as we know the possibility that the customer may not exist in our Customer object or that their details may need amending. This is shown on the diagram as a dotted line from the Customer object back to itself. If this is indeed the case, we know that the flow of events will be somewhat more complicated than shown in this diagram.

> *As I mentioned earlier, the purpose of this diagram is to help us visualize the communication between our components. We could make a more detailed diagram showing all of these possibilities in full, but for the moment we should just be trying to get an overview of the process of making an order. Editing and creating a customer are not important to our overview of creating an order. For these reasons, we should leave these possibilities out of the diagram.*

The Customer component then passes the CustomerID onto the Order object, as this object will need to know which customer this Order belongs to. The Order object will also need to create an OrderID. Once the Customer object has returned the details about a particular customer, the Sales Representative requests the user interface to get products that belong to a certain category. The Interface passes this message along to the Product component, which returns the products to the user. Let's take a look and see how our sequence diagram is coming along:

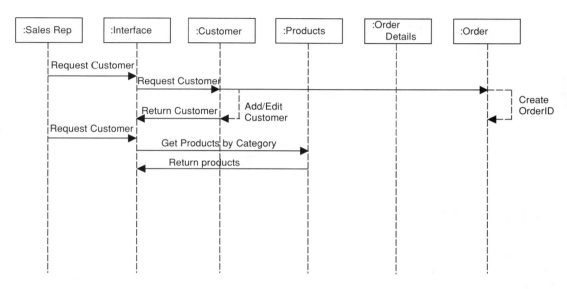

The Sales Representative will then choose a particular product and add it to the Order Detail component. The Sales Representative can then select more products from this category or make another request for products from a different one. The Sales Representative will repeat this process until they have completed the Order that the customer desires. This iterative process is shown by a dashed line at the Interface object.

Once the Sales Representative has finished, they can tell the Interface to save the order. This request is passed to the Order component and the Order Details components, which will then add this new record to the disconnected recordset and send the recordset to the middle tier. From here, it is passed to the database so that the database can be updated. As this final part of the operation is outside the realm of our client objects, it will not be shown our diagram:

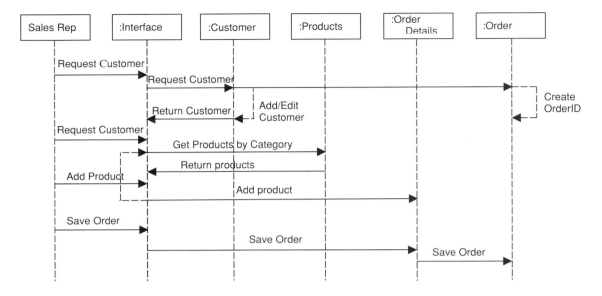

How Not to Make a GUI

While some of the IES Inc. development team were busy talking to the employees of the Northwind company in order to make the necessary use cases, some of the remaining workers at IES were getting a bit impatient. One bright spark already had experience of creating GUIs, and felt that he knew enough about the project to get started. So in an effort to impress his boss he came up with this:

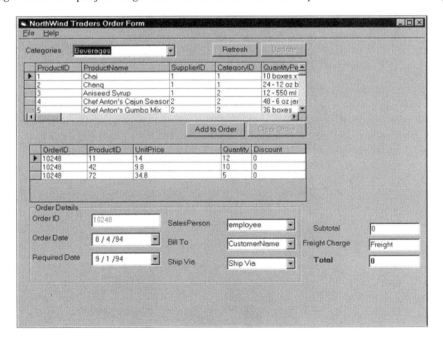

At a glance, this prototype seems quite reasonable. It appears to have all the basic elements. There's a drop down box for choosing the categories and a grid to choose the particular product from. We can add new products to the order with the Add to Order button. There's a section for the order details such as the OrderID and the order date, and essentially there is an identifier for the customer in the Bill To drop down box. Our IES developer thinks that this is a pretty good-looking form.

However, this Order Entry prototype would never get to the client because it has some serious flaws. Let's step back and look at this interface with our Create Order use case and sequence diagram in mind.

We now know that adding and editing customers is a subtask of entering an order. Do you see any way of adding or editing a customer on this form? This form only has the Bill To section to select a customer. There is simply no way to add or edit a customer.

To add a customer, the Sales Representative would have to:

- Close the Order Entry form
- Open a Customer form
- Make the changes to the customer
- Save the changes
- Close the Customer form
- Open the Order Entry form
- Click Refresh

I call this user-abusive rather than user-friendly. Clearly the developer is not always the best person to create a GUI. It should be the users that dictate its design.

Actors and Use Case Focused Forms

Let's explore a better way of making a GUI. To do this we need to look at the use case and the sequence diagram that we've just made. From these we can see that the first thing that happens is a customer will ring in to place an order. At this point the Sales Representative will take their name and details. Now there are three possible things that can be happening:

- The customer already exists and their details are correct
- The customer is new and the Sales Representative will need to add them to the system
- The customer's details have changed and the Sales Representative will need to amend them

Since the customer information is only modified or added while adding an order, it would make sense to add and modify customers on the Order Entry form. Now a customer can be added or edited without interrupting the flow of the order by moving in and out of several forms. This part of the GUI could look like this:

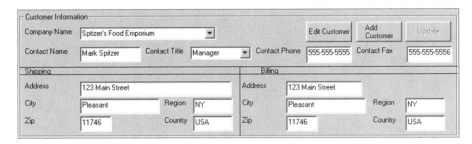

Everything that the Sales Representative needs to carry out this initial part of her task is available to her on this form. There is no need to swap between forms to complete this part of the task.

The next part of the Order Entry task is to pick out the products that the customer wants and to add them to the order. This sub-task is quite distinct from taking the customer details and so should occupy a separate part of the form. It could looks as follows:

Categories and Products

Category	Beverages
Category Description	Soft drinks, coffees, teas, beers, and ales

General Information / Product Search

Product	Chai	Quantity Ordered	5
Cost	$3.98	Unit	Each
		Units In Stock	100

Add to Order

Using Tabs

We have chosen to use tabs in this section. Using tabs on a form can prevent the form from becoming overcrowded and difficult to follow. Here, our user needs to check information about a product, such as cost and availability. So there is a tab to display this general information about the product. Sometimes, particularly when new products have been entered into the system the Sales Representative is not sure to which category the products belong. Therefore we have provided a tab to perform a product search. For most of the time this option will not be used and the tab would not be selected. When it is needed it can be pulled up quickly with a single click of the tab.

The alternative is to open a special product form that allows the user to search for a product. The Sales Representative would then have to close this form when they had finished and return to the Order Entry form. If the user needs to do this a number of times while taking an order, the solution would involve moving back and forth between the forms a lot of times. This doesn't seem very efficient.

> *We could improve the situation by linking the product in the Product Search form to the Order Entry form. Now we can open the Product Search form, find the product we want and choose whether or not to add it to the current order. While this is not a bad solution, it is still easier to click on a tab in the Order Entry form.*

The final part of the Order Entry task is to select a shipper, check the order details with the customer and that they find the total price for the order acceptable and then to cancel the order or go ahead and save it. This information should therefore be grouped together and the final part of the form would probably look as follows:

Putting It All Together

Putting all the separate parts together the Order Entry prototype GUI would create one large form as follows:

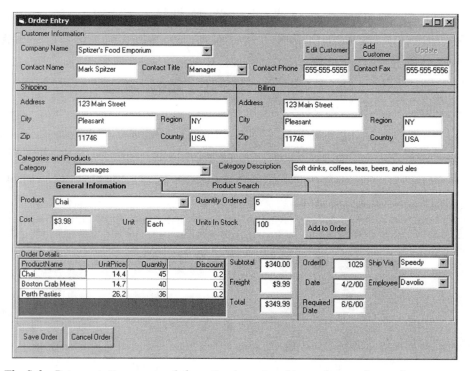

The Sales Representative can spend the entire day using this one form and never have to move away from it.

Most of the information we used to create this GUI came from the use case Create New Order. However, there is at least one aspect of the GUI that follows from the sequence diagram. We have learnt that sequence diagrams place a temporal emphasis on an interaction.

They give us the order in which events occur. Bearing that in mind, take another look at the sequence diagram that we created earlier. You can see that the user first selects a customer, then a category and then a product. Once the product is selected, the user enters the required quantity of that product. If you look at the form it is arranged in this order from the top down:

- ❑ First, comes the customer information section
- ❑ Next, is a product category dropdown listbox
- ❑ Next, is a product dropdown listbox
- ❑ Finally, the order details and order information

This allows the user to easily perform the task without having to move all over the form. We are not only using our UML diagrams to keep a user within a single form to perform a single task, but we are also using our diagrams to arrange the sections on the form in the order the user is going to use them.

Are Two Forms Better Than One?

So far, we've been extolling the virtues of a single form where the actor can perform all the duties associated with his particular role. If some of these duties are identical for different actors we need to ask the question "Are two forms for the same activity better than one?"

To address this issue, let's imagine that there is another use case called Review All Customers performed by the Sales Manager actor. Part of this Review All Customers use case is to check if a customer's information is correct. If the information is incorrect, then the Sales Manager has to modify the customer record. If the only place to modify customer information were on the Order Entry form, the Sales Manager would have to perform this task in the Order Entry form, which would make no sense, as this task has nothing to do with Order Entry.

We could make a separate form that is specifically for Customer Review. While this may seem redundant, as there are now two places to edit information, there are advantages to doing this. What if the Sales Manager needed to look at a customer's past sales history, balance information, and products purchased as part of the customer review? Now it makes sense to have one individual form to handle customer review.

Most likely the top half of the form will have customer information on it, the bottom half will be a tab control: one tab for sales history, a second for balance information, and a third for products purchased:

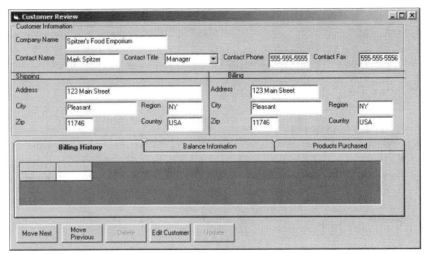

Security

An application that has different actors with different responsibilities will usually have a log in screen and some form of security. If our application employs the Review All Customers use case, the application should have security added and only allow a person logged in as a Sales Manager to view the Customer Review form. The Customer Review form would not be accessible to a Sales Representative.

The Sales Representative has one main role, entering orders. There will only be one form she should have access to, the Order Entry form. The Sales Representative would come in at the beginning of the day and log in as a Sales Representative. The application would go directly to the Order Entry form, as this is the only form a person in this role can access.

As for our Sales Manager, when he logs in there will either be special forms related to his role, such as the Customer Review form, or one form which will provide different functionality for different users, such as the Order Entry form.

Internet Applications

There is one other advantage to this single user interface style of programming. Building Internet and intranet applications is becoming more and more common. While we do have the ability to create dynamic web pages that can build new pages on the fly, these only work with certain browsers. Users are usually not too happy when they are constantly waiting for new pages to load. In this case, the usual standard is to minimize the number of pages and try to complete a single task on one page. Internet solutions seem to work best with a single user interface such as the one we have built above.

If we wanted to use an Internet browser to run this application on an intranet, we would not have to make any major changes in the design of my user interface. As this application is being built from the three-tier model, moving the entire project to an intranet solution would be fairly easy.

> *We must build our applications with a focus not only on current needs but also on future needs. The technology is definitely moving toward building Internet and intranet solutions, and our Visual Basic applications should be able to adapt to these changes.*

A Form in Many Guises

In our example, the Order Entry form allowed the Sales Representative to add orders, but not to edit or delete them. This same form *could* also provide the ability to edit an order for someone logged in as a Sales Manager. We can create one application, which presents each user with forms that are appropriate for the tasks they need to perform. Each form will provide the actor with everything they need to complete a task in the most efficient manner possible.

This approach does not mean that two different actors may not use the same forms.

In our example, the Sales Representative is allowed to create an order, but not to delete or modify them. The Sales Representative is also allowed to create and modify customers, but not delete them. The Sales Manager, on the other hand, can modify and delete the orders and delete customers. It makes sense that the Sales Manager uses the same form to edit and delete orders as the Sales Representative uses to create them, as both of them will require the same information to perform their task, i.e. order details and customer information.

Even though they are using the same form, the form may present itself differently to the two actors. When a Sales Representative views the Order Entry form, they would only have the ability to add a new order, and edit or add a customer. The buttons to delete or modify an order or delete a customer will be invisible to the Sales Representative. However, when a Sales Manager logs into the system and accesses the same form, they will have the command buttons allowing them to edit and delete orders, and delete customers - as these are tasks this actor can do.

Thus, we have one form that performs several different tasks for two different actors, but this form is designed to perform these tasks in the most efficient manner. This one form will add, delete, and modify both customers and orders.

With this type of form there is always the possibility that it will become quite complex. This is something to take account of when deciding the best way to create the GUI for a particular application.

Although this choice may be guided by the amount of coding that it requires, the main criterion when creating forms should be the user requirements.

Delete Customer GUI

As a final example of making GUI prototypes, we are going to take a look at deleting a customer. Below is the Delete Customer use case:

USE CASE: DELETE CUSTOMER

Overview

The purpose of this use case is to remove customer information.

Primary Actor

Sales Manager

Secondary Actor

Vice President of Sales

Starting Point

The actor must have displayed a list of customers.

Ending Point

The customer is either deleted or the delete is canceled by the system.

Measurable Result

A customer is deleted.

Flow of Events

This use case is started when the actor requests to review an existing customer. The actor then requests to delete the customer information.

If there are outstanding unfilled customer orders or debts for the customer the actor will be advised of this by the application and the delete will not be allowed. If there are no outstanding orders or debts the actor is prompted to accept or cancel the operation. If the actor accepts the operation, the customer is deleted from the system and the customer list is updated.

Alternative Flow of Events

The actor tries to cancel a customer who has an outstanding order or debt. The customer delete will be canceled.

Use Case Extensions

None

Outstanding Issues

None

This use case for deleting a customer shows that the Sales Manager is the actor for this task. As this task requires a review of the customer's billing history, sales history, and current balance information, this should also be performed on a separate form that has a tab control on the bottom showing views of the information required to perform this task.

The GUI Effect

The approach we've seen here may force our users to change their habits a bit. Users can no longer begin one task, stop in the middle, open a second window and begin a second task, open another window and start a third task, etc. The user should focus on one task at a time. This is not to say that one task can always be done in one form; sometimes it may require several. This is especially true when a use case uses many other use cases.

What I am saying is that a use case represents a task being performed by a user; it has a beginning and an end. Once a user begins a use case, they must follow it through to the end - remember that use cases always have cancel as one of the options for the end point. If that task requires three windows to be open at once, fine, but the user is not allowed to move on to perform another unrelated task until the current one is complete. This allows the user to focus on one task at a time and prevents the user from being in the middle of a task and forgetting to complete it.

If one use case ends up using a large number of other use cases, it may be worthwhile to review the system and see if the use case can be broken up. There is no magic number of use cases. There is no amount that is too small or too large. Every system is unique.

Summary

In this chapter, we've explored the best ways to create a GUI prototype. Although there may be other considerations that govern the GUI design, the most important factor should always be the requirements of the user. Once a prototype has been made it must be shown to the relevant users. They can then review it and the necessary changes can be made.

Later, when we build activity diagrams that will map out the sequence of events that will occur in each section, we'll be able to order the section according to how the user enters information into that section. For example, we can create an activity diagram showing the detailed set of steps the user takes to enter the customer information. Using this information, we can further optimize the customer section on this form by putting the customer textboxes in the order that the user normally will enter the customer information.

That is all in the future though. We have already covered a great deal in these first chapters of the book. In the next chapter, we'll perform an important review of the stages of the UML design process that we've been through so far, and see exactly where we're at and how we're going to move into the development stage of our Northwind project.

7
External and Internal Factors

At this point in our design process, we've arrived at a critical junction. You may remember how I said that the design of our project would be influenced by two sets of considerations:

- ❑ External factors
- ❑ Internal factors

The source of these *external* considerations has been the user requirements, which we began to draw up as soon as we interviewed some of the employees at Northwind. The *internal* considerations will be determined by the technologies that we choose to use. In this chapter, we will take stock of the UML development so far, and ready ourselves for the coming together of external and internal considerations for our Northwind project.

> *In fact, we are at the junction in our design process between user requirement analysis and technology framework analysis.*

The purpose of the internal design of the project was to fulfill the external requirements of the users. Put more simply, we know *what* we want our project to do; and we must now discover *how* to make it do it.

Although designing the user requirements and designing the internal aspects of our system are quite different activities, there will of course be some common ground between them:

> *The design of user requirements and the design of internal system requirements can both be made easier with the use of appropriate UML models.*

In addition, both internal and external design activities are iterative processes. Just as we found the defining the user requirements was not a one-step procedure, we shall soon see, over the next few chapters, that internal design is far from a smooth ride. The iterative process will be paramount to finding the best way to build out project.

Review of the UML Process (so far)

We've spent the first half of this book determining the user requirements. To achieve this, we have used a number of different UML diagrams. Let's review the process so far.

Use Cases

The starting point for the external design should always be the **use case** model. To successfully conduct this stage of the UML process, it is always necessary to find a representative group of users.

We should be able to find a representative group of users by talking to someone in management. From the list of employees they give us, we then need to interview each person to find out exactly what they do. From these interviews, we may find that some of these people perform identical tasks and may be considered to be one user. We are also likely to find that many other tasks exist and that we have many more users than we originally thought.

This is the first evidence that our design process will be an iterative affair.

We can then turn these interviews into a set of **use cases**, which are a verbal description of the tasks that each user or **actor** will perform. We can also make **use case diagrams**, which show the relationships between actors and use cases.

At this point, the use cases and use case diagrams should be shown to the users so that they can review them. It is very unlikely that they will contain all the right information first time round. They can then be amended as appropriate.

Interaction Diagrams

The next step is to build **interaction** diagrams. These can be **sequence** or **collaboration** diagrams. Sequence and collaboration diagrams represent essentially the same information. However:

❑ Sequence diagrams emphasize the temporal sequence of events in an interaction
❑ Collaboration diagrams emphasize the structural organization of the objects.

For Visual Basic projects, we found that sequence diagrams are more appropriate - since they better represent the particular steps the user will follow.

Sequence diagrams are made by transforming the use cases from a verbal description into a pictorial representation. These diagrams show the communication between objects that must take place for a task to be accomplished, as well as the steps that the actor actually performs during these tasks.

Once again, these sequence diagrams must be reviewed and any amendments made. It is quite possible that at this stage we may find that the use cases also need to change.

Activity Diagrams

From our use cases and sequence diagrams, we then go on to make the **class diagrams**. A class diagram shows a collection of classes and how they are related to one another. It offers a simple static view of the classes of a system.

Class diagrams also show the methods and properties of the classes. The properties are derived from the use cases via **business rules**, while the methods can be found from sequence diagrams. Once again it will be necessary to review these diagrams to ensure that we know everything about the user requirement that we need.

GUI Prototype

Finally, we can consider a **GUI prototype**. This is how we build a GUI prototype from the UML analysis thus far:

- ❏ The essential elements that the GUI should contain will depend on the tasks performed by an actor, and are therefore found from use cases.
- ❏ The order in which these elements appear on the form will be influenced by the order that the actor would perform them in, and are therefore derived from the sequence diagrams.

Building a prototype GUI allows us to show it to the potential users. After such a review, alterations can be made.

The Iterative Process

This iterative process can seem pretty heavy going, but I make no apologies when I tell you that it will feature just as much in the second half of this book. The procedure is, however, made a much less painful procedure by the use of UML diagrams.

> *It would be great if we could have started from the very beginning with the perfect design. Unfortunately, this is not realistic. Working through much iteration is a natural process of designing any system. If we accept the fact that a project's design will go through many refinements, we can quickly see the advantage of using UML to design our project: diagrams are easy to change.*

UML diagrams give us a very powerful tool that allows us to map out the design of the project. These diagrams give us a deeper insight into how the system will work. They will help us to find all the components our system will require to perform its tasks. When the UML diagrams are shown to the user, he or she can understand the diagrams and recommend improvements, refinements and changes. These changes can be made with little effort.

If, on the other hand, we do not use UML diagrams to design our project - but instead just dive in and start coding, we will need to change our code with each refinement of the design. At this point, we would have to ditch the original code and start again. This is time consuming but will work. We could also try to revise the original project by chopping out the bad code, adding new code and trying to revise the original project to reflect the new design. This method, though very common, will always result in code that is unmanageable and usually filled with bugs.

Hopefully, you're beginning to see how UML diagrams make our lives much easier as a developer.

Where We Are Right Now

Right now, we've completed the initial part of our design phase, and we've built all of our use cases and sequence diagrams. The users have reviewed these diagrams and the GUI prototype. After careful revisions, we have arrived at a final set of use cases and sequence diagrams. We've drilled down to our class diagrams. We now know all the tasks the user wants the system to perform, and what components and messages are needed to perform these tasks. This is where the big shift occurs. Until now, everything has been centered on finding out what the user wants. The internal workings of the system have not played much of a role in our design.

A few of the items that the user wants will be related to how the internal system will work. The user wants our system to be able to operate over an intranet. To make this happen, the user effectively does not want a continuous connection to the database. Instead, the user needs the information to be coming from a client side component. Looking back at our sequence diagrams for adding or modifying a customer, we can see that a request for a customer record only goes to the client customer component. The request for the record is not passed back to the server component. There has been no discussion of how this will actually be done; we have been strictly talking about how the user wants the system to work.

The second part of our design phase will center on finding out how we can perform the tasks that the user requires. It is quite possible that what the user wants is simply impossible. Hopefully, we will know this when the user makes the request, but sometimes things seem possible at first but then turn out to be impossible, difficult, or inefficient.

What Next?

The rest of the design phase will focus on how the system can perform the user-required tasks. Just as we had to go through a series of steps to find out what these tasks were, we will also need to go through a well-defined series of steps to find out how the system can perform these tasks.

There is only one realistic way to find the best way to perform the different tasks required by the system: build small **test projects**. These test projects will find the best techniques to build the most critical portions of our system.

If we think about our Order Entry application, we have already said that we're going to use disconnected ADO recordsets through RDS. What we have not said is how we are going to do this!

The solution to this and similar questions will come from building a test project using ADO and RDS. This project will simulate our final project, performing the same critical tasks that our system will perform. The test project will find the best way of performing these tasks.

How UML Fits In: Activity Diagrams

Each of the messages in our sequence diagrams is a task that the components must perform. These components will perform each message by using a method.

> For every message, we must ask, "How will our method perform this task?"
> This now becomes the critical question.

Wouldn't it be great if we could make a diagram to answer this question for every method? Well, guess what? UML has a model specifically designed to turn these steps into a diagram. This diagram is the UML **activity diagram**.

Activity diagrams will turn all of the 'how to' steps into a diagram that can show us the relationship between each step. Activity diagrams show each sub-task that a method must perform to complete its required overall task. Decision points will be easy to see, and we will be easy to understand the general flow of the code.

Activity diagrams allow us to design the way a method will be coded, without writing a line of code. We can easily create many different ways of performing a single task by making a different activity diagram for each possible solution. When we have completed them, we can compare all of the activity diagrams and find the best technique for coding the method.

> *I will supply a more detailed discussion of how to use activity diagrams, and the benefits of using them, in Chapter 9.*

Activity diagrams are very close to actually being code, but they still are not Visual Basic code. We still have to make the final transition from the pseudo-code in our activity diagrams to real Visual Basic code. This final transition, though, will be fairly simple. Every step has been mapped out: we just have to follow the activity diagrams.

The first code we should produce, however, should *not* be for the final project - but for a test project. Each system is unique. What works well in one environment may crash in a different environment. We test our methods to see if our solution actually works, and how it can be improved. From these tests, we will find out which technique really answers our question, "How do we perform this task?"

Using this information, we will go back and make a final set of activity diagrams that will reflect our final design. Using these activity diagrams, we will make the final component.

As I said earlier, **every step of the way the design process is iterative**.

- ❏ For the first stage of the design, we must keep refining our design based on the user requirements
- ❏ In the second stage, we must refine our design based on the results of our test projects

The end result of this type of iterative approach is a well-polished design that has the maximum chance of producing code that will work correctly and efficiently.

Now let's cross this junction and focus on answering the question, "How do we perform these tasks?" We'll start by looking at the frameworks and technologies that we are going to use.

```
                    ▼
        ┌──────────────────────┐
        │      Get ADO         │
        │    connection        │
        └──────────────────────┘
                    │
                    ▼
                 ◇       ◇
              ◇             ◇
              ◇             ◇
                 ◇       ◇

          [Successful]
                    │
                    ▼
        ┌──────────────────────┐
        │    Set Recordset     │
        │   cursor location    │
        └──────────────────────┘
                    │
                    ▼
        ┌──────────────────────┐
        │    Set Recordset     │
        │       source         │
        └──────────────────────┘
                    │
                    ▼
        ┌──────────────────────┐
        │    Set Recordset     │
        │     connection       │
        └──────────────────────┘
                    │
                    ▼
```

Frameworks and Technologies

So far, we've only really considered how our project design is shaped from the outside. If you recall from previous discussions, this refers to the particular user requirements that we've been working on since we interviewed the Northwind employees. However, this is only half the story, and before we begin to implement our design we need to consider how our project is shaped from the inside; or more precisely, how the technologies and frameworks we have chosen will impact on our design so far.

These technologies and frameworks are complex. Trying to understand them is difficult. Trying to work out the best way to use them in your project is even more difficult. That is why this chapter will give a general explanation of the frameworks and technologies that will be used in the second half of the book, when we come to complete the design of our project and move into Visual Basic development.

As we meet these technologies or frameworks in the following chapters, we will build upon the general information I present in this chapter, expanding and clarifying our understanding of them through more detailed descriptions and code samples.

If you remember back to Chapter 2, we discussed frameworks and how to choose the correct frameworks for our project.

In this chapter, we will:

- ❑ Review our choice of frameworks
- ❑ Give a description of each of the technologies
- ❑ Examine how to combine these frameworks with our UML designs

The particular technologies we'll be discussing in this chapter are:

- ❑   Client-server architecture
- ❑   The DNA architecture
- ❑   ADO (ActiveX Data Objects)
- ❑   RDS (Remote Data Services)
- ❑   The Visual Basic Class Hierarchy framework

It may be that you are already familiar with the technologies that we'll be discussing here. If so you can probably skip these descriptions, although you will probably want to read the sections on how the technologies impact on our UML design so far.

Review of our Technical Requirements

In Chapter 2 we looked at some of the basic requirements that our system needed to meet. To recap, these were:

- ❑   The system needs to function over an Internet and a local intranet.
  The main order entry application will be a Visual Basic executable program, connected to a middle tier server component that will communicate with the database and perform various functions.
- ❑   There will also be an intranet application that will allow Northwind managers to access reports on sales.
- ❑   Northwind requires the ability to track every order, and generate reports on the status of every order.
- ❑   The application will also be accessible to shipping, so that information on items shipped can be entered immediately.
- ❑   There is a planned e-commerce web site for selling the products over the web. The system should be designed with this in mind.
- ❑   The bulk of these applications should be built from the same reusable components.

We also made some preliminary decisions about some of the technologies and frameworks that we are going to be using. We decided to build a three-tier system using ADO as our data access technology of choice.

Now that we have a pretty good external design in place, we need to start thinking about how best to implement it. This requires us to examine the technologies in more detail.

Client-Server Architecture

Basic client-server applications are built by creating a Visual Basic front-end on the client that keeps a continuous connection to the database. The database on the back-end has stored procedures and views to handle the database business logic and to limit the amount of information being returned to the client. As many of you know, this client-server project has a few problems:

❑　This basic client-server relies on stored procedures. This makes the framework difficult to work, since every database has its own way of building stored procedures and views. We would need to hire and train developers in a wide range of SQL versions. SQL is a difficult language to work with, to debug, and has many limitations.

❑　In addition, applications that run over the Internet don't allow a client to maintain a continuous connection to the database. Standard Internet applications allow the client to remain connected only long enough to make a request to the web server and retrieve information. Once the web server has sent the information to the client, the connection is severed. The client-server framework requires a continuous connection to the database so this framework won't work over the Internet. As Northwind eventually wants to add Internet capability to this project, the client-server framework is not a very good choice for this project.

There is fairly new variation on the above framework, which would be ideal for our project, called DNA. Let's take a look at the DNA framework now.

Distributed iNternet Applications (DNA)

DNA is rather new. However, it's really nothing more than a three-tier architecture, which has also been called n-tier, except it has an emphasis on the Internet. Looking at the diagram below, we can see that DNA architecture divides a project into three layers.

One layer is on the **client**, which is the interface that the user employs. The second layer comprises one or more servers that contain the **business logic**, which deals with communicating all of the transactions (editing, updating, adding and retrieving records) to the database.

> **Business logic is a set of rules that defines how the data will be presented, what type of data is valid, how the value of something is calculated, etc. These rules are not all the same and they don't all belong in the same place.**

The third layer contains one or more **databases**. DNA therefore looks rather like this:

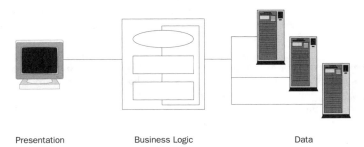

Presentation　　　　　Business Logic　　　　　Data

At first glance, it may not seem that we have gained too much. We have removed the transaction business logic from the database's stored procedures, and put them into a component in the middle-tier. However, take a closer look and you'll see that there are several important benefits to this approach.

The Middle-Tier

Unlike a SQL stored procedure, a Visual Basic component on the middle-tier handles the transaction business logic. It has code that is easy to read, write and debug and has very few limitations. One can also create a single component that can work with a multitude of databases on different servers. A very powerful component can be built that can even do the most complex manipulation and massaging of the data. Extremely complex activities, which used to be done on the client in client-server applications, can now be performed in the middle-tier. This makes the client smaller, lighter and easier to work over the Internet.

The middle-tier works as a middleman, taking requests from the client for a particular set of information formatted according to a certain set of business rules. The middle-tier gets the data, transforms it according to the business rules and returns the data to the client. The client no longer has to worry about database connections, tables or transforming data. The client simply requests the information it needs and the middle tier returns it. We now have a client that makes a request to the middle-tier for data, and once the client has the data, it disconnects from the middle tier. This is how the Internet works, so it sounds like we are on the right track.

Building with Components

Putting this framework together with OOP can create very powerful projects. If we begin to build components out of objects that perform certain tasks, we can then build applications out of these components. Using these components to build our n-tier applications allows us to place different components on different tiers, and in different locations within a tier, depending on the particular needs of the application. We will discuss this in more depth in a moment, but it is important to understand what this really means.

> **We are now moving away from building one huge application that tries to do everything and ends up doing nothing well. Instead, we are building components that can be put together in different ways to build different applications.**

We can arrange the components in one way for applications used by a company's internal workers; a different arrangement for an application being used over the Internet; and a third way to build decision-making applications for management. Building new applications will be easy and take little time. These separate object-oriented applications will replace one huge application trying to perform many completely different tasks, each with a different set of requirements.

Using DNA and OOP offers another advantage. If for some reason the business-logic changes, it is likely only one, or perhaps two, components will have to be changed. This component should be in the middle-tier, which means you will only have to upgrade the server. In a company where there are hundreds of clients, this will mean simply updating one or a few servers rather than having to upgrade each individual client.

DNA sounds really good: it is scalable, works with the Internet, works well with object-oriented programming techniques, and allows a thin or fat client. Yet, unless we can come up with a good method to implement this architecture, it is useless.

Now that we have a rough idea of the basic three-tier framework that we are going to be using, we need to think about some of the technology frameworks that we are going to need to pull it off.

ActiveX Data Objects (ADO)

ADO is a set of ActiveX controls; so any programming or scripting language that can instantiate and use ActiveX controls can also use ADO. This means that ADO is language-neutral and can be used within Visual Basic, Delphi, Visual C++, Java, JavaScript and VBScript.

ADO provides programmatic access to an underlying data access technology called OLE-DB. OLE-DB is a defined set of interfaces that all data sources can implement through special drivers known as providers. These data sources may be Access or SQL Server databases, but they might also be mail or video.

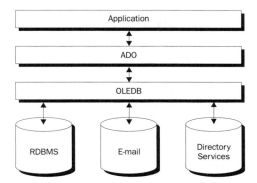

The ever-increasing role and importance of the Internet in application development has also driven the design concepts of ADO. It provides a range of ways that remote data access can be achieved over the Internet, using a Web browser or through custom applications written in a range of programming languages.

Prior to ADO, you would have used a variety of technologies to access the various data stores. RDO would be used to access SQL Server, DAO would access your Microsoft Access database and if you wanted to access data in Microsoft Excel, you'd have to use ODBC.

There are many downsides to this method. Technologies such as ODBC are difficult to use. Other technologies such as RDO and DAO (which actually provide the user with another interface to ODBC) add an extra layer of code to the application and performance can drop. An alternative access method was needed.

OLE-DB is that alternative and is designed to be the successor to ODBC. OLE-DB provides access not only to relational data sources such as databases, but also to non-relational data such as mail and text. Additionally, we can use ADO to talk to data sources, via OLE-DB.

Using ADO

ADO is very simple to use. It equates well to DAO (Data Access Objects), where you create an object, and call its methods and properties. ADO is quick and painless to use when programming, as data can be retrieved from a data source with as little as one line of code.

This has been achieved by 'flattening' the object model. In other words, although there is still an object hierarchy, such as that of DAO or RDO, some of the lower level objects can exist on their own and the higher level objects are built behind the scenes. This means that a programmer can use the object most suitable for a particular task, without having to create a lot of objects that aren't really required in their program. If ADO requires these objects then it creates them and uses them without the programmer needing to know that they are there.

There are three main objects within ADO:

- ❑ `Connection`
- ❑ `Command`
- ❑ `Recordset`

The object model in its strictest sense shows a hierarchical relationship between the `Connection` object and the `Command` and `Recordset` objects, but these can exist independently of a `Connection`.

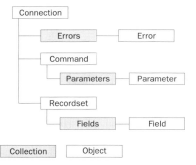

The Connection Object

The `Connection` object is the hub of ADO. We use its properties and methods to connect to the data store, linking the consumer and the provider. We can also use the `Connection` object to run commands and create recordsets.

The `Connection` object is also where any errors that occurred during the ADO operation are stored. We don't need to explicitly create `Connection` objects: we can simply pass a `Connection String` directly to a `Command` or `Recordset`. However, creating a `Connection` object is worthwhile if you are going to be getting data from the data source more than once, because the connection won't have to be established each time.

The Command Object

The `Command` object is designed to run single commands, especially those that require parameters. This is an important point, because the use of stored queries and procedures is a great way to improve speed and segment your application. The `Command` object can exist with or without a `Connection`.

The Recordset Object

If the `Connection` object was the hub then the `Recordset` object is the heart. It is probably the most used object, and consequently has more properties and methods than the other objects. Like the `Command` object, a `Recordset` can exist on its own or attached to a `Connection`.

We use recordsets to examine and manipulate data from the data store. The `Recordset` object provides the facilities to move about through the records, find records, sort records in a particular order and update records.

ADO and DNA

One of the primary reasons that we have chosen to use ADO is that we can pass recordsets between the business logic tier and the user interface tier, where they can be manipulated locally. This saves database resources, which can be critical on large-scale applications, as well as minimizing network traffic. These recordsets are called **disconnected recordsets**.

Disconnected Recordsets

These allow the recordset to be disassociated from the server, and then re-associated later. A user can update the disconnected recordset and save the changes locally. When it is reconnected later, the server can be updated.

The use of client-side data manipulation also allows you to sort data, find records, and generally manage recordsets without resorting to a trip back to the server. As you can see this idea primarily fits in with the nature of the Web, but it can work just as well for the standard type of applications running on a LAN. So you can see it is suited for both our thick and thin client models.

In summary, ADO is designed to access data from any data source (through special OLE-DB providers) and you can use ADO from any programming or scripting language (as long as it supports ActiveX). Applications that use ADO can also work in the disconnected and stateless environment of the Internet. All this means that ADO is ideal for use as the method of data access in the Windows DNA architecture.

> *If you want to learn more about ADO, I recommend the 'ADO Programmer's Reference', also published by Wrox Press.*

Remote Data Services (RDS)

The three-tier framework offers us many advantages over the old client-server framework. Unfortunately, the three-tier framework was extremely difficult to implement. DCOM required a difficult procedure to configure both the client and server. Security was handled by systems outside of the component, such as MTS. A system with thousands of clients quickly became nearly impossible to configure properly.

A way to work around this problem was the use of the **HyperText Transport Protocol (HTTP)** to pass information to a server and retrieve information from the server. The major advantage of this technique was that the client only had to be configured to have an Internet or an intranet connection. Once the client was set up to use HTTP, nothing else had to be done. Security, though, would now have to be dealt with inside the component. Using the HTTP protocol shifted the responsibility of keeping the system secure to the component. This was usually accomplished through log-in screens, UserIDs and passwords.

Before RDS, making a connection to the server-object through HTTP was very complicated. To use the HTTP protocol we needed to have a Web Server on the server. The client-side application had to pass information to the server formatted for the HTTP protocol inside a query string. In order to pass this formatted information to the Web Server the client had to use the WinInet APIs. When using an IIS Web Server the following would happen when a request arrived at the server:

❑ An Active Server Page would receive the request from the server and unformat the request
❑ The Active Server Page would pass the request to an Active-X DLL server-object
❑ The server object would retrieve data or perform a function
❑ The server object would pass the information back to the ASP page
❑ The Active Server Page would then pass the information back to the client

If this sounds very complicated, that's because it was. Passing information to a server object through HTTP used to look as follows:

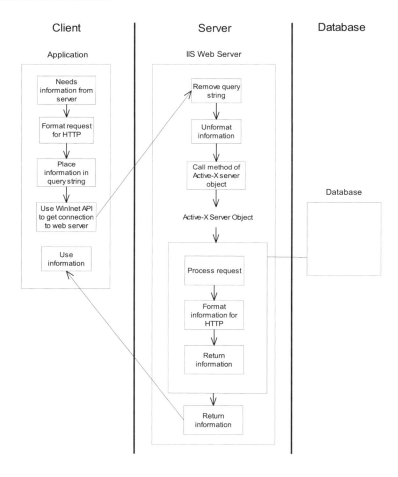

While this technique made distributing the solution very easy, it made coding the client and server components extremely complex. Information had to be formatted to the HTTP protocol and unformatted back to regular text. This resulted in parsing routines in all of the components, and complicated code to use the WinInet APIs.

Fortunately, Microsoft has offered us a much easier solution for connecting to IIS Web Servers: Remote Data Services (RDS). RDS 2.0 makes connecting to an object on a Web Server simple. The connection to a server object using RDS now looks as follows:

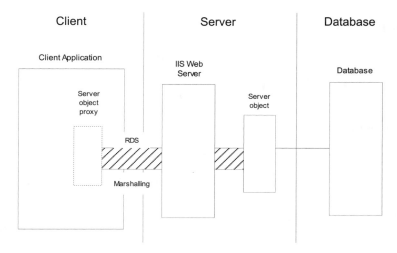

RDS will make a proxy of the server-object on the client. A proxy will be something that looks exactly like the server-object, i.e. it will have the same public properties and methods as the server-object. As far as the client application is concerned, the Proxy object is identical to the server-object. The client will make requests to the Proxy object, and the RDS will pass this request to and from the server-object on the server. This is called marshalling. When RDS uses HTTP, marshalling is done through an IIS Web Server.

The only disadvantage of using RDS with HTTP is that it requires an IIS Web Server. For connecting to other operating systems, such as a UNIX system, we will still have to use the old work around. Fortunately for us, we know our system will only be using a Windows platform so we don't have to worry about this.

Like our previous HTTP solution, RDS using HTTP allows users to access the database on any client with an Internet connection. Another advantage of RDS is that it also allows the client to connect through DCOM over an intranet, though this still requires a special configuration of the firewall on the client side.

When using RDS with HTTP the connection to the server may be made through a Domain Server Name (DSN). Therefore, the client needs no knowledge of the server's actual address or, in fact, any information on the server whatsoever. This allows the DSN address to act as a gateway that may actually represent any number of actual Web Servers.

The Components of an RDS Project

You will need to have several components set up on your machine to use RDS with the HTTP protocol. If you do not have access to a Microsoft Internet Information Server (IIS), you can still run these applications by using COM instead of HTTP. Below is a list of components required for making an RDS project that uses HTTP:

- ❑ **ADO:** This is the latest framework that Microsoft provides for connecting into any source of data. We've already discussed ADO.

- ❑ **RDS DataSpace Object:** RDS on the client is made from two objects: the **DataSpace** object and the **DataControl** object. The `DataSpace` object allows you to access the methods of an ActiveX DLL on a Server through the Internet using HTTP, COM, or DCOM. The `DataSpace` object has one method, `CreateObject()`, which allows you to access an object on the server. There is one property, `InternetTimeOut`, which is the amount of time allowed to make a connection to the server. On the server, there is a corresponding **DataFactory** object that communicates with the data store.

- ❑ **Visual Basic ActiveX DLL:** Although we don't have to have a business object, it is usually prudent to separate the client from the business rules, especially those that deal mostly with database functions. You can actually build your server components as a Visual Basic ActiveX DLL or as a Visual Basic IIS application. The ActiveX DLL will give you a greater degree of control over who can access your data over the Internet than an IIS application. IIS applications, though, give you more flexibility and perform better when there are dozens of forms.

- ❑ **Microsoft Internet Information Server:** This is required for RDS to connect to the server using the HTTP protocol and the Internet. This must be an NT 4.0 Web Server with the Option Pack installed (RDS is installed with the Option Pack by default).

- ❑ **Database:** A database for which there is an OLE DB provider.

- ❑ **Client Machine:** This computer must also be connected to the Internet - usually through an Internet service provider (ISP). To deploy the client application, use the Visual Basic Package and Deployment wizard, which will ensure that both ADO and RDS are installed on the client machine.

Security

We can secure an application at several different levels. The first is by building a password system into the client form. A user must log in with a user name and password before getting access to the server-object. The client object will have to save the user name and password in a private variable for subsequent reuse with every transaction. This information cannot be saved in server-object as it is stateless, which we're just about to discuss.

A higher level of security can be reached by using MTS. This will be described in a later section. Finally, if the information you expect to send over the Internet requires security, such as passwords, you can create a secure HTTP server that uses the HTTPS (Secure HTTP) protocol.

These passwords and IDs can be stored in a membership directory, like the one used in Microsoft Site Server 3.0. Using this membership directory, the server component of an RDS application can verify if a user is allowed access to the server component. In this way, we can build a security feature that is similar to the typical Windows NT user security. For detailed information on membership directories see the Wrox Book Site Server 3.0 Personalization and Membership.

Stateless Transactions

When we build RDS applications using HTTP we must create a stateless project. This means that every call the client application makes to the server-object is viewed as a new client. Afterwards, the server-object has no memory of the client. This works the same way as an HTML page: using a browser you connect to a server, which returns the page you are requesting. Once the data has been returned to the client, the server and the browser have no knowledge of each other. Building a stateless project will mean that retrieving and updating data from the database will have to be done in a completely different way from the standard client-server project.

Therefore, we can see how simply choosing to use RDS is beginning to define how our project will be constructed. Our server component will be an ActiveX DLL and we will have to design its behavior so that it complies with the stateless model that RDS dictates.

Visual Basic Data Providers

Before we look at how Data Providers work, I need to introduce the two terms: **Data Provider** and **Data Consumer**.

> **As the names suggest, the Data Consumer uses data from an external source, while a Data Provider is the source that supplies that data.**

Data Providers have been around for some time. They are basically anything that provides data. For example, any of the Data Control objects that you can drag off the Visual Basic toolbox and drop onto a form act as a Data Provider. You can set the properties of the Data Provider so that it knows what database and table to connect to, and then set a data source property on the control (such as a text box or grid control) so that the control can get data from the Data Provider.

When the application is run, the data appears in the control. You can use the data source to move through records and all of the controls bound to that data source refresh automatically. Data Providers allow you to create running programs by setting properties and calling only a few methods, such as `AddNew` or `Edit`.

These data controls also have properties and methods that allow you to access the data in your code *directly*, instead of binding a control to your Data Provider. This is a much simpler way to program.

Data Source Classes as Data Providers

Prior to Visual Basic 6, we could not build classes that functioned as Data Providers. With Data Source classes, we now can. We will refer to Visual Basic Data Source classes as Data Provider classes - since they provide data for Data Consumers.

A Data Provider class will have a private recordset variable associated with it. A reference to this private recordset variable is passed to the Data Consumer (a grid control, a text box, etc). The Data Consumer can then retrieve data from the recordset, as well as update, edit, add and delete data from the recordset.

The recordset is passed from the Data Provider to the Data Consumer by an event called `GetDataMember` that is automatically added to a Visual Basic Data Provider class. The `GetDataMember` event will be raised whenever a Data Source binds to our Data Provider class.

It is possible to have more than one recordset object in a Data Provider class. Using the `DataMember` property, one can determine which recordset the Data Source wants to bind to. This means that Data Provider classes can be polymorphic: they can perform in different ways for different Data Consumers. This is a very powerful feature.

Visual Basic Class Hierarchy Framework

A class hierarchy orders objects with increasing degrees of abstraction. This helps us to stay in control of complex components. We have already met a two-tier class hierarchy in Chapter 5. There are certain rules concerning the movement of information between different levels of the hierarchy.

Information Flow in a Class Hierarchy

Communication can easily go down the hierarchy. A higher class will have a copy of a lower class within it so it can easily pass information to the lower class. Information can flow down the hierarchy with no problem.

The higher class can give information to the lower class, but can the lower class get information from the higher class?

The lower class has no parent object. It has no reference to the higher class that created it and it cannot access information in the higher class. The only thing the lower class can do is raise an event that the higher class can then capture and respond to. However, the lower class cannot actually access any properties or information from the higher class; it can only pass information to the higher class.

> **A lower class in a hierarchy cannot get information from a higher class.**

Let's look at an example to see how this works and see how communication goes up and down a class hierarchy.

The Four Rules of Visual Basic Class Hierarchies

Because of the way Visual Basic classes are designed we will find that there are certain limitations to building class hierarchies. These limitations result in four rules that can be used to build a Visual Basic class hierarchy.

Imagine we have two classes, `Class1` and `Class2`, which are in a hierarchy. `Class1` is at the top of the hierarchy and above `Class2`.

Class1 would contain a copy of Class2 within it by using a declaration as follows:

```
Private m_objClass2 as New Class1
```

Class Hierarchy Rule 1

If Class1 needs to pass information down to Class2 it can do so using a property inside Class2. If Class2 has a friend property (a property that can be seen by other components in the project, but not by components outside of the project) called ClassID then Class1 could set this property by calling:

```
m_objClass2.ClassID = 2
```

This gives us our first rule.

> **Rule 1: A class in a hierarchy can pass information into the class below it by using a property in the class below it.**

Class Hierarchy Rule 2

If Class1 requires Class2 to perform some task and not return anything, Class1 can call a Sub in Class2. If Class1 needs Class2 to perform a task and return one piece of information, then a function can be used. If Class1 needs Class2 to return more than one piece of information, then a Sub or function in Class2 with by reference parameters could be used. Using this last technique, we could have a Sub in Class2 that would look as follows:

```
Friend Sub DoSomething (ByRef Param1, ByRef Param2)
  Dim x, y
  'Do something
  Param1=x
  Param2=y
End Sub
```

In Class1 we can now call this method as follows:

```
Dim a, b
m_objClass2.DoSomething (a, b)
```

a and b will now have been changed by the method in Class2.

> **Rule 2: A class in a hierarchy can get a class below it to perform a task by using a method in the class below it. The method can return no information, be a function that returns one piece of information, or return many pieces of information by using By Ref parameters.**

Class Hierarchy Rule 3

Class2 has no reference to the instance of Class1 that created it. There is no parent class. There is no private variable in Class2 that references Class1 in Class2. Class2 cannot access a property or method in Class1. This gives us the third rule.

> **Rule 3: A class in a hierarchy cannot access information in the class above it, through a property or through a method. Any information that a class may need from the class above it will have to be passed to the lower class by the higher class using properties in the lower class according to Rule 1.**

Class Hierarchy Rule 4

If Class2 wants to send a message to Class1, it can do this by using an event. If Class2 has the following event defined:

```
Public Event RaiseMe()
```

This can be called in Class2 as follows:

```
RaiseEvent RaiseMe
```

In Class1 we would need to change our declaration to:

```
Private WithEvents m_objClass2
```

We will now have the following event added to Class1:

```
Private Sub_RaiseMe()

End Sub
```

We can add code in the Sub to respond to the event. This gives us our final rule of class hierarchies.

> **RULE 4: A class can pass information up to a higher class by using events.**

Now that we have the architecture we need to think about how we can map the architecture to our existing design.

Fitting Our UML Design Into the Frameworks

Having a basic understanding of these frameworks is only the first step towards being able to determine how to use these frameworks in our project. These frameworks are all fairly new, and sometimes they do not work as they are supposed to. Even when they work as advertised, they may not work for our particular project. The information we gather is just the starting point. Once we understand the technology, we must figure out how to make it work for our project.

Architectural Views

We've come quite a long way with the design of our project and we have an idea of the frameworks that we are going to be using. Now we need to combine these two sets of information so that we can "see" what are final project is actually going to look like. This can be achieved by examining the project from a series of **architectural views**.

The Logical View

The **logical view** is the most comprehensive architectural view. It provides an overarching view of the system as a whole. We filter through the various layers of abstraction to understand the larger picture. The class diagrams were like the trees and the logical view allows you to step back and see the forest.

UML provides us with **package diagrams** to represent logical software modules. Each module is a folder-shaped icon. Links between packages are represented by dashed-arrows. Package names are generally shown inside the package, although if there are sub-packages then the super-package name can be written on the tag of the largest folder:

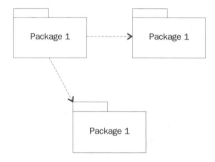

The Deployment View

The **deployment view** is only relevant to distributed systems and describes how a design is distributed physically across the architecture of a system.

UML provides **deployment diagrams** to help describe this view. Each node or processing element in the system is represented by a three-dimensional cube. If two cubes communicate, through a network for example, then this relationship is depicted by a solid line:

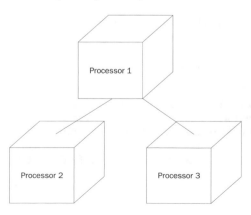

The Process View

The **process view** deals with issues such as concurrent tasks and helps us to work out multithreading and multiple processing issues. This view is not really relevant to us.

The Implementation View

The **implementation view** is essentially related to the specific issues arising from the actual coding. We'll see more of this when we start coding from Chapter 10 onwards.

These views have a tendency to overlap as they are all essentially based on the same set of information. Thus you may not find a need to use them all if indeed any. Typically though you would switch between them when appropriate.

Building Three-Tier Visual Basic Components

Often there are many ways we can build a component using a framework. Some solutions will work very well for our system, and others will not work at all. For example, where is the best place to put the middle-tier component? Do we put the middle-tier component on its own server, or do we put it on the same server as the database? Each choice can result in a drastically different overall performance of the entire system.

Placing the Server Component

While our first thought might be that the system will always work faster if the middle-tier component is on its own server, this is not necessarily the case. Placing the middle-tier component on its own server means that communications between this component and the database must now be made over the network. If the network is already overloaded, or we are moving large quantities of data back and forth, this could take a considerable amount of time. If this special server has all of the company's middle-tier components or is performing other functions, it may not be able to handle another component.

Placing the middle-tier component on the database server, on the other hand, means that the database and the component can communicate directly to each other. However, now we run into the possibility of overwhelming the database server. Whether the database server can handle the middle-tier component depends on the amount of RAM on the machine, the speed of the processor and the other tasks the server might be performing.

The position of the middle-tier component may also affect how we use ADO. ADO `Connection` and `Recordset` objects both have properties that can be set to different values to optimize the performance of the ADO. The size of the data, the location of the middle-tier component, and the capacity of the server and network will all determine what the best values are for these properties.

> There is not one solution that works for every three-tier project. Each project will have its own arrangement of components using frameworks in a way that results in the best performance for the system.
>
> Working through a test project is the best way to find the best techniques for using a framework in our project.

Client-Side Components

A three-tier Visual Basic project will have the user interface on the client. In an Order Entry application, the interface will allow the user to do things such as enter orders, add and review customers, etc. As this will be an object-oriented project, we will create objects to represent things such as orders, customers, products, etc. For example, we can have a Customer object that supplies customer information to the GUI. All of the objects will supply information to the user interface, which in turn is supplying information to the user. The user will also be providing information to the User Interface, which will pass this information back to the objects.

What we are going to do with these objects is a bit strange. The object's properties (things that describe the object or state) will be on the client. Properties for the Customer object might be the customer name, their phone number, etc. It is the job of the client to keep track of what is being done to this object. Maintaining a history of what has happened is called "maintaining state". When we say that the client maintains state, it means the client remembers what it has been doing, and the objects on the client can remember the values of their properties over time.

Distributing the Objects

An object, though, does not just have state. Objects also have behavior, or methods. This is where things get a little weird with the DNA framework. Any methods that are simple and not associated with getting or massaging data are placed on the client. All the methods that are doing heavy-duty work or dealing with transactions now go in the middle-tier. There are really two objects, one object on the middle-tier and one on the client, but they will both be part of the same component.

In a way we have spread our component over two or more computers, putting its methods and properties where they work best. This client object will have nothing to do with connecting to the database, retrieving records, sorting records or manipulating data. The only thing the client will be doing, with regard to the database, is telling the business object in the middle-tier, "I need this particular record set" or "I need this particular set of information". For example, the client may request all of the customers or all of the customers whose title is 'owner'.

Our Visual Basic DNA implementation would look like this:

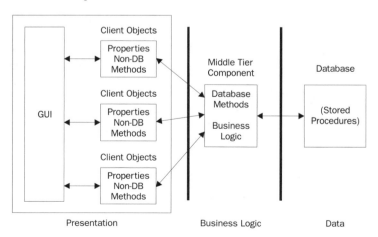

For example, we may want to build a `Customer` component. On the client there will be a `Customer` object that will have all of the `Customer`'s properties and methods that do not communicate with the database, such as `Move Next` to browse through the customer list.

Meanwhile, on the middle-tier, there will be methods to retrieve the customer records and update the customer records. Putting these together will create the entire customer component, which is actually spread across both tiers. The component itself will not actually be aware that it is split across two tiers. We can build the `Customer` components so that they are separate from the graphical user interface. This will allow us to use these components in any application, even one that does not have a graphical user interface.

Client Size and State

What we're building here is still a fairly **fat client**. The client will have numerous objects that will communicate with the interface and the middle-tier. These client components will not have a connection with the database, so they will have to be either constantly communicating with the database to get data or they will have to store data on the client-side. Storing data on the client-side is the best solution. The client can read the records and return the records to the middle-tier to make changes to the database. Yet, having records on the client-side makes this an even fatter client. If this is an Order Entry application being used by order entry clerks connected to the server through the network, this is a good solution. You want the information to be readily available. As long as you place limits on the amount of information on the client and don't allow huge amounts of data on the client, this will work efficiently.

Yet, this is not a very workable solution for the Internet that requires a **thin client**. If we wanted a thin, dynamic, interactive Internet client, we could only allow very small sets of data to reside on the client. We could also place the client-side objects onto a web server. These objects could pass the data to an ASP page, which properly formats the information and passes it back to the client in a standard HTML page.

> *Remember, an ASP page is a web page associated with IIS, that allows a request to be passed to a server, be processed, and a return page built on the fly.*

In this way, we could create a `Products` object that works in our `Order Entry` project on the client, but resides on the web server in an Internet application, which allows customers to view the products. The Internet application will pass back HTML pages with product information to the client. Therefore, we can use one object to build two applications that have completely different requirements, i.e. a thin and a fat client.

Our middle-tier object has no properties and so it will have no history and no memory of what was requested, i.e. the server does not have any state. The middle-tier objects are simply performing a task. When the task is done they have no memory that they did it.

Implementing a Class Hierarchy

Here we are going to consider how to build a three-tier class hierarchy for a client component. We will discover how the Data Provider and Visual Basic Class Hierarchy frameworks affect our solution.

We have already seen, in Chapter 5, how the `Customer` component can be divided up into two tiers:

❑ The Managed Class, containing particular class properties
❑ The Managing Class, containing common methods that will be shared by different components

However, consider the following hypothetical situation. Different users at Northwind may actually need to look at different types of customers. For instance, a Sales Representative may need to view all customers during their working day; but a Sales Analyst at Northwind might need to look at all the customers who have made orders very recently. Or a rather interested Sales Manager somewhere may need to view all customers who are regularly spending over $1000 an order, say. Clearly, what's happening here is that different users would be viewing different collections of customers.

Now this is a hypothetical situation, I must stress: nothing like this came up in our interviews back in Chapter 3 when we drew up the use cases. However, what quickly becomes clear, here, is that if Northwind do ever require customer views like this, we are going to have not one collection of customers to deal with, as we have currently thought, but three collections of customers:

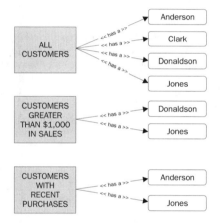

How would we deal with not one but *three* collection of customers like this? The best way would be to extend our original two-level class hierarchy so that there were three levels, like this:

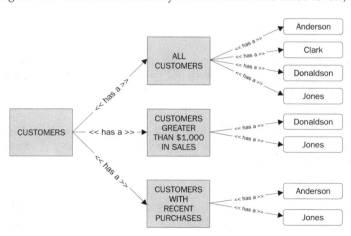

In this diagram, it's clear that we will have three different groups of customers:

- ❑ All Customers
- ❑ Customers greater than $1,000 in sales
- ❑ Customers With Recent Purchases.

and that there are **Customer Collections** which will be three separate objects. So what's happening in this diagram? Well if you remember back to our two-level class hierarchy, you'll recall that we had a Managing Class that managed the Managed Class. In the diagram above, our Managed Class is represented by the rightmost collections of actual customer details. And our Managing Class is right there in the middle of the diagram, managing those collections of customer details. The problem is: if there are actually three customer views in our hypothetical situation, how do we manage these views?

What's new in the above diagram is that we've now introduced a third level class - which itself manages what was our original Managing Class. Clearly the hierarchy has become more complex!

Now you might be thinking: that was a hypothetical situation, we don't really need to change anything in our Northwind system. In fact, I've presented in hypothetical terms something that we were always going to have to address: that different Northwind users would need to view different collections of customers, orders etc. As we approach the implementation of our system, new issues become clear to us. As our design considerations and various implementation issues - such as the class hierarchy framework - come together, we must continue to accept the iterative process that is involved in designing and developing a real-world project.

Our new class hierarchy therefore looks like this:

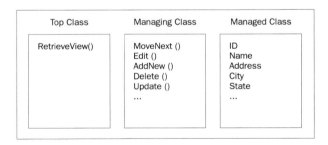

What was, in our two-level hierarchy, the Managed class, is now the **Bottom Class** - and this class will still be managed by what was the Managing class in our two-level hierarchy. Meanwhile, what was our Managing class in the two-level hierarchy, is now the **Middle Class**, and will itself be managed by a new **Top Class**.

This is a fairly complex hierarchy. To actually build this component, we will need to map out what each class will do and how it will communicate with the other classes. It might be useful, at this point, to make what is commonly called a CRC card.

CRC Cards

We mentioned CRC cards earlier in our discussion of collaboration diagrams. CRC stands for **Class**, **Responsibility**, and **Collaboration** (classes with which this class communicates directly). CRC cards are usually made using an index card and look as follows:

Class Name	
Responsibilities	Collaborations

As with other UML models, the CRC cards are just a tool. They help us to get things clear in our minds. Making CRC cards forces us to consider in a logical way the methods and interactions that a class may have. These cards will be particularly helpful when we're considering our hierarchy.

The diagram below depicts the CRC card for our Bottom Class, the `Customer Managed` class. This CRC card supplies a description of the various responsibilities of the `Customer Managed` class plus any classes with which it will directly communicate.

Looking at the **Responsibilities** section, we can see that the Bottom Class has three main responsibilities:

- ❑ To provide data
- ❑ To validate input
- ❑ To communicate property changes to the Middle Class

The Bottom Class has direct communication with the Middle Class, and any Data Consumers for which the Bottom Class is the source:

CLASS: Customer Managed Class	
Responsibilities	**Collaborations**
Provide direct access to Customer information through Properties.	Customer Managing Class.
Provide information about a Customer as a Data Provider by supplying a recordset to the Data Consumer.	Data Consumers.
Validate any changes made to a Customer property or field by a data consumer.	
Communicate all changes of properties to the Customer Managing Class.	

Now let's take a look at the Middle Class. It's clear that the Middle Class will have to act as bridge between the Top Class and the Bottom Class. This will be reflected in its responsibilities and collaborations:

CLASS: Customers Managing Class	
Responsibilities	**Collaborations**
Provide access to the Customer Bottom Class.	Customer Managed Class.
Maintain a collection of Customer Objects.	Customer Collection Managing Class.
Provide information on a collection of Customers as a Data Provider by	Data Consumer.
Supplying a recordset containing all Customers in the collection to a Data Consumer.	
Validate any changes made to a Customer field by the Data Consumer.	
Manage Customer edits, add new Customers, delete Customers, move through Customers in the collection, Customer count, etc.	
Must communicate all changes of properties down to Customer Managed Class.	

Our final CRC card is for the Top Class, the `Collection Manager` Class. Although this class will communicate indirectly with the Bottom Class, this will be achieved through the Middle Class. Therefore, the Bottom Class should not feature in the **Collaborations** section:

CLASS: Customer Collection Manager Class	
Responsibilities	**Collaborations**
Retrieve a particular customer	Client Application.
Collection.	Customer Managing Class.
Pass requests, such as Add New or Edit, to the appropriate customer collection.	

We can see that the main responsibility of the Top Class, the `Collection Manager` Class, is to retrieve a particular customer collection, which would be achieved by a method such as `RetrieveView`.

From our UML diagrams and these CRC cards, we can see that all of the methods that we've found from our sequence diagrams belong to the Middle Class, the `Customer Managing` Class.

There will also have to be a way to validate any changes, which will be made in the Bottom Class, the `Customer Managed` Class. This class will mostly consist of `Customer` properties: `CustomerID`, `Region`, etc. which came from our **Customer Fields** definition Business Rule. The validation rules for these properties will come from the Business Rules that we made for each field.

We also know from our use cases that a request to **Edit** or **Add a New Customer** must be sent to the **Customer** object before the activities can be performed. We will therefore need a property called `EditMode` so that the class can determine if an edit or add new is in progress.

Properties in the Data Provider Managed Class

The Bottom Class is mostly made up of properties. The `Customer Managed` object can provide information on a particular customer either through these properties, or through a recordset to a Data Consumer. We will begin by looking at the best way to code the properties of the Bottom Class so it can be an efficient Data Provider class.

If you remember back to the description of the Data Provider technology, we considered the possibility of using Data Source Classes. We will not be able to use them in our example though, as they would greatly complicate the code and would not allow us to make the middle class generic.

Normally a class like the `Customer Managed` class would have private variables associated with each property. The properties would set and get these private variables. The properties would also validate new information and contain rules for accessing information

In the case of the `Customer Managed` class, however, we are going to do something a little different. Looking at the CRC diagram for this class, we can see that its class responsibilities include:

❑ Returning Customer information through **properties**
❑ Returning Customer information through **recordset**

To be a Data Provider, our class will need a private ADO Recordset, which it can pass to a Data Consumer. Do we really want to keep the identical information in two places, i.e. the private variables (such as `m_strCustomerID`) and a separate private recordset variable?

Keeping the information in *two* places means that we will have to keep the recordset and the private variables synchronized. When a Data Consumer changes a field in the recordset, we will also have to change the private variables associated with the property that corresponds to that field and vice versa.

If we have both private variables and a private recordset for each property, we are going to have to write a great deal of code to keep everything synchronized. A golden rule of programming is to keep it simple.

There is no rule written in stone, however, that says that every property must have a private variable associated with it. Using private variables for each property is the easiest implementation and makes sense for most classes. However, when it comes to our Data Provider class, it makes more sense to store the information of the `Customer Managed` class in the private recordset variable. Then, when Customer information is changed through a property, we simply set the recordset's field associated with the property to the new value. When we retrieve information about a Customer through a `Get` property, we will retrieve the current value of the field associated with this property from the recordset.

Using this technique, we now only have *one* private recordset variable holding all of the Customer information. This recordset can be passed to a Data Consumer or it can be used by the properties to get and set customer information.

Let's now look at how we can use UML diagrams, combined with our knowledge of how to code a Visual Basic class hierarchy, to further refine our design of the `Customer` component. We will look at the Bottom Class to find some of the basic issues of coding the `Customer` component.

Synchronizing the Middle and Bottom Classes

While using a recordset for the properties greatly simplifies the `Customer Managed` class, there is still one issue we need to explore. The `Customer Managed` class and the `Customer Managing` class both in fact act as Data Providers!

Let's consider what the Middle and Bottom classes provide:

❑ The Middle Class (`Customer Managing` class) provides a recordset containing *all* of the Customers in the collection.

❑ The Bottom Class (`Customer Managed` class) provides the view of a *single* customer. This single customer is the current record of the `Customer Managing` class recordset.

> **We see that we once again have an issue of keeping two things synchronized: the recordset in the Bottom Class, and the recordset in the Middle Class.**

In my initial idea for this project, I tried to build the Customer Component with two recordsets: one in the Bottom Class and one in the Middle Class. This leads to some major synchronization problems, however, a few of which are listed here:

❑ A Data Consumer bound to the Middle Class edits a record or moves to another record. (Example: A grid control is bound to the Middle Class, and the user of the application edits a record in the grid control.) These changes would have to be communicated down to the Bottom Class recordset.

❑ The Client Application uses a `Move` method, which is located in the Middle Class. The recordset in the Bottom Class would have to be rebuilt to reflect this new Customer.

❑ A property in the Bottom Class is changed. This change would have to be passed back up to the recordset in the Middle Class.

❑ A Data Consumer bound to the Bottom Class changes a field. This change would have to be passed back up to the recordset in the Middle Class. (Example: A text box with the Customer Address is bound to the Managed Class and the user of the application updates the information in the text box.)

I began to draw this all out with pencil and paper using sequence diagrams. Just by looking at those few possibilities, I think you can imagine how complicated these diagrams were. This would be lead to very complicated code.

Often the hardest part of finding a solution is not finding the right answer, but finding the right question.

To find the optimum solution, I had to ask this question: "What type of components will be Data Consumers for the Bottom Class?" Please consider this question. The Bottom Class is only going to provide the Data Consumer with a recordset with one single Customer record.

That is certainly not something we would want to stick into a gridbox.

If we were making an application and we wanted to show Customer information in text boxes, then it would make sense to bind these text boxes to the `Customer` object. We only want information on one customer at a time in these text boxes, so we'd want the recordset with only one customer record in it.

I hope that you agree with me on this; I am now making a design decision for us:

> The Bottom Class (`Customer Managed` **class**) **can only be used as a Data Provider for textboxes; it cannot be used for grid controls.**

Now, one of the nice things about binding textboxes to a data source is this: the recordset that the text boxes are bound to can have more than one record. The record that you see in the text boxes is the current record in the recordset.

What this means is that we don't have to pass a recordset with only one record back to the data consumers bound to the Bottom Class. We could pass back a recordset with all the records in it - as long as the recordset's current record is the Customer we want to return.

Perhaps you see where this is going. The Middle Class will always have a recordset whose current record is the Customer we want. In other words: **we use the same recordset for the Middle Class and the Bottom Class.** Suddenly, all of the complexity of writing about twenty pages of code to keep two recordsets synchronized disappears.

Catastrophic and Harmless Problems

There is still a problem with this implementation. If we attach a `Customer Managed` class to a data grid, we will not see one customer - we will see all of them.

This is obviously wrong. For our application, this would never be the case. A grid control should never be a Data Consumer for the `Customer Managed` class. Grid Controls should be bound to the Middle Class, which provides a collection of customers.

> *As we explore class hierarchy implementation, we find that some technologies are simply not suitable, while others can be used but place constraints on our design. As we consider the possibilities we need to weigh up how serious these constraints are and the potential problems that may arise.*

Let's look at the last problem that we came up against. Does it make sense that we should make the code several times more complex and add many pages of code just because someone will get the wrong information if they do something that they should not - such as connecting a Grid control to a Bottom Class?

When we design an event driven project, we must always think of every possible thing the user can do to blow up your application. It doesn't matter how ridiculous it is, if the user can do it, they probably will. This is where use cases and sequence diagrams come in. They can show us all of the alternative flows.

When a user does something they should not, there can be two types of outcomes: **catastrophic** outcomes and **harmless** outcomes. My list of catastrophic outcomes includes:

- ❑ A violation of a business rule.
- ❑ Something that would corrupt the integrity of the database.
- ❑ Something that would cause the application to lock up, blow up, GPF (General Protection Fault), or any other possibility along these lines.
- ❑ Something that would cause information to become incorrect or corrupt.

Catastrophic outcomes must always be handled. We must write code to prevent them from happening. We must carefully design our project using UML, search for every possible alternative flow, and figure out everything the user can do. From this list of alternative flows, we find the ones that are catastrophic and prevent them. We have little choice here. **Catastrophic outcomes can never be allowed to happen!**

All outcomes that are not catastrophic, we can put into the harmless category. These are things that we should prevent from happening, if it is possible. They are usually things that will annoy a user when they do something wrong, but will not affect anything in the application.

As long as the cost is not too high to stop these things from happening, we should write the necessary code to protect against harmless outcomes. While using one recordset would cause some weird behavior if for some bizarre reason someone wants to see a single Customer in a grid control, this is a harmless outcome. This is not a violation of a business rule, it does not affect the database or information integrity, and it will not cause a GPF. It might annoy the users of our application, but it is does not do any damage.

To summarize what I'm saying here, we must not confuse our ideal world with the real world. In an ideal world, we would never make such a compromise: we would make perfect code that did everything it was supposed to do and that would never work in a way it shouldn't. Harmless outcomes would never happen in our applications. In the real world, we have deadlines, budgets and other things that limit us and prevent us from using an ideal solution.

Placing the Recordset

Now that we've decided to use only one recordset, there's still one major problem with this implementation. The shared recordset should be placed in the `Customer Managing` class, as this call will maintain the recordset. If we do this, however, the `Customer Managed` class will only be able to get the recordset from the `Customer Managing` class if it has a reference to the `Customer Managing` class.

From our earlier discussion of Visual Basic Class Hierarchy framework, we know that there are certain rules governing the flow of information between classes. If the shared recordset is located in the `Customer Managing` class, then there's no way to get access to this recordset from the `Customer Managed` class.

It is for this reason that we must put the shared recordset into the Bottom Class - the `Customer Managed` class. As we shall see, this will force us to add events into the Bottom Class to pass information up to the Middle class. This will also affect the location of other methods.

Putting It All Together

We have seen, through this chapter, that the DNA framework, combined with the ADO and RDS frameworks using OOP techniques, can allow us to build either:

- ❑ a fat client that maintains state
- ❑ a thin Internet client that may or may not maintain state

These frameworks allow us to create server objects, in the form of an ActiveX DLL, which can be easily scaled. In addition, the server component can minimize the amount of data that is being transferred back and forth between the client and the server.

The ADO and RDS frameworks will be a critical part of our application. Here is how we will be deploying these technologies in our Northwind project:

- ❑ RDS will provide the connection between the client and the middle tier
- ❑ ADO will provide disconnected recordsets that can be passed between the two

We can pass these disconnected recordsets from the middle-tier to the client-tier. The client-tier can then look at these records, or update these records and return them to the middle-tier, which will then pass them on to the database. Our client side objects will contain a disconnected recordset object that will be used to review and update that object's information. This would look as follows:

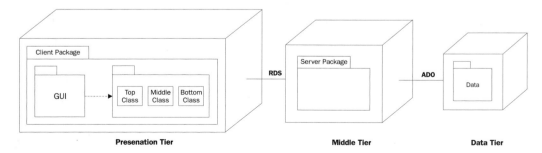

To summarize our architecture then: the user interface interacts with the appropriate object, such as a `Customer` object. The `Customer` object has all of its properties on the client, and can give the user interface any information on the client that it needs. If the user interface makes a request that requires a connection to the database, the object will have to pass that request to the middle-tier. The middle-tier will then connect to the database, get the information, transform it, and pass it back to the client.

We will be implementing this architecture throughout the second half of this book.

Summary

In this chapter, we've started to think about the implementation of our system design. Up until now, although we had a pretty good idea of the design of the Northwind system, we didn't really know how that design would be translated into code.

Although we haven't actually seen any code yet, we have begun the process of defining the technologies and frameworks that we will be using to build our system. We have examined the technologies in more detail to find out how they will affect our code when we come to the implementation stage.

In this chapter, we looked at our Northwind project in relation to these technologies:

❑ Client-server architecture
❑ The DNA architecture
❑ ADO (ActiveX Data Objects)
❑ RDS (Remote Data Services)
❑ The Visual Basic Class Hierarchy framework

In the next chapter, we will start to refine this implementation stage by using activity diagrams to model some of our components' more complex behaviors. We'll also see how some of the frameworks in this chapter affect our coding.

```
              ┌─────────────────┐
              │     Get ADO     │
              │   connection    │
              └─────────────────┘
                       │
                       ▼
                    ◇       ◇
                  ◇           ◇──────────────
                    ◇       ◇
                       │
     [Successful]      ▼
              ┌─────────────────┐
              │  Set Recordset  │
              │ cursor location │
              └─────────────────┘
                       │
                       ▼
              ┌─────────────────┐
              │  Set Recordset  │
              │     source      │
              └─────────────────┘
                       │
                       ▼
              ┌─────────────────┐
              │  Set Recordset  │
              │   connection    │
              └─────────────────┘
                       │
                       ▼
```

Designing A Test Project With Activity Diagrams

Using our UML use cases, we created sequence diagrams. These diagrams determined the public properties and methods that our project's components would need to perform their required tasks. Sequence diagrams, though, are very general and provide us with very little, if any, information on how to perform these tasks.

Therefore we now proceed to the next stage of the UML Process, **activity diagrams**, so we can find the best way to code these public properties and methods.

Activity diagrams will also help to determine what **private** methods and properties our components require.

Since activity diagram deal with specifics, we're also going to start working towards the implementation of our Northwind system. We're not just going to jump straight in to the main project code however. First, we're going to design and build a test project to see how well our frameworks and UML design perform. This test project will help us find the best way to implement our DNA architecture.

Using this information, we will design and build a final version of the server component in Chapter 11.

In this chapter we'll cover:

- ❑ Activity diagrams and what they are
- ❑ Designing a Test Project for our system
- ❑ Using activity diagrams to map out complex behaviors
- ❑ Planning VB code from activity diagrams
- ❑ Effective testing strategies

Activity Diagrams

An activity diagram is the point at which the user requirements, as described in the use cases and sequence diagrams, finally meet the requirements of our frameworks. It's at this stage of the UML process, therefore, that we create a detailed mapping of the code within each Property and Method of the system's components.

Each message in our sequence diagrams can represent a `Public` method of one of the system's components. We can use our activity diagrams to expand these messages out, showing how the component will respond to the message and what tasks the component is required to perform when it receives that message.

> *For example, the server object may get a request for a* `Customer` *object from the client application. An activity diagram would show the series of activities the server object would have to perform to get and return a* `Customer` *object.*

Although we could create activity diagrams for every message we've developed, it is often unnecessary to actually do this. Activity diagrams are good at capturing the details of complex operations. For simple messages, then, sequence diagrams are often sufficient.

For more complex messages, especially between logical tiers, we really need a more detailed breakdown of the process. We shall therefore only need to expand out some of the messages in our Order Entry application in this chapter.

The Parts of an Activity Diagram

An activity diagram models the flow of activities in a procedure or message. In essence, then, they are rather like flowcharts.

> **An activity is a step in the internal processing of a message or procedure.**

An activity diagram begins with a starting point and finishes with a ending point:

 Starting Point

Ending Point

Each activity is placed in a lozenge shape. The text inside can be as specific or as general as we like:

An arrow connects one activity to another showing the movement of the procedure in step-wise fashion:

If there is a decision point where the flow can go in more than one direction, then a diamond is used. The two arrows coming out of a decision point will have text placed over them showing what is required to go in one or the other direction. The text over the arrow is called a **guard** and must be Boolean in nature (either the guard is True, or it is False):

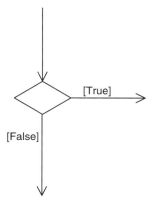

For every split in the flow caused by a decision point, there has to be a place in the diagram where the flows come back together, even if this is the end point of the diagram.

One of the powerful features of activity diagrams is that they are able to show a sequence of events happening in parallel. This is modeled through the use of a horizontal bar, where the number of flows will either join or fork:

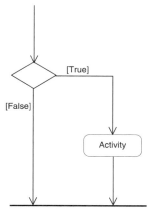

Therefore, an activity diagram for making a cup of coffee might look like this:

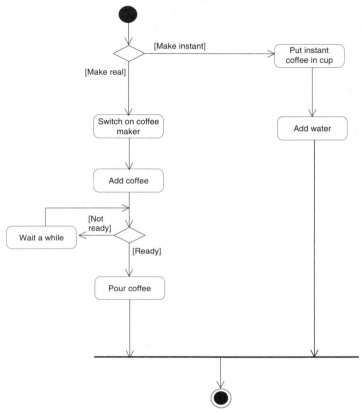

Now let's look at how to turn our use cases and sequence diagrams into some specific activity diagrams so we can start coding Visual Basic in the next chapter.

Designing a Test Project

We will now turn our attention to designing the server component for an experimental server component test project. This activity will involve diagrams.

The first step in designing any project is deciding what the project is going to do. An experimental project should test the part of the system you are about to build. Our test project will test the server component to make sure that the frameworks we are using are actually going to work for our project.

The use cases that we built allowed us to group the user requirements into tasks. Each use case contained a series of events that we modeled with sequence diagrams. The use case and sequence diagrams gave us a good understanding of the user requirements, the components the system needs, and the public methods and properties these components must have to accomplish the tasks the users require of the system.

From this point onward, we must begin to use activity diagrams to map out the internal workings of each method and property of the system's components. The choice of frameworks, whether we build our project using MTS, RDS, ADO or any other technology, will shape the code that we model with the activity diagrams. Therefore, before we can continue designing our project, we need to determine what technologies will work best for our system. To answer this question, we have to create a test server component.

The Test Server Component

There will be certain tasks that must be performed by each component in the system. We can find these by reviewing the sequence diagrams. Once we know what these tasks are, we can then begin to design methods using activity diagrams, that will perform a series of tests to find the best way to perform each task.

Activity Diagrams in Action

Let's start by looking at the following sequence diagram for modifying customer information:

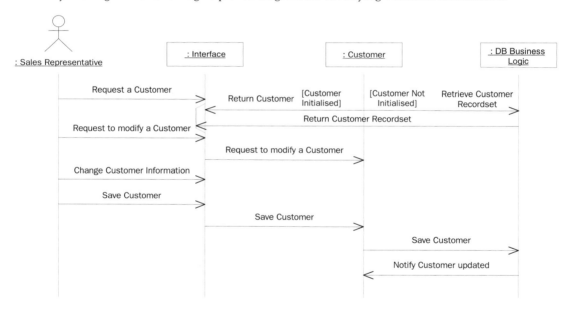

We have added to this sequence diagram the conditional step of retrieving the recordset if the client `Customer` object is not initialized. When the `Customer` object is not initialized, we use the message **Retrieve Customer Recordset**.

The server component will then have to retrieve the category information from the database and return this information to the client in the form of a disconnected recordset.

Although every message in this diagram can be expanded out into an activity diagram, we are focusing on the server component at the moment, so let's just look at the messages being sent to and from the server component. These messages include:

- ❑ Retrieve Customer Recordset
- ❑ Return Customer Recordset
- ❑ Save Customer
- ❑ Notify Customer Updated

We can group these first two messages into a `Retrieve Recordset` method, and the second two messages into an `Update Recordset` method.

> **So this test server component will test retrieving and updating disconnected recordsets.**

These recordsets are not just any type of recordset: they are ADO disconnected recordsets. We made this decision based on the needs of our system: primarily, the condition that our system should be stateless.

Building an ADO disconnected recordset is like building anything else: we must follow a certain set of rules when we're putting it together for it to work properly. The hardest part is finding what these rules are. Throughout the rest of book, I'll be explaining the rules of our frameworks.

For now, let us return to retrieving a customer recordset.

Building Activity Diagrams: Retrieve Customer

How do we take the message Retrieve a Customer, which is being sent to the server component, from the Modify Customer sequence diagram and expand this message into an activity diagram? Let's create a new activity diagram called Retrieve Customer Recordset and find out.

We will start with the knowledge that there are variables for a private ADO connection object and a private customer recordset variable in our server component. The necessary steps for retrieving a customer recordset are as follows:

- ❑ Initialize the recordset variable
- ❑ Set the properties of the recordset so that it will contain all of the customer records
- ❑ Connect the recordset to the database
- ❑ Retrieve the customer records from the database
- ❑ Disconnect from the database
- ❑ Return the recordset variable filled with customer records to the client

These steps are very high-level. They do not really get into any discussion of the ADO or how the ADO works. They are just a logical series of steps that we need to perform to get information from the database and return it to the client. The next step is to determine exactly how we do each of these steps using the ADO.

Looking into the Wrox book on the ADO (the ADO Programmers Reference), we can determine how to perform each of these steps using the ADO. For example, to create a disconnected recordset, we need to create a client side cursor. We can go through the book and find what properties need to be set, how to connect to the database, and how to get the records from the database.

I have done this for you, and below is a table of the steps required to perform the general tasks we listed above using the ADO. These are the specific steps our server component must perform to get a customer recordset and pass back a disconnected recordset with the client information in it using ADO. Each step also includes the framework that places this requirement on the system, so you can see where you might have found information on how to perform this step.

Activity	Framework that requires this activity	Requirement
Create ADO connection	ADO Framework	You must make a connection to the database by either creating a connection object prior to retrieving data or passing in a connection string in the open method of the recordset
	Three-Tier framework	No information can be stored from one call to the next. Therefore a connection object must be created first for every request to get information
If there is an error getting the connection, raise an error and end	ADO Framework	All errors must be handled
If there is no error, initialize the customer recordset object	Three-Tier framework	No information can be stored from one call to the next; must initialize the Recordset for each request
Set customer recordset cursor location to the client	ADO/RDS framework	Updateable disconnected recordsets are required; these recordsets need a cursor location to be on the client
Set customer recordset source equal to the appropriate query string	ADO framework	If a recordset is going to retrieve data from the database, there must be a Query string that specifies what information from which tables will be retrieved (a query string is not required if you accessing a stored procedure)

Activity	Framework that requires this activity	Requirement
Set customers recordset connection	ADO framework	To connect a recordset variable to a database you must set the recordset variable's connection property to a valid connection string
If there is an error getting the connection, raise an error and end	ADO Framework	All errors must be handled
If there is no error, set the customer recordset LockType to the appropriate lock type and set the Recordset's connection object to the connection object.	ADO framework	Must set LockType of a recordset before retrieving data from the database (not required for the default optimistic lock)
Open the customer recordset object	ADO framework requirement	Must open a recordset to retrieve the data into the recordset
If there is an error opening the recordset, raise an error	ADO framework requirement	All errors must be handled
If there is no error, return the recordset	Three-Tier framework	Return disconnected recordsets
Close the ADO recordset and set the recordset and connection object to nothing.	ADO framework	Failing to close the connection object leaves it open until it times out. There is a limited number of connection objects, so letting them close by timing out ties up valuable resources

This table says a great deal about programming in Visual Basic. To make this chart, I had to understand three frameworks (RDS, ADO and Three-Tier). Programming Visual Basic goes beyond knowing just the language syntax. To make Visual Basic projects, we now have to understand the frameworks that our projects are going to work under. We therefore need to do the following:

❑ Map out the general steps a message requires

❑ Determine what frameworks you will be using to perform these steps

❑ Get out your reference books on these frameworks, and find for each framework the specific sub-steps that are required for each general step

If you follow this guide you should end up with a table like the one above. It might take some time but the rewards are worth it.

From this table, we can now draw out our activity diagram for Get Customers. Each activity in the chart above will map to some element of the activity diagram.

Let's take the first step: **Create ADO connection**

We know that our diagram should begin with a starting point and an arrow pointing to the first activity, so the first part of the diagram will look like this:

The next two rows in the chart make up a decision point. **Either** an error occurs **or** it does not:

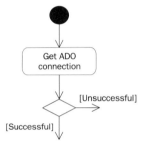

If no error occurs, a sequence of activities follows and is depicted by a description of each activity connected by arrows:

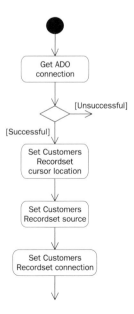

The rest of the chart can be mapped out similarly until the whole activity diagram is created:

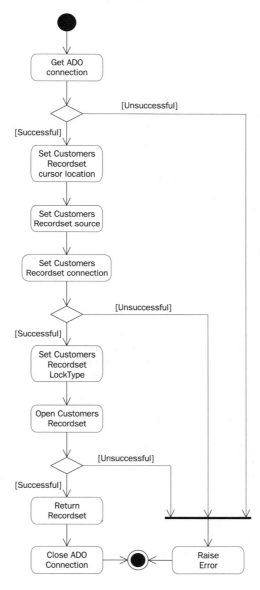

The simultaneous flows that have arisen due to the possibility of errors will come back together at the thick horizontal bar or concurrent join. Of course, as with any activity diagram, the ending point must be shown.

Benefits of Activity Diagrams

We've gone through a lot of work to make this diagram, so once again we have to ask the question, "What do we gain by making a UML Activity diagram?" The two main advantages are that activity diagrams allow us to

- ❑ Effectively map and review methods
- ❑ Find patterns

Let's consider each of these in turn now. Once we're done here, we'll move on to create some more activity diagrams and see if we can identify any patterns emerging.

Mapping and Reviewing Methods

Using an activity diagram replicates one of the best techniques of writing code. You should write detailed comments in your methods prior to actually writing the code for the method. The comments map out what the method should do and how it will do it. You can follow the activity diagram to map out your code, and then use the diagram to comment your code.

When we're working on a team, we can map out a method's sequence of events together, or have a single person work them out and then put them into an activity diagram. Once we have this diagram, the whole team can then review the diagram and decide what they want to add, remove or simply change.

Trust me, it's far easier to look at an activity diagram and see the flow of a method than it is to try to look through code to find the same flow. When I hand someone an activity diagram, I do not have to explain the diagram; the diagram is telling him or her everything that is happening. If I hand you two pages of code, you will be staring at it for ages. If the code is complex, with many alternative flows, it may take a very long time to understand the code. Even when you have figured the code out, it is still very hard to visualize the flow and to spot any step that might be missing.

Listing all of the steps of each of our methods gives a clear, readable way of seeing everything your code must do to perform this task. An activity diagram can be passed around to all of the team members. Each member of the team can quickly understand it, read it and determine if any changes need to be made. Making changes requires adding activities, decision points, etc., and can even be made with a pencil on the diagram and later added to the final copy in the repository.

Finding the best solution is usually an iterative process. First you have your initial concept, refine it, test it, then you refine it more and test it more, etc. Activity diagrams will let us go through many refinements of our object's methods before we even write one line of code. Removing something from an activity diagram, means deleting a graphic image. This takes about a second. Changing code means deleting lines of code that may have taken hours to create and adjusting the rest of the code to deal with the deletion. Which one would you rather do?

Finding Patterns

There is one other thing activity diagrams are useful for: patterns. Just as our sequence diagrams revealed patterns, which could be used to simplify coding, activity diagrams should also reveal patterns, but at a more detailed level. To demonstrate this, we will go ahead and make the tables and activity diagrams for Retrieve Product and Retrieve Category.

Activity Diagram: Retrieve Product

Following exactly the same steps as for the Retrieve Customer table, we should get the following table for Retrieve Product.

As you can see, it is almost identical. This means that not only are we identifying a pattern but also it should only take a fraction of the time to produce that the first one did:

Activity	Framework that requires this Activity	Requirement
Create ADO connection	Three-Tier framework	No information can be stored from one call to the next, therefore a connection object must be created first for every request to get information
	ADO framework	You must make a connection to the database by creating a connection object prior to retrieving data
If there is an error getting the connection, raise an error and end	ADO Framework	All errors must be handled
If there is no error, initialize the products recordset object	Three-Tier framework	No information can be stored from one call to the next; must initialize recordset for each request
Set products recordset cursor location to the client	ADO/RDS framework	An updateable disconnected recordset is required; these recordsets need a cursor location to be on the client
Set products recordset source equal to the appropriate query string	ADO framework	If a recordset is going to retrieve data from the database, there must be a query string which specifies what information from which tables will be retrieved
Set products recordset connection	ADO framework	To connect a recordset variable to a database you must set the recordset variable's connection property to a valid connection string.
If there is an error getting the connection, raise an error and end	ADO Framework	All errors must be handled
Set the products recordset LockType	ADO framework	Must set LockType of a recordset before retrieving data from the database
Open the products recordset object	ADO framework requirement	Must open a recordset to retrieve the data into the recordset

Table Continued on Following Page

227

Activity	Framework that requires this Activity	Requirement
If there is an error opening the recordset, raise an error	ADO framework requirement	All errors must be handled
If there is no error, return the recordset	Three-Tier framework	Return disconnected recordsets

The corresponding activity diagram would look as follows:

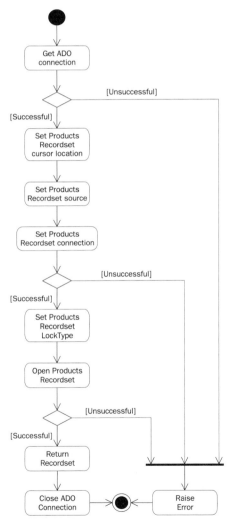

Of course, this is almost identical to the activity diagram for the Retrieve Customer.

Activity Diagram: Retrieve Category

When we analyze the situation for Retrieve Category we end up with the following activity diagram:

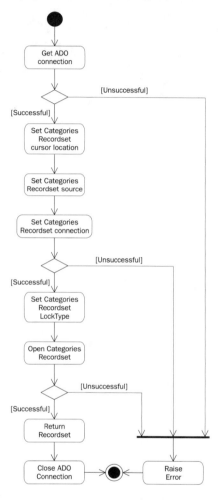

Is this looking familiar? Let's see how we exploit the emerging pattern.

Taking Advantage of Patterns

Now that we know that retrieving a customer, product and category all work in an extremely similar manner, how are we going to implement this? We could just make one retrieve method with a parameter that will tell us how we want to retrieve the information. We can use a `Select Case` statement to determine whether we are retrieving a customer, product or category. The only problem is that the code can become quite complex and very long. We should try to keep our methods small; there really shouldn't be more than a page of comment-free code for a method.

Putting the retrieve into one method could result in multiple `Select Case` statements, optional parameters (products may have some special requirements for retrieval), and lines and lines of code to work through all of this. Code should not only work, but also be readable. Keeping separate methods for retrieving customers, products and categories will result in more methods, but is cleaner. Revising our activity diagrams, we can make a general retrieve recordset diagram that would look as follows:

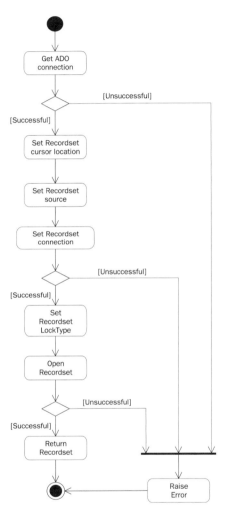

For each type of recordset that we need to retrieve, we would have a method like this. For example, we would have `RetrieveCustomers`, `RetrieveProducts` and `RetrieveCategories` methods. As each method would be used to retrieve only one type of recordset, we do not need any steps in the code to determine what the correct recordset is.

As for the code that is the same in each of these methods, we could also create a separate, private method to perform these tasks so the same code is not repeated within each method.

Efficient and Effective Testing

So now we can see that Retrieve Recordset is a task that is required by nearly every client component. Therefore the majority of the tasks the client will be performing will depend on this tasks functioning correctly. If we had made the appropriate activity diagrams for updating recordsets, we would have found a pattern also emerged for this task. Tasks that are essential to the entire system, such as these two tasks, should always be thoroughly tested during the design phase. If either one of these tasks fails to work, or works inefficiently, the entire project will fail.

With regard to retrieving recordsets from and updating recordsets to the server component, we will need to answer these questions:

❑   How efficiently will disconnected recordsets work for the Northwind Order Entry system?
❑   Does RDS actually work?
❑   If RDS works, does it work efficiently enough for this system?
❑   Does this system require MTS?

The test project should be designed to find the best way to retrieve a disconnected recordset from the server component and pass it on to the client. It also must find the best way to pass a disconnected recordset to the server component so it can pass any updates on to the database. We will want to put methods into the test project that will retrieve and update disconnected recordsets.

For updating information, we find that we have something special to test because we are using disconnected recordsets. What happens if two users both have disconnected products recordsets? Both users get the product information, which is stored on the client machine. One makes a change to a product, soup, and updates the database with this change. The second person now has old information, which is on their client. If the second person updates this soup product, there will have to be some way to reconcile this inconsistency. We will also have to include a test to find the best way to handle the inconsistencies in our test project.

The next step is to determine is the nature of recordsets we will be retrieving and updating:

❑   Do we want to test recordsets with one hundred records?
❑   Maybe we should use recordsets with ten thousand records?
❑   Should we do tests to see if we can resolve conflicting records?

There is only one way to find the answers to these questions, and that is to look at the system and see what type of recordsets the final project will be using. It would make little sense to be performing tests on disconnected recordsets of ten thousand records when the final project will never use a recordset with more than fifty records.

When considering how our recordsets should perform, we will look at the database that our final production system will be using. We will then determine the conditions that will exist for the disconnected recordsets. We must make sure that the retrieve and update methods in our test project meet all of these conditions. For example, we could make the following chart for the different tables in the Northwind database:

Table Name	Conditions
Categories	Less than twenty records. Changes very rarely and updated by only one actor so not likely to have any conflicts. Not likely to increase in size. Contains images.
Customers	Under one hundred records, records added and updated infrequently, updated by several actors, yet still not likely to have any conflicts. Likely to increase in size over the next few months.
Employees	Under twenty records, records added and updated very rarely, updated by several actors, yet still not likely to have any conflicts. Not likely to increase by more than a few records
Orders	Large recordset, yet not likely to view all records. More likely to view only recent records from this table, under one thousand records. Frequent AddNews, infrequent edits or deletes. Accessed by several actors, yet conflicts are unlikely. Will increase over time, yet number of records being retrieved should remain approximately the same.
Products	Moderate size recordset, less than one hundred records. Frequently changing, likely to have conflicts, may increase in size
Order Details	Large recordset, yet not likely to view all records. More likely to view only records relating to a particular order, fewer than fifty records. Frequent AddNews, infrequent Edits or Deletes. Accessed by several actors, yet conflicts are unlikely. Will increase over time, yet number of records being retrieved should remain approximately the same.
Shippers	Small table, not likely to change. Changed by one person, not likely to change.
Suppliers	Small table, not likely to change. Changed by one person, not likely to change.

We could make a method to test retrieving a recordset from each table. If there is enough time to make a test project this detailed, then this is the most accurate test. However, there is rarely time or a need to do this.

We have made activity diagrams for retrieving a customer, product and category recordset. The three activity diagrams show us that the task of retrieving a recordset will be basically the same whether we are retrieving a customer, product or category recordset. We can choose to design and implement only one `Retrieve` method in our test project, providing we test this `Retrieve` method over a wide range of conditions that represent the full range of possibilities that will exist for all of the `Retrieve` functions.

Looking at the above table, we can see that our `Retrieve` methods will need to retrieve anywhere from a few records to a few hundred. The Categories table has fields of many data types: OLE object, fixed and variable length strings, and long data types. This is a small table with only a few records. Building the `RetrieveCategory` method will allow us to test a small recordset with a wide range of field data types. This makes the Categories table a good candidate for our test project. Therefore, we will use the `Retrieve Category` method in our test project.

The Products table, though, is not very well represented by the Categories table. The Products table is likely to have conflicts on an update, which is not true for the Categories table. The Products table will also have larger recordsets built from it than the Categories table. We will therefore have to include a series of tests on the Products table as well.

From this discussion, we design a test project that runs through the following sequence of events:

- ❑ The client will request a disconnected category recordset using the server component.
- ❑ The server component will get the recordset from the database and return it to the client.
- ❑ The client will select a category.
- ❑ The client will request a disconnected recordset containing the products in the selected category using the server component.
- ❑ The server component will get the recordset from the database and return it to the client.
- ❑ The client will update the disconnected recordset.
- ❑ The client will pass the recordset back to the server component.
- ❑ The server component will check for any inconsistencies in the data.
- ❑ The server component will try to fix any inconsistencies in the data.
- ❑ The server component will update the database if there are no inconsistencies in the data.

These tasks will allow us to test retrieving and updating disconnected recordsets from the Products and Categories tables.

In the next chapter, we will actually build this test server component project. We will need to design and implement a `GetProducts` and `GetCategories` methods, and an `UpdateProducts` method. We will also need several private methods to reconcile any inconsistencies. We will design these methods by creating activity diagrams for each of them. We will also make an activity diagram for any additional private methods that we will need for our server component.

Summary

In this chapter, I have given you an introduction to activity diagrams. These simple diagrams give us a visual model of the flow of our code. Using these diagrams, we can find the best way to code our properties and methods. We can carefully check the model and make sure every possible situation has been covered, and that all possible alternative flows have been properly addressed.

These are the topics we've covered in this chapter:

- ❑ Activity diagrams and how to build them
- ❑ Using activity diagrams to map out complex behaviors
- ❑ Designing a Test Project for our system
- ❑ Testing strategies
- ❑ Planning VB code from activity diagrams

Making a set of activity diagrams is only the first step in making our application however. The next step is to turn these activity diagrams into Visual Basic code. In the next chapter, we will work out several more activity diagrams for the server component of our test project. We will then see how we can turn these activity diagrams into Visual Basic code.

10

Building and Testing A Server-Object

In the previous chapter, we looked at how we can use activity diagrams to help us model some of the more complex operations that we will be coding. We also saw how the choices of technology that we made affected they way we intend to code these operations.

We've spent a lot of time discussing and planning the system and now it's time to get our hands dirty. As you can see, we've come a long way without seeing any code - quite the opposite of the common development strategy of diving straight into code.

Don't think we've finished designing yet though. We're building this test project to find out how feasible our design is. As you'll find out, we still have some modifications to make. But I'm getting ahead of myself.

In this chapter we will:

- ❏ See how to convert our activity diagrams into Visual Basic code
- ❏ Continue to design new operations with activity diagrams
- ❏ See how our activity diagrams patterns can be used as a template
- ❏ Learn the benefits of building a test project
- ❏ Assess how well our experimental server project works
- ❏ Build a strategy based on the results of this test

With all the discussing and drawing of diagrams, we've almost forgotten how to code. Let's jump right in and get coding.

Building the Experimental Server Object

Open Visual Basic and create a new ActiveX DLL project. Name the project prjServerTest and the default class clsServerTest.

Now we need to open the References dialog, and set a reference to Microsoft ActiveX Data Objects 2.0 Library. All connections to the database will be made with the ADO:

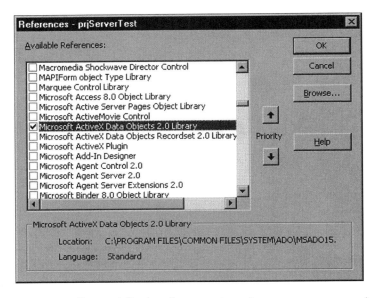

Add the following code to the General Declarations section of clsServerTest class:

```
Option Explicit

Private m_objADOConn As ADODB.Connection
```

The variable m_objADOConn is an ADO Connection object variable that we will use to connect to the current database. With each call to the server component, the Connection object variable is recreated.

We are creating a module-level variable for the Connection object, as it will be created in one function, and then used in one or more other functions. Use a module-level variable whenever you don't want to be passing the Connection object from one function to another.

Connecting to the Database

A connection to the database must be created every time the business object is created because the application is stateless. Connections are a pooled resource and they should be managed carefully.

If we do not close our `Connection` object when we've finished with it, the `Connection` object will remain until it times out. The default timeout is sixty seconds. If we don't close `Connection` objects, unused ones will quickly pile up and use up valuable resources. Creating the `Connection` object when we need it, and closing and destroying it when we're done, will allow ADO to function more efficiently, which in turn will make our system work better and faster.

We will create a `Public` function to make a connection to the database. We will use this function to perform two services:

- ❑ To test whether a user's UserID and Password are correct
- ❑ To make a connection to the database every time the server object is asked to retrieve data from or update data to the database

The final project will need to know which actor is using the system. To do this, a user will have to log into the system. Therefore, we need to have some way of verifying if a user is allowed into the system and what their role in the system is.

> *We will not determine the user's role in the test project, but we will verify if the user's Password and UserID are valid. In the Northwind database, there are no logins, but in a real application, there would be some form of security on the database.*

The methods of the server component are going to be "connecting to the database" and "returning data to the client". This function will provide a way of doing this.

We are only allowing for one database. If there was more than one database, we might need multiple connection objects.

> **This is not coded in the best way possible: a function should only be performing one task, not two completely separate tasks. However, it will provide a good example that I will later use to go into a detailed discussion of why methods should only perform one task. We will do this when we design the final version of the server component. Writing the function this way will not affect the performance of the test project, so it will not affect our tests of the three-tier framework.**

The test project is not meant to be perfect. A test project is a *first attempt*, a rough draft that is more concerned with finding out if a framework will work with our project, and, if it does work, how to make it function efficiently. As we run through our tests we will find weaknesses in our code, poor decisions concerning how we have chosen to implement our methods, and techniques that are unworkable. We should *document* this information, and be sure not to repeat these mistakes in the final project. If these mistakes will affect the performance of our test project, we will have to rewrite the test project to remove them. If these mistakes have no effect on our tests, then we can remove them if we have time, or just leave them. Writing code is an iterative process. It's better to work the kinks out in a small test project that takes a few weeks to design, build, debug and rebuild, than a final project that has taken months to build and may require many more to rebuild.

The activity diagram for creating a connection would be as follows:

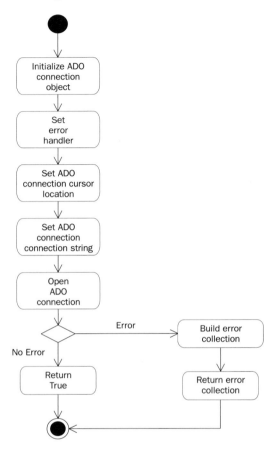

This function will have two parameters: the user name and password. ADO may return an Errors collection.

An Errors collection are errors that are concatenated and passed back to the calling function (the client). The client can then pass the error to the user, or in this example, log it to a file to be viewed later.

Create a Public function with two optional parameters, one for the user name and one for the user password:

```
Public Function ADOConnection(ByVal v_strUserID As String, _
                              ByVal v_strPassword As String) As String
```

Please note that the section headings that follow correspond to the activity diagram we're using to build this code. We're actually building one function through these sections.

Initialize the ADO Connection Object

```
Set m_objADOConn = New ADODB.Connection
```

Set Error Handler

```
On Error GoTo ADOConnectionError
```

Set ADO Connection Cursor Location

```
With m_objADOConn
    .CursorLocation = adUseClient
```

For disconnected recordsets, we want to set the CursorLocation to the client otherwise we'll end up with a continuous connection, which defeats the point.

Set ADO Connection Connection String

```
.ConnectionString = "Driver={Microsoft Access Driver (*.mdb)};" & _
    "Dbq=C:\Program Files\Microsoft Visual Studio\VB98\Nwind.mdb;" & _
    "Uid=" & v_strUserID & ";Pwd=" & v_strPassword
```

Of course, you may need to modify the ConnectionString so that it points to the correct directory on your computer.

> *If the DBMS requires a user name and password, these will be added to the connection string. To keep it simple, we are using the Microsoft Access version of the Northwind DBMS, which is not password protected.*

Open ADO Connection

```
    .Open
End With
```

Return True (if there is no error)

Set the return value of the function to True to let the calling function know that the connection was successfully made and exit the function:

```
ADOConnection = True

Exit Function
```

Build Error Collection (if there is an error)

Create the error handler. As there may be several errors in the ADO error collection, we must loop through all of them and add them to a string variable (strErrors). We will then set the return value of the variable to this error so that the client can retrieve it:

```
ADOConnectionError:

    Dim lngErrorCounter As Long
    Dim strErrors As String
```

```
strErrors = Err.Number & ": " & Err.Description
If m_objADOConn.Errors.Count > 0 Then

    For lngErrorCounter = 0 To m_objADOConn.Errors.Count - 1
        strErrors = strErrors & m_objADOConn.Errors(lngErrorCounter).Number & _
            ": " & m_objADOConn.Errors(lngErrorCounter).Description & vbCrLf
    Next lngErrorCounter

End If
```

Return Error Collection

```
ADOConnection = strErrors

Exit Function

End Function
```

That's our first function complete, build directly from our activity diagram. This function now allows the server object to make an ADO connection. However, as a final step, we must add a line of code to the class' `Terminate` event to make sure the `Connection` object is closed and destroyed before we leave the function:

```
Private Sub Class_Terminate()

If Not m_objADOConn Is Nothing Then
    If m_objADOConn.State = adStateOpen Then
        m_objAdOConn.Close
    End If
    Set m_objADOConn = Nothing
End If

End Sub
```

Retrieving Categories Recordset

In the previous chapter we made an activity diagram for Retrieving Categories:

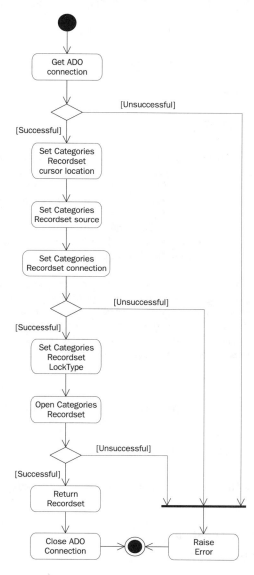

So create a new Public function with two parameters, one for the user name and one for the user password.

> *Remember that the client has no memory of the UserID or Password from the* ADOConnection *function because it is stateless. These two parameters must be passed into every function that requires them.*

This function will return a disconnected recordset to the client:

```
Public Function GetCategories(ByVal v_strUserID As String, _
                            ByVal v_strPassword As String) As Recordset
```

We will now create a local recordset variable that we can use to retrieve the category records into:

```
Dim recCategories as New ADODB.Recordset
```

Now we will set the error handler:

```
On Error Goto GetCategoriesError
```

We did not include these previous two steps in our activity diagram. Having a recordset variable is a prerequisite to this function. We cannot set properties of a recordset unless we have a recordset variable to work with. We could therefore explicitly add "Create local recordset variable" into the diagram if we felt that someone reading the diagram may not figure this out.

As for error handling, the arrows going to "Raise Error" indicate that there will be an error handler in the routine, so again we did not explicitly show "Create Error Handler". We can make your activity diagrams as fine-grained and detailed as we like.

What we include in our diagram depends on how we will be using the diagram, and who will be using it. If we were giving this diagram to an inexperienced programmer, we would probably want to get very fine-grained and show every step. If this diagram were only going to be used by experienced programmers, they would probably want to see the big picture, and would be less concerned with the detailed steps that an experienced programmer would expect. UML models are tools. It's up to us to determine the best way to use the tool in each situation.

Get ADO Connection

Create the connection to the database by passing the user ID and password to the `ADOConnection` function:

```
ADOConnection v_strUserID, v_strPassword
```

Once again, the section headings I've used here reflect the stages we've analysed in our activity diagram.

Set Categories Recordset Cursor Location

It's a disconnected recordset so the location is the client:

```
With recCategories
    .CursorLocation = adUseClient
```

Set Categories Recordset Source

For the purpose of our test project we are just using a general SELECT * FROM SQL statement to retrieve all of the records:

```
        .Source = "SELECT * FROM Categories"
```

As this is a test application, we'll hard-code the query into the code instead of using a string constant.

As a general rule, we'd rather the user didn't have the control over what information is returned or what types of queries are performed. If we allow a user to pass in any query to the function, they could write a query that deletes tables, records, or any number of destructive actions. It's critical to always keep security in mind; there are some very malicious users out there!

The downside of not allowing queries to be passed in is that we now have to provide functions to handle each query that may be wanted. Another solution to this is to allow an additional parameter to be passed in that will determine what query is to be used, such as returning all customers, all customers who have orders greater than one-thousand dollars, etc.

Set Categories Recordset Connection

We need to use the `Connection` object we opened in the call to `ADOConnection`:

```
        Set .ActiveConnection = m_objADOConn
```

Set Categories Recordset Cursor Type

We're using a static cursor type because it fixes the data at the time the cursor is created:

```
        .CursorType = adOpenStatic
```

Set Categories Recordset Lock Type

Optimistic locking means that records are locked on a row-by-row basis when they are updated. It also means that we'll have to cater for conflicts ourselves:

```
        .LockType = adLockOptimistic
```

Open the Categories Recordset

```
        .Open
    End With
```

Return the Recordset (if there is no error)

Once we have set all of the data in the `Categories Recordset` object, we can set the return value of the function to the `Recordset` and set the `Connection` object and the private `Categories` object to `Nothing`.

Again, I have not shown the steps of setting the two objects to Nothing; this step is a standard part of programming objects and should not have to be explicitly shown. If you feel you, or the developers reading the diagram, may not remember this, you can add these steps into your diagram.

```
    Set recCategories.ActiveConnection = Nothing
    Set GetCategories = recCategories
    Set recCategories = Nothing

    Exit Function
```

Raise Error (if there is an error)

The error handler in this case simply returns the error information and the name of the routine where the error occurred:

```
GetCategoriesError:

    Err.Raise Err.Number, "GetCategories", Err.Description
    Set recCategories = Nothing

End Function
```

Retrieving Products Recordset

We will create a function that is similar to the GetCategories function, except this time we'll add an additional parameter to give the user some control over the data that is returned. If you refer back to our activity diagram in the last chapter, you will see that it also follows the diagram every step of the way:

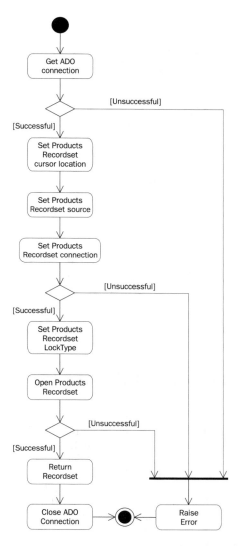

This function is essentially identical to GetCategories, except that we have added a parameter for the CategoryID to give the user some very limited control over the query. In this way, we can only return the Product belonging to a particular Category:

```
Public Function GetProducts(ByVal v_strUserID As String, ByVal v_strPassword As _
                            String, CategoryID As Long) As Recordset
  Dim recProducts As New ADODB.Recordset

  On Error GoTo GetProductsError

  ADOConnection v_strUserID, v_strPassword

  With recProducts
    .CursorLocation = adUseClient
```

```
      .Source = "SELECT ProductID, ProductName, " & _
                "UnitPrice, UnitsInStock FROM Products " & _
                "WHERE CategoryID = " & CategoryID
      .Open , m_objADOConn, adOpenStatic, adLockOptimistic
   End With

   Set recProducts.ActiveConnection = Nothing
   Set GetProducts = recProducts
   Set recProducts = Nothing

   Exit Function

GetProductsError:

   Err.Raise Err.Number, "GetProducts", Err.Description
   Set recProducts = Nothing

End Function
```

You'll also notice that instead of setting the recordset's properties, such as CursorType,
individually we are setting them as parameters of the Open *command:*

```
.Open , m_objADOConn, adOpenStatic, adLockOptimistic
```

We now have the necessary routines to get data for the test project from the database. So let's turn
our attention to the reverse process of updating the database.

Updating the Recordset in the Database

This is a complex function that passes a recordset back to the database. This is where things get very
interesting with disconnected recordsets. We could just simply return the records to the database, but
what happens if the record we are updating was changed while the recordset was sitting on the client?
We then have a serious problem. We need some way to make the correction. But how?

The secret is in the recordset object itself. ADO allows us to apply a filter to the recordset object so
that we can remove all the records that have not been changed. We can then try to update these
records to the database. When that fails, the recordset object will contain three copies of the
information:

❑   The values that were originally sent to the client
❑   The new values that were set while at the client
❑   The current values that are in the database

We will create a special function called Reconcile that will use these three values to reconcile any
changes that occurred to updated records while the recordset was at the client.

This is a fairly intense piece of code, but once you understand it, you will understand the basis for
any future three-tier reconciliations. As this is a complex function, it has been broken down into three
activity diagrams.

The first looks as follows:

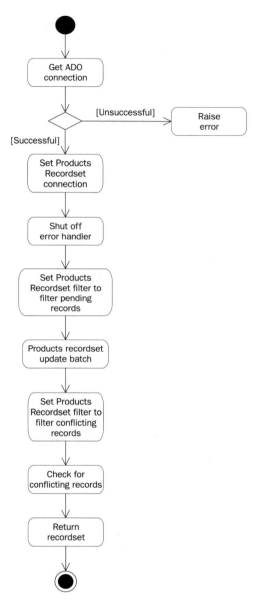

The second diagram will be checking for conflicting records and the third will be Reconcile itself. Both of these will be presented below. Let's start creating the code.

UpdateProduct

Begin by creating a `Public` function called `UpdateProduct` with our standard `UserID` and `Password` parameters. We will also have an additional parameter, `v_recClient`, which will pass in the client's modified Products recordset. We will use this recordset to update the database:

```
Public Function UpdateProduct(ByVal v_strUserID As String, ByVal v_strPassword _
                     As String, ByVal v_recClient As Recordset) As Recordset
```

Also add the recordset variable and set up the error handler:

```
Dim recProducts As ADODB.Recordset

On Error GoTo UpdateProductError
```

Get ADO Connection

We will once again begin by making a connection to the database using `ADOConnection`:

```
ADOConnection v_strUserID, v_strPassword
```

You're probably getting used to the idea now that my section headings reflect the stages in our activity diagram.

Set Products Recordset Connection

We next set the private `Products` recordset in the server object equal to the Recordset object that was passed back from the client:

```
Set recProducts = v_recClient
```

The `recProducts` Recordset object does not have its `Connection` object set to the `Connection` object we have just created. Before we can move on, we must do that:

```
Set recProducts.ActiveConnection = m_objADOConn
```

Disable Error Handle

We are now going to turn off our error trap and begin handling any errors ourselves. We have to do this because the `UpdateBatch` method of the ADO will raise an error if one of the records has been changed whilst the recordset was at the client. Instead of raising an error, we want to reconcile these differences ourselves:

```
On Error Resume Next
```

Set Products Recordset to Filter Pending Records

The next step is to remove any records that have not been changed. To do this we set the `Filter` of the Products recordset object equal to `adFilterPendingRecords`:

```
recProducts.Filter = adFilterPendingRecords
```

This filter allows us to view only those records that have changed but not been sent to the server.

Products Recordset UpdateBatch

We will now try to update the records:

```
recProducts.UpdateBatch adAffectGroup
```

The `adAffectGroup` constant means that the `UpdateBatch` operation only effects the records specified by the current filter.

Set Products Recordset to Filter Conflicting Records

We will now filter the Products recordset object again, this time we are setting the filter equal to `adFilterConflictingRecords`, which will only leave the records in which there was a conflict:

```
recProducts.Filter = adFilterConflictingRecords
```

Check For Conflicting Records

Now if there are any records remaining in the recordset, they are conflicting records and must be dealt with.

Our function is not yet finished; but we need now to look at the activity diagram for Checking for Conflicting Records:

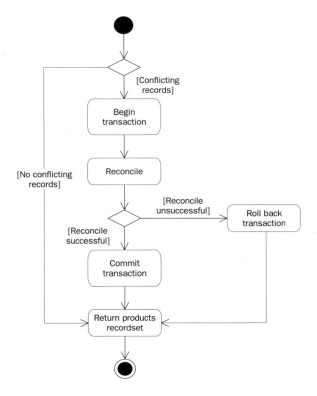

We can tell if there are any conflicting records because the record count will be greater than 0. If there are conflicts, we will call the function Reconcile that will try to reconcile these differences. Reconcile will return True if the changes were successful and False if they fail. (We'll look at Reconcile in a moment.)

We are using a feature of the Connection object called a **transaction** here. A transaction provides atomicity to a series of data changes to a recordset within a connection, meaning that the entire operation either succeeds or fails as a whole. The transaction starts before we call the Reconcile function. Any changes that we make to the recordset in the Reconcile function will not be committed until we return from the Reconcile function, and the function returns True. Only at that time, we will commit the transaction, and the changes to the database.

If in the middle of attempting to reconcile the records in the Reconcile function, the function fails, then it will return False. We can then **rollback** the transaction. The rollback causes any values in the recordset that were changed after the transaction began to be returned to their values prior to the start of the transaction:

```
If recProducts.RecordCount > 0 Then
' Begin Transaction
  m_objADOConn.BeginTrans

' Reconcile
  If Reconcile (recProducts) Then
    ' Commit Transaction
      m_objADOConn.CommitTrans
  Else
    ' Roll Back
      m_objADOConn.RollbackTrans
  End If

End If
```

Return Recordset

The recordset we now have may be different from what is on client, so we want to return a recordset to the client that is complete and current. To make the recordset complete, we must remove all of the filters, and then set the function's return value equal to the unfiltered recordset:

```
recProducts.Filter = adFilterNone
Set UpdateProduct = recProducts

Exit Function
```

Raise Error

Once again, we have a standard error handler:

```
UpdateProductError:

  Err.Raise Err.Number, "UpdateProducts", Err.Description

End Function
```

Let's now take a look at the Reconcile function.

Reconciling Product Inconsistencies

The activity diagram for this function looks like this:

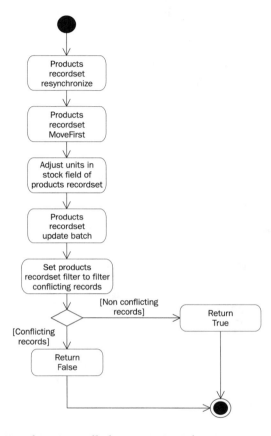

So now create a `Public` function called `Reconcile` that accepts a recordset parameter By Reference and returns a `Boolean`. By passing in the recordset `ByRef`, any changes to the Product recordset in the `Reconcile` function will also be made to the Product recordset in the `UpdateProduct` function:

```
Public Function Reconcile(ByRef r_recProducts as ADODB.Recordset) As Boolean

   On Error GoTo ReconcileError
```

As ever, my section headings here reflect the stages in our activity diagram.

Products Recordset Resynchronize

As I mentioned earlier, we're going to need three copies of the out-of-synch records:

❑　The values that were originally sent to the client
❑　The new values that were set while at the client
❑　The current values that are in the database

To do this we need to call the Products recordset's `Resync` method as follows (remember that this recordset only contains records that were out of sync with the database):

```
r_recProducts.Resync adAffectGroup, adResyncUnderlyingValues
```

We've already seen the `adAffectGroup` constant before so we don't need to discuss it here. However, the `adResyncUnderlyingValues` constant is new to us. It means that the data is not overwritten and the pending updates are not cancelled. (The default value here is `adResyncAllValues`, which does overwrite any pending updates.)

> *The Resync method of the ADO Recordset object only works for recordsets that have a client cursor and are being batch updated.*

Products Recordset MoveFirst

We will move to the first record by calling the `MoveFirst` method:

```
r_recProducts.MoveFirst
```

Adjust UnitsInStock Field of Products Recordset

What happens here will need a bit of explaining. What we are in essence trying to do is to reconcile a difference in the `UnitsInStock` field. Let's imagine that the following series of events occur:

Order Entry Clerk, Mike, has a customer call in. Mike starts a new order on his client application. Mike's client retrieves the current product information and stores it on Mike's client in a disconnected recordset. In this recordset, the product called ACME has the value of 10 for the `UnitsInStock` field.

Order Entry Clerk, Dana, has a different customer call in. Dana starts an order on her client application. Dana's client retrieves the current product information and stores it in a disconnected recordset. In this recordset, the product called ACME also has the value of 10 for the `UnitsInStock` field (it has not yet changed since Mike started his order).

Mike's customer makes a request for three cans of ACME. Mike enters them into the order. Mike's client changes the field in his Product disconnected recordset to seven cans. This recordset is not connected to the database, so this change only occurs in the recordset on his client.

Dana's customer orders two cans of ACME. Dana's client updates the disconnected recordset on her client to eight cans. Dana completes the order and sends the disconnected recordset to the server object to update the database.

The database now says that there are eight cans of ACME. How do we fix this when Mike's client sends its update to the database?

It's harder to understand the problem than the solution. The original value in Mike's recordset was ten and the current value is seven. If we subtract seven (the number on Mike's machine) from ten (the original value sent to Mike's machine) we get three. Therefore, if we know the original value in the recordset and the new value in the recordset, we know how many of cans have been removed. We only need to subtract the total number removed from current value in the database to get the correct value in the database. Are you still with me?

Note that it's basically the same process for adding stock - except that the sums go backwards.

An ADO Recordset object with a client cursor, performing batch updates, will have three properties that can be used to resolve conflicts:

- ❑ Value - The current value of the field in the database at the time the batch update was performed
- ❑ OriginalValue - The value of the field that was originally sent to the client
- ❑ UnderlyingValue - The value the client changed the field to

UnderlyingValue − OriginalValue **= the amount of items that were removed.**

In our case, the UnderlyingValue is 7 and the OriginalValue is 10, so we have 7 − 10= -3. There were 3 items removed by Mike.

The current value in the database is 8, so 8 + -3 = 5. Hey Presto! We have the correct value.

The situation would work as the following sequence diagram:

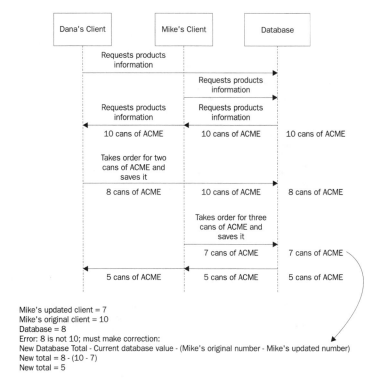

Mike's updated client = 7
Mike's original client = 10
Database = 8
Error: 8 is not 10; must make correction:
New Database Total - Current database value - (Mike's original number - Mike's updated number)
New total = 8 - (10 - 7)
New total = 5

The code looks like this:

```
While Not r_recProducts.EOF
   With r_recProducts.Fields("UnitsInStock")
      .Value = .UnderlyingValue + .Value - .OriginalValue
   End With
   r_recProducts.MoveNext
Wend
```

> **We are not taking into account the possibility of dropping below zero items.
> We will address this issue when we are designing the final server-
> component.**

Products Recordset Update Batch

We now attempt to update the records again:

```
r_recProducts.UpdateBatch
```

Set Products Recordset to Filter Conflicting Records

And just the same as before for this task:

```
r_recProducts.Filter = adFilterConflictingRecords
```

Check for Conflicting Records

If there are still conflicts (which could be caused by another field having been changed), we will just return False so that these changes can be rolled back:

```
If r_recProducts.RecordCount > 0 Then
   Reconcile = False
Else
   Reconcile = True
End If

Exit Function
```

Error Handler

Let's create the error trap:

```
ReconcileError:

   Err.Raise Err.Number, Err.Source & " Reconcile" & Err.Description

End Function
```

Actually, this function is not complete. We have not dealt with the possibility of one of the other fields changing. If the name or the price of a product changes, the entire transaction would be dropped. This certainly is a bit poor, as the user will have to re-enter the order.

If there were any other changes, such as price, product name, etc. these changes don't need to be reconciled, we only need to update the disconnected recordset to reflect these new values.

To do this, we could just set the `Value` property (the value of the field currently in the disconnected recordset) to `UnderlyingValue` (the value currently in the database). The following code segment could therefore have been added after we had reconciled the `UnitsInStock` field:

```
Dim lngFieldCounter as Long

While Not r_recProducts.EOF
  For lngFieldCounter = 0 to r_recProducts.Fields.Count
    With r_recProducts.Fields(lngFieldCounter)
        .Value = .UnderlyingValue
    End With
  Next
    r_recProducts.MoveNext
Wend
```

In this situation, if we attempted to the update and it failed again, there would have to be an error in the `UnitsInStock` field that couldn't be reconciled.

If you're concerned that working with disconnected recordsets will result in pages of code to reconcile inconsistencies, relax: this should not happen. In the Northwind system, only the Sales Coordinator makes changes to the product. The only change that is likely to occur is a change in price. A method could be added to the system to input these changes during business hours, but actually change the database after hours. The only possible conflict that could exist for a Product recordset is the `UnitsInStock` field.

> *If the Order Entry clerks were working twenty-four hours a day, we would have to do the update while orders were being taken. We can still do an update at a scheduled time, but in this system the client component would automatically get a new version of the Products recordset after the table update was complete. For example, the Product update could occur at 12:00 a.m. and the client component can request an update of the Products recordset at 12:05 a.m. If you are worrying about what will happen in the five minutes between, you do not have to.*

Using disconnected recordsets requires a shift in thinking. We must look for ways of minimizing conflicts in the records. A carefully designed system will only have a few possible circumstances where there can be conflict, and they can be handled by writing methods such as the `Reconcile` method we have created. Most of the possible conflicts can be easily resolved. For example, if there is conflict in the field containing the name of the product, we can just change the value in the disconnected recordset to the new value.

GetServerTime Function

To properly stress test this component, we will want several copies of the client test application to be running at the same time making requests to the server at exactly the same time. The only way several different clients can make a request at exactly the same time is if they are all synchronized. If all of the clients get the time from the server and set their clocks to the server's time, they will all be synchronized. We therefore need to write a function that will return the time on the server for the clients (a property will not work with RDS and HTTP):

```
Public Function GetServerTime() As String

  GetServerTime = Format(Time, "hhnnss")

End Function
```

When using the `Format` *function, the letter "m" is for month, "n" is for minute.*

Compiling the Server Object

Compile the `prjServerTest` DLL. Visual Basic will then automatically register your DLL when it is compiled.

If we only had to compile our object once, we could leave this topic now. Unfortunately, we often compile our DLL, find there are bugs, fix the bugs and recompile. If we don't make some changes to the way the project is compiled, Visual Basic will create new registry entries every time we recompile our DLL. It would be really nice if the old entries were removed from the registry when the new one is created; but it isn't. As we compile our project over and over again, more and more entries will be associated with our DLL in the registry. In theory, only the last entry should be used and everything should be OK. In the real world, these old registry entries will usually cause our DLL to fail, usually in a way that is completely unpredictable and incomprehensible. To prevent this from happening, we must compile the DLL once. Once we've done that, we can bring up the **Project Properties** window and select the **Component** tab:

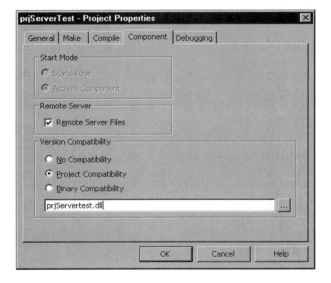

We can then change the compatibility to <u>B</u>inary and select our compiled DLL. This forces Visual Basic to compile the DLL with the same registry entries as the DLL listed.

This works great as long as we don't change the **public interface**, i.e. the public methods and properties. If we do change the public interface after we compile the DLL, there is only one option: to switch Version Compatibility to No Compatibility, remove all references of the DLL from the registry, and recompile. Once we've done this, we can set Version Compatibility back to Binary Compatibility.

Registering the Server Object

In a moment, we will build the client-side of our test project and connect our client component to our server component through the RDS. Before we can do this, though, we have to register the server component on the server.

To do this we can use the **Package and Deployment Wizard** to create a proper setup package, but this is too much work for a simple test project. We *would* want to consider doing this for the final component of course.

For our test purposes, we can simply copy the `prjServerTest.dll` to the server and use the `Regsvr32.exe` program to register the DLL:

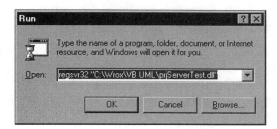

We're not quite ready yet though. The server component must be properly registered before RDS can create the component. This is to keep our server secure. If any object on the server could be connected through RDS, then anyone could get access to any application or DLL on a server simply by knowing the correct name. There is a special key in the registry that must have the name of the server component as a subkey. To register a server component, we must add this subkey.

Unfortunately, this registration does not automatically occur, we have to do it ourselves. We could do this the hard way and add the key directly to the registry but that's a rather messy way to do it. Instead, let's write a very small piece of Windows scripting that will allow us to register not only our test server, but any object in the future.

To run this script you will need to have the Windows Scripting Host installed on the server. It comes with the Windows NT Option Pack:

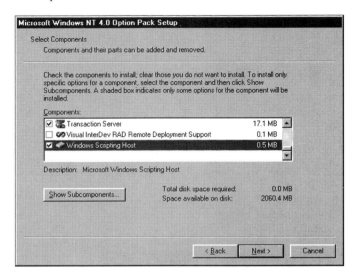

You should have the Option Pack installed to access MTS for the next chapter, but in case you don't, I've provided this registry hack in Appendix B.

If you haven't scripted before, don't worry: we're only going to be writing a few lines of code that resemble Visual Basic very closely.

Using Notepad, create a new blank file and enter the following code:

```
Dim ProgID
Dim WSHShell

On Error Resume Next

ProgID = InputBox("Enter the ProgID of the ActiveX server you're interested in?")

Set WSHShell = WScript.CreateObject("WScript.Shell")

If Trim(ProgID) = "" Then
    WSHShell.PopUp "Aborting ..."
    WScript.Quit(1)
End If

'Now create the key
WSHShell.Regwrite
"HKLM\SYSTEM\CurrentControlSet\Services\W3SVC\Parameters\ADCLaunch\" & ProgId _
          & "\", ""

WSHShell.PopUp progID & " successfully entered"

WScript.Quit
```

Save the text file with a .VBP extension. We can now simply double-click on it in Windows Explorer to run it.

We will be presented with an input box:

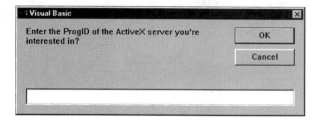

Enter the progID for the component we want to register – in this case it's our prjServerTest.clsServerTest:

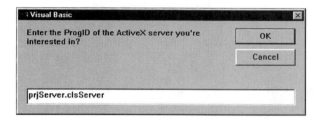

Hit OK and an empty key will be added to the registry. If you want to check if it's worked, refer to Appendix B to find out where the key was entered.

At this point, our server object is ready to rock and roll. All we need is a client.

The Client-Side Component

The time has come for us to build the client component of the stress test application. The purpose of the client component is to answer the questions we have raised about disconnected recordsets and RDS. Our client component will do this by trying to retrieve and update recordsets, and see how long it takes the server component to perform these tasks. From this information, we can make a decision on the best way to build our system.

Personally, I find it rather fun trying to build an application that can kill the system. You can use your imagination trying to find fun, new ways to put your system through a series of thorough, brutal tests. Just don't get too carried away. You don't want Dr. Watson to become your best friend.

In a real project, we would ideally first make sure there are no bugs in our server code. This is done by performing unit tests, i.e. testing the server-component by itself by adding methods into the server component. Once the server component passes these tests, it is bug free and ready to be hammered by our client stress test application. We will skip this step here, but I will show you how to build a test module in a later chapter.

The client component will make a call to the server object, request several recordsets, and then repeat this operation a set number of times at a set interval (for example, every ten seconds). Once the client application is built, it can be distributed to several testers who will start the program at the same time. At a specified time, the application will begin making its calls to the server. In this way, there will be multiple client requests coming into the server at exactly the same time. This application will not only determine whether RDS works, but also how many users the server component can handle at one time, i.e. how scalable is the server component? A sequence diagram for this project might look as follows:

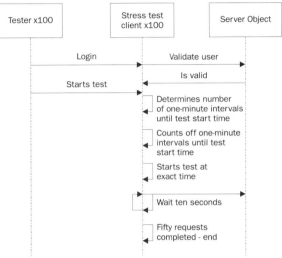

Building the Client Component

Create a new Visual Basic Standard EXE project and call it `prjStressTest`.

In the References dialog, add references to the Microsoft ActiveX Data Objects 2.0 Library and the Microsoft Remote Data Sources 2.0 Library:

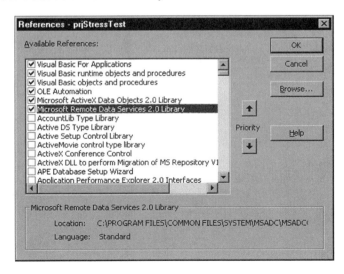

The project will use two forms: a main form called `frmTest` and a log-in form, called `frmLogin`. These forms will perform all of the tasks shown in the sequence diagram above.

This project will start up in a main form that will open the log-in form, allowing the user to try to log-in. Name the default form `frmTest`. Add another form but use the Login dialog template:

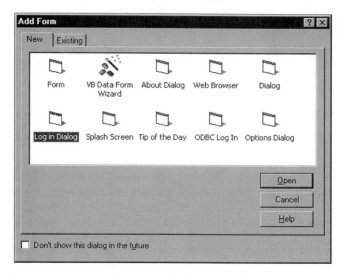

Make sure `frmTest` is set as the Startup Object in the Project Properties dialog:

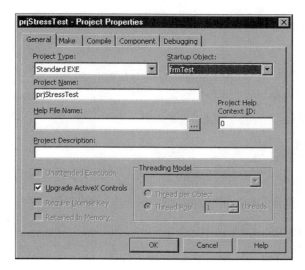

The Login Form

The login form will allow the tester to enter a User ID and a Password if one is required. Once the user clicks OK, the login form will try to make a connection to the server object to verify that the user has authorized access to the database.

If you open the code window, you will find that there is certain amount of code already there:

```
Option Explicit

Public LoginSucceeded As Boolean

Private Sub cmdCancel_Click()
    'set the global var to false
    'to denote a failed login
    LoginSucceeded = False
    Me.Hide
End Sub

Private Sub cmdOK_Click()
    'check for correct password
    If txtPassword = "password" Then
        'place code to here to pass the
        'success to the calling sub
        'setting a global var is the easiest
        LoginSucceeded = True
        Me.Hide
    Else
        MsgBox "Invalid Password, try again!", , "Login"
        txtPassword.SetFocus
        SendKeys "{Home}+{End}"
    End If
End Sub
```

The `cmdCancel_Click` event handler is suitable for our purposes, but we do need to modify the `cmdOK_Click` event:

```
Private Sub cmdOK_Click()

  On Error GoTo cmdOKError

  Dim strConnectResult As String

  strConnectResult = frmTest.m_objProxy.ADOConnection(txtUserName.Text, _
                                        txtPassword.Text)

  LoginSucceeded = True

  If strConnectResult = "True" Then
    frmTest.UserID = txtUserName.Text
    frmTest.UserPassword = txtPassword.Text
    LoginSucceeded = True
  Else
    MsgBox "Login failed:" & strConnectResult
    Exit Sub
  End If

  Exit Sub

cmdOKError:

  frmTest.WriteInfo "Error frmLogin:cmdOK Error: " & _
    Err.Description , " Error Number: " & Err.Number

End Sub
```

As we'll discuss in a moment, `frmTest` has an object variable called `m_objProxy`. This object is a reference to the server object. Therefore:

```
frmTest.m_objProxy.ADOConnection(txtUserName.Text, txtPassword.Text)
```

calls the `ADOConnection` method of the server object, passing in the username and password. The `ADOConnection` method will attempt to make a connection to the database using the password and user ID that are passed in as parameters. If a connection is made to the database, this function returns `True`. Otherwise, it returns the errors. The routine `WriteInfo` is also in `frmTest` and will write error information to a log file.

The Test Form

Add the Microsoft DataGrid Control 6 (OLEDB) to our project using the Components Dialog:

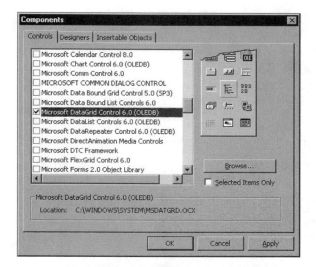

And now add the following controls to the form so that it looks something like this:

The controls names are as follows:

Control	Name
Label	lblIterationCount
Timer	tmrStartTest
Timer	tmrExecute
Data Grid	grdProducts
Combo Box	cboCategories
Command Button	cmdStart
Command Button	cmdStop
Command Button	cmdExit
List Box	lstError
Label	lblStatus

Open the code window and add the following code:

```
Option Explicit
```

```
Public m_objProxy

Private m_lngNumberOfIntervals As Long
Private m_intFileNumber As Integer
Private m_blnStop As Boolean
Private m_lngIterations As Long
Private m_lngTimeDifference As Long
Private m_strTimeToStart As String
Private m_lngNumberOfTests As Long
Private m_strPassword As String
Private m_strUserID As String
Private m_lngStartingTime As Long
Private m_objRDSDataSpace As RDS.DataSpace
Private m_recCategories As ADODB.Recordset
Private m_recProducts As ADODB.Recordset

Private Const cNumberOfIterations = 50
Private Const cStartingTime = " 2:55PM" ' Change this to an approptriate time
Private Const cFileName =  "C:\Wrox\VBUML\StressTest.txt"
```

These variables have the following functions:

Variable Name	Variable Function
m_objProxy	Proxy object representing server object. You'll see why it is a variant in a moment.

Variable Name	Variable Function
m_lngNumberOf_Intervals	When the test is first started there will be a certain number of minutes until the test will actually start. We will therefore need to know how many minutes have passed since the application has started. This variable is the number of one-minute intervals that have passed since the application started.
m_intFileNumber	FileNumber is for the log file that will log all errors that occur during the test.
m_lngIterations	Keeps track of the number of times the test has been run.
m_strTimeToStart	The time in military time that the test is to start.
m_lngNumberOfTests	How many times the test is supposed to run.
m_strPassword	UserPassword, set if login is successful.
m_strUserID	UserID, set if login is successful.
m_lngStartingTime	The number of 1-minute intervals that must pass before the test begins.
cNumberOfIterations	A constant that is equal to the total numberof times the test will run.
cFileName	Path and name of log file.
cStartingTime	A constant that is equal to the starting time in military time (you will need to change this to an appropriate time).
m_objRDSDataSpace	The DataSpace object that will be used to get a reference to the server object.
m_recCategories	Categories Recordset object.
m_recProducts	Products Recordset object.
m_blnStop	When a user stops the program, this variable will let the looping routine know the test has been stopped so it can stop the test.
m_lngTimeDifference	The difference between the time on the server and the time on the client. Used to synchronize all clients to the server time.

Getting a Reference to the Server Object

RDS can make a connection from the client object to the server object in four possible ways, through COM, DCOM, HTTP and SHTTP.

If you wish to use HTTP, you will need IIS running on the server where your server object will be running. If you do not have an IIS web server, you can run the server component using COM. COM will only work with RDS when the server and client components are on the same machine. To use DCOM you will need to configure the server and client to use DCOM. You can now see why we declared m_objProxy as a variant!

Create a `Public Sub` called `Get Proxy`:

```
Public Sub GetProxy()
```

This sub will use the `DataSpace` object. This object contains the following:

- ❑ `InternetTimeout` - This property determines the number of milliseconds allowed to make a connection to the component.
- ❑ `CreateObject (progID, Server)` - This method creates a connection to an ActiveX object. The `progID` is the name of the ActiveX component. `Server` is the name of the server where the ActiveX component is located.

The exact syntax for the `CreateObject`'s server parameter depends on whether COM, DCOM, SHTTP or HTTP is used. The proper syntax for `CreateObject` is, for each technology, as follows:

COM - `Set Object = DataSpace.CreateObject("ProgId", "")`

DCOM - `Set Object = DataSpace.CreateObject("ProgId", "machinename")`

HTTP - `Set Object = DataSpace.CreateObject("ProgId", "http://awebserver")`

SHTTP - `Set Object = DataSpace.CreateObject("ProgId", "http://awebserver")`

> *COM can only be used with RDS when the server and client components are on the same machine.*

Set the `DataSpace` object to a new `DataSpace` object. Once you've done this, set the `InternetTimeout` property to 30 seconds:

```
Set m_objRDSDataSpace = New RDS.DataSpace

m_objRDSDataSpace.InternetTimeout = 30000
```

Set the variable `m_objProxy` equal to the server object by using the `CreateObject` method.

If you have the server object running under IIS you can use the following code:

```
Set m_objProxy = m_objRDSDataSpace.CreateObject _
                    ("prjServerTest.clsServerTest", "HTTP://ServerName")

End Sub
```

> *You will need to replace* `ServerName`, *with the name of your server of course.*

If you do not have IIS and have the server object running on the client machine, use the following code:

```
Set m_objProxy = m_objRDSDataSpace.Createobject _
                    ("prjServerTest.clsServerTest", "")
End Sub
```

This is all there is to setting up RDS. If you've ever tried to configure hundreds of clients to connect through DCOM to a server, you'll certainly appreciate how simple RDS is. While it is a bit of a nuisance adding the registry entry to the server for RDS, once you've done this, you're done setting up RDS.

Of course, we could add extra security to RDS through MTS, but we will not cover that here. The question is not whether RDS is a simpler solution to implement than DCOM, as it is obvious that RDS is easier, but whether RDS will actually work. To establish that answer, we have created this test application.

Form_Load Event Handler

We'll be using two variables to keep track of the starting time, and the number of times the test should be performed. We'll begin by setting the starting time variable and the number of tests variable equal to their default values by setting them equal to their two constants:

```
Private Sub Form_Load()

    m_strTimeToStart = cStartingTime
    m_lngNumberOfTests = cNumberOfIterations
```

We've used constants because we can easily change their values (they are in the very beginning of our code and easy to find). We are also using the two variables m_strTimeToStart and m_lngNumberOfTests in case we want to override these default values. To keep it simple, we'll use the default values for our code sample, but we can add text boxes so the user could input a value to override them. This is a lot easier than changing the code for every test. Other options are using an INI file on a public network drive that all of the clients have access to, or using the registry.

We next call the function GetProxy to set the variable m_objProxy equal to the Server object:

```
    GetProxy
```

Now we bring up the login form:

```
    frmLogin.Show vbModal
```

If the login failed, LoginSucceeded will be False, and we will want to give the user a message and exit out of the application:

```
    If frmLogin. LoginSucceeded = False Then
      MsgBox "Login failed. Please try again later"
      Unload Me
      Exit Sub
    End If

End Sub
```

Starting the Test

This Sub will begin the countdown to the stress test:

```
Private Sub cmdStart_Click()

    lblStatus.Caption = "Status: Running"
```

```
        cmdStart.Enabled = False
        Initialize

    End Sub
```

Initialize Routine - Determines Number of One Minute Intervals

Create a subroutine `Initialize`. We'll set the variable, `m_lngTimeDifference`, so that it will measure the time difference between the server machine and the client machine.

We can use this to synchronize the clients with the server. We'll also set up the log file by setting the `m_intFileNumber` to the next free file number, and using this to open the file specified by the variable `cFileName`:

```
Private Sub Initialize()

  On Error GoTo InitializeError

  m_intFileNumber = FreeFile

  Open cFileName for Output as #m_intFileNumber
```

We next need to find the time difference between the server and the client. The time from the server is formatted `hhnnss`, so we will format the client time to be the same. Then we can use the `DateDiff` function to find the difference between the two times:

```
    m_lngTimeDifference = DateDiff("n", m_objProxy.GetServerTime(), _
                          Format(Time, "hhnnss"))
```

Next, we need to figure out how many minutes there are until the beginning of the test. This will be the time the test begins minus the current time. To make this subtraction we will use `m_strTimeToStart`, the time the test will begin, minus the current time:

```
    m_lngStartingTime = DateDiff("n", DateAdd("n", m_lngTimeDifference, Time), _
                        m_strTimeToStart)
```

We'll use the timer control, `tmrStartTest`, to count down the time between when the program actually starts, and when the test is supposed to begin running.

This timer control's interval property will be set to one minute. When the timer control has run `m_lngStartingTime` intervals, we know that we're within a minute of the starting time. We could set the interval to every second, but this could use up a lot of the client's resources, and the start time may be hours before the actual test time. We don't want the program interfering with the user's ability to work on the client; so one-minute intervals will be better. Let's see what happens when we are measuring in minutes.

Let's say our test is supposed to start at 2:00 p.m. From 2:00 p.m. on the clients are all supposed to be accessing the server every 30 seconds for one hour. The time the first client starts the program is 1:00:45 p.m. (45 seconds after 1:00 p.m.).

The time difference between the start time and the current time is 59 minutes and 15 seconds (2:00:00 – 1:00:45 p.m.).

Since our time is measuring time in one-minute increments, we could begin the test when the timer has run 59 times. Yet, 59 times is 59 minutes. Adding the starting time (1:00:45) to 59 minutes means we will start the test at 1:59:45, fifteen seconds early.

The whole point of the test is to see how the server handles simultaneous requests, yet using a one-minute interval on our counter means that our clients can be starting the tests at different times. A few minutes of calculations will show you that the clients could begin anywhere between fifty-nine seconds early and right-on-time.

To catch up on these missing seconds, we'll have a second timer control, `tmrExecute`, that will have its interval property set to a second. We'll initialize this timer when the number of times `tmrStartTest_Timer` event has been raised `m_lngStartingTime` intervals. Using this control, we can delay the start of the test to the actual time the test is supposed to begin. If we limit our start times to being exactly on the minute, we can find the number of seconds till the start of the test by calculating the number of seconds to the beginning of the next minute.

We're going to use `tmrStartTest` to count the minutes until the test will begin. We will now initialize the timer and set the interval to one millisecond so the timer will run immediately. We'll reset the time to one minute the first time the timer event fires:

```
tmrStartTest.Interval = 1
tmrStartTest.Enabled = True

Exit Sub
```

Finally, we'll put in the error trap, and write all errors to the log file:

```
InitializeError:

    WriteInfo "Sub Initialize :" & Err.Description, Err.Number

End Sub
```

tmrStartTest - Counts Off One-Minute Intevals

This timer will be set to run every minute and `m_lngNumberOfIntervals` will be incremented by one every time this sub executes. As this sub starts when the user clicks the Start button, `m_lngNumberOfIntervals` will measure the number of minutes that have passed since the Start button was clicked. `m_lngStartingTime` is the number of minutes from the time the Start button was clicked until the time the test will begin. Therefore, when `m_lngNumberOfIntervals` equals `m_lngStartingTime`, it's time to begin the test.

We still have to make up for those missing seconds we ignored when we started this timer in the `Initialize` sub. The number of seconds to the beginning of the next minute will be sixty minus the current number of seconds.

Open the `tmrStartTest_Timer` event. If this is the first time the event is being called, the timer will be set to one millisecond. We'll therefore need to reset the interval to one minute, so we begin by adding code to set the interval to one minute if that is not already the value:

```
Private Sub tmrStartTest_Timer()

    On Error GoTo tmrStartTestError
```

```
      If tmrStartTest.Interval <> 60000 Then
        tmrStartTest.Interval = 60000
      End If
```

We now check to see if enough minutes have passed to start the test. If it's time to start the test, we set the `Interval` on the `tmrExecute` timer to be the number of seconds until the beginning of the next minute. If it's not time to start the test, we change the status label to show the number of remaining minutes:

```
      If m_lngNumberOfIntervals >= m_lngStartingTime Then
        tmrExecute.Interval = (60 - Format(Time, "ss")) * 1000
        tmrExecute.Enabled = True
      Else
        lblStatus.Caption = "Status: Running:" & (m_lngStartingTime _
                      - m_lngNumberOfIntervals) & " minutes to start"
      End If
```

We increment `m_lngNumberOfIntervals` by one and exit:

```
      m_lngNumberOfIntervals = m_lngNumberOfIntervals + 1

      Exit Sub
```

Finally, put an error handler in:

```
    tmrStartTestError:

      WriteInfo "tmrExecute: " & Err.Description, Err.Number

    End Sub
```

tmrExecute - Starts Test at Exact Time

This timer will start at exactly the time the test begins. The timer interval will be set to ten seconds here, but you can create a variable to set the timer interval to different values.

Open the sub `tmrExecute_Timer` and setup the error handler:

```
    Private Sub tmrExecute_Timer()

      On Error GoTo tmrExecuteError
```

Next, change the status label to Executing and disable the `tmrStartTest` timer:

```
      lblStatus.Caption = "Status: Executing"
      tmrStartTest.Enabled = False
```

Call the sub `PerformTest` to run the test:

```
      PerformTest
```

Next, we increment the number of iterations by one, and change `lblIterationCount` to show the new number of times the test has been run:

```
m_lngIterations = m_lngIterations + 1
lblIterationCount = m_lngIterations
```

The value in the variable `m_lngNumberOfTests` is the number of times we should run the test. When `m_lngIterations` equals `m_lngNumberOfTests` we have completed the required number of tests and must stop:

```
If m_lngIterations >= m_lngNumberOfTests Then
    tmrExecute.Enabled = False
    lblStatus = "Status: Stopped"
    cmdStart.Enabled = True
End If

Exit Sub
```

Finally, put an error handler in:

```
tmrExecuteError:

    WriteInfo "tmrExecute: " & Err.Description, Err.Number

End Sub
```

Retrieve Records From the Server Object

We could perform a multitude of tests on the server object and ideally we should - but we could be here for weeks, and I'm sure you would rather move on to the next chapter. Therefore, this test simply retrieves records from the database. You could also write a test that tries to have all of the clients change the same product record and see what happens.

Firstly, create the sub called `PerformTest` that we called in the last routine:

```
Private Sub PerformTest()

    On Error GoTo PerformTestError
```

In the first step of the test, we will get the Categories disconnected recordset from the server object:

```
Set m_recCategories = m_objProxy.GetCategories(m_strUserID, m_strPassword)
```

Next, we place all of the records into the combo box and move to the first item in the combo box:

```
While Not m_recCategories.EOF
  cboCategories.AddItem m_recCategories!CategoryName
  m_recCategories.MoveNext
Wend

cboCategories.ListIndex = 0
```

Next, we move the Categories recordset to the first record, and using the value for `CategoryID` from the Categories recordset, we use the server object to get all the products with that ID:

```
m_recCategories.MoveFirst
Set m_recProducts = m_objProxy.GetProducts _
  (m_strUserID, m_strPassword,m_recCategories.Fields("CategoryID").Value)
```

Finally, if we have the records, set the grid's `DataSource` equal to the Products recordset to display them:

```
Set grdProducts.DataSource = m_recProducts

Exit Sub
```

Finally, we build the error trap:

```
PerformTestError:

  WriteInfo "Perform Test Error: " & Err.Description, Err.Number

End Sub
```

Writing Information to a Log File

We want to handle our errors by simply writing them to a log file. However, we haven't yet written the routine that does this writing.

This is a very generic simple sub. You could add another parameter to determine what type of information should be written if you wanted. You could have error information, timing information, and information specific to your application. You could write this information to different log files. You could also write a specific application to analyze the data in the log files and print summary reports. Use your imagination and make your own specialized function.

Create a `Public Sub` called `WriteInfo` with two parameters for error details and error number:

Normally, this would be in a `bas` *module so all forms could use it, but to keep it simple we will include it in this form.*

```
Public Sub WriteInfo(ByVal v_strErrorDescription As String, ByVal _
                        v_lngErrorNumber As Long)

  On Error GoTo WriteInfoError
```

Here's the code to write the information to the log file and include the time this error occurred (this allows you to compare log files and see if all the clients had a problem at this particular time):

```
Write #m_intFileNumber, "Error :" & v_strErrorDescription & " Number " & _
                        v_lngErrorNumber & " Time: " & Now

  Exit Sub
```

Now we'll add an error trap. Since this means there was a problem writing to the log file, we will display the error on the form itself (lstError):

```
WriteInfoError:

  LstError.AddItem "Error In WriteInfo: Description:" & Err.Description & _
                   " Error Number: " & Err.Number
  Err.Clear

End Sub
```

Coding the Rest of the Test Form

We have a few bits and pieces of code that still need to be implemented before we can run the project:

The cmdStop button will stop the test. To do this, we must close all of the files with the Close command, set the number of intervals back to 0, shut off the timers, and enable the cmdStart command button:

```
Private Sub cmdStop_Click()

  lblStatus.Caption = "Status: Stopped"
  Close   'Close the files
  m_lngNumberOfIntervals = 0
  m_lngIterations = 0
  tmrStartTest.Enabled = False
  tmrExecute.Enabled = False
  cmdStart.Enabled=True

End Sub
```

We'll now go into the cmdExit_Click routine and write code notifying the user they are stopping the application; then we'll set the server object m_objProxy to Nothing and end the application:

```
Private Sub cmdExit_Click()

  lblStatus.Caption = "Status: Stopping"
  Set m_objProxy=Nothing
  End

End Sub
```

Finally, we need two Property Lets to hold to set the UserPassword and the UserID:

```
Public Property Let UserPassword(ByVal vNewValue As String)
  m_strPassword = vNewValue
End Property
```

```
Public Property Let UserID(ByVal vNewValue As String)
  m_strUserID = vNewValue
End Property
```

Our client is now complete and ready to be run.

Running the Test Project

The next step is actually running this project. To try a test of this project, set the constant `cStartingTime` equal to a time that is five minutes ahead of your current time. Step through the code and watch how everything is done.

> *You can run through the server code by starting Visual Basic on the Server Machine, and running the server project. You will need to have the server component registered, and Binary Compatibility set for the server component. Once you have the server component running under Visual Basic, begin the client object. You should be able to step through the code in both projects.*

This project is very simple, and at this point can only be used to determine if we can successfully retrieve recordsets using RDS. We can run this test by distributing the client application to several different users, have them run the application, and then review the logs. We can write the logs to a database on a server, or to comma delineated text files that can be read into a database. We can then combine the information from all the clients into one report and see how your different components ran.

The next step would be to add code to determine how efficiently RDS actually works. I modified the client test application a little so we could measure the time it took to perform the test. The code looked something like this, but you can design your own testing procedures:

```
Private Sub PerformTest()

   On Error GoTo PerformTestError

   WriteTimeInfo "Before Test: "

   Set m_recCategories = m_objProxy.GetCategories(m_strUserID, m_strPassword)

   WriteTimeInfo "GetCategories: "

   While Not m_recCategories.EOF
      cboCategories.AddItem m_recCategories!CategoryName
      m_recCategories.MoveNext
   Wend

   cboCategories.ListIndex = 0
   m_recCategories.MoveFirst

   WriteTimeInfo "Before get Product: "

   Set m_recProducts = m_objProxy.GetProducts _
      (m_strUserID, m_strPassword, m_recCategories.Fields("CategoryID").Value)

   WriteTimeInfo "After get Product: "
   Set grdProducts.DataSource = m_recProducts
   Exit Sub

PerformTestError:

   WriteInfo "Perform Test Error: " & Err.Description, Err.Number

End Sub
```

And the `WriteTimeInfo` method would look something like this:

```
Public Sub WriteTimeInfo(ByVal v_strText As String)

   On Error GoTo WriteInfoError

   Write #m_intFileNumber2, v_strText & " Time: " & _
         DateAdd("n", m_lngTimeDifference, Now) & vbCrLf

   Exit Sub

WriteInfoError:

   lstError.AddItem "Error In WriteInfo: Description:" & _
         Err.Description & " Error Number: " & Err.Number
   Err.Clear

End Sub
```

On my network with one user, the time to perform the test is always well below one second. When ten users started making requests, the time to retrieve the Product and Category recordsets averaged between two and three seconds, with a few responses as long as six seconds. It would seem that our system can only handle a few simultaneous requests before it is bogged down. Of course, with clients using disconnected recordsets, it is likely that they will be making requests fairly infrequently. One hundred users working on this system may only occasionally result in ten simultaneous requests. It's possible that this server object, serving one hundred or less users will be OK. Try to use only the tools that are required, and perform extensive tests to find out what is really needed. To be safe, however, I concluded that we ought to think about hosting the component under MTS to improve scalability. We'll explore MTS in the next chapter.

If you are working with Visual Studio Enterprise, than you will have a tool called the **Application Performance Explorer**. The Application Performance Explorer does not come with the Visual Basic Enterprise, only with Visual Studio Enterprise. This tool can do a thorough diagnostics of your components, giving you enough detailed information to fine-tune your components.

Summary

Try expanding out the test application. Step through the server code. Run a few stress tests of your own and see what is happening in the code. You can use `INI` files in a public directory that all the clients have access to for the starting time, length of intervals between requests, and number of tests. The only limit is your imagination. Try writing out what the larger functions and subs are doing in the client application, and turning these into activity diagrams. Using your activity diagrams, add more functionality to the Client Test Application. Take these changes in your diagrams and turn them in Visual Basic code.

In answer to our questions, we can see that the RDS works as advertised. In regards to how well it works without MTS, our component seems to be only able to handle a few simultaneous requests before it gets bogged down. This may be acceptable with a small number of users, but this system would start having serious performance problems if the number of users began to increase to hundreds or thousands of users. If this system were required to handle a large number of users, we would have to upgrade our server component to run under MTS and run another series of tests. Based on tests like these, we will find that using MTS with RDS is a simple, workable DNA solution.

I will show you how to design a server component that runs under MTS in the next chapter. Once again, we will determine what methods are required for the server component by looking at what messages are being passed to and from the server component in our sequence diagrams. We will expand these messages out into activity diagrams to map the internal working of our server component. Once the server component is complete, we will build the Order Entry component of our client.

Building The Final Server Object With MTS

In the previous chapters, we created UML diagrams that we used to design and build our first test version of the server object. Based on the information we learned from our test project, we will now build our server component with no public properties (so it can work with RDS and HTTP) running under MTS.

Once again, the design of our server component will focus on the two messages: return recordset and update recordset. In the course of this chapter, we'll also add one more message for logging an Actor into the database.

We're going to have to revise our activity diagrams for our server object because we're adding the MTS framework to our other frameworks. The MTS framework will provide additional steps in our activity diagrams. In addition, based on the test project we created earlier, we're going to make some improvements to our code.

Therefore, in this chapter we will cover:

❑   Microsoft Transaction Server (MTS)
❑   Modifying our activity diagrams to include MTS
❑   Building our final server object

This chapter will be quite intensive, so strap yourself in and let's mush.

Microsoft Transaction Server (MTS)

Before we can move on to our activity diagrams, we have to understand **Microsoft Transaction Server (MTS)**. Running our component in MTS will add a few activities to our activity diagrams. At the very least, we have to discuss these MTS activities.

MTS is actually something of a misnomer. Although it does having something to do with **transactions**, it can do so much more.

> A transaction can be thought of as a series of steps in which every step must be completed successfully or nothing will happen at all. If one step fails then all steps effectively fail, and any changes that have taken place are rolled back as if they had never happened.

Imagine a customer, named Mr. Anderson, who places an order for fifty cans of soup. The order is put in the system by an Order Entry Clerk and sent to the server object to be saved to the database. The first thing the server object does is remove fifty cans of soup from the Products table in the database. Next, the server object sends the order to the shipping department. Finally, the server object tries to charge Mr. Anderson's credit card for the fifty cans of soup. When the server object tries to do this, the credit card company rejects the charge because Mr. Anderson has bad credit.

Without a transaction, we'd have to put the fifty cans of soup back into the Products table and notify shipping to cancel the order. If there are many steps in a process, going backwards and undoing everything could become extremely complex. Even worse, an error could occur in a step and the previous steps might not be reversed. If shipping isn't notified, Mr. Anderson will get fifty free cans of soup.

If we make all of the steps part of a single transaction, we can undo all of the changes any time before the end of the transaction. Our Add New Order transaction would now consist of the following:

- ❑ Request to add a new order
- ❑ Begin transaction
- ❑ Remove product from Products table
- ❑ Send order to shipping
- ❑ Bill credit card
- ❑ End transaction

If we cancel the transaction at any step before we reach the end transaction point, all the changes made after begin transaction will be undone automatically. This is the power of transactions. When working with databases and middle-tier business logic, transactions are an essential part of maintaining database integrity and simplifying our code.

Another of the major benefits of MTS is that it provides an easy means of **scaling** our components without worrying about implementing a complex infrastructure - all we need to add are a few lines of code here and there.

Scaling Our Components with MTS

MTS is perhaps best thought of as a component manager. It provides scalability by managing your object's lifetimes and through resource pooling.

Object Life Times Under MTS

One of the principal reasons that MTS can easily allow many users to access our objects is that they are only around as long as we need them. When we create an object that is being hosted in MTS, which requires transactional support, the request is intercepted by MTS, which creates an MTS **Context Wrapper** object for our object. Note that our 'real' object is not actually created.

It is only when we actually call a routine on the object that an instance of your object is actually created. This is known as **Just In Time (JIT) activation**. This saves on resources because we don't actually have an instance of the object hanging around until we actually need it. Finally, when the routine ends the 'real' object is destroyed. This is known as **As Soon As Possible (ASAP) deactivation**. The client is completely unaware of any of this happening because it's holding a reference to the Context Wrapper object and not the 'real' object.

Resource Pooling

Another resource saving performed by MTS is that it is able to pool resources. This allows limited resources, such as database connections, to be shared amongst a greater number of clients. Traditionally, a client would be allocated resources for the lifetime of the application. This quickly uses up the available resources and hence limited the number of clients.

Under MTS, the resources are pooled so that clients only demand resources when they need them and release them back into the pool when they are done.

Resource pooling, JIT activation, ASAP deactivation, and many other MTS features are all enabled by another MTS object called the Context object.

Managing Transactions

In order for us to take advantage of many of the features that MTS offers, we need tell MTS when we have finished a transaction and whether it was successful or something went wrong. In order to do this, we need to use the **Context object**. Each of our objects created under MTS has its own Context object. This object contains information about the 'real' object's execution environment, such as transactional status and security information.

More importantly, the Context object also has two methods:

- ❑ `SetComplete`
- ❑ `SetAbort`

If the transaction was successful then we need call `SetComplete`, and the changes will be committed. If for any reason an error occurred, then we need to call `SetAbort` and all changes will be rolled back.

We could therefore represent the transaction sequence as follows:

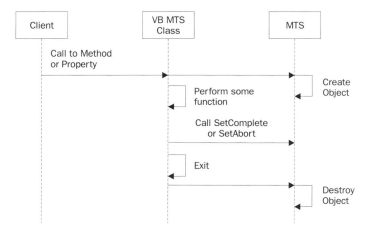

We only have to call `SetComplete` and `SetAbort` in public routines before we exit. In private methods or properties, we don't have to worry about finishing the transaction because we are not ready to destroy the server object. When the private method or property is done, control will be passed back to the calling routine, which will be responsible for telling MTS to `SetAbort` or `SetComplete`. Remember this rule for making MTS properties and methods:

> **Every public method or property must end the transaction, one way or another, before they finish.**

Think of our public methods as the entry and exit points of our object. When we enter, MTS will create the object; when we leave, we'll be good guests and let our host know we are leaving, by calling `SetComplete` or `SetAbort`.

If we need to call several properties or methods, there should be one method that starts the transaction, calls all of the other private routines, and (if everything is successful) the initial method will close the transaction when it is done.

MTS and Database Transactions

MTS also allows us to perform our database updates under transactions. MTS will do this by using an additional component installed with MTS, or SQL Server, called the **Distributed Transaction Coordinator (DTC)**. All communication to the database will occur through the DTC. Because all updates to the databases go through the DTC, it can control these updates, committing or rolling them back when necessary.

The language that DTC uses to communicate with databases is based on a standard, and most databases conform to this standard.

When a method or property of an object hosted in MTS makes a connection to the database, the DTC will automatically start a database transaction. Yet, to end or cancel the transaction, the component must send a message to the DTC through MTS that the transaction is complete, or has failed.

A sequence diagram for a component running under MTS performing updates to the database using an ADO Connection object would look as follows:

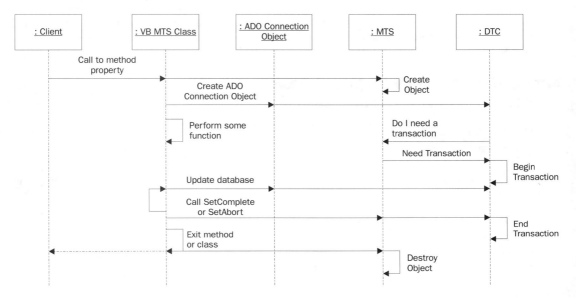

Non-Transactional Objects

The best part of MTS is that it can manage any object, even one that is not participating in a transaction. MTS does not care if our component does not have any transactions: it will still manage our component so that many clients can access it efficiently. When our non-transactional component tells MTS that is done, MTS will destroy our component at the appropriate time, just like it did with transactional components. The only difference is that MTS will not pass any messages onto the DTC.

Security Under MTS

As we mentioned before, MTS can also handle **security**. MTS uses the Windows NT role-based security model. This allows us to assign different roles to different users for a single component. If we get a reference to the Context object, we can determine what a person's role is, and using this role allow different users access to different parts of your program. For example, a manager could see employee salaries, while an employee could only access employee names and phone numbers.

A Stateless Programming Model

As objects in MTS only exist for the length of a single call into a public method, any state that they possess is, therefore, very short-lived. This is a resource saving process, so that the objects are not left holding large sets of data or vital resources longer than absolutely necessary. If a transactional object requires state then we have to pass it in as additional parameters to each method call.

Fortunately for us, because RDS is also a stateless model, we have already designed our object to be stateless.

MTS and Visual Basic

It is very easy to write MTS compatible components with Visual Basic, since all the issues (such as scalability) are handled transparently by MTS. Provided that we use the Context and Control MTS objects (we'll see these in action soon), we should have no problem. However, there are a few issues that do need briefly explaining.

Creating MTS Objects with Visual Basic

Visual Basic provides two ways of creating objects:

- ❏ The New keyword
- ❏ The CreateObject method

MTS works differently with the New keyword and the CreateObject method, and also introduces a third method itself:

- ❏ The CreateInstance method

We'll run through these three ways of creating objects with MTS and Visual Basic now, and then move on to consider how to make these objects support transactions.

The New Keyword

The New keyword, although it acts jut like CreateObject when creating an object from another ActiveX server, actually bypasses some COM processing when it creates an instance of a class within the same server.

Let me explain that a little more practically. Using the New keyword only creates a **Private** instance of the object - that's why we must use it for creating instances of classes with an Instancing property of 1- Private or 2 - PublicNotCreatable. And because it is a private instance, MTS won't know anything about our object: a Context object won't be created for it, and our object won't be able to be involved in any transactions. It will simply run as a regular code.

The CreateObject Method

The CreateObject method is almost the exact opposite of the New keyword - it always uses COM to create an instance of class - regardless of whether the class is in the same server or not.

If an object in MTS is created using CreateObject then MTS will treat it as if it had been created by client; that is, it will get its own context object. This means that it won't contain any information about the context of the component that created it and so will outside of the current transaction.

The CreateInstance Method

The CreateInstance method of the context object is the best way to create objects within MTS. CreateInstance works just like CreateObject except that it performs a bit more work behind the scenes.

Again, let me state that in a more practical fashion. When a new object is created with CreateInstance, MTS copies the context information of the creating object into the new object's Context object. This means the new object will inherit the same security and transactional environment from its creator.

Making Objects Support Transactions

Visual Basic 6 makes it very easy for us to specify that our objects be used in MTS. Each public class now has an MTSTransactionMode property that MTS uses to determine how the object handles transactions:

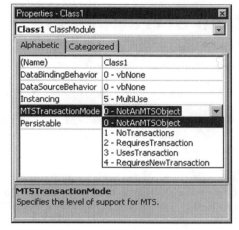

Here are the possible values for this MTSTransactionMode property, and what these values mean to our objects.

NotAnMTSObject

Specifies that the object will not be involved with MTS. This is the default option.

NoTransactions

The class will not support transactions. An object context will still be created, but will not participate in any transactions. This value is useful for when we are just using MTS as a central repository for a component class. With this value, there will not be a transaction as part of the class.

RequiresTransactions

This MTSTransactionMode value mandates that the object must run within a transaction. When a new instance of the object is created, if the client has a transaction already running then the object's context will inherit the existing transaction. If that client does not have a transaction associated with it, MTS will automatically create a new transaction for the object.

UsesTransactions

This choice indicates that should a transaction be available when the object is created, then that object will use the existing transaction. If no transaction exists then it will still run - but without any transactional support.

RequiresNewTransaction

This MTSTransactionMode value indicates that the object will execute within its own transaction. When a new object is created with this setting, a new transaction is created regardless if the client already has a transaction.

If you want to learn more about MTS, then I recommend you try 'Professional MTS and MSMQ with VB and ASP', also published by Wrox Press.

Building the Revised Server Object

We're going to be improving on the test version, which we created in Chapter 10. We're going to improve both the design and implementation, and also finesse our coding techniques.

The improvements in our code will include a more sophisticated technique for handling the updating of the product Units In Stock, additional recordset retrieval methods, and additional update methods. We will also add parameters to our retrieving and updating methods. Our last example used `Private` variables that were being set and retrieved directly in various parts of the code. While this may be acceptable in a small test application, it isn't good coding practice in a large, final application.

Using `Private` variables that can be changed at will by any method or property within the class, usually results in a variable being changed incorrectly somewhere in the code. This is usually impossible to find and can result in hours or even weeks of debugging. By using `ByRef` parameters, we can make sure variables are only changed in routines where we want them to change. If the variable is not supposed to be changed in a routine, we pass it in `ByVal`. If there is a problem with a variable, then the problem could only be located in the places where the variable is passed in by reference. In general, this makes a more readable, less error-prone component. We will discuss this in more detail later.

Setting the Project Up

Open Visual Basic and create a new Visual Basic ActiveX DLL project. Call the Project `prjServer` and the default class `clsServer`.

Set the MTSTransactionMode property of `clsServer` to 2 - RequiresTransaction:

Open up the References dialog and add a reference to the Microsoft ActiveX Data Objects 2.0 Library, Microsoft Remote Data Services Server 2.0 Library and the Microsoft Transaction Server Type Library:

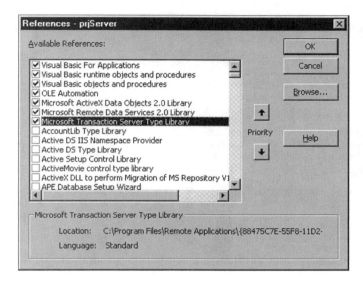

Adding the Declarations

Enter the following declarations into `clsServer`:

```
Option Explicit
```

```
Enum TableName
  e_Customers = 0
  e_OrderDetails = 1
  e_Orders = 2
  e_Products = 3
  e_Shippers = 4
  e_Employees = 5
  e_Suppliers = 6
End Enum

Private Const m_cstrEmployeesQuery As String = "Select * From Employees"
Private Const m_cstrCustomersQuery As String = "SELECT * FROM Customers"
Private Const m_cstrCategoriesQuery As String = "Select * From " & _
        " Categories"
Private Const m_cstrShipperQuery As String="SELECT ShipperID, " & _
        " CompanyName FROM Shippers"
Private Const m_cstrOrderDetailsProductNameQuery As String = _
    "SELECT Products.ProductName, [Order Details].UnitPrice," _
        & " [Order Details].Quantity, [Order Details].Discount, " & _
        " [Order Details].ProductID, [Order Details].OrderID " _
        & " FROM Products INNER JOIN [Order Details] ON " & _
        " Products.ProductID = [Order Details].ProductID "
Private Const m_cstrOrderDetailsQuery As String = "SELECT * From" & _
        " [Order Details]"
Private Const m_cstrProductQuery As String = "SELECT ProductID, " & _
```

```
                  " ProductName, UnitPrice, ReorderLevel, QuantityPerUnit, " & _
                  " UnitsInStock, UnitsOnOrder, Discontinued FROM Products "
     Private Const m_cstrOrdersQuery As String = "Select " & _
              "OrderID,CustomerID,EmployeeID,OrderDate,RequiredDate,ShippedDate," _
              & "ShipVia,Freight,ShipName,ShipAddress,ShipCity,ShipRegion, " & _
              " ShipPostalCode,ShipCountry From Orders "

     Private Const m_cstrCustomersCustomerIDField As String = "CustomerID"
     Private Const m_cstrOrderDetailsOrderID As String = "OrderID"
     Private Const m_cstrOrderDetailsProductNameField As String = "ProductName"
     Private Const m_cstrProductsUnitsInStockField As String = "UnitsInStock"
     Private Const m_cstrOrderDetailsQuantityField As String = "Quantity"
     Private Const m_cstrOrderDetailsProductIDField As String = "ProductID"
     Private Const m_cstrProductsUnitsOnOrderField As String = "UnitsOnOrder"
     Private Const m_cstrProductsReorderLevelField As String = "ReorderLevel"
     Private Const m_cstrOrderDetailsOrderIDField As String = "OrderID"
     Private Const m_cstrProductsProductIDField As String = "ProductID"

     Private Const m_cstrDatabasePath As String = "C:\Microsoft Visual" & _
              " Studio\VB98\Nwind.mdb"

     Private m_objADOConnection As ADODB.Connection

     Private m_strErrorDetails As String
     Private m_strQueryString As String
     Private m_objContext As ObjectContext

     Implements ObjectControl
```

These variables and constants have the following functions:

Variable Name	Function
m_cstrEmployeesQuery m_cstrCustomersQuery m_cstrOrderDetailsQuery m_cstrOrderDetailsProductNameQuery m_cstrCategoriesQuery m_cstrShipperQuery m_cstrProductQuery m_cstrOrdersQuery	Queries have field and table name information in them, and therefore should not be located inside the code. We'll therefore use these constants for our queries. If a field or table name needs to be changed, we only have to redefine the constant. The queries must be in the server component to limit the possible queries the user can perform. Otherwise, a malicious user could pass in a destructive query such as one that will delete all the records in the database.
Implements ObjectControl	The MTS ObjectControl Interface should be used when our component runs under MTS. The interface has three methods that must be exposed: Activate, Deactivate, and ObjectCanBePooled.

Variable Name	Function

`m_cstrProductsUnits_In_StockField`
 	
`m_cstrOrderDetailsOrderIDField`
 	
`m_cstrOrderDetailsProductNameField`
 	
`m_cstrProductsProductIDField`
 	
`m_cstrCustomersCustomerIDField`
 	
`m_cstrOrderDetailsQuantityField`
 	
`m_cstrProductsUnitsOnOrderField`
 	
`m_cstrProductsReorderdLevelField`
 	
`m_cstrOrderDetailsProductIDField`
	Several fields need to be referenced in the code to reconcile values that have changed in the database and in the disconnected recordset while the recordset was at the client. Again, we will use constants to avoid referencing field names in the code.

`m_cstrDatabasePath`	A constant for the name and path to the database. *Change this to your path and database.* It would be better to place this value in an `INI` file or in the registry, but to keep it simple we are using a constant.
`m_objContext`	We will need a reference to the MTS object context. We will use this object context to notify MTS when we are done with our transaction. This variable allows us to communicate with MTS.

*We are using the * in our queries to return all of the fields. In general, this is not a very good practice. In a final release application there will be many different queries, some of which will return only certain fields and others where you will want all fields. To keep it simple we are using the * .*

Also, instead of using string constants for the queries, we could have also used stored procedures in the database.

Coding for MTS

While we intend our object to run under MTS, it would also be nice if it were possible for it to also run without MTS.

For example, we may want to debug our application without the component running under MTS. We may also want to test the component running under both circumstances. There is also the possibility that for some reason MTS is not running on the server. If the object is supposed to run under MTS, but MTS has failed for some reason, we will get an error when we attempt to set any of the Context object properties, or use the Context object methods.

We can code for the two possibilities by checking for the presence of the Context object. If it doesn't exist, we have two options: either to raise an error, or work without the object context (that is, run our component without MTS).

Which option we choose here depends upon the system itself. If the object can still function without MTS, but perhaps very slowly, we might want to allow the component to still run. If there are many simultaneous hits and the object will simply lock up without MTS, we would probably want to raise an error. We can, of course, choose to do both: allow the component to run but still create an error message. The error message could be placed in the event log, written a function to e-mail the administrator, or whatever is appropriate.

For this project, we will allow the function to run without MTS, as the current system doesn't have that many users. If the system later changes, we may have to upgrade the component so that it raises an error when MTS is not running.

Coding the ObjectControl Interface

When we're using a class working under MTS, we won't be using the Initialize and Terminate events of the class. As I said earlier, the real object instance is created and destroyed with each method call. It therefore makes little sense to have to run through any code in these events every time we call a method.

We can avoid this problem by placing any code that was in the Initialize and Terminate events into the Activate and Deactivate events, respectively, of the ObjectControl interface we implemented.

The Activate event is fired the first time a client invokes a method on the object. The Deactivate event is fired every time the method is complete.

Begin by adding the following line of code to the Activate event:

```
Private Sub ObjectControl_Activate()

    Set m_objContext = GetObjectContext

End Sub
```

the call to GetObjectContext returns a reference to the Context for our object, if it's running under MTS. If it's not running under MTS, it will return Nothing. Since GetObjectContext doesn't raise an error when the object is not running under MTS, we can still run our component without MTS.

If we could pass in the UserID and Password to the Activate method, we could create the ADO Connection object in this method. Unfortunately, we cannot add parameters into the Activate event. This means that all of our public methods will need a UserID and a Password parameter to create the ADO Connection object.

In the Deactivate event we need to release resources such as the ADO Connection:

```
Private Sub ObjectControl_Deactivate()

    Set m_objADOConnection = Nothing

    Set m_objContext = Nothing

End Sub
```

We're not quite done yet though. Because we are using the Implements statement Visual Basic is expecting us to provide implementation for all the methods on the ObjectControl interface. There is one remaining method: CanBePooled.

The CanBePooled method allows us to set whether our object can be pooled, rather like other resource type can be pooled. Unfortunately, the current version of MTS has no support for this facility. We do still have to implement is though, so we shall set it to False:

```
Private Function ObjectControl_CanBePooled() As Boolean

    ObjectControl_CanBePooled = False

End Function
```

Methods For the MTS Object Context Properties

Since many of the methods of this object will be creating other objects, and using SetComplete and SetAbort, it makes sense to write a generic function to perform these tasks.

> *As we discussed earlier, when using MTS, objects should be created the* CreateInstance *method of the Context object.*

A Generic CreateInstance Function

This function will use the CreateInstance method of the MTS Context object if it exists; if it does not exist, then it will create the object using the New keyword:

```
Private Function CreateInstance(ProgID As String) As Object

  On Error GoTo CreateInstanceError

  If Not m_objContext Is Nothing Then
    Set CreateInstance = m_objContext.CreateInstance(ProgID)

  Else

    Select Case ProgID

      Case "ADODB.Connection"
          Set CreateInstance = New ADODB.Connection

      Case "ADODB.Recordset"
          Set CreateInstance = New ADODB.Recordset

    End Select

  End If

  Exit Function

CreateInstanceError:

  Err.Raise Err.Number, Err.Source & " CreateInstance" , Err.Description

End Function
```

The Generic SetComplete and SetAbort Methods

These two methods will simply call `SetComplete` or `SetAbort` if the Context object exists:

```
Public Sub SetComplete()

  If Not m_objContext Is Nothing Then
     m_objContext.SetComplete
  End If

End Sub
```

```
Public Sub SetAbort()

  If Not m_objContext Is Nothing Then
     m_objContext.SetAbort
  End If

End Sub
```

Working with the ADO Connection Object

One of the most essential parts of our server object will be our ADO Connection object. This object provides us with connection to the database. As all of our `Public` methods have to interact with the database, we can do nothing until we have the Connection object.

Revisiting the Test ADOConnection Function

The original version of this function, which we made for our test project, did not really use the best possible coding. If you look back at it, you will see our original function returned a string:

```
Public Function ADOConnection(ByVal v_strUserID As String, _
                ByVal v_strPassword As String) As String
```

This was because this one function had to do two completely different things:

- ❏   It was being used by the client to test if a user's ID and Password were valid
- ❏   It was being used by the server object to set the ADO connection

These are two, totally unrelated tasks. If a routine has to perform more then one task, these tasks should at least be related to each other. This is not the case here, so we should make them into two separate routines.

We'll first create a function to set the ADO Connection object and then later we'll create a separate function to test if the UserID and Password are valid.

Making the ADO Connection

Once we've removed the validation from this routine it becomes fairly straightforward.

Our new `SetADOConnection` sub would look as follows:

```
Private Sub SetADOConnection(ByVal v_strUserID As String, _
            ByVal v_strPassword As String)

  On Error GoTo SetADOConnectionError

  Set m_objADOConnection = CreateInstance("ADODB.Connection")

  With m_objADOConnection
      .CursorLocation = adUseClient
      .ConnectionString= "Provider=Microsoft.Jet.OLEDB.3.51;Persist " & _
            "Security Info=False;Data Source=" & m_cstrDatabasePath
      .Open
  End With

  Exit Sub
```

If we wanted to connect through SQL Server to we would use the following `ConnectionString`:

```
.ConnectionString = "Provider=SQLOLEDB.1;Integrated " & _
    " Security=SSPI;Persist Security Info=False;Initial " & _
    " Catalog=Northwind;Data Source=IES-4G8KBH3XSYE" & _
    ";uid=" & v_strUserId & ";pwd=" & v_strPassword
```

Build the error trap like you did last time, except this time raise an error to be passed back to the calling routine. We will create our own error number. This is not technically the best way to assign an error number, but it will do for now.

> We will discuss error handling in more detail in Chapter 12, as this chapter is already complicated enough.

```
SetADOConnectionError:

  Dim lngErrorCounter As Long
  Dim strErrors As String

  strErrors = Err.Number & ": " & Err.Description

  If m_objADOConnection.Errors.Count > 0 Then

      For lngErrorCounter = 0 To m_objADOConnection.Errors.Count - 1
          strErrors = strErrors & _
            m_objADOConnection.Errors(lngErrorCounter).Number & _
            ": " & m_objADOConnection.Errors(lngErrorCounter).Description & vbCrLf
      Next lngErrorCounter

  End If

  Err.Raise 2000 + vbObjectError, "SetADOConnection " & Err.Source, strErrors

End Sub
```

Notice that we made the error source both the name of our function and the name of any source that may be in the Error object. By combining sources like this, the final error message that reaches the client will list all of the methods and objects that this error has passed through. This is extremely useful when debugging.

Retrieving the ADO Connection Object

Once we've called SetADOConnection, we want to be able to retrieve the Connection object created and use it in our code. In our test project, we just allowed our code to use the private Connection object variable whenever it wanted to. This gives us little control over how the variable is actually used, and it could be very easy to accidentally put the variable on the wrong side of the equal sign.

> *Making the mistake of setting the variable equal to something that it should not be can often result in one of the hardest bugs to find, as it is a subtle error that can often be missed as you go through the code. By only allowing your private variables to be set and retrieved in either a function or a property (or a sub by using by reference parameters) you can never make the mistake of setting the routine on the wrong side of an equal sign.*

We will create a function called GetADOConnection that will cause the Visual Basic compiler to raise an error should this happen. Using functions or properties to set and retrieve the Private variables will allow the compiler to make sure we do not place something on the wrong side of the equal sign. We can also do validation checks in our functions and properties that we couldn't do if we just use Private variables.

The function SetADOConnection must be called before calling GetADOConnection so that the m_objADOConnection variable is set to a Connection object (we cannot get a connection that has not been created yet!). Therefore, we will check to see if the variable m_objADOConnection has been set, if it has not, we will raise an error.

Our GetADOConnection function looks as follows:

```
Private Function GetADOConnection() As ADODB.Connection

   If m_objADOConnection Is Nothing Then
      Err.Raise 2001, "GetADOConnection", _
            "Trying to Get Connection prior to setting it"

   Else
      Set GetADOConnection = m_objADOConnection

   End If

End Function
```

We have assigned a value of 2001 for the error. We can use this number on the client to handle this particular error.

Closing the ADO Connection Object

We could simply use the Close method of the Connection object but if for some reason the Connection object doesn't exist then we will get an error.

The CloseADOConnection routine looks like this:

```
Private Sub CloseADOConnection()

   With GetADOConnection
```

```
        If .State = adStateOpen Then
            .Close
        End If

    End With

End Sub
```

Validating UserID and Password

Looking over our use cases, we can see that there is no actual use case for logging-in. We might want to go back to the user to find out the exact procedure - but logging-in is a fairly generic task, so we can create the use case ourselves, or we may already have one from a previous job. Logging-in meets all of the criteria for a use case and would look as follows:

USE CASE: LOG-IN

Overview:
The purpose of this use case is to give the Actor access to the system.

Primary Actors
Sales Representative, Vice President Sales, Sales Manager, Inside Sales Coordinator

Secondary Actors
None

Starting Point
The Actor attempts to enter the system

Ending Point
The Actor is either granted or denied access to the system

Measurable Result
An Actor is granted access to a system

Flow of Events
The Actor enters their UserID and Password
The Actor submits the information to the system
The Actor is granted access to the system

Alternative Flow of Events
The Actor does not put in a valid UserID and is denied access
The Actor does not put in a valid Password and is denied access

Business Rules
Invalid UserID and Password

Use Case Extension
None

Outstanding Issues
None

You could add some more business rules. For example, a rule defining the UserID and Password.

The function that we'll create, to check the UserID and Password, will check if the user is allowed into the database by attempting to make a connection to the database using the private `SetADOConnection` function.

This brings up an interesting point. The `SetADOConnection` function will raise an error if the user is denied access. This error will be passed up to our check UserID and Password function. It wouldn't be too user-friendly to raise this error back to the client if the user is not allowed to use the database. It's possible that the developer of the client may want to ignore an invalid sign-in, and they would have to use `On Error Resume Next` and handle all errors themselves.

It's much friendlier to simply return a value of `False` for the function. If the programmer, making the client, wants to raise an error when the function returns `False` they can. If they don't want to raise an error, they can just ignore the `False` value.

We are still missing one thing, though. It's likely the programmer does want to inform the user that they failed validation on the database. The best way to return the error values is to add an extra parameter that is passed in by reference. We can then set the value of the error variable on the client by setting the by reference parameter in our validation routine.

There is one word of caution here. If we stop to think about it for a moment, By Reference variables are fairly complicated when we are working with a server object. The RDS (DCOM) is providing us a connection between the server object on the server and the client application on the client. A by reference parameter that is being updated on the server must result in the variable on the client also being updated. This requires quite a bit of communication. By Reference parameters are extremely expensive when we are using DCOM or RDS with HTTP.

In this case, we only call this function once when the user initially logs-in. A by reference variable is acceptable here, but by reference variables should generally be used sparingly with server objects.

The activity diagram for this looks as follows:

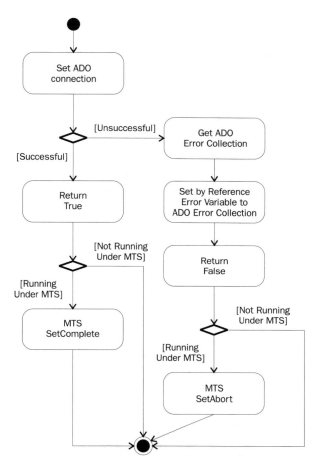

Make a function called `ValidUserIDPassword` with two by value parameters, `v_strUserID` and `v_strPassword`, and one by reference parameter `r_strErrorDetails` with a default value of `Empty`. Add in an error handler:

```
Public Function ValidUserIDPassword(ByVal v_strUserID As String, _
    ByVal v_strPassword As String, Optional ByRef r_strErrorDetails As String _
    = "Empty") As Boolean

On Error GoTo ValidUserIDPasswordError
```

Call the `SetADOConnection` function and try to make a connection to the database. If the connection failed, `SetADOConnection` will raise an error, and we will jump down to the error trap `ValidUserIDPasswordError`. If there is no error, then we will continue to the next line of code:

```
SetADOConnection v_strUserID, v_strPassword
```

If we have not jumped into the error trap, there are no errors and we can set the return value of `ValidUserIDPassword` to `True` and call `SetComplete`:

```
    ValidUserIDPassword = True

  SetComplete
```

Exit out so we don't fall into the error trap:

```
  Exit Function
```

If there was an error making the connection, get the ADO error collection and set the by reference parameter r_strErrorDetails equal to these errors.

```
  ValidUserIDPasswordError:

  If r_strErrorDetails <> "Empty" Then
    r_strErrorDetails = "Error Details:" & Err.Description & vbCrLf & _
          " Error Number: " & Err.Number & vbCrLf & " Error Source: " & _
          "ValidUserIDPassword " & Err.Source
  End If
```

When working with optional parameters, you can only use the IsMissing function to determine if an optional parameter has been passed in if the parameter is a variant. IsMissing does not work with all other data types. This is the reason why I gave the optional parameter a default value: Empty. If the value of the optional parameter is equal to Empty, then we know nothing was passed into this parameter, and you can ignore it. In our case, we are giving the user the option of retrieving the error details with this optional parameter. The client application could then build a message box to inform the user the reason why their log-in failed.

Next, we have to notify MTS that our object is no longer needed. We have had an error, yet do we really need to call SetAbort? SetAbort is used to rollback changes, and we have not actually done any updates or changes in this function.

We can use MTS as an object manager even when we are not technically doing a database transaction. In this case, we are not doing any transaction; we are calling a method in our server object to find out if a user is allowed into the database. We only need to notify MTS that we are done with the server object; both SetComplete and SetAbort will inform MTS that we are done and the server object is no longer needed. We will use SetAbort in all our error traps for consistency:

```
  SetAbort
```

Finally, we will set the return value to False:

```
  ValidUserIDPassword = False

End Function
```

We could also use MTS security to make sure a user is allowed to access the component. MTS security is an advanced topic, so we won't discuss it here.

Our object now has all the basic functionality that it needs to handle MTS and ADO. Now let's move onto creating the functions and methods that will allow our object to fulfill its main purpose.

Retrieving a Recordset

In the last chapter we drew activity diagrams for retrieving Products, Customer and Category recordsets. To keep things simple in our test application, the three different types of data were all retrieved in the same way.

We could build a generic routine to retrieve data for any type of data. This routine will use a Select Case statement to determine the correct type of data to retrieve. Our generic routine would have an activity diagram that would look as follows:

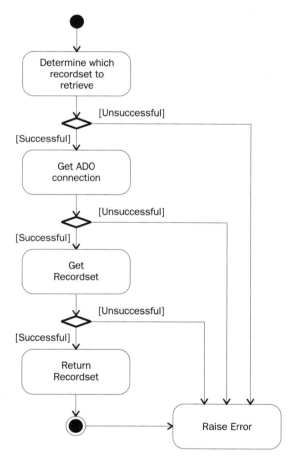

This diagram seems deceptively simple. You have to realize that everything here is pseudo code, and some of these steps are a complex operation in themselves.

Take a look at Determine which Recordset to Retrieve. To determine the recordset, we would need a parameter that would identify which records we want to retrieve. If we make it an enumerated type then the programmer could select the correct type from a drop list if they were programming in Visual Basic. Using that parameter in a Select Case statement we would be able to select the correct record. Sounds good so far.

Now, we'll also want to retrieve different views of the different tables. For example, we may only want to retrieve an Employee's last name and ID when filling in an order, but we might not want their address and other information. On the other hand, when the manager is editing an employee's record they will want all of the information on the employee. This means that we might want several different views for each table.

Let's say we want three different views of each table. Since there are seven tables, we will need seven times three or twenty-one `Cases` in our `Select Case`. Figuring five lines of code per case that comes out to 105 lines of code just to figure out which recordset we need. Have you ever tried to debug a function with over 100 lines of code? It isn't much fun. Once we start adding sophisticated error handling and checking, then this routine could quickly bloat to several hundred lines of code. We may have made one super function that can be used to retrieve any recordset, but we have also created a huge, bloated monster that could be a maintenance and debugging nightmare.

A good rule of thumb is that functions should do as few things as possible. Everything in the routine should be related to accomplishing one task. The task Update Order will add the order to the database, bill the customer, and remove products from stock. There is no way to make it smaller without sacrificing good design structure. Each activity, though, is part of one single task: Updating an Order.

> *There is no connection between retrieving an Order and retrieving a Customer, it just so happens that we do both of these things in the same way.*

This does mean that our server component will have a lot of separate methods in it to handle retrieving different types of data. Yet, these methods are small, perform only one task, and it will be very clear to the programmer using the object which method to use when. If two tasks are part of a larger task, they belong in one routine. If two tasks do similar things (i.e. they are based on the same pattern) but are not part of some larger task, they should be in separate routines and there should be a private function that performs the tasks they have in common.

Creating the Generic GetRecordset Method

Not having a super-function to return all possible recordsets doesn't mean that there is no room for creating generic routines. All the Return Recordset functions that we are about to code will all require that a new recordset with specific properties be created. It therefore makes more sense if we create a generic `GetRecordset` routine that does this for all the Return Recordset routines.

The activity diagram for the generic method `GetRecordset` looks as follows:

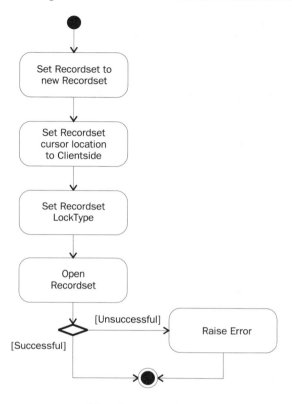

Let us now turn these activities into Visual Basic code:

```
Private Sub GetRecordSet(ByRef r_recRecordset As ADODB.Recordset, _
                         ByVal v_strSource)

    On Error GoTo GetRecordSetError

    Set r_recRecordset = New ADODB.Recordset
    r_recRecordset.CursorLocation = adUseClient
    r_recRecordset.Open _
            v_strSource, GetADOConnection, adOpenStatic, adLockOptimistic

    Exit Sub

GetRecordSetError:

    Err.Raise Err.Number, "ReturnRecordSet" & Err.Source, Err.Description

End Sub
```

You'll note that we have passed our recordset parameter in by reference. This is so that any changes we make will actually be made to our recordset variable.

While passing parameters by reference between the client object and the server object is an expensive task, when it is done within the server component there is no extra overhead. This is because everything within the object is in the same process.

Now the generic method is in place we can start to deal with some more specific retrieval functions.

Creating the Function to Return a Products Recordset

Now that we've created a generic GetRecordset routine our activity diagram looks as follows:

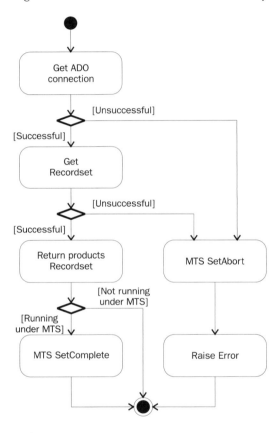

This function will require three parameters:

Parameter Name	Purpose
v_strUserID and v_strPassword	These are needed because the server object does not maintain state, and we must pass these in every time.
v_strParameter	v_strParamater is an optional parameter that can be used to provide information for the WHERE clause. For example, if you want only Products with the Category of "Beverage" this parameter could be set to Where Category = 'Beverage'.

Begin by creating a function called `ReturnProductRecordset` with the three above variables:

```
Public Function ReturnProductsRecordSet(ByVal v_strUserID As String, ByVal _
    v_strPassword As String, Optional ByVal v_strParameter As String) As _
    ADODB.Recordset
```

Declare a temporary recordset variable that can be used to place the records in, and if successful, return to the client. Put in an error handler:

```
Dim recProducts As ADODB.Recordset

On Error GoTo ReturnProductsRecordSetError
```

We have to first create an ADO Connection object using the `SetADOConnection` object:

```
SetADOConnection v_strUserID, v_strPassword
```

Notice that our activity diagram has a decision point here; if there is an error, we are supposed to raise the error, cancel the transaction and exit the Function. Where is this code?

Well, we set an error handler in our first line of code. Therefore, if there is an error, the error will be passed to `ReturnProductsRecordset`, which will then jump into its error trap. The error trap will provide all of the activities listed in the activity diagram for the error path.

Next we call `GetRecordset`, passing in the temporary Products recordset and the query to retrieve the record:

```
GetRecordSet recProducts, m_cstrProductQuery & v_strParameter
```

If everything was successful, return the recordset:

```
Set ReturnProductsRecordSet = recProducts

Set recProducts.ActiveConnection = Nothing
```

Before we leave the function, we must call `SetComplete` to let MTS know that we are done with this object. Once again, we have not made any changes to the database. This method is using MTS to manage the server object, not to manage a database transaction:

```
SetComplete
```

We must now close the connection, destroy our local variable and exit the function so we do not fall into the error trap:

```
CloseADOConnection
Set recProducts = Nothing

Exit Function
```

Write the error trap:

```
ReturnProductsRecordSetError:

  CloseADOConnection
  SetAbort

  Err.Raise Err.Number, "ReturnProducts" & " " & Err.Source & " " & _
      m_strErrorDetails

End Function
```

Now that we've built one of these Return Recordset functions we can knock up the others in no time. As we saw with the Test project all these routines are very similar.

Creating the Function to Retrieve a Customer Recordset

It probably will not surprise you that our Return Customer activity diagram looks practically the same as the Return Products activity diagram. It looks as follows:

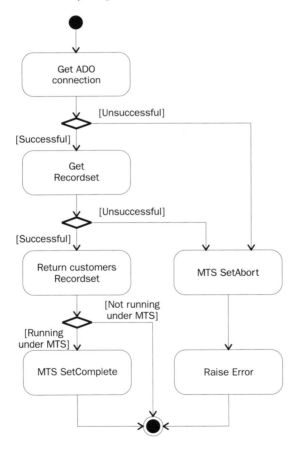

The code for this function would be:

```
Public Function ReturnCustomerRecordSet(ByVal v_strUserID As String,ByVal _
        v_strPassword As String, Optional ByVal v_strParameter As String) As _
        ADODB.Recordset

  Dim recCustomers As ADODB.Recordset

  On Error GoTo ReturnCustomerRecordSetError

  SetADOConnection v_strUserID, v_strPassword

  GetRecordSet recCustomers, m_cstrCustomersQuery & v_strParameter

  Set recCustomers.ActiveConnection = Nothing

  Set ReturnCustomerRecordSet = recCustomers

  SetComplete
  CloseADOConnection
  Set recCustomers = Nothing

  Exit Function

ReturnCustomerRecordSetError:

  CloseADOConnection
  SetAbort

  Err.Raise Err.Number, "ReturnCustomers" & Err.Source, _
      Err.Description

End Function
```

Creating the Other Get Functions

Now that we've created two Return Recordset methods the rest are easy:

```
Public Function ReturnOrdersRecordSet(ByVal v_strUserID As String, _
    ByVal v_strPassword As String, _
    Optional ByVal v_strParameter As String) As ADODB.Recordset

  Dim recOrders As ADODB.Recordset

  On Error GoTo ReturnOrdersRecordSetError

  SetADOConnection v_strUserID, v_strPassword

  GetRecordSet recOrders, m_cstrOrdersQuery & v_strParameter
  Set recOrders.ActiveConnection = Nothing
  Set ReturnOrdersRecordSet = recOrders

  GetADOConnection.Close
  SetComplete
  Set recOrders = Nothing

  Exit Function

ReturnOrdersRecordSetError:
```

```
      SetAbort
      Err.Raise Err.Number, "ReturnOrders" & " " & Err.Source, _
         m_strErrorDetails

   End Function

   Public Function ReturnOrderDetailsRecordSet(ByVal v_strUserID As String, _
      ByVal v_strPassword As String, _
      Optional ByVal v_strParameter As String = "Empty") As ADODB.Recordset

      Dim strReturnValue As String
      Dim recOrderDetails As ADODB.Recordset

      On Error GoTo ReturnOrderDetailsRecordSetError

      SetADOConnection v_strUserID, v_strPassword

      If v_strParameter <> "Empty" Or v_strParameter <> "" Then
            GetRecordSet recOrderDetails, m_cstrOrderDetailsProductNameQuery _
               & " " & v_strParameter
      Else
            GetRecordSet recOrderDetails, m_cstrOrderDetailsProductNameQuery
      End If

      Set recOrderDetails.ActiveConnection = Nothing
      Set ReturnOrderDetailsRecordSet = recOrderDetails

      GetADOConnection.Close
      SetComplete
      Set recOrderDetails = Nothing

      Exit Function

   ReturnOrderDetailsRecordSetError:

      GetADOConnection.Close
      SetAbort
      Err.Raise Err.Number, "ReturnOrderDetails" & " " & Err.Source, _
         m_strErrorDetails

   End Function
```

It's a short step to also add routines for Employees and Shippers.

Updating the Database

Our server component now has all the necessary methods to pull data, in the form of recordsets, from the database. That was the easy part. All we really had to do was choose what view we wanted and then read the data.

Now we come to the tricky part - writing data back to the database. In the previous chapter we spent some time discussing how to handle such issues as multiple disconnected recordsets and conflicts that might arise as a result. You'll see some of what we developed in the last chapter here but we'll also consider some additional problems that might occur.

When we start getting into updating records, we may have to start looking at the use cases and the rules associated with them before we can decide how to make some of the update methods.

A Generic Update Method

We steered away from making a generic `Get` method because we could have had so many queries that we would end up with a huge `Select Case`. When it comes to the `Update` methods, we don't have to worry about views and so our `Select Case` statement will only have four branches. The whole statement should take about fifteen lines of code so is within acceptable limits.

Our generic function will be very simple and do the following:

- ❏ Determine which table is being updated
- ❏ Call the correct function to update the recordset
- ❏ Call `SetComplete` if there were no errors
- ❏ Call `SetAbort` to cancel the transaction if there were errors

Creating a generic Update routine that is Public allows us to make the more specific Updates Private so that the transaction can be set and controlled by this routine.

The activity diagram for `UpdateRecordset` would therefore be as follows:

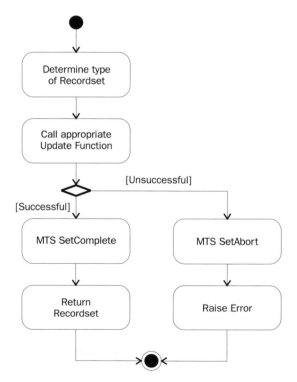

Our `UpdateRecordset` function will have the following parameters:

Parameter Name	Type	Purpose
`v_strUserID`	String	Required user ID for making ADO connection.
`v_strPassword`	String	Required user password for making ADO connection.
`v_recClientRecordset`	Recordset	Recordset being passed from the client that has pending changes. These changes must be added to the database.
`v_eName`	An enumerated type	The enumerated type `TableName` is a list of all of the tables. It's Public and can be used in the client as well. We defined this enum in the declarations section of this class.
`v_strWhereClause`	String	Optional parameter for Queries.

Begin by making a public method called `UpdateRecordset` that has the above parameters:

```
Public Function UpdateRecordset(ByVal v_strUserID As String, _
        ByVal v_strPassword As String, _
        ByVal v_recClientRecordSet As ADODB.Recordset, _
        ByVal v_eName As TableName, _
        ByVal v_strWhereClause As String) As ADODB.Recordset
```

We are not passing the recordset variables in by reference as this function will be called many times and by reference is very expensive when working with DCOM or RDS over HTTP.

Add an error handler and set the ADO Connection object:

```
On Error GoTo UpdateRecordsetError

SetADOConnection v_strUserID, v_strPassword
```

Next, we will determine which record to use with a `Select Case`. Once we know which records are being updated we can call the appropriate method:

```
Select Case v_eName

  Case e_Customers
     Set UpdateRecordset = UpdateCustomerRS(v_recClientRecordSet)

  Case e_Products
     Set UpdateRecordset = UpdateProductsRS(v_recClientRecordSet)

  Case e_OrderDetails
     Set UpdateRecordset = UpdateOrderDetailsRS(v_recClientRecordSet)
```

```
       Case e_Orders
          Set UpdateRecordset = UpdateOrderRS(v_recClientRecordSet)

   End Select
```

If the update was successful, call `SetComplete`:

```
   SetComplete
```

Close the ADO connection object:

```
   CloseADOConnection

   Exit Function
```

Create the error trap:

```
   UpdateRecordsetError:

   CloseADOConnection
   SetAbort

   m_strErrorDetails = "Error Number: " & Err.Number & " Error " & _
             "Description: " & Err.Description
   Err.Raise Err.Number, "ReturnCustomers" & " " & Err.Source, m_strErrorDetails

   End Function
```

Now that the generic routine is in place we need to code the four Update methods that are called. Although there is a great deal of similarity between them, they all have their own particular considerations.

Creating the UpdateCustomer Function

We've already seen the basics of the `UpdateCustomerRS` function in the `UpdateProduct` routine of the previous chapter.

> *The reason why we're not creating* `UpdateProductRS` *first is because Updating Products has some new considerations but Updating Customers is almost identical.*

To keep this function simple, we are not going to handle any conflicts arising from a Customer record being edited by more than one person. This doesn't seem too much of a cheat because realistically, a Customer record should not be being changed by two people at the same time. If a conflict does occur, `UpdateCustomerRS` will simply raise an error.

The steps for Updating Customers are:

- ❑ Set local recordset variable equal to passed in client recordset
- ❑ Set ADO Connection
- ❑ Check if it's a new customer or an edit
- ❑ If new simply update

❏ If edit, turn off error handler
❏ Perform batch update
❏ If conflict raise error
❏ Close connection
❏ Return recordset

The activity diagram will look quite reminiscent to that for Update Product in the previous chapter:

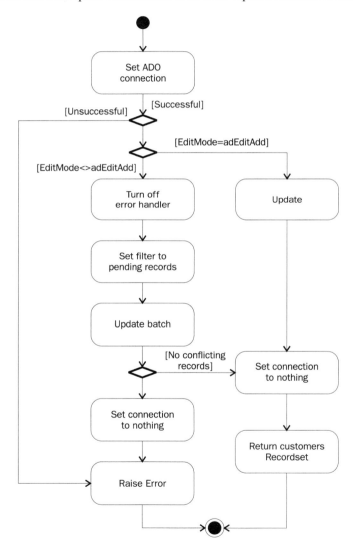

Start the function by setting a local recordset variable to the passed in Customer recordset:

```
Private Function UpdateCustomerRS(ByVal v_recClientRecordSet As Recordset)
```

```
        Dim recCustomers As ADODB.Recordset

        Set recCustomers = v_recClientRecordSet
        Set recCustomers.ActiveConnection = GetADOConnection
```

You'll see from the activity diagram that there is a decision at his point. This is because updating the recordset can occur in two situations:

- ❑ Adding a new customer
- ❑ Editing an existing customer

We can tell if the update is adding a new record or simply editing an existing record by checking the `EditMode` property of the Recordset object.

```
        If recCustomers.EditMode = adEditAdd Then
```

Adding a new Customer is easy all we have to do is call Update. Other updates have a few more complications, and we'll get to them in due time:

```
            recCustomers.Update
```

Editing an existing record is trickier as we have to perform a batch update and then check for conflicting records:

```
        Else
            On Error Resume Next

            recCustomers.Filter = adFilterPendingRecords
            recCustomers.UpdateBatch adAffectGroup
            recCustomers.Filter = adFilterConflictingRecords
```

In this case, we simply want to raise an error if there are any conflicts. In some of the other updates, however, we will need to do something about it:

```
            If recCustomers.RecordCount > 0 Then
                Err.Raise 2009, "UpdateCustomerRS " & Err.Source, _
                        "Customer Update Conflict"
            End If

        End If
```

Finally, close the connection and return the recordset.

```
            recCustomers.Filter = adFilterNone
            Set recCustomers.ActiveConnection = Nothing
            Set UpdateCustomerRS = recCustomers
            Set recCustomers = Nothing

        End Function
```

Now we've seen the basics of an `UpdateRS` function, let's consider a more complex example.

Updating Products

The Products table can be updated in two different ways, changes in the Units In Stock field when an order is placed, and when product information is changed because of a change in inventory, product name, etc. If we look at the use cases associated with Products (Update, Edit and Delete Product use cases), we can see that these can affect all of the Products table's fields except ProductID. It would be highly unlikely that two people in charge of Products would change the same product at exactly the same time. In our case, there is only one person in charge of products anyway.

Scenarios

What would happen, though, if someone accidentally knocked a whole case of *Rössle Sauerkraut* off the top shelf while doing inventory, destroying five cans? The person in charge of products would have to remove five cans of *Rössle Sauerkraut* from the Products table.

However, adding or removing items from the inventory is something that is not only done by the person in charge of Products; the Order Entry clerks also do it when they are taking orders. Imagine the following scenario:

The Products person goes to the Edit Product screen and pulls up information on *Rössle Sauerkraut*. The Order Entry person takes an order for four cans of *Rössle Sauerkraut* and sends the order to the database. Four cans of *Rössle Sauerkraut* are removed from the database. The Products person removes five cans of *Rössle Sauerkraut*, but the number of products that is on the Products person's client computer does not show the cans removed by the Order Entry person. When the Products person goes to update the information, there will be a conflict.

These descriptions of what may happen are called **Scenarios**.

> **A scenario shows the details of how an actor interacts with the system using real data.**

There are an unlimited number of possible scenarios. Working out a few, representative scenarios, helps us see the different ways an Actor uses the system. Scenarios can be grouped by the tasks that they accomplish. These tasks will then become a use case. There will only be a limited number of use cases that describe these single tasks. A scenario represents one of the many different real occurrences of that single task. By looking at several scenarios for a single task, one can see all the possible steps in the task and all of the possible alternative flows.

We will have to add activities into our activity diagrams that deal with these conflicts, and add code into our Update methods to reconcile these differences. Keep in mind that it is also possible that the Products person makes the update first and that the Customer's update will need to be reconciled. We can also see that our current Create Order use case is not complete. We have not mapped out any of the details of how the database is actually updated. It's fairly common to find that your initial use cases are not complete, and that you have to gather more information. Let us turn to our Create Order use case first.

As each order is placed and updated to the database, the products ordered must be subtracted from the Units In Stock for that product. Looking back at our Business Rules associated with Order Entry, we see that we do not have any rules about removing the ordered products from stock.
We are also missing Business Rules on what to do when there is not enough of a product in stock to fill an order, an ordered product is out of stock, or a particular product is running low. These are all situations that must have rules associated with them. We would obviously need to ask a few more questions to our users.

Extending the Use Cases

Looking at the original use case, we see that we have a step in our use case where the Order is saved to the database. This is actually another full use case, it has a beginning (the Actor requests to save the Order), it has an ending (the Order is either saved or not saved) and it has an outcome (an Order is added to the database). All of our missing Business Rules would belong to this new Save Order use case. Save Order use case would extend our already existing Create Order use case. It would look as follows:

USE CASE: SAVE ORDER

Overview
The purpose of this use case is to update the database with the Order information, remove ordered items from stock, and bill the customer.

Primary Actor
Sales Person

Secondary Actor
None

Starting Point
The Actor requests to save an order

End Point
An Order is saved or not saved to the database

Measurable Result
The Order is added to the database

Flow of Events
The Actor requests an Order be saved

Business Rules
Remove ordered Products from Units in Stock
Bill Customer

Use Case Extension
None

Outstanding Issues
None

While it may seem strange to be removing items before they are actually shipped, this should not create a problem. We can perform a query on the Order Details table that retrieves all of the products that have not shipped, i.e. there is no entry for the shipped date. If this query is grouped by product, we can determine the number of units of each product that have been ordered but not shipped. If we add this number to the current units in stock, we will get the number of units that are actually in stock. Thus, if we need to do an inventory of the products, we can quickly determine the number of units that are actually in stock.

Create Order use case will now look as follows:

USE CASE: CREATE ORDER

Overview
The main purpose of this use case is to create a new product order for a customer.

Primary Actor
Sales Representative

Secondary Actor
None

Starting Point
The Actor requests to make a new order.

End Point
An Order is either created or cancelled.

Measurable Result
An Order is created.

Flow of Events
The actor received the phone call from a customer. The actor is asked by the customer to place an order. The actor opens up the order entry form. The actor retrieves the name and address from the customer. The actor enters the name in the system. The actor confirms that the customer's personal information is correct. If the information is correct, the actor requests the order information. If the customer information is incorrect the actor updates the customer information. The actor selects a product category. The actor selects the products. The actor types a quantity for each product. The actor selects a shipper. The actor confirms with the customer that all the information is correct. The actor completes the order details. The actor saves to the database.

Business Rules
Restrict Order Create
Customer can place Orders
Order
Order Fields

Use Case Extension
Add Customer
Edit Customer
Save Order

Outstanding Issues
None

You may be wondering why we haven't created a use case for Remove Ordered Products from Units In Stock. The main reason it cannot be a use case is that nothing external to the system is requesting these items to be removed. An internal process (the request to update orders) is making a request to remove items from stock. No Actor is actually making this request. This has to be a Business Rule.

When we actually sit down and try to figure out how to code all of these rules, we want to try to keep things as simple as possible. Let's imagine that we decide to keep a Products recordset on the client side, and adjust this recordset's Units In Stock field as items are added to Order Details. When we return this Product recordset to the server, we will first have to reconcile it with the information in the database (as it is possible that the Units In Stock have changed by someone else placing an order).

On the other hand, we could also make no changes to the Products recordset on the client. In this case, the client's Product recordset would only be used to let the Order Entry Clerk know what the different products are and how many are in stock at the time the order began. The adjustment to the Units In Stock field would occur on the server object instead. When an Order is sent to the server to be saved, the server object would get a copy of the Products table, change the Units In Stock field for each item ordered, and then save the changes. As long as the records were locked as the edits were made, there would be no need to for any reconciliation. This is definitely a lot easier then making the changes on the client side and later reconciling values. After an Order is completed, the client application could request an updated Product recordset from the server object.

In the case of the Products person changing the Units In Stock, the changes would obviously have to be made on the client. We will look at how both of these different situations are actually handled. Let's continue with the Create Order. Using these new rules and use cases, and the MTS, ADO, and three-tier frameworks we will make the activity diagrams.

Updating Products Directly

The Products person will be directly manipulating the Products table. We only have one Products person, so conflicts should only arise while editing a record in the Units In Stock field. This is because sales people are entering orders and constantly changing the Units In Stock field. When we updated customers we considered all conflicts an error. This doesn't hold for Updating Products. We must first try to reconcile all conflicts.

The steps for Updating Products are therefore as follows:

- ❑   Pass a copy of the client's Products recordset into the `UpdateProductsRS` function
- ❑   Test to see if it's a new Product or an edit
- ❑   If it's new then add new product
- ❑   If it's an edit then create local Products recordset and set it equal to client recordset
- ❑   Set local Products recordset ADO Connection
- ❑   Set local Products recordset to `PendingChanges` to limit records to those that were changed
- ❑   Batch update the Products recordset
- ❑   Reconcile any conflicts. If there were no errors, set connection object to nothing, remove the filter, return the recordset, and close the ADO connection
- ❑   If there were any conflicts or error raise an error

The activity diagram would look something like this:

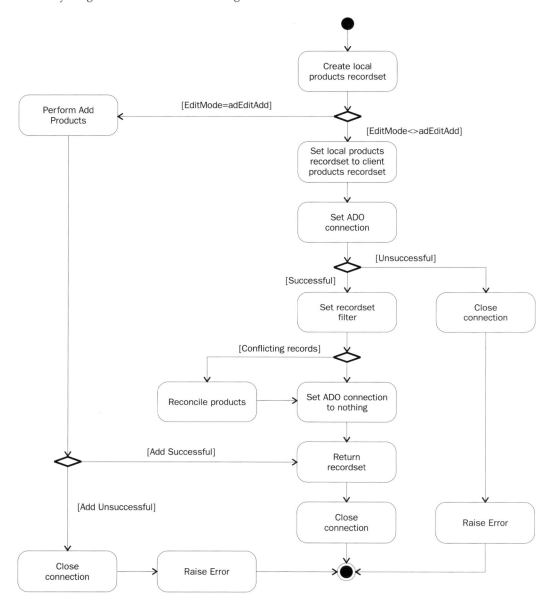

Reconcile Products is a complete function and will have its own activity diagram.

Creating the UpdateProducts Method

The Update Products function will perform in two completely different ways depending on whether we are adding a new record, or updating an existing record:

❑ If we are working with an existing record, we must take into account the possibility of there being a conflict in the records.

❑ If we are adding a new record, then we do not have to be concerned about reconciling records.

Make the `UpdateProductsRS` function with one ADO recordset parameter, `v_recClientRecordset`, and a return type of ADO Recordset:

```
Private Function UpdateProductsRS(ByVal v_recClientRecordSet As _
        ADODB.Recordset) As ADODB.Recordset
```

Create a Products recordset variable and a long variable that we'll need later loop through the fields:

```
Dim recProducts As ADODB.Recordset
Dim lngFieldCounter As Long
```

Set up the error handling:

```
On Error GoTo UpdateProductsRSError
```

Then add the main decision branch for adding a new record or editing an existing:

```
If recProducts.EditMode = adEditAdd Then
```

We will begin with adding a new record. The Products table has an auto-incrementing ProductID field. However, in order for this to work we need a continuous connection to the database. If we call the `AddNew` method on a disconnected Products recordset, it can not assign a value to the ProductID field. We will therefore have to create a recordset variable that we can attach to the database using a server-side cursor - `recProducts`. We can then perform an `AddNew` on the recordset, and the database will supply us with the next available ProductID. We can then set all of the fields in the connected recordset, `recProducts`, to the new values that were passed in from the client in the disconnected recordset variable, `v_recClientRecordset`.

We will create the connected recordset by performing a query on the Products table requesting the record with `ProductID = 0`. As there is no record with this value, we will get a recordset with no values. We can then use this recordset to perform an `AddNew`.

Begin by creating the new recordset using the `CreateInstance` function we made earlier:

```
Set recProducts = CreateInstance("ADODB.Recordset")
```

Set the `Connection`, the `LockType`, the `CursorLocation`, and open the recordset:

```
With recProducts
        .Source = m_cstrProductQuery & " Where " & _
            m_cstrProductsProductIDField & "=" & 0
        .ActiveConnection = GetADOConnection
        .LockType = adLockPessimistic
        .CursorLocation = adUseServer
        .CursorType = adOpenKeyset
        .Open
```

Start an `AddNew`:

```
        .AddNew
```

Loop through all of the fields of the disconnected recordset to map their values to the corresponding fields on the connected recordset:

```
        For lngFieldCounter = 0 To v_recClientRecordSet.Fields.Count - 1
            If Not IsNull(v_recClientRecordSet.Fields(lngFieldCounter).Value) Then
                .Fields(v_recClientRecordSet.Fields(lngFieldCounter).Name)= _
                        v_recClientRecordSet.Fields(lngFieldCounter).Value
            End If
        Next
```

No we will attempt to perform an update. We don't have to worry about conflicts as this is a new record:

```
        .Update
    End With
Else
```

When we are editing, we could have a conflict. To handle this, we will have to check the records using a reconciliation function.

Since the client recordset is passed in `ByVal`, we cannot make any changes to it. We will therefore use our local recordset variable equal to the client variable that we can manipulate.

Start by setting the local recordset variable equal to the client recordset variable:

```
    Set recProducts = v_recClientRecordset
```

Set the active connection:

```
    Set recProducts.ActiveConnection = GetADOConnection
```

Shut off the error handle so an error is not raised if there are conflicting records:

```
    On Error Resume Next
```

Set the filter to pending records:

```
    recProducts.Filter = adFilterPendingRecords
```

Attempt the update:

```
    recProducts.UpdateBatch adAffectGroup
```

Using the `adFilterConflictingRecords` filter we can reduce our recordset to rows containing conflicts:

```
recProducts.Filter = adFilterConflictingRecords
```

We can test for conflicts by checking the `RecordCount` property of the recordset. If there no conflicts all records would have been filtered out and so the count would be zero. A count of anything else indicates that there are conflicts. We want to try and reconcile the conflicts and so we'll call a separate function (which we'll build next) to handle the reconciliation for us.

However, suppose there was an error in the Reconcile function. This would also cause `UpdateProductsRS` to fail, all because of a few records. This would rollback everything we'd accomplished, i.e. all the records that didn't have a conflict. This seems counter productive and the most obvious way to avoid this happening is if we started a new transaction for the reconciliation. So we could code:

(Do not enter this code!)

```
If recProducts.RecordCount > 0 Then
   GetADOConnection.BeginTrans

   If ReconcileProducts(recProducts) Then
       GetADOConnection.RollbackTrans
   End If

End If
```

Looks great, but there is one serious flaw in this logic. MTS does not support nested transactions.

The above code tries to start a second transaction within the first. Remember, we built our component to run under transactions, which means a transaction will have begun when our component was initialised. This will be the first transaction. The above code attempts to start a second one. This is a **nested transaction**.

> **MTS does not support nested transactions! You can run separate concurrent transactions but not transactions with transactions.**

There are some fairly complicated ways to perform separate transactions. These can involve creating another component that runs under transactions, and calling this component from your current component. We won't get into these methods, as we can solve the problem in a much easier way.

Our solution is to try to the fix the conflicting records one record at a time. If our attempt to fix the record fails, we will move on to the next record. In this way, we'll only update the conflicting records that can be fixed, and ignore the ones that cannot be fixed. The correct code would simply be:

```
If recProducts.RecordCount > 0 Then
   Dim strReturn
   strReturn = ReconcileProducts(recProducts)
   If strReturn <> "" then
       Err.Raise 2011, "UpdateProducts " & _
          Err.Source, "Can not reconcile products" & strReturn
   End If
End If
```

Next, we shut the filter off and clean up:

```
        recProducts.Filter = adFilterNone

    End If

    Set recProducts.ActiveConnection = Nothing
    Set UpdateProductsRS = recProducts

    CloseADOConnection
    Set recProducts = Nothing

    Exit Function
```

Finally, we set the error handling:

```
    UpdateProductsRSError:

        recProducts.Filter = adFilterNone
        Set recProducts.ActiveConnection = Nothing
        CloseADOConnection

        Err.Raise Err.Number, "Error UpdateProductsRS" & " " & _
            Err.Source, Err.Description

    End Function
```

Now we have to code the `ReconcileProducts` function that caused so much trouble earlier.

Creating the Reconcile Products Function

Although we created a `Reconcile` function in the previous chapter, because we can't use nested transactions we are going to have to rewrite it so that we check each conflicting record in turn. The basic algorithm to reconcile the Units In Stock will remain the same though.

Our new activity diagram will look like this:

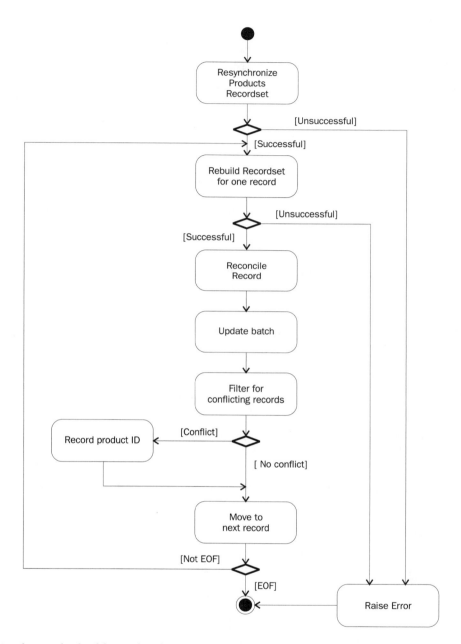

The function begins by building a local recordset variable. This variable will contain the product that has a `ProductID` equal to one of the conflicting records. We'll perform an edit on the local recordset variable, and set the value of the Units In Stock field of the local variable, the one we are checking for a conflict, equal to the value passed in from the client.

Begin by declaring the required variables:

```
Private Function ReconcileProducts(ByRef r_recProducts As _
                ADODB.Recordset) As String

 Dim recProducts As New ADODB.Recordset
 Dim strError As String
```

Set the error handler and initialize the recordset variable:

```
 On Error GoTo ReconcileProductsError

 Set recProducts = CreateInstance("ADODB.Recordset")
```

Call the `Resynch` method, like before, to get the underlying values currently in the database:

```
 r_recProducts.Resync adAffectGroup, adResyncUnderlyingValues
```

Start the loop to iterate through all the rows that are conflicting:

```
 Do Until r_recProducts.EOF
```

For each row, rebuild the recordset variable by setting the `ProductID` of the query equal to the current conflicting row:

```
 With recProducts
     .Source = m_cstrProductQuery & " WHERE " & m_cstrProductsProductIDField _
         & "=" & r_recProducts.Fields(m_cstrProductsProductIDField)
     .ActiveConnection = GetADOConnection
     .LockType = adLockPessimistic
     .CursorLocation = adUseServer
     .CursorType = adOpenKeyset
     .Open
```

Now we will set the Units in Stock Field in the local recordset variable equal to the value in the recordset from the client:

```
 If Not IsNull(r_recProducts.Fields(m_cstrProductsUnitsInStockField).Value) _
    Then
         .Fields(m_cstrProductsUnitsInStockField).Value = _
             r_recProducts.Fields(m_cstrProductsUnitsInStockField).Value
 End If

 With .Fields(m_cstrProductsUnitsInStockField)
     .Value = _
         r_recProducts.Fields(m_cstrProductsUnitsInStockField).UnderlyingValue _
         + (.Value - _
             recProducts.Fields(m_cstrProductsUnitsInStockField).OriginalValue)

 End With
```

Note that we are only checking for conflicts in the Units In Stock field. We are ignoring the other fields, but in a real application you should do something to check if perhaps another field was the problem.

Next, we will once again try to update the record:

```
        .UpdateBatch
```

We'll check for problems once again by checking for conflicting records. At this point, there should not be any, as we have a lock on the recordset at the moment:

```
        .Filter = adFilterConflictingRecords
```

If there were still errors, we'll have a `RecordCount` greater than 0:

```
        If .RecordCount > 0 Then
```

We will simply build a string with the ProductIDs of the products whose update failed:

```
            strError = strError & .Fields(m_cstrProductsProductIDField)
```

We will now cancel the update, which will throw away this change:

```
            .CancelUpdate
        End If
```

Now we close the recordset:

```
            .Close
        End With
```

Then we move to the next record and loop the whole process:

```
        r_recProducts.MoveNext
        Set recProducts = Nothing
    Loop
```

We'll return the value of `strError` to the calling procedure. If there were no problems then this will be empty, otherwise it will contain the ProductIDs of the problem items:

```
    ReconcileProducts = strError
    Exit Function
```

Finally we will put in the error handler:

```
ReconcileProductsError:
    Err.Raise Err.Number, "Reconcile Products:" & Err.Source, _
        Err.Description & " " & strError
End Function
```

Product Updates from Adding an Order

Whilst Updating Products directly was a fairly straightforward procedure, well kind of at least, Updating Products indirectly through an Order is a different kettle of fish.

When a new Order is placed it actually updates both the Orders and the Order Details table. Therefore, we need an update function for both tables. We will focus on the Order Details table first, as it contains information on the Products.

This routine will actually be quite simple. This is because it requires two quite complex and separate processes, each of which we'll split off into their own function. Therefore, all we really need to do is call each of them.

Creating The UpdateOrderDetails Function

We first need to begin by creating the `UpdateOrderDetailsRS` function that returns an ADO recordset. This function has one parameter, `v_recClientRecordset`, which is also an ADO recordset:

```
Private Function UpdateOrderDetailsRS(ByVal v_recClientRecordSet As _
    ADODB.Recordset) As ADODB.Recordset

Dim recOrderDetails As ADODB.Recordset

On Error GoTo UpdateOrderDetailsRSError
```

I've chose to create a separate function, at this point, to deal with updating the Order Details. This is because there are two scenarios in which Order Details need to be updated. It can either be updated directly, as in this case, or, as we'll see later, by placing a order. Therefore, as the code would be the same, I've chosen to create another function called `SaveOrderDetailsRS` that can be called when appropriate.

```
Set recOrderDetails = SaveOrderDetailsRS(v_recClientRecordset)
```

The second routine that we need to call deals with removing items from stock:

```
With recOrderDetails

    While Not .EOF
        RemoveFromStock .Fields(m_cstrOrderDetailsProductIDField), _
                    .Fields(m_cstrOrderDetailsQuantityField)
        .MoveNext
    Wend

End With
```

We'll now close the recordset variable and set the Connection and the object to `Nothing`:

```
recOrderDetails.Close
Set recOrderDetails.ActiveConnection = Nothing
Set recOrderDetails = Nothing

Exit Function
```

Finally we will make the error handler:

```
UpdateOrderDetailsRSError:

    Err.Raise Err.Description, "Error UpdateOrderDetailsTable " & _
    Err.Source, Err.Description

End Function
```

This function only deals with adding an entry and not editing an existing one. It should be too much effort however for you to add the edit code.

Now that this function is complete we need to code the two routines it calls: `SaveOrderDetailsRS` and `RemoveFromStock` method.

Creating the SaveOrderDetailsRS Function

Like Products there is an auto-incrementing filed that requires us to use a connected recordset, and so most of the code we've already seen.

Once again, we'll create a local recordset variable, copy the fields into this variable from the client recordset, and then update the local recordset to the database. The only real difference is that we also have to set the OrderID.

The function has an optional `OrderID` parameter for when we are using this function to add a new `OrderID` through the `SubmitNewOrder` method that we'll code later.

```
Private Function SaveOrderDetailsRS(ByVal v_recClientRecordset As _
    ADODB.Recordset, Optional ByVal v_lngOrderID As Long = 0) As ADODB.Recordset

Dim recOrderDetails As New ADODB.Recordset
Dim lngFieldCounter As Long
Dim lngRowCounter As Long

Set recOrderDetails = CreateInstance("ADODB.Recordset")

With recOrderDetails
    .Source = m_cstrOrderDetailsQuery & " Where " & _
        m_cstrOrderDetailsOrderIDField & "=" & 0
    .ActiveConnection = GetADOConnection
    .LockType = adLockPessimistic
    .CursorLocation = adUseServer
    .CursorType = adOpenKeyset
    .Open

    Do Until v_recClientRecordset.EOF
        .AddNew

        For lngFieldCounter = 0 To v_recClientRecordset.Fields.Count - 1

            If LCase(v_recClientRecordset.Fields(lngFieldCounter).Name) <> _
                LCase(m_cstrOrderDetailsProductNameField) Then

                If Not IsNull(v_recClientRecordset.Fields(lngFieldCounter).Value) Then
                    .Fields(v_recClientRecordset.Fields(lngFieldCounter).Name) = _
                        v_recClientRecordset.Fields(lngFieldCounter).Value
                End If
```

```
        End If

    Next

    v_recClientRecordset.MoveNext
    If v_lngOrderID <> 0 Then
        .Fields(m_cstrOrderDetailsOrderIDField).Value = v_lngOrderID
    End If
    .Update

Loop

Set SaveOrderDetailsRS = recOrderDetails

End With

End Function
```

Creating the RemoveFromStock Method

The purpose of this function is self-evident and will perform the following steps:

- ❏ Create a local Products Recordset.
- ❏ Set the Source, ActiveConnection, LockType, CursorLocation and CursorType of the Product recordset.
- ❏ Open the recordset.
- ❏ If there are not enough in stock, remove all the items currently in stock, and add the difference between the number ordered and the number in stock (the number the order is short) to the On Order field. Set Units In Stock to zero.
- ❏ If there is enough in stock, remove the amount ordered from the number in stock. If the number in stock is now less then the Reorder number, add more to the On Order field. Set Units In Stock to zero. There would have to be some Business Rule to determine what happens when there are not enough units in stock to fill an order. For Northwind, we will say that they have can replenish stock with twenty-four hours so shortages will be ignored.
- ❏ Update the Products table.

The activity diagram will be:

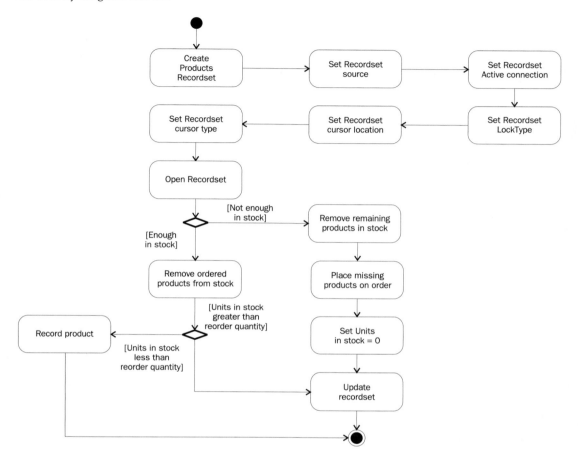

Create the Private subroutine RemoveFromStock with two parameters, both of long type, one called v_lngProdID for the ProductID, and the other v_lngQuantity for the amount of the product to be removed from the Products table:

```
Private Sub RemoveFromStock(ByVal v_lngProdID As Long, ByVal v_lngQuantity As_
                            Long)
```

Create a variable for the Products recordset and initialise it:

```
Dim recProducts As ADODB.Recordset

On Error GoTo RemoveFromStockError

Set recProducts = CreateInstance("ADODB.Recordset")
```

Set all of the properties of the Products recordset. We are going to set the LockType to be pessimistic because we don't want someone changing this record while we are editing it:

```
With recProducts
   .Source=m_cstrProductQuery & " Where " & m_cstrProductsProductIDField _
          & "=" & v_lngProdID
   .ActiveConnection = GetADOConnection
   .LockType = adLockPessimistic
   .CursorLocation = adUseClient
   .CursorType = adOpenKeyset
   .Open
End With
```

It's unlikely that the product was deleted while the order was being entered, but we should still check to make sure a record came back:

```
If recProducts.RecordCount = 0 Then
   Err.Raise 2004, "RemoveFromStock", "Product is not in the database"
End If
```

First, we are going to check if there is enough of this item in stock:

```
If recProducts.Fields(m_cstrProductsUnitsInStockField) < v_lngQuantity Then
```

If there are not enough, add the amount that is missing to the On Order field:

```
Dim intDifference As Integer

intDifference = v_lngQuantity - _
      recProducts.Fields(m_cstrProductsUnitsInStockField)
recProducts.Fields(m_cstrProductsUnitsOnOrderField) = _
      recProducts.Fields(m_cstrProductsUnitsOnOrderField) + intDifference
```

Set the total number Units In Stock to zero:

```
recProducts.Fields(m_cstrProductsUnitsInStockField) = 0
```

If there are enough in stock, first remove the amount ordered from Units In Stock:

```
Else
   recProducts.Fields(m_cstrProductsUnitsInStockField) = _
      recProducts.Fields(m_cstrProductsUnitsInStockField) - _
      v_lngQuantity
```

Check to see if this order has put the total units in stock below the reorder level:

```
If recProducts.Fields(m_cstrProductsUnitsInStockField) < _
      recProducts.Fields(m_cstrProductsReorderLevelField) Then
```

If we need to reorder, add these to the Units On Order:

```
                recProducts.Fields(m_cstrProductsUnitsOnOrderField) = _
                    recProducts.Fields(m_cstrProductsUnitsOnOrderField) + _
                    v_lngQuantity
        End If

    End If
```

Update the recordset:

```
    recProducts.Update
    Set recProducts = Nothing

    Exit Sub
```

Finally, add in an error handler:

```
    RemoveFromStockError:

      Err.Raise Err.Number, "RemoveFromStock " & Err.Source, Err.Description

    End Sub
```

> *I would like to make one comment here. If there are shortages, we are simply increasing the*
> *number of units on order. While this good, it may not be good enough. The Products person could*
> *periodically check the database for all products that have more than zero units on order to find*
> *products that need to be ordered, but it would be better if our server object notified the Products*
> *person. We could create another server component that sends an e-mail message to the Products*
> *person, or sends a report to them. There are any number of possibilities, just make sure whatever*
> *you choose works for your users.*

Creating the UpdateOrders Method

Another part of updating an Order is updating the Orders Table. So far we have ignored the Orders table. As updating Orders and Order Details often needs to made simultaneously, we either create one big function that does both or two separate functions. We've chosen the separate function option to make the code simpler. However, updating both table should really be done under one transaction, therefore, we'll code another function that does this later.

This method will be similar to the other update methods. The Orders table also has an auto increment ID field. We will have to perform the AddNew in the same manner as we did for Products and Order Details. If there is a conflict with the records we'll just raise an error.

The activity diagram is:

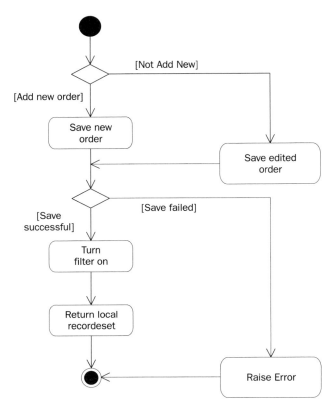

The function looks as follows:

```
Private Function UpdateOrderRS(ByVal v_recClientRecordSet As _
                              ADODB.Recordset) As ADODB.Recordset

    Dim recOrder As ADODB.Recordset
    Dim lngFieldCounter As Long
    Dim lngRowCounter As Long

    On Error GoTo UpdateOrderRSError

    If v_recClientRecordSet.EditMode = adEditAdd Then
        Set recOrder = CreateInstance("ADODB.Recordset")

        With recOrder
            .Source = m_cstrOrdersQuery & " Where " & m_cstrOrderDetailsOrderID & _
                        "=" & 0
            .ActiveConnection = GetADOConnection
            .LockType = adLockPessimistic
            .CursorLocation = adUseServer
            .CursorType = adOpenKeyset
            .Open
            .AddNew
            For lngFieldCounter= 0 To v_recClientRecordSet.Fields.Count- 1
```

```
            If Not IsNull(v_recClientRecordSet.Fields(lngFieldCounter).Value) Then
                .Fields(v_recClientRecordSet.Fields(lngFieldCounter).Name) _
                        = v_recClientRecordSet.Fields(lngFieldCounter).Value
            End If

        Next

        .Update
    End With

Else

    Set recOrder = v_recClientRecordSet
    Set recOrder.ActiveConnection = GetADOConnection

    On Error Resume Next

    recOrder.Filter = adFilterPendingRecords
    recOrder.UpdateBatch
    recOrder.Filter = adFilterConflictingRecords

    If recOrder.RecordCount > 0 Then
            Err.Raise 2002, "UpdateOrderRS", "Conflicting Errors"
    End If

    recOrder.Filter = adFilterNone

End If

Set UpdateOrderRS = recOrder
Set recOrder = Nothing

Exit Function

UpdateOrderRSError:

Err.Raise Err.Description, "Error UpdateOrderRS" & " " & Err.Source, _
        Err.Description

End Function
```

That's the last Update routine that I'm going to show. You should, however, be able to go ahead and make ones for Employees and Shippers if you so desire.

Our server object is almost complete. We just need to add a single routine for adding a new order that will deal with updating multiple tables.

Creating a New Order

We now have all of the methods we are going to need to build a method to update a new order. Since we need to update several tables at the same time, we want to perform the two updates under one transaction. In this way, if there are any error during the update of Order Details, Orders, or Products tables when we remove the Units In Stock, we can rollback all of the changes. Since we need to pass in two recordsets, we will not use the generic update function. Instead, we will create a special function for updating an Order.

Creating a Sub to Submit an Order

Submitting a new order requires us to coordinate with several other routines as it involves updating so many different elements. The steps of submitting an Order are:

❑ Set ADO Connection
❑ Update Orders
❑ Update Order Details
❑ Remove Products from Stock
❑ Close ADO Connection

This would look like the following activity diagram:

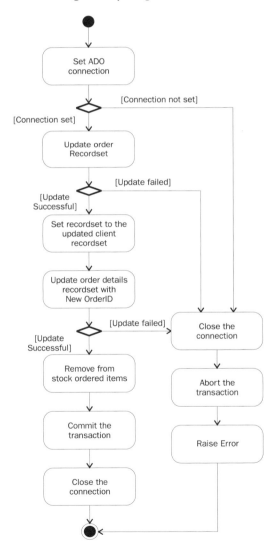

Create a new public subroutine called `SubmitNewOrder`. We will be passing in the UserID and password, and the Orders and Order Details recordsets. We do not need the Products recordset, as we can determine what items to remove from stock by using the Order Details table:

```
Public Sub SubmitNewOrder(ByVal v_strUserID As String, ByVal v_strPassword As _
    String, ByVal v_recOrders As ADODB.Recordset, ByVal v_recOrderDetails As _
                ADODB.Recordset)
```

Create local recordset variables for the Order Details and Order recordsets:

```
Dim recOrder As ADODB.Recordset
Dim recOrderDetails As ADODB.Recordset
```

Set the error handler and the ADO Connection:

```
On Error GoTo UpdateOrderError

SetADOConnection v_strUserID, v_strPassword
```

We want to update the Order Details, Orders, and Products recordset under one transaction, however, as we saw earlier we can't use nested transactions. To get round this we'll use the `SaveOrderDetailsRS` routine we built earlier, you can see now why we added an Optional parameter.

First, though, we need to update the Order recordset:

```
Set recOrder = UpdateOrderRS(v_recOrders)

Set recOrderDetails = SaveOrderDetailsRS(v_recOrderDetails, _
        recOrder.Fields(m_cstrOrderDetailsOrderID))
```

Then, we want to remove the ordered products from stock:

```
With recOrderDetails

    While Not .EOF
      RemoveFromStock .Fields(m_cstrOrderDetailsProductIDField), _
            .Fields(m_cstrOrderDetailsQuantityField)
    .MoveNext
    Wend

End With
```

Finally, we'll call `SetComplete` and clean up:

```
SetComplete

CloseADOConnection

Set recOrder = Nothing
Set recOrderDetails = Nothing

Exit Sub
```

If there are errors, we call SetAbort and raise the appropriate error:

```
UpdateOrderError:

  CloseADOConnection
  SetAbort

  m_strErrorDetails="Error Number: " & Err.Number & " Error Description: " _
                    & Err.Description
  Err.Raise Err.Number, "ReturnCustomers" & " " & Err.Source, m_strErrorDetails

End Sub
```

The code for our server object is now complete. We still have to compile it and host it in MTS though. I won't go into that here, as it's quite straightforward. However, you can refer to Appendices C and D for information on running and debugging with MTS.

Summary

As you may have gathered, a server object built to run under the three-tier framework contains some very complex methods.

No matter how complicated this process was using UML diagrams, trying to do the same thing without them would have been a thousand times more difficult. When I was trying to figure out how to design the system, I had to draw it all out. OK, I confess, I used a pencil and made some rather ugly looking activity diagrams mapping everything out. The initial concepts were, well, extremely different from the final diagrams above.

The process of mapping it all out using diagrams was fairly easy. If you don't believe me, sit down and try to figure out how to code the methods like UpdateProducts without activity diagrams. I guarantee you, a few hours of shuffling code around and you will quickly turn to UML diagrams.

For simple methods and properties, you can rely on other UML diagrams, such as sequence diagrams, to map out your code. Complicated methods, though, need activity diagrams to help you visualize your methods, see the flow of your code, and work out the best possible code solution.

We have created a Server Component that can do the following:

- ❏ Maintain the integrity of the database with methods that correct data conflicts.
- ❏ Pass disconnected recordsets to the client through DCOM or HTTP using RDS.
- ❏ Safely update the database

This is a very powerful server object, and I hope that you will be able to use it as the basis for your future projects.

In our next few chapters, we will be designing and building the other half of our system: the client-side objects.

Get ADO
connection

[Successful]

Set Recordset
cursor location

Set Recordset
source

Set Recordset
connection

12

Coding the Customer Client Component

So far, we've coded the middle-tier, which handles the fine details of retrieving, updating and reconciling recordsets. This server component has all the necessary implementation to handle almost every aspect of the Northwind system. However, this server component is next to useless unless it has a client to talk to. This is what we're going to build in this chapter.

In Chapters 5 and 8, we saw how we would be constructing a three-tier class hierarchy. Now we have to think about how to implement it. This architecture has a few interesting points of its own that we'll be exploring in this chapter.

In this chapter you will learn:

- ❑ How to apply the four rules of building Visual Basic Class Hierarchies
- ❑ How to make Visual Basic 6 Data Provider Class Hierarchies
- ❑ How to build a generic DNA Client Object

We'll concentrate, in this chapter, on building only one of the client components, the one that belongs to the Customer. Once we've built one client component, the others are easy. When we come to building the other components in the next chapter, you'll be able to see the power and beauty of our design.

Before we begin to code a client component, let's take a quick look at the design we've been developing since the earlier chapters.

The Client Component Design

In Chapter 5, we decided to implement a class hierarchy with one class primarily responsible for properties, and the other primarily responsible for methods.

Then in Chapter 8, we saw how we needed to add a third class at the top of the hierarchy to provide different views of the Middle and Bottom classes.

Our design, therefore, looks like this:

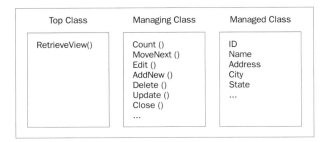

We've got a lot of code to get through in this chapter, so let's get started.

Setting Up the Customer Component

We'll be creating a Standard Visual Basic EXE in Chapter 14 on which to build the GUI, so we'll be putting the entire client component into one application. This will make it easier for us to build the project, and to run and test it. If we were going to reuse our components, we could easily move the components into a separate project and compile them as a separate DLL, or DLLs.

This component, and the others, will be built using the class hierarchy of two data source classes and a user control that we developed in the last chapter.

> *I've chosen to build the components as ActiveX controls because we may later want to add a user interface and property pages to our components. The user inteface could just be buttons that allow move next, move previous, move first, move last like the standard Visual Basic data control.*
>
> *If you don't want to use the interfaces, you can make the controls windowless. However, there's very little stopping you from building them as ActiveX DLLs.*

So let's begin by creating a new ActiveX Control project in Visual Basic. Name the control `ctlCustomers` and add two standard class modules. Name the first class `clsCustomer` and the second `clsCustomerManager`:

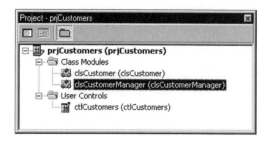

Here is how these Visual Basic elements relate to our class hierarchy design, which we developed in Chapter 8:

❑ The `ctlCustomers` user control will be the **Top Class** of our hierarchy.

❑ The `clsCustomerManager` class will be the **Middle Class** in our hierarchy. As we wish to reuse this class for our other components, we'll try to use to make it as generic as possible.

❑ Finally, `clsCustomer` will be the **Bottom Class** in our hierarchy, and it will mostly contain the Customer properties.

Make sure both the `clsCustomerManager` and the `clsCustomer` classes have the following properties:

Property	Setting
DataBindingBehavior	0 - vbNone
DataSourceBehavior	1 - vbDataSource
Instancing	2 - Public Not Creatable
Persistable	0 - Not Persistable

Now add the following references to your project:

❑ The Remote Data Service Library 2.0
❑ Microsoft ActiveX Data Objects 2.0 Library
❑ Microsoft Data Sources Interfaces

The Data Source Interfaces reference will probably already be added because we set the classes to be data sources.

Now that we have the basic object heirarchy in place we can move on to some code.

Adding a BAS Module

There will be several enumerated types and a few functions that we want to be accessible to all ranks of our hierarchy.

Add a regular BAS module to your project. Call this module `basCMain`.

We are going to start using an enumerated type for our errors, so add the following code:

```
Option Explicit

Public Enum CustomerErrors
   errChangeFieldNoEdit = 1001
   errEditPrimaryKey = 1002
   errPrimaryKeyLength = 1003
   errCustomerTitleType = 1004
End Enum
```

We've just included a few of the error codes. These errors are:

❑ errChangeFieldNoEdit - For trying to change a record without first starting an Edit session
❑ errEditPrimaryKey - For trying to edit the primary key
❑ errPrimaryKeyLength - For entering a primary key of the wrong length
❑ errCustomerTitleType - For the wrong value of a Customer Title

> *In the final application, there would be many more possible errors, but this will be sufficient to show how we'll handle errors.*

We never want to place field names into the code, so we shall create constants for them; add the following code right after the previous lines:

```
Public Const g_cstrFieldCustomerID As String = "CustomerID"
Public Const g_cstrFieldAddress As String = "Address"
Public Const g_cstrFieldCity As String = "City"
Public Const g_cstrFieldCompanyName As String = "CompanyName"
Public Const g_cstrFieldContactName As String = "ContactName"
Public Const g_cstrFieldContactTitle As String = "ContactTitle"
Public Const g_cstrFieldCountry As String = "Country"
Public Const g_cstrFieldFax As String = "Fax"
Public Const g_cstrFieldPhone As String = "Phone"
Public Const g_cstrFieldPostalCode As String = "PostalCode"
Public Const g_cstrFieldRegion As String = "Region"
Public Const g_cstrFieldProductName As String = "ProductName"
```

There are two ways that a user might request to view the Customer data. They will either want to see all the Customers or just those with a particular Customer Title. For every different Customer view that the data consumers might need, there will have to be a ClientDataMember type entry. Therefore, we'll be using the DataMember property to determine the type of information a data consumer wants from our class.

To do this, we will create two constants representing the two possible values of the DataSource property:

```
Public Const g_cdmAllCustomers As String = "AllCustomers"
Public Const g_cdmCustomersContactTitleEquals As String = _
         "CustomersContactTitleEquals"
```

We're also going to add in a function to retrieve error detail information from a resource file. A resource file (RES file) is a special type of file that can be added to projects, which can contain string information as well as images. We are going to use it to associate an error number with the string that contains the error details for that number.

So let's create the following function to retrieve the error detail information:

```
Public Function GetErrorText(ByVal v_lngErrorNumber As Long)

  On Error GoTo GetErrorText_Error

  GetErrorText = LoadResString(v_lngErrorNumber)

  Exit Function

GetErrorText_Error:

  If Err.Number <> 0 Then
     GetErrorText = "An unknown error has occurred, the error was not found"
  End If

End Function
```

`LoadResString` is a Visual Basic function that retrieves the string associated with a particular number from the resource file.

Adding a Resource File

To use the RES Editor it first needs to be added using the Add-In Manger found in the Add-Ins menu:

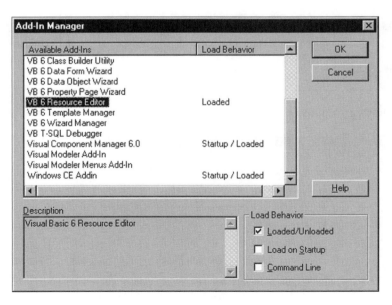

Now select Resource Editor from the Tools menu. When it fires up it will look like this:

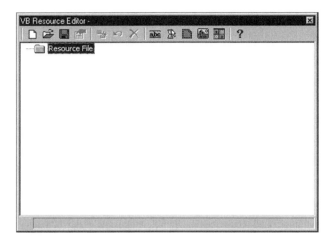

Click on the abc button, and you'll see this:

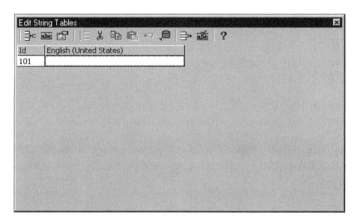

Now add the following strings to the string editor:

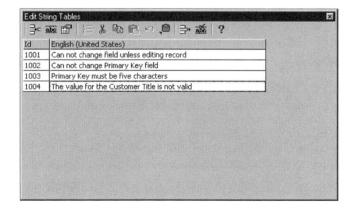

These are the actual messages that we will show to the user when these errors occur. In this way, we can use an enumerated type to identify the error in our code, then associate this enumerated type with a number. This number is then associated with an error message in the RES file. This gives us the benefits of both using an enumerated type in our code, and also the ability to store our error messages in one file.

Save the RES files as `ClientError.RES`.

Now we've got these preliminaries out the way, let's move on to develop the Bottom Class, which in Visual Basic is our class called `clsCustomer`.

Implementing The Bottom Class

This Bottom Class, or Managed Class, is used to hold most of the *properties* for our Customer component. We'll be spending most of our time implementing `Property Lets` and `Property Gets` for this class, therefore.

We'll need a fair few other supporting elements to get this class up and running, of course. So let's start by adding the following module-level declarations to the `clsCustomer` class we created a little bit earlier:

```
Private m_blnValidatingFieldChange As Boolean
Private m_eEditMode As ADODB.EditModeEnum
Private m_strErrorDetails As String
Private m_blnIgnoreFieldChange As Boolean
Private m_blnInFieldChange As Boolean
Private m_avarAcceptableValuesTitle As Variant
Private m_strManagedObjectDataMember As String

Private WithEvents m_recManagedObjects As ADODB.Recordset

Public Event RefreshDataMember()
Public Event EditInProgress(ByVal v_strEditMode)
```

These variables have the following purposes:

Variable Name	Purpose
m_blnValidatingFieldChange	Because we'll be using properties to validate a change in one the recordset's fields, we need this variable to prevent an endless loop (see below).
m_eEditMode	To keep track of when an edit is occurring, we'll use this variable to monitor the current Edit status of the recordset.
m_blnIgnoreFieldChange	This Boolean variable will alert the FieldChange event that it was itself raised as a consequence of a change of the field within by a property.
m_blnInFieldChange	This is a Boolean variable to let the object know that it's currently in a FieldChange event. It will be used to prevent a possible endless loop.

Table Continued on Following Page

343

Variable Name	Purpose
m_recManagedObjects	This is the recordset that is shared between the Bottom Class and the Middle Class. It's created with events so that any changes to a field by a data source can be verified before they are committed.
RefreshDataMember	This event will be raised whenever the Data Provider changes the value of a field in the recordset.
EditInProgress	This event will be raised when the EditMode has changed in the Bottom Class. It will be used to pass the change onto the Middle Class.
m_avarAcceptableValuesTitle	This is an array of the acceptable values for the CustomerTitle field.
m_strManagedObjectDataMember	This variable will contain the value of the DataMember for this instance of the class.

Next we need to shall code for the class events.

Bottom Class: Coding the Class Events

Because we have set clsCustomer class to be a Data Provider, Visual Basic has automatically added the GetDataMember event to the other intrinsic class events.

Bottom Class: The Class_Initialize Event

We'll set up our error handler and set our Booleans to False in the Class_Initialize:

```
Private Sub Class_Initialize()

    m_blnValidatingFieldChange = False
    m_blnIgnoreFieldChange = False
    m_blnInFieldChange = False

    On Error Goto InitializeError
```

Next, we'll set the Edit mode to none and initialize the ADO Recordset variable:

```
    m_eEditMode = adEditNone

    Set m_recManagedObjects = New ADODB.Recordset
```

We also need to load our array m_avarAcceptableValuesTitle with a list of Contact Titles that are acceptable. We'll use this list later on when validating a new Contact Title:

```
    m_avarAcceptableValuesTitle = Array("Owner", "Sales Representative", _
                                  "Order Administrator", "Marketing Manager", _
                                  "Accounting Manager", "Sales Agent", _
                                  "Sales Associate", "Owner")

    Exit Sub
```

Finally, we will put our error trap in:

```
InitializeError:

   MsgBox "Error In Class Initialize"
```

End Sub

Bottom Class: The Class_GetDataMember Event

The GetDataMember event will be called every time a Data Consumer bound to the class binds to the project or changes its DataMember property. If the DataMember being passed is not the correct one for this instance of the class, then we'll exit. Otherwise, we'll return the recordset:

```
Private Sub Class_GetDataMember(DataMember As String, Data As Object)

   If ItemsDataMember <> DataMember Then
      Exit Sub
   End If

   Set Data = m_recManagedObjects
```

End Sub

ItemsDataMember is a property that we'll create to retrieve the value of the private variable m_strDataMember, which describes which view this instance of the class is using.

Bottom Class: The Class_Terminate Event

In our Terminate event, we'll Close and destroy the Recordset object:

```
Private Sub Class_Terminate()

   If Not m_recManagedObjects Is Nothing Then
      With ItemsRecordset

         If .State = adStateOpen Then
            If Not .BOF And Not .EOF Then
               If .EditMode <> adEditNone Then
                  .CancelUpdate
               End If
               .Close
            End If
         End If
      End With

      Set m_recManagedObjects = Nothing

   End If
```

End Sub

Now let's look at how we're going to deal with validation.

Bottom Class: Validating Fields - Part One

Our Bottom Class will consist primarily of properties that represent the fields in the recordset. Each field will have a property associated with it. For example, there is a ContactTitle field in the recordset, and so there will be a corresponding property called ContactTitle.

We have Business Rules that have placed limitations on the possible values of our Customer fields. Therefore, we'll write validation code in the Property Lets that enforces these Business Rules.

This would be all very fine and well, except that this class will also be a Data Provider. This means the fields can also be changed directly through the Recordset object. These changes also need to be validated.

The ADO Recordset object provides us with several events that get fired when a field is changed. Choosing which one to use, however, proved to be somewhat tricky.

I had several problems. I began in the most logical place, the WillChangeEvent. It made sense to check the value of the field before it was actually changed. I came across one problem. I could not find any way to get the value that the field was about to be changed to while in the WillChangeEvent. Without knowing the pending change, it was impossible to provide any validation. So, I had to try something else.

The next choice was to try the RecordChangeComplete, but I had problems with that too. In the end, I settled on using the FieldChangeComplete method. I am not saying this was the best method. I could not find any documentation on validating fields and rolling back invalid changes, so I settled on what worked. I admit that it was not the prettiest solution, but it worked. You, of course, are more than welcome to spend a few weekends playing with the ADO recordset events to try to come up with a better solution.

However, we certainly do not want to rewrite all of our validation rules in the FieldChangeComplete event of the recordset especially as we already have the validation code in the Property Lets. Thus, to avoid placing our Business Rules in two places, we'll call a function from our FieldChangeComplete event that will check if the field's new value is valid. Since there is already validation code in the Property Lets, we can use them to validate the new field values.

This allows us to localize all of our validation routines in our properties, instead of several different places.

We have localized all of our validation into our properties. Another possibility is to create a separate function for every Business Rule that requires validation code. This allows you to map your Business Rules directly to a function and easily make sure every rule has been implemented. It also allows a Business Rule to be used by several methods or properties. Obviously, if a Business Rule requires dozens of lines of code to enforce it, then it makse sense to make it into a separate function. Nearly all of our rules associated with properties though, require only a few lines of code to enforce, and they only relate to a single property. For this reason I keep them inside the Property routines.

However, can you see the problem with using the Let properties to test if a field change is valid? Let's step through this:

❑ A data source (e.g. bound text box) changes a field value.

❑ The FieldChangeComplete event is raised.

❑ The FieldChangeComplete has code within it that calls ValidateFields to check if the field is valid.

❑ ValidateFields will attempt to set the property associated with this field to the new value.

❑ The Property Let will try to set the field associated with the property to the new value. This will cause the FieldChangeComplete to be fired. This in turn will call ValidateFields, which means we now have an infinite loop.

To prevent this, we must have a Boolean variable to tell the Property Lets that they are only being used to validate a field, and that they shouldn't try to actually change the field in the recordset. This is what the m_blnValidatingtFieldChange variable is for.

Bottom Class: Creating a Function to ValidateFields

ValidateFields will return a Boolean of False if the field is not valid and True if it is.

Begin by creating the function as a Friend, because we don't want to expose it outside the project. The function will have two parameters: v_vFields and v_recCustomerRS.

The parameter v_vFields is an array of the fields that have been changed. It's actually a parameter from the FieldChangeComplete event that we are simply passing directly to our function. As we are checking when each field has been changed, we only need the last field that has been changed. This will always be the first field in the array, v_vFields(0).

The parameter v_recRecordset is also from the FieldChangeComplete event. It's a copy of the Customer recordset with the new underlying values:

```
Friend Function ValidateFields(ByVal v_vFields As Variant, _
    ByVal v_recRecordset As ADODB.Recordset) As Boolean
```

To test the validity of the new field values, we shall attempt to set the property associated with the field to the new value. If the value is invalid, the property will raise an error. So if we code an error trap in ValidateFields, then we can know when a field is invalid by catching the error. The next step is to add an error handler:

```
On Error GoTo ValidateFieldsError
```

We now set the m_blnValidatingFieldChange variable to True, so that our function knows it's only supposed to be performing validation:

```
m_blnValidatingFieldChange = True
```

Next, using the first entry of the v_vFields array, we can find out the field that has been changed, and using a Select Case validate the field by calling its corresponding property:

```
    Select Case LCase(v_vFields(0).Name)

        Case g_cstrFieldAddress
            Address = v_recRecordset.Fields(g_cstrFieldAddress)

        Case g_cstrFieldCity
            City = v_recRecordset.Fields(g_cstrFieldCity)

        Case g_cstrFieldCompanyName
            CompanyName = v_recRecordset.Fields(g_cstrFieldCompanyName)

        Case g_cstrFieldContactName
            ContactName = v_recRecordset.Fields(g_cstrFieldContactName)

        Case g_cstrFieldContactTitle
            ContactTitle = v_recRecordset.Fields(g_cstrFieldContactTitle)

        Case g_cstrFieldCountry
            Country = v_recRecordset.Fields(g_cstrFieldCountry)

        Case g_cstrFieldCustomerID
            CustomerID = v_recRecordset.Fields(g_cstrFieldCustomerID)

        Case g_cstrFieldFax
            Fax = v_recRecordset.Fields(g_cstrFieldFax)

        Case g_cstrFieldPhone
            Phone = v_recRecordset.Fields(g_cstrFieldPhone)

        Case g_cstrFieldPostalCode
            PostalCode = v_recRecordset.Fields(g_cstrFieldPostalCode)

        Case g_cstrFieldRegion
            Region = v_recRecordset.Fields(g_cstrFieldRegion)

        Case Else
            ValidateFields = False

    End Select
```

If the field name is not one of the listed fields, then there is an error and we set `ValidateFields` to `False` in the `Case Else` statement.

We can now set our `m_blnValidatingFieldChange` event to `False`, since we have finished performing our validation process:

```
    m_blnValidatingFieldChange = False
```

Since there were no errors the field change was valid and we can set `ValidateFields` to `True`:

```
    ValidateFields = True

    Exit Function
```

If the change was not valid, we can set the `ValidateFields` to `False` and clear the error:

```
ValidateFieldsError:

  ValidateFields = False
  m_blnValidatingFieldChange = False
  Err.Clear

End Function
```

Bottom Class: Validating Fields - Part Two

If only things were that simple. I mentioned earlier that we'd be coding the `FieldChangeComplete` event to handle direct changes to the fields. Unfortunately, using this event causes some problems of its own.

Once again, there's the possibility of it creating an infinite loop. The sequence goes like this:

❑ A user changes a field through a Data Consumer control.

❑ `FieldChangeComplete` event is raised, and the new value is checked.

❑ The new value is invalid, so the value is changed in the `FieldChangedComplete` event back to the original value. This change causes the `FieldChangedComplete` event to be raised again.

This is an infinite loop. We'll set the Boolean `m_blnInFieldChange` to `True` before we change the field value so that the next time we come into the `FieldChangeComplete` event we can just exit out. If the original value is wrong, we will ignore it.

There is still one more issue to be considered. When we change the value of a field in a property, we will also raise the `FieldChangeComplete` event. As the code in the `FieldChangeComplete` event performs validation, and the properties validate the code before setting the field, we don't need `FieldChangeComplete` to validate the new value. We will need to set the Boolean `m_blnIgnoreFieldChange` to `True` when we are changing a field value in a property.

Bottom Class: Coding the FieldChangeComplete Event

Go to the Object drop-down on the left of the Visual Basic code window and select **m_recManagedObjects**. You will now have all of the events in the right drop-down list. Select `FieldChangeComplete`. The field change event declaration will look like this:

```
Private Sub m_recManagedObjects_FieldChangeComplete(ByVal cFields As Long, _
    ByVal Fields As Variant, ByVal pError As ADODB.Error, _
    adStatus As ADODB.EventStatusEnum, ByVal pRecordset As ADODB.Recordset)
```

There are a lot of parameters here. Let's look at what these values are:

Parameter Name	Purpose
cFields	This variable is the number of fields that have changed. I have not seen any situations where more than one value is returned, but you may want to add code to check this value, and loop through all of the changed fields.

Table Continued on Following Page

Parameter Name	Purpose
Fields	This is an array of fields, listing the fields that have changed. Using this, we can get the name of the changed field.
pError	This is an ADO error object listing any errors that occurred.
adStatus	This is the status. In theory, you can set this to cancel and stop the field change. I have not seen this work consistently.
pRecordset	This is the ADO recordset that contains the new values. We will use this to get the changed value, and if it is not valid, get the old value from this recordset using the Underlying property of the recordset. This is the same property as we used in the server component to reconcile products.

Now add an error handler to this:

```
    On Error GoTo FieldChangeError
```

We will begin by checking whether the event has been raised by from property routine by checking the m_blnIgnoreFieldChange variable. If m_blnIgnoreFieldChange is True, we have changed the value of the field from a property and can just exit the sub:

```
    If m_blnIgnoreFieldChange = True Then
        m_blnIgnoreFieldChange = False
```

Before we leave the sub, though, we need to update all of the Data Consumers by calling the DataMemberChanged method and also raising the RefreshDataMember event. The RefreshDataMember event will be trapped by the Middle Class, which will then refresh the controls bound to it:

```
        DataMemberChanged ItemsDataMember
        RaiseEvent RefreshDataMember
        Exit Sub
    End If
```

As we saw, it's possible to get an infinite loop if an invalid field is entered. To prevent this loop we'll be setting the m_blnInFieldChange to True before we change an invalid field back to its original value. Therefore, we must check for the value of m_blnInFieldChange to see if it has been set to True. If so, we must exit the sub:

```
    If m_blnInFieldChange = True Then
        m_blnInFieldChange = False
        Exit Sub
    End If
```

Next, we need to check if there is anything that needs validation. If there are no records (RecordCount = 0) or the recordset has not been initialized (recordset state not equal to adStateOpen) then we have nothing to validate and should just exit the sub:

```
      If m_recManagedObjects.RecordCount = 0 _
               Or m_recManagedObjects.State <> adStateOpen Then
         Exit Sub
      End If
```

If we are performing a Delete, we have no need to validate the field change; we will simply exit the sub:

```
      If EditMode = adEditDelete Then
         Exit Sub
      End If
```

Data Consumers can allow an edit without explicitly calling an Edit function. We will allow this to happen, but we must set our EditMode property to adEditInProgress. We will check to see if the property is currently set to adEditNone, and if it is change it to adEditInProgress:

```
      If EditMode = adEditNone Then
         EditMode = adEditInProgress
         RaiseEvent EditInProgress(adEditInProgress)
      End If
```

If we've got this far then we're finally ready to do the validation. We begin by calling the ValidateFields function that we created earlier. It will return False if the field is not valid, which means we must roll back to the old value:

```
      If ValidateFields(Fields, pRecordset) = False Then
```

If we go into the If statement, we need to first set m_blnInFieldChange equal to True so we don't loop when we come back into the FieldChangeComplete event when we set the field back to its old value:

```
         m_blnInFieldChange = True
```

As there is only one field that has been changed, that field will be the zero element in the Fields array, v_vFields(0).We can use the UnderlyingValue property of the field to get the original value before the field was changed:

```
         m_recManagedObjects.Fields(Fields(0).Name).Value = _
                     pRecordset.Fields(Fields(0).Name).UnderlyingValue
```

Since we have changed the underlying recordset we must update the Data Consumers:

```
         DataMemberChanged ItemsDataMember
         RaiseEvent RefreshDataMember
```

Finally, we must set m_blnInFieldChange to False and exit the If statement and the sub:

```
      m_blnInFieldChange = False
   End If

   Exit Sub
```

And put in the error trap:

```
FieldChangeError:

   Err.Raise Err.Number, "FieldChange " & Err.Source, Err.Description

End Sub
```

Bottom Class: Creating the Customer Object Properties

Now that we're all set up to perform validation on new field values, we need to code the validation rules themselves. As we said earlier, each field will have corresponding `Property` routines.

These `Property` routines represent every possible property of a Customer. It's possible, though, that the underlying recordset is not based on all of the Customer fields. We might only need a table with the Contact and Company Name fields. If we retrieved a recordset that did not have the CustomerID field and we try to retrieve the field, an error would be raised. The error would be `3265`, which is raised when someone tries to get a field that is not in the recordset. In this case, we want to ignore the error and just return nothing. In this way, even if someone tries to get a field that is not in the recordset, they'll simply get back an empty string.

Customer Object Property: CustomerID

Within our `clsCustomer` class, create a new `Get` property for the CustomerID:

```
Public Property Get CustomerID() As String
```

We will turn off error handling right here within the property `Get`:

```
   On Error Resume Next
```

Next, we get the value of the CustomerID from the recordset using the parent function `ItemsRecordset` that returns the Customer recordset:

```
   CustomerID = ItemsRecordset.Fields(g_cstrFieldCustomerID)
```

We'll check to see if there was an error. If it was not `3265` (the field is not present) then we will raise an error; otherwise we will ignore the error:

```
   If Err.Number <> 0 Then

      If Err.Number <> 3265 Then
         Err.Raise Err.Number, "CustomerID.Get", Err.Description
      End If

   End If
End Property
```

We will allow the application using the control to build the CustomerID. Unfortunately, the CustomerID is, according to our Business Rules, based on the Customer name. This is not the best choice, especially when we are using foreign names with non-standard characters. A better choice would have been an auto-incrementing number, but we have to work with what is already in the Northwind database.

Therefore, let's create the following Let property for CustomerID within our clsCustomer class:

```
Public Property Let CustomerID(ByVal v_strNewCustomerID As String)

    On Error GoTo CustomerIDLetError
```

Our Business Rule restricts the CustomerID to a field that is five characters long. If the value passed in is not five characters, then it's not a valid value and an error must be raised:

```
If Len(v_strNewCustomerID) <> 5 Then
    m_blnIgnoreFieldChange = True
    Err.Raise GetErrorText(errPrimaryKeyLength), "Customer.CustomerID.Let"
End If
```

If the Edit mode is adEditNone we want to raise an error, as we can edit the ID field:

```
If m_eEditMode = adEditInProgress Then
    Err.Raise GetErrorText(errEditPrimaryKey), "Customer.CustomerID.Let"
End If
```

If m_blnValidatingFieldChange is True (i.e. we're just validating the field, not trying to change it), we can exit the property now as we have already performed the validation:

```
If m_eEditMode = adEditNone Or m_blnValidatingFieldChange = True Then
    Exit Property
End If
```

Finally, if the Edit mode is adEditAdd then we can set the field:

```
If m_eEditMode = adEditAdd Then
    ItemsRecordset.Fields(g_cstrFieldCustomerID) = v_strNewCustomerID
End If

Exit Property
```

Lastly, we set the error handler:

```
CustomerIDLetError:

    Err.Raise Err.Number, "CustomerID Let " & Err.Source, Err.Description

End Property
```

Customer Object Property: Company Name

The CompanyName Get function will be practically identical to that for CustomerID:

```
Public Property Get CompanyName() As String

  On Error Resume Next

  CompanyName = ItemsRecordset.Fields(g_cstrFieldCompanyName)

  If Err.Number <> 0 Then

    If Err.Number <> 3265 Then
       Err.Raise Err.Number, "CompanyName Get", Err.Description
    End If

  End If

End Property
```

The only Business Rule we have for the Company Name is: "the length of the field cannot exceed a certain value". If the user enters a field that's too long, is it really one worth raising an error? The database will simply truncate it to the correct length. While this may not be particularly user-friendly, raising an error is a bit too severe for such a minor error.

> *You can deal with this situation by raising an event so that the mistake can be detected by the application using the component. If the user of your control wants to raise the error, they can do so. If they do not want to raise an error for this event, they can choose to ignore the event. It's better to give the user options. To simplify an already complicated example, we will not raise the event but simply ignore the error.*

This leaves us with no validation to perform for CompanyName so we end up with this Let property for Company Name:

```
Public Property Let CompanyName(ByVal v_strNewCompanyName As String)

  On Error GoTo CompanyNameLetError

  If m_blnValidatingFieldChange = True Then
     Exit Property
  End If
```

We will need to make sure that before calling the Property Let the Edit mode has been set to adEditInProgress or adEditAdd:

```
  If m_eEditMode = adEditInProgress Or m_eEditMode = adEditAdd Then
     m_blnIgnoreFieldChange = True
        ItemsRecordset.Fields(g_cstrFieldCompanyName) = _
          v_strNewCompanyName

  ElseIf m_eEditMode = adEditNone Then
     Err.Raise 1001, "CompanyName Let:", GetErrorText(errChangeFieldNoEdit)
  End If

  Exit Property
```

Finally, we will build the error trap raising any errors:

```
CompanyNameLetError:

   Err.Raise Err.Number, "CompanyName Let " & Err.Source, Err.Description

End Property
```

Customer Object Property: ContactTitle

The `Property Get` will be the same as for CustomerID and Company Name:

```
Public Property Get ContactTitle() As String

   On Error Resume Next

   ContactTitle = ItemsRecordset.Fields(g_cstrFieldContactTitle)

   If Err.Number <> 0 Then

      If Err.Number <> 3265 Then
         Err.Raise Err.Number, "ContactTitle Get", Err.Description
      End If

   End If

End Property
```

Our Business Rule for this field limits the values of ContactTitle, so we must make sure that ContactTitle is a valid value. We created the array m_avarAcceptableValuesTitle to hold all of the acceptable values. We will use this array to check the value inputted. So now add the following Let property:

```
Public Property Let ContactTitle(ByVal v_strNewContactTitle As String)

   Dim lngArrayCount As Long
   Dim blnCorrect As Boolean
   Dim lngUpperLimit As Long

   On Error GoTo ContactTitleLetError

   If m_blnValidatingFieldChange = True Then
      Exit Property
   End If

   If m_eEditMode = adEditInProgress Or m_eEditMode = adEditAdd Then

      blnCorrect = False
      lngUpperLimit = UBound(m_avarAcceptableValuesTitle)
         For lngArrayCount = 1 To lngUpperLimit
            If UCase(v_strNewContactTitle) = _
               UCase(m_avarAcceptableValuesTitle(lngArrayCount)) Then
               blnCorrect = True
            End If
         Next

         If blnCorrect = False Then
            Err.Raise 1004, "ContactTitleLet:", _
               GetErrorText(errCustomerTitleType)
         End If
```

```
            ItemsRecordset.Fields(g_cstrFieldContactTitle) = _
                    v_strNewContactTitle

    ElseIf m_eEditMode = adEditNone Then
        Err.Raise 1001, "ContactTitle Let:", GetErrorText(errChangeFieldNoEdit)

    End If

    Exit Property

ContactTitleLetError:

    Err.Raise Err.Number, "ContactTitle Let " & Err.Source, Err.Description

End Property
```

We also need a `Public` property that allows the user to get the `m_avarAcceptableValuesTitle` array. So add the following property to our `clsCustomer` class:

```
Public Property Get GetCustomerContactTitleValues() as Variant

    GetCustomerContactTitleValues = m_avarAcceptableValuesTitle

End Property
```

The rest of our fields do not have any constraints beside size, so we can code them without any specific rules. They are presented below; add each on to our `clsCustomer` class.

Customer Object Property: ContactName

```
Public Property Get ContactName() As String

    On Error Resume Next

    ContactName = ItemsRecordset.Fields(g_cstrFieldContactName)

    If Err.Number <> 0 Then

        If Err.Number <> 3265 Then
            Err.Raise Err.Number, "ContactName Get", Err.Description
        End If

    End If

End Property

Public Property Let ContactName(ByVal v_strNewContactName As String)

    On Error GoTo ContactNameLetError

    If m_blnValidatingFieldChange = True Then
        Exit Property
    End If

    If m_eEditMode = adEditInProgress Or m_eEditMode = adEditAdd Then
        m_blnIgnoreFieldChange = True
        ItemsRecordset.Fields(g_cstrFieldContactName) = _
                v_strNewContactName
```

```
      ElseIf m_eEditMode = adEditNone Then
         Err.Raise 1001, "ContactName Let:", GetErrorText(errChangeFieldNoEdit)

    End If

    Exit Property

ContactNameLetError:

    Err.Raise Err.Number, "ContactName Let " & Err.Source, Err.Description

End Property
```

Customer Object Property: Address

```
Public Property Get Address() As String

  On Error Resume Next

  Address = ItemsRecordset.Fields(g_cstrFieldAddress)

  If Err.Number <> 0 Then

    If Err.Number <> 3265 Then
       Err.Raise Err.Number, "Address Get", Err.Description
    End If

  End If

End Property
```

```
Public Property Let Address(ByVal v_strNewAddress As String)

  On Error GoTo AddressLetError

  If m_blnValidatingFieldChange = True Then
     Exit Property
  End If

  If m_eEditMode = adEditInProgress Or m_eEditMode = adEditAdd Then
     m_blnIgnoreFieldChange = True
     ItemsRecordset.Fields(g_cstrFieldAddress) = v_strNewAddress

  ElseIf m_eEditMode = adEditNone Then
     Err.Raise 1001, "Address Let:", GetErrorText(errChangeFieldNoEdit)

  End If

  Exit Property

AddressLetError:

  Err.Raise Err.Number, "Address Let " & Err.Source, Err.Description

End Property
```

VB6 UML

Customer Object Property: City

```
Public Property Get City() As String

  On Error Resume Next

  City = ItemsRecordset.Fields(g_cstrFieldCity)

  If Err.Number <> 0 Then

     If Err.Number <> 3265 Then
        Err.Raise Err.Number, "City Get", Err.Description
     End If

  End If

End Property

Public Property Let City(ByVal v_strNewcity As String)

  On Error GoTo CityLetError

  If m_blnValidatingFieldChange = True Then
     Exit Property
  End If

  If m_eEditMode = adEditInProgress Or m_eEditMode = adEditAdd Then
     m_blnIgnoreFieldChange = True
     ItemsRecordset.Fields(g_cstrFieldCity) = v_strNewcity

  ElseIf m_eEditMode = adEditNone Then
     Err.Raise 1001, "City Let:", GetErrorText(errChangeFieldNoEdit)

  End If

  Exit Property

CityLetError:

  Err.Raise Err.Number, "City Let" & Err.Source, Err.Description

End Property
```

Customer Object Property: Region

```
Public Property Get Region() As String

  On Error Resume Next

  Region = ItemsRecordset.Fields(g_cstrFieldRegion)

  If Err.Number <> 0 Then

     If Err.Number <> 3265 Then
        Err.Raise Err.Number, "Region Get", Err.Description
     End If

  End If

End Property
```

```
   Public Property Let Region(ByVal v_strNewregion As String)

     On Error GoTo RegionLetError

     If m_blnValidatingFieldChange = True Then
        Exit Property
     End If

     If m_eEditMode = adEditInProgress Or m_eEditMode = adEditAdd Then
        m_blnIgnoreFieldChange = True
        ItemsRecordset.Fields(g_cstrFieldRegion) = v_strNewregion

     ElseIf m_eEditMode = adEditNone Then
        Err.Raise 1001, "Region Let:", GetErrorText(errChangeFieldNoEdit)

     End If

     Exit Property

RegionLetError:

     Err.Raise Err.Number, "Region Let " & Err.Source, Err.Description

End Property
```

Customer Object Property: Postal Code

```
   Public Property Get PostalCode() As String

     On Error Resume Next

     PostalCode = ItemsRecordset.Fields(g_cstrFieldPostalCode)

     If Err.Number <> 0 Then

        If Err.Number <> 3265 Then
           Err.Raise Err.Number, "PostalCode Get", Err.Description
        End If

     End If

End Property
```

```
   Public Property Let PostalCode(ByVal v_strNewPostalCode As String)

     On Error GoTo PostalCodeLetError

     If m_blnValidatingFieldChange = True Then
        Exit Property
     End If

     If m_eEditMode = adEditInProgress Or m_eEditMode = adEditAdd Then
        m_blnIgnoreFieldChange = True
        ItemsRecordset.Fields(g_cstrFieldPostalCode) = v_strNewPostalCode

     ElseIf m_eEditMode = adEditNone Then
        Err.Raise 1001, "PostalCode Let:", GetErrorText(errChangeFieldNoEdit)

     End If
```

```
      Exit Property

PostalCodeLetError:

   Err.Raise Err.Number, "PostalCode Let " & Err.Source, Err.Description

End Property
```

Customer Object Property: Country

```
Public Property Get Country() As String

   On Error Resume Next

   Country = ItemsRecordset.Fields(g_cstrFieldCountry)

   If Err.Number <> 0 Then

      If Err.Number <> 3265 Then
         Err.Raise Err.Number, "Country Get", Err.Description
      End If

   End If

End Property
```

```
Public Property Let Country(ByVal v_strNewCountry As String)

   On Error GoTo CountryLetError

   If m_blnValidatingFieldChange = True Then
      Exit Property
   End If

   If m_eEditMode = adEditInProgress Or m_eEditMode = adEditAdd Then
      m_blnIgnoreFieldChange = True
      ItemsRecordset.Fields(g_cstrFieldCountry) = v_strNewCountry

   ElseIf m_eEditMode = adEditNone Then
      Err.Raise 1001, "Country Let:", GetErrorText(errChangeFieldNoEdit)

   End If

   Exit Property

CountryLetError:

   Err.Raise Err.Number, "Country Let " & Err.Source, Err.Description

End Property
```

Customer Object Property: Phone

```
Public Property Get Phone() As String

   On Error Resume Next

   Phone = ItemsRecordset.Fields(g_cstrFieldPhone)
```

```
        If Err.Number <> 0 Then

            If Err.Number <> 3265 Then
                Err.Raise Err.Number, "Phone Get", Err.Description
            End If

        End If

End Property


Public Property Let Phone(ByVal v_strNewPhone As String)

  On Error GoTo PhoneLetError

  If m_blnValidatingFieldChange = True Then
     Exit Property
  End If

  If m_eEditMode = adEditInProgress Or m_eEditMode = adEditAdd Then
     m_blnIgnoreFieldChange = True
     ItemsRecordset.Fields(g_cstrFieldPhone) = v_strNewPhone

  ElseIf m_eEditMode = adEditNone Then
     Err.Raise 1001, "Phone Let:", GetErrorText(errChangeFieldNoEdit)

  End If

  Exit Property

PhoneLetError:

  Err.Raise Err.Number, "Phone Let " & Err.Source, Err.Description

End Property
```

Customer Object Property: Fax

```
Public Property Get Fax() As String

  On Error Resume Next

  Fax = ItemsRecordset.Fields(g_cstrFieldFax)

  If Err.Number <> 0 Then

     If Err.Number <> 3265 Then
        Err.Raise Err.Number, "Fax Get", Err.Description
     End If

  End If

End Property


Public Property Let Fax(ByVal v_strNewFax As String)

  On Error GoTo FaxLetError

  If m_blnValidatingFieldChange = True Then
     Exit Property
  End If
```

```
       If m_eEditMode = adEditInProgress Or m_eEditMode = adEditAdd Then
          m_blnIgnoreFieldChange = True
          ItemsRecordset.Fields(g_cstrFieldFax) = v_strNewFax

       ElseIf m_eEditMode = adEditNone Then
          Err.Raise 1001, "Fax Let:", GetErrorText(errChangeFieldNoEdit)

       End If

       Exit Property

    FaxLetError:

       Err.Raise Err.Number, "Fax Let " & Err.Source, Err.Description

    End Property
```

We've now implemented Property routines for all the possible Customer attributes, but there are a few additional properties that our Bottom Class (`clsCustomer`) requires.

Bottom Class: EditMode Property

Our `EditMode` property will not have any validation; it will simply return the value of the private variable `m_eEditMode`. The `Editmode` will be set by the Middle Class, `clsCustomerManager`, when its own Edit Mode property changes. We will make this `Property Let` in our Bottom Class a `Friend` function - so that the Middle Class can change the value of the Bottom class' `EditMode` property.

It's impossible, though, for the Bottom Class to set the Edit Mode in the Middle Class (see Object Hierarchy Rule 3). Whenever a record is changed, the `FieldChanged` event will be called in the Bottom Class. We will set the EditMode to `adEditInProgress`. To tell the Middle Class that the `EditMode` property has changed in the Bottom Class, we raise our user-defined event called `EditInProgress`.

This property will use the ADODB enumerated type for `EditMode`.

Bottom Class: The EditMode Properties

```
    Public Property Get EditMode() As ADODB.EditModeEnum

      EditMode = m_eEditMode

    End Property
```

In the `Let` property, we will raise the `EditInProgress` event to notify the Middle Class of the new value:

```
    Friend Property Let EditMode(ByVal v_eNewEditMode As ADODB.EditModeEnum)

      m_eEditMode = v_eNewEditMode
      RaiseEvent EditInProgress(v_eNewEditMode)

    End Property
```

Bottom Class: Updating the Data Consumers

We made the decision to allow each Middle Class to have only one DataMember. When we wanted different views of the Customer information, we would create different instances (copies) of the Middle class, one for each collection, each having their own unique DataMember.

Bottom Class: Retrieving the DataMember

In the Customer example, there are two possible views:

- ❑ All customers
- ❑ Customers whose title is equal a certain value

We will want to save this DataMember in a `Private` variable, and be able to retrieve it. We will make the `Property Let` a friend property, so that the Middle Class can set this property.

Add these Properties to our `clsCustomer` Bottom Class:

```
Friend Property Let ItemsDataMember(ByVal v_strNewCustomerDataMember As String)

   m_strManagedObjectDataMember = v_strNewCustomerDataMember

End Property
```

```
Private Property Get ItemsDataMember() As String

   ItemsDataMember = m_strManagedObjectDataMember

End Property
```

Bottom Class: Refreshing the Data Consumers Information

Every time the recordset changes, we must call the `DataMemberChanged` method to force all controls bound to the recordset (Data Consumers) to refresh their copy of the recordset. This will not happen automatically, i.e. a change in the recordset will not cause the controls to refresh automatically, so we need to force the issue, so to speak.

Therefore add the following `Friend Sub` to the `clsCustomer` class:

```
Friend Sub RefreshDataMember()

   DataMemberChanged ItemsDataMember

End Sub
```

Every control bound to this Customer class which has its `DataMember` property set to `ItemsDataMember`, will now know the recordset has changed. When the Data Consumers are informed that the recordset has changed through the `DataMemberChanged` method (which is part of a Visual Basic Data Provider class) they will call the class `GetDataMember` method.

We have nearly finished with our Bottom Class. The Middle Class will need to get the recordset from this Bottom Class. As we only need to retrieve the recordset, and do not need to have the Middle Class perform any actions, we will use Object Heirarchy Rule 1, and create a property to retrieve the recordset.

Bottom Class: Retrieve the Recordset

These properties will be `Friend` properties because we only want the recordset to be available from within the component. The `Property Get` will just return the recordset variable `m_recManagedObjects`.

So add this to our `clsCustomer` class:

```
Friend Property Get ItemsRecordset() As ADODB.Recordset

  Set ItemsRecordset = m_recManagedObjects

End Property
```

While the Bottom Class will be holding the recordset, because of the rules of object hierarchies, the Middle Class will be performing the Management for this class.

The functions of the Middle Class include starting edits, add news, and retrieving the recordset from the server component. When the Middle Class retrieves the recordset, we will need to pass the recordset down to the Bottom Class. Therefore, we will need a `Property Set` (a recordset is an object, so we need to use `Set`, not `Let`).

Add this final piece of code to our `clsCustomer` class:

```
Friend Property Set ItemsRecordset(ByVal v_recNewRecordset As ADODB.Recordset)

  Set m_recManagedObjects = v_recNewRecordset

End Property
```

This completes the Bottom Class. Now we will move on to the Middle Class.

Implementing The Middle Class

This Middle or Managing class is used to hold most of the *methods* for our Customer component. We can therefore expect to be implementing more methods than we did for the Bottom Class, and significantly less properties.

As we are using RDS to connect to our server object, we don't need to add a reference to the server object in this this project. However, we will need the Public enumerated types that are in the server component for configuring our updates.

Therefore, copy the `TableName` enumerated type from the server object to the `clsCustomerManager` class.

> Or you may wish to just copy the relevant `Enum TableName` *lines below, that I haven't shaded.*

Now add the following enumerated types to our `clsCustomerManager` Middle Class:

```
Option Explicit

Enum TableName
  e_Customers = 0
  e_OrderDetails = 1
  e_orders = 2
  e_Products = 3
  e_Shippers = 4
  e_Employees = 5
  e_Suppliers = 6
End Enum
```

```
Public Enum BOFActionType
  adMoveFirst = 0
  adStayBOF = 1
End Enum
```

```
Public Enum EOFActionType
  adMoveLast = 0
  adStayEOF = 1
  adAddNew = 2
End Enum
```

BOFActionType and EOFAction type will determine how our object will behave when we pass the first and last records:

```
Private m_eRecordsetName As TableName
Private m_strWhereClause As String
Private m_strDataMember As String
Private m_strPrimaryKey As String
Private m_eBOFAction As BOFActionType
Private m_eEOFAction As EOFActionType
Private m_strUserName As String
Private m_strPassword As String
Private m_eEditMode As ADODB.EditModeEnum

Private WithEvents m_objManagedObject As clsCustomer

Public Event ChangeManagedObjects()
```

Variable Name	Purpose
m_eRecordsetName	We need to know what table we are referencing when we call the server object to update information. As this is going to be a generic object, we will place this information into this class. We will pass this variable down from the Collection Managing Class.
m_strWhereClause	This is the WHERE clause that will be passed to the server object to return the correct Customer Collection. It will also be passed down from the Top Class.
m_strDataMember	The DataMember for this class, also set by the Collection Managing Class.

Table Continued on Following Page

Variable Name	Purpose
m_strPrimaryKey	This is the field that is the primary key. It will be needed in several places.
	This is also passed down from the Top Class.
m_eBOFAction	This will determine what the Managing object should do when it moves before the first customer.
m_eEOFAction	This will determine what the Managing object should do when it moves after the last customer.
m_strUserName	The name of the application user, required to get access to the database.
m_strPassword	The password of the application user, required to get access to the database.
m_objManagedObject	The object that is being managed, in this case a Customer Object. This line of code will have to be changed when building other Components, such as an Employee Object.
m_eEditMode	To determine what edit mode the class is in.

Next, we will add some constants that will be used to initialize some of our variables. Add the following lines to our `clsCustomerManager` class:

```
Const m_def_BOFAction = BOFActionType.adMoveFirst
Const m_def_EOFAction = EOFActionType.adMoveLast
Const m_def_UserName = ""
Const m_def_Password = ""
```

The next lines of code create the RDS proxy object - add them right along into our `clsCustomerManager` class:

```
Private m_objDataSpace As RDS.DataSpace
Private m_objProxy 'As prjServer.clsServer
```

The variable `m_objProxy` will hold a pointer to the server object.

> *If you created a reference to* `prjServer`, *you can uncomment the part of this code that reads* `As prjServer.clsServer`. *This allows you to run under straight COM and can be helpful for debugging purposes.*

Middle Class: Coding the Class Events

Like the Bottom Class, this Middle Class is a data source and, as such, gains the GetDataMember as an intrinsic class event.

Middle Class: The GetDataMember Event

This is the event raised when a Data Consumer has set its DataSource property equal to the clsCustomerManager Object. The DataMember for the class is set by the Collection Managing Object. If the Data Provider's DataMember property is not the same as the DataMember for this class, we will be returning the wrong recordset. Therefore we must first make sure that the DataMember parameter that was passed in is the same as the DataMember of this instance of the class.

So add this method to our clsCustomerManager class:

```
Private Sub Class_GetDataMember(DataMember As String, Data As Object)

    On Error GoTo GetDataMemberError

    If ItemsDataMember <> DataMember Then
        Exit Sub
    End If
```

Next, we must pass back the DataMember:

```
    Set Data = m_objManagedObject.ItemsRecordset

    Exit Sub
```

Last, we'll make the error trap:

```
GetDataMemberError:

    Set Data = Nothing

End Sub
```

Middle Class: Initializing the Class

When this Middle Class initializes, we will also need to initialize our Bottom Class Customer object:

```
Private Sub Class_Initialize()

    On Error GoTo IntitializeError

    Set m_objManagedObject = New clsCustomer
```

We also have to initialize the Proxy object. We'll be coding a separate method in a minute that sets up the proxy to connect with the server object through RDS, so we can just call it from here:

```
    GetProxy
```

If you made a reference to the server object in your Project's references you could *alternatively* add:

```
Set m_objProxy = New prjServer.clsServer
```

You can use this if you do not want to try using the RDS with HTTP, or you don't have an IIS web server to run RDS with HHTP.

Now let's set the default values for our member variables:

```
m_eBOFAction = m_def_BOFAction
m_eEOFAction = m_def_EOFAction
m_strUserName = m_def_UserName
m_strPassword = m_def_Password
m_eEditMode = adEditNone
```

Next, we'll make the error handler. We must use a message box here, since we can't raise an error in the `Initialize` event:

```
Exit Sub

IntitializeError:

    MsgBox "Collection Managing Class cannot be initialized"

End Sub
```

Middle Class: The GetProxy Method

The `GetProxy` method is very simple and doesn't do anything we haven't already seen in the test project. The only issue is how to use RDS, e.g. through COM, HTTP etc.

```
Public Sub GetProxy()

    Set m_objDataSpace = New RDS.DataSpace

    m_objDataSpace.InternetTimeout = 30000

    Set m_objProxy = m_objDataSpace.CreateObject
    ("prjServer.clsServer", "webserver")

End Sub
```

You'll need to adjust the `CreateObject` *statement for your own particular setup.*

Middle Class: Coding The Terminate Event

The `Terminate` event must destroy any objects created:

```
Private Sub Class_Terminate()

If Not m_objManagedObject Is Nothing Then
    Set m_objManagedObject = Nothing
End If

End Sub
```

Middle Class: Getting Information From the Top Class

We have several variables that will need to be passed down from the Top Class (the Collection Managing Class) to the Middle Class. To keep it simple, we will pass all of the variables in at once into one function. This will prevent us from having to make many separate calls, which could take a significant time. As most of these variables are concerned with the server object, which we are referring to as a Proxy object, we will call this function `SetProxyInformation`.

Middle Class: Coding SetProxyInformation

We will make this a `Friend Function` with parameters for the table name, the WHERE clause, the primary key and DataMember:

```
Friend Function SetProxyInformation(ByVal v_eRecordsetName As TableName, _
    ByVal v_strWhereClause As String, ByVal v_strPrimaryKey As String, _
    ByVal v_eDataMember As String)
```

We will now set the `clsCustomerManager` class' private variables to these values:

```
    m_eRecordsetName = v_eRecordsetName
    m_strWhereClause = v_strWhereClause
    m_strPrimaryKey = v_strPrimaryKey
    m_strDataMember = v_eDataMember
    m_objManagedObject.ItemsDataMember = v_eDataMember

End Function
```

Middle Class: General Properties

We will have to make several general properties for our `clsCustomerManager` class.

Middle Class: Creating a Property to Get the DataMember

We will need a property to get the DataMember. By using only a Get property we can make this property read-only. The Top Class will set the DataMember, so this will be a `Friend Property`:

```
Friend Property Get ItemsDataMember() As String

    ItemsDataMember = m_strDataMember

End Property
```

Middle Class: Get Properties for the Table, WhereClause, and PrimaryKey Information

The `Get` Properties for these would be as follows. Add them to our `clsCustomerManager` class:

```
Private Property Get PrimaryKey() As String

    PrimaryKey = m_strPrimaryKey

End Property
```

`RecordsetName` is the name of the recordet we are using. It will be used to retireve the correct recordset from the database:

```
Private Property Get RecordsetName() As TableName

  RecordsetName = m_eRecordsetName

End Property
```

The `WhereClause` property will be built when a recordset is being built using a WHERE clause.

```
Private Property Get WhereClause() As String

  WhereClause = m_strWhereClause

End Property
```

Middle Class: Creating a Property to Retrieve a Customer Object

We want to create a property that will retrieve a Customer object. This is a hierarchy and the only way to access this Customer Bottom Class is through this property. There will be no `Let` property as the Customer can only be created by the Middle Class:

```
Public Property Get Item() As clsCustomer

  Set Item = m_objManagedObject

End Property
```

Middle Class: Creating a Property to Get the Number of Customers

We will need a property that will return the number of customers. The ADO recordset will have a `RecordCount` property that we can use to determine the number of customers:

```
Public Property Get ItemCount() As Long

  ItemCount = m_objManagedObject.ItemsRecordset.RecordCount

End Property
```

There will be no `Let` property as this value cannot be changed by the user.

Middle Class: Creating a Property to Return the Recordset

We've already seen that the Bottom Class needed a `Public` property called `GetItemsRecordset` to get the ADO Recordset that is used to store/retrieve/update information.

This will be a `Friend Get Property`, as we do not want this recordset accessed outside of the component:

```
Friend Property Get ItemsRecordset() As ADODB.Recordset

  Set ItemsRecordset = m_objManagedObject.ItemsRecordset

End Property
```

Middle Class: Private Properties Related to the Database

Middle Class: Creating the EditMode Property

We will make the Get Property public here - so that the Edit mode can be checked. Add the following property to our clsCustomerManager class:

```
Public Property Get EditMode() As ADODB.EditModeEnum

   EditMode = m_eEditMode

End Property
```

The Let Property will be a Friend Property as the Edit mode should only be set internally - it can only be set through either the Edit or AddNew methods that we'll code shortly. We need to sync the EditMode of both the Bottom and Middle Class. So if the value of the EditMode in the Bottom Class is not the same as that in the Middle Class, then we need to change the Bottom Class' EditMode so they're both the same:

```
Friend Property Let EditMode(ByVal v_eNewEditMode As ADODB.EditModeEnum)

   m_eEditMode = v_eNewEditMode

   If m_objManagedObject.EditMode <> v_eNewEditMode Then
      m_objManagedObject.EditMode = v_eNewEditMode
   End If

End Property
```

Middle Class: Public Properties Related to the Database

We will need a Refresh method so the user can refresh the records. Once we have finished with the refresh, we also want to put the user back to the record they were on prior to the refresh. To keep this simple, we'll do this by getting the value of the primary key field the recordset is currently at. After we refresh the recordset, we can then reset the recordset to the original recordset using that value.

Middle Class: The Refresh Sub

So we start with the Refresh Sub. Add a variable to store the value of the current record's primary key field. Do this by adding the following lines to our clsCustomerManager class:

```
Public Sub Refresh()

   Dim strPrimaryKeyValue As String 'Use to keep to current record
```

We will want to begin by saving the value of the current record's primary key field. If the recordset is not initialized or there are no records, there will be no current value.

We proceed by checking to see if the recordset has been initialized by checking the recordset's State property:

```
   If m_objManagedObject.ItemsRecordset.State = adStateOpen Then
```

Next, we make sure there are records, and if there are, we will save the primary key value:

```
        If Not m_objManagedObject.ItemsRecordset.BOF And _
            Not m_objManagedObject.ItemsRecordset.EOF And_
            NotIsNull(m_objManagedObject.ItemsRecordset.Fields(PrimaryKey)) Then
            strPrimaryKeyValue = _
                    m_objManagedObject.ItemsRecordset.Fields(PrimaryKey)
        End If
    End If
```

Next, we will call a method that will update the recordset:

```
    UpdateManagedObjects
```

If there is value for the Primary Key field, we can use it to move to that record:

```
    If strPrimaryKeyValue <> "" Then
        m_objManagedObject.ItemsRecordset.Find PrimaryKey & "='" & _
                strPrimaryKeyValue & "'",,,1
    End If

End Sub
```

There is one little quirk with using the `Find` method. If the record is not found, it will move the recordset to the last record. It might be better if you checked to see if this happens and, if it does, move to the first record. I will leave this up to you.

Middle Class: The Edit Sub

The `Edit` subroutine is used to set the current edit mode of the recordset to indicate that it is being edited. We first need to check that the `EditMode` is set to `adEditNone` because you cannot start an `Edit` in the middle of an `AddNew` or `Delete` (and you do not want to start an `Edit` if you are already editing).

If the `EditMode` is set to `adEditNone`, we need to set both the Middle and Top Class' `EditMode` to `adEditInProgress`. We've already created a property to do this so it's quite straightforward. Add the following code to the `clsCustomerManager` class:

```
    Public Sub Edit()

        If EditMode = adEditNone Then
            EditMode = adEditInProgress
        End If

    End Sub
```

We're not going to handle any errors here, but you can add in an `Else` clause to do so. You would probably want to ignore the error of being in an `Edit`, but handle the error of being in an `AddNew`.

Middle Class: Deleting a Record

To delete a record, we first delete the current record from the recordset and then send the updated recordset to the database. This function will use the variables passed in by the Collection Managing function to delete the current record. Add the following code to the `clsCustomerManager` class:

```
Public Sub Delete()

    On Error GoTo DeleteError
```

We do not want to allow a delete if an AddNew or Edit is in progress. Because the EditMode property is not set when a delete is performed, the EditMode property should be set to adEditNone:

```
    If EditMode = adEditNone Then
```

If the delete is allowed, delete the current record and update the database:

```
    If EditMode = adEditNone Then
      m_objManagedObject.ItemsRecordset.Delete
        Set m_objManagedObject.ItemsRecordset = _
          m_objProxy.UpdateRecordset(UserName, Password, _
          m_objManagedObject.ItemsRecordset, m_eRecordsetName, WhereClause)
```

We will include an Else statement:

```
    Else
      GetErrorText "CanNotDeleteDuringEdit/AddNew"
    End If

    End If
```

Finally, we'll exit the Sub and make the error trap:

```
    Exit Sub

DeleteError:

    Err.Raise Err.Number, "Delete " & Err.Source, Err.Description

End Sub
```

Middle Class: Creating the AddNew Method

This sub will allow an AddNew session to begin. We will first check if there is already an AddNew or an Edit in progress by checking the EditMode property. It should be set to adEditNone. Add the following code to the clsCustomerManager class:

```
Public Sub AddNew()

    On Error GoTo AddNewError

    If EditMode = adEditNone Then
```

If there is no AddNew or Edit in progress, perform an AddNew on the recordset:

```
      m_objManagedObject.ItemsRecordset.AddNew
      EditMode = adEditAdd
   Else

   End If
```

Again, you can add error handling to the `Else` statement if you wish.

Finally, let's add the error trap:

```
   Exit Sub

AddNewError:

   Err.Raise Err.Number, "AddNew " & Err.Source, Err.Description

End Sub
```

Middle Class: Creating the Cancel Sub

This method is very simple. All we do is check to make sure an `Edit` or `AddNew` is in progress, and if it it we cancel it:

```
Public Sub Cancel()

   If EditMode = adEditAdd Or EditMode = adEditInProgress Then
      ItemsRecordset.CancelUpdate
      EditMode = adEditNone
   End If

End Sub
```

Middle Class: Creating the Update Sub

The `Update` method will begin by getting the current record's primary key value. We'll save this value so we can return to this record after the update. Add the following code to our `clsCustomerManager` class:

```
Public Sub Update()

   Dim strPrimaryKeyValue As String

   On Error GoTo UpdateError

   If m_objManagedObject.ItemsRecordset.State = adStateOpen And _
         m_objManagedObject.ItemsRecordset.EditMode <> adEditDelete Then
            If m_objManagedObject.ItemsRecordset.RecordCount <> 0 Then
               strPrimaryKeyValue = _
                  m_objManagedObject.ItemsRecordset.Fields(PrimaryKey)
            End If
   End If
```

We will make sure an `AddNew` or `Edit` is in progress by checking the `EditMode`:

```
   If EditMode <> adEditNone Then
```

Then we'll send the `Update` to the server object:

```
Set m_objManagedObject.ItemsRecordset = m_objProxy.UpdateRecordset(UserName, _
        Password, m_objManagedObject.ItemsRecordset, m_eRecordsetName, _
        WhereClause)
EditMode = adEditNone

m_objProxy.UpdateRecordset UserName, Password, _
        m_objManagedObject.ItemsRecordset, RecordsetName, WhereClause
```

Next, the `EditMode` has to be reset to `adEditNone`:

```
EditMode = adEditNone
```

It's possible that there are other Customer objects that are using different Middle Class objects with a different Customer Collection. As we just changed the Customer recordset, we need to raise an event to let the Top Collection Managing class know to refresh all of the Customer Collections:

```
    RaiseEvent ChangeManagedObjects
End If
```

Now we'll reset the current record:

```
If strPrimaryKeyValue <> "" Then
    m_objManagedObject.ItemsRecordset.Find PrimaryKey & "='" & _
        strPrimaryKeyValue & "'"
End If
```

And finally, exit the sub and put in the error trap:

```
Exit Sub

UpdateError:

    Err.Raise Err.Number, "Update: " & Err.Source, Err.Description

End Sub
```

Middle Class: Finding a Record

In the `Find` function, we will be finding a Customer by their Company Name. As a Company Name is registered (®), it's unlikely two companies could have the same name. For simplicity, we will assume there is only one Customer with a particular Company Name. If this were not the case, we would have to add a `FindNext` method also. Add the following code to the `clsCustomerManager` class:

```
Public Function Find(ByVal v_strCompanyName As String)

    Dim strCompanyName As String
```

If no company name was passed in, then exit the sub:

```
   If v_strCompanyName = "" Then
     Exit Function
   End If
```

Unfortunately, one of the Company Names, in the Northwind database, has an apostrophe character (') in it, which will affect our queries. We'll simply truncate off the rest of the name after this character for simplicity:

```
   If InStr(v_strCompanyName, "'") > 0 Then
       strCompanyName = Mid(v_strCompanyName, 1, InStr(v_strCompanyName, "'") - 1)
   Else
       strCompanyName = v_strCompanyName
   End If
```

Finally, we will find the correct record:

```
   ItemsRecordset.Find g_cstrFieldCompanyName & "= '" & _
           strCompanyName & "'", 0, adSearchForward, adBookmarkFirst
```

Now we must refresh all of the Data Consumers so they also move to this new record:

```
   Refresh

End Function
```

Middle Class: Database - Returning the RecordCount

The RecordCount property will simply return the recordset's recordcount. Add the following code to the clsCustomerManager class:

```
Public Property Get RecordCount() As Long

   RecordCount = m_objManagedObject.ItemsRecordset.RecordCount

End Property
```

Middle Class: Coding the Move Methods

The MoveFirst and MoveLast methods will first make sure the recordset exists, and then move to the correct record:

```
Public Sub MoveFirst()

   On Error GoTo MoveFirstError

   If m_objManagedObject.ItemsRecordset Is Nothing Then
       Exit Sub
   End If

   If m_objManagedObject.ItemsRecordset.Recordcount > 0 Then
       m_objManagedObject.ItemsRecordset.MoveFirst
   End If

   Exit Sub
```

```
   MoveFirstError:

     Err.Raise Err.Number, "Move First " & Err.Source, Err.Description

   End Sub

   Public Sub MoveLast()

     On Error GoTo MoveLastError

     If m_objManagedObject.ItemsRecordset Is Nothing Then
        Exit Sub
     End If

     If m_objManagedObject.ItemsRecordset.Recordcount > 0 Then
        m_objManagedObject.ItemsRecordset.MoveLast
     End If

     Exit Sub

   MoveLastError:

     Err.Raise Err.Number, "Move Last " & Err.Source, Err.Description

   End Sub
```

The rest of the Move functions are more complicated because they can move past the last or first record. What we do depends on the BOFAction and EOFAction properties:

For the MoveNext we start by checking if the recordset exists. Carry on adding code to the clsCustomerManager class as follows:

```
   Public Sub MoveNext()

     On Error GoTo MoveNextError

     If m_objManagedObject.ItemsRecordset Is Nothing Then
        Exit Sub
     End If
```

Next we perform the MoveNext:

```
     If m_objManagedObject.ItemsRecordset.EOF = False Then
        m_objManagedObject.ItemsRecordset.MoveNext
     End If
```

We check to see if the recordset has moved past the last record:

```
     If m_objManagedObject.ItemsRecordset.EOF = True Then
```

If we are past the last record, how we will handle this depends on the value of m_eEOFAction. EOFAction is a public property that will be set by the user of the component:

```
      Select Case EOFAction
          Case EOFActionType.adAddNew
              m_objManagedObject.ItemsRecordset.AddNew
          Case EOFActionType.adMoveLast
              m_objManagedObject.ItemsRecordset.MoveLast
          Case EOFActionType.adStayEOF
              Exit Sub
          Case Else
              Exit Sub
      End Select

   End If

   Exit Sub

MoveNextError:

   Err.Raise Err.Number, "Move Next " & Err.Source, Err.Description

End Sub
```

`MovePrevious` will work in a similar manner:

```
Private Sub MovePrevious()

   On Error GoTo MovePreviousError

   If m_objManagedObject.ItemsRecordset Is Nothing Then Exit Sub

   If m_objManagedObject.ItemsRecordset.BOF Then
      Select Case BOFAction
          Case BOFActionType.adMoveFirst
              m_objManagedObject.ItemsRecordset.MoveFirst
          Case BOFActionType.adStayBOF
              Exit Sub
          Case Else
              Exit Sub
      End Select

   Else
       m_objManagedObject.ItemsRecordset.MovePrevious

   End If

   Exit Sub

MovePreviousError:

   Err.Raise Err.Number, "Move Previous Error" & Err.Source, _
           Err.Description

End Sub
```

Middle Class: Creating the UpdateManagedObjects Method

We will use this method to update the Data Consumers by calling the `DataMemberChanged` method. Add the following code to our `clsCustomerManager` class:

```
Private Sub UpdateManagedObjects()

  On Error GoTo UpdateManagedObjectsError

  Set m_objManagedObject.ItemsRecordset = _
      m_objProxy.ReturnCustomerRecordSet(UserName, Password, WhereClause)

  DataMemberChanged ItemsDataMember

  m_objManagedObject.RefreshDataMember

  Exit Sub

UpdateManagedObjectsError:

  MsgBox Err.Description & Err.Source

End Sub
```

Middle Class: Creating the UserName and Password Properties

These properties are standard properties using private variables. Add the following code to the `clsCustomerManager` class:

```
Public Property Get UserName() As String

  UserName = m_strUserName

End Property
```

```
Public Property Let UserName(ByVal New_strUserName As String)

  m_strUserName = New_strUserName

End Property
```

```
Public Property Get Password() As String

  Password = m_strPassword

End Property
```

```
Public Property Let Password(ByVal New_strPassword As String)

  m_strPassword = New_strPassword

End Property
```

Middle Class: Creating the Properties For BOFAction and EOFAction

These will also be standard properties:

```
Public Property Get BOFAction() As BOFActionType

  BOFAction = m_eBOFAction

End Property
```

```
Public Property Let BOFAction(ByVal New_BOFAction As BOFActionType)

  m_eBOFAction = New_BOFAction

End Property
```

```
Public Property Get EOFAction() As EOFActionType

  EOFAction = m_eEOFAction

End Property
```

```
Public Property Let EOFAction(ByVal New_EOFAction As EOFActionType)

  m_eEOFAction = New_EOFAction

End Property
```

Middle Class: Coding the Events From the Managed Object

We have to handle the two Events that are raised from the Bottom Class. If the Edit Mode changes on the Bottom Class then we need to resync the Middle Class by setting the `EditMode` property. Add the following code to our now rather lengthy `clsCustomerManager` class:

```
Private Sub m_objManagedObject_EditInProgress(ByVal v_strEditMode As Variant)

    EditMode = v_strEditMode

End Sub
```

If the Bottom Class indicates that the recordset needs to be refreshed we can call the `DataMemberChanged` method:

```
Private Sub m_objManagedObject_RefreshDataMember()

    DataMemberChanged ItemsDataMember

End Sub
```

Implementing The Top Collection Manager Class

Finally, we have reached the point of coding our Top Class. This class will manage all of our Customer Collections. We will hold these different collection objects in an array called `m_acolDataMemeberArray`.

We will only create two Customer Collections:

- ❑ m_colCustomerAll
- ❑ m_colCustomerTitle

`m_colCustomerTitle` will be a collection of customers whose title equals a certain value. The value that the title should be equal to will be stored in this Top Class and accessed through properties. Any values that will be part of WHERE clauses of our collections should be stored in the Middle Class and have properties associated with them.

It's time to code the Top Class, `ctlCustomers`. So add the following declarations to `ctlCustomers`, which we created earlier:

```
Option Explicit
```

```
Public Enum ClientDataMember
    e_AllCustomers = 1
    e_CustomersWhoseTitle = 2
End Enum

Const m_def_NumberOfCustomerCollections = 2
Const m_def_ContactTitleEquals As String = "Owner"

Private WithEvents m_colCustomerAll As clsCustomerManager
Private WithEvents m_colCustomerTitle As clsCustomerManager

Private m_acolDataMembersArray() As clsCustomerManager
Private m_ablnDataMembersInitialized() As Boolean
Private m_strContactTitleEquals As String
```

These variables have the following purposes:

Variable Name	Purpose
m_colCustomerAll	This is the Customer collection that contains all of the Customers.
m_colCustomerTitle	This is the Customer Collection that contains all of the Customers whose title is equal to the ContactTitlesEqual property.
m_acolDataMembersArray	This is the array containing all of the Customer Collections.
m_ablnDataMembersInitialized	This is an array of Booleans that determine if a Customer Collection has been initialized. We do not want to create a collection unless it is required.
m_strContactTitleEquals	The variable for the Where Clause for the Customer Title Collection.
m_def_ContactTitleEquals	A default value for the Customer Title.
m_def_NumberOfCustomerCollections	A default value for the number of Customer Collections.
ClientDataMember	The types of customer collections the managing class can have.

Top Class: Coding the Class Events

When the Top Class is initialized we want to create our **Array of Customer Collections**. What we do not want to do is fill these collections with values. There could be dozens of collections. We do not want to hoard endless resources by having dozens of objects with filled recordsets when the user only wants one collection object.

This is one very large potential danger of using disconnected recordsets. A user could easily use your objects to create dozens of customer collections, which would quickly overwhelm the client computer and the network. The users of your object have to understand that they must destroy a collection when they have finished with it.

Top Class: The Inititialize Event

Begin by initializing the two Customer Collection objects. Add this code to our control called `ctlCustomers`:

```
Private Sub UserControl_Initialize()

    Set m_colCustomerAll = New clsCustomerManager
    Set m_colCustomerTitle = New clsCustomerManager
```

Set the private variable `m_strContactTitleEquals` to its default value:

```
    m_strContactTitleEquals = m_def_ContactTitleEquals
```

Redim the two arrays, they will be 1 based (they will start at element 1):

```
    ReDim m_acolDataMembersArray(1 to m_def_NumberOfCustomerCollections)
    ReDim m_ablnDataMembersInitialized(1 to m_def_NumberOfCustomerCollections)
```

Place the collection objects into the collection array:

```
    Set m_acolDataMembersArray(e_AllCustomers) = m_colCustomerAll
    Set m_acolDataMembersArray(e_CustomersWhoseTitle) = m_colCustomerTitle
```

Place `False` into the array, which indicates if the collections have been populated with data:

```
    m_ablnDataMembersInitialized(e_AllCustomers) = False
    m_ablnDataMembersInitialized(e_CustomersWhoseTitle) = False

End Sub
```

Top Class: Coding Class Terminate

We have to clean up all of the objects:

```
Private Sub UserControl_Terminate()

    Set M_colCustomerAll = Nothing
    Set M_colCustomerTitle = Nothing

End Sub
```

Top Class: A Function to Retrieve the Customer Collection

We need a function that will return a Customer Collection. Using this class, one can gain access to the Middle Class. If the collection being requested is not yet created, then we must initialize the collection.

Top Class: Creating the GetCustomerCollection Object

Create a `Public Function` called `GetCustomerCollection` within our `ctlCustomers` control:

```
Public Function GetCustomerCollection(ByVal v_eDataMember As ClientDataMember) _
        As clsCustomerManager
```

The parameter `v_eDataMember` will indicate which Customer collection to retrieve. Begin by checking if the Customer collection that was requested has been initialized:

```
If m_ablnDataMembersInitialized(v_eDataMember) = False Then
```

If the collection has not been initialized, initialize it by passing the appropriate parameters down to the Middle Class using the `SetProxyInformation` function:

```
Select Case v_eDataMember

    Case e_AllCustomers
        m_acolDataMembersArray(e_AllCustomers).SetProxyInformation _
            e_Customers, "", g_cstrFieldCustomerID, g_cdmAllCustomers

    Case e_CustomersWhoseTitle
        m_acolDataMembersArray(e_CustomersWhoseTitle).SetProxyInformation _
            e_Customers, " WHERE ContactTitle='" & ContactTitleEquals & "'", _
            g_cstrFieldCustomerID, g_cdmCustomersContactTitleEquals

End Select
```

Now call the `Refresh` method of the Middle Class:

```
m_acolDataMembersArray(v_eDataMember).Refresh
```

Set the initialized array member for this collection to `True`:

```
m_ablnDataMembersInitialized(v_eDataMember) = True

End If
```

And finally return the Customer collection:

```
Set GetCustomerCollection = m_acolDataMembersArray(v_eDataMember)

End Function
```

Top Class: Refreshing All the Customer Collections

Whenever one Customer collection changes the value of the recordset, we have to refresh all of the other Customer collections so that they also have this new recordset. We'll create a sub that will be called when the Middle Class raises the event `ChangeManagedObjects`.

Top Class: The ChangeManagedObjects Sub

The collection raising the event does not need to be updated, but any other collections will. Therefore, we can use the DataMember associated with the collection that raised the event, to configure which collections to ignore and which need updating.

Create the sub with these variables, within our `ctlCustomers` control:

```
Private Sub ChangeManagedObjects(ByVal v_strDataMember As String)

    Dim lngCustomerCollNumber As Long
    Dim lngIgnoreCustomerNumber As Long
```

Set `IgnoreCustomerNumber` equal to the collection that we do not need to update:

```
Select Case v_strDataMember
    Case g_cdmAllCustomers
        lngIgnoreCustomerNumber = 1
    Case g_cdmCustomersContactTitleEquals
        lngIgnoreCustomerNumber = 2
End Select
```

Now move through the Customer collections and call the `Refresh` methods of all the collections except the one we are to ignore:

```
For lngCustomerCollNumber = 1 To m_def_NumberOfCustomerCollections

    If lngCustomerCollNumber <> lngIgnoreCustomerNumber Then
        If m_ablnDataMembersInitialized(lngCustomerCollNumber) = True Then
            m_acolDataMembersArray(lngCustomerCollNumber).Refresh
        End If
    End If

    Next

End Sub
```

Top Class: Coding the Events from the Managing Class

Each collection will have an event associated with it. For each event, call the `ChangedManagedObjects` sub:

```
Private Sub m_colCustomerAll_ChangeManagedObjects()

    ChangeManagedObjects g_cdmAllCustomers

End Sub
```

```
Private Sub m_colCustomerTitle_ChangeManagedObjects()

    ChangeManagedObjects g_cdmCustomersContactTitleEquals

End Sub
```

Top Class: Coding the ContactTitleEquals Property

`ContactTitleEquals` is for the `WHERE` clause of the Title Equals collection. This will be a standard property:

```
Public Property Get ContactTitleEquals() As String

    ContactTitleEquals = m_strContactTitleEquals

End Property

Public Property Let ContactTitleEquals(ByVal v_strNewContactTitleEquals As String)
    m_strContactTitleEquals = v_strNewContactTitleEquals

End Property
```

Summary

This has been a very long chapter - making a client component is not a simple task. By using UML diagrams earlier, however, we were able to see a pattern in our Client component that allowed us to build our components in an efficient and effective way. As such, we'll be able to use practically the same code in all the Middle classes.

We can now crank out the rest of our Client components with very little effort. The total time to make this component will probably be about a day. This is what patterns are all about. Once you find the patterns, you can use them to make a framework to build your code from. Our Server and Client components make up a Visual Basic DNA framework that allows you to quickly build projects.

In the next chapter we'll use the template we have made in this chapter to build three more Client components: Order Details, Orders and Products.

13

Coding the Other Client Components

In the last chapter, you saw how we coded the implementation for the Customer component on the client-side of our Northwind system. We must now proceed with the implementation of the:

- ❏ OrderDetails component
- ❏ Order component
- ❏ Product components

Fortunately, because of our design, coding these additional components requires less work than you might think. Using a hierarchy means that there is little to change in the Middle and Top Classes for them to work with any of our components. All we really need to concentrate on is the Bottom Class, which has properties specific to its purpose. We've essentially created a code template that we can apply to all of our components and then tweak for that component's specifics.

Therefore, in this chapter we'll be concentrating more on the differences between the components rather than the actual implementation.

Implementing the OrderDetails Component

We will proceed by building the Middle, Bottom and Top Classes for our OrderDetails component.

We'll be able to build this component using the code template that we created when we built the Customer component. The majority of the code in the Customer component can again be reused when we build the other component.

We will be building all our components within the same project group to make them easier to build and debug, but there's nothing to stop you creating them each separately.

To begin with, add a new ActiveX Control project to the `Customer` project.

Save Project Group as `OrderEntry.vbg` and the new project as `prjOrderDetails.vbp`.

Now call the control `ctlOrderDetails`.

Add two regular classes to the project. Call them `clsOrderDetail` and `clsOrderDetailManager`. Set the properties of the classes as follows:

DataBindingBehavior	0 - vbNone
DataSourceBehavior	1 - vbDataSource
Instancing	2 - Public Not Creatable
Persistable	0 - Not Persistable

Now add the following references in our project:

- ❑ The Remote Data Service Library 2.0
- ❑ Microsoft ActiveX Data Objects 2.0 library
- ❑ Microsoft Data Sources Interfaces

Here is how these Visual Basic elements map to our class hierarchy:

- ❑ **OrderDetails Top Class**: `ctlOrderDetails` control
- ❑ **OrderDetails Middle Class**: `clsOrderDetailManager` class
- ❑ **OrderDetails Bottom Class**: `clsOrderDetail` class

OrderDetails: basODMain

As with our `Customer` component, we'll need to create a bas module for constants and shared functions. So add a standard BAS module to the project, and call the module `basODMain`.

We will first use an Enum for error and constants for all of the fields in the `Order` table:

```
Public Enum OrderDetailErrors
  errChangeFieldNoEdit = 1001
End Enum

Public Const g_odFieldOrderID As String = "OrderID"
Public Const g_odFieldProductID As String = "ProductID"
Public Const g_odFieldUnitPrice As String = "UnitPrice"
Public Const g_odFieldQuantity As String = "Quantity"
Public Const g_odFieldDiscount As String = "Discount"
Public Const g_odFieldProductName As String = "ProductName"
Public Const g_oddmAllOrderDetails As String = "OrderDetails"
```

Next, we'll use the same `GetErrorText` module as we used in the Customer component.

OrderDetails: Coding the GetErrorText Method

This is the same as before:

```
Public Function GetErrorText(ByVal v_lngErrorNumber As Long)

  On Error GoTo GetErrorText_Error

  GetErrorText = LoadResString(v_lngErrorNumber)

  Exit Function

GetErrorText_Error:

  If Err.Number <> 0 Then
     GetErrorText = "An unknown error has occurred! "
  End If

End Function
```

You may want to think about creating a separate Error component that holds all error messaging, etc.

Next, we'll code the OrderDetails Middle Class, which happens to be the VB class we've already created and called `clsOrderDetailManager`.

OrderDetails: Middle Class - OrderDetailManager

Now we'll be able to appreciate the power of the design we've created. We'll only need to change a few lines of code here and there for the Middle Class we created for the Customer component (`clsCustomerManager` of course) to be useable by our OrderDetails component, in its own class called `clsOrderDetailManager`.

In fact, you'll need to delete some routines such as Find *or you'll get compile errors. Although it wouldn't actually take much effort to configure them for this class component.*

Copy all the code from the Customer component `clsCustomManager` class into our `clsOrderDetailManager` class, and in the declarations section change:

```
Private WithEvents m_objManagedObject As clsCustomer
```

to this:

```
Private WithEvents m_objManagedObject As clsOrderDetail
```

This variable is initialized in the `Class_Initialize` event:

```
Private Sub Class_Initialize()

  On Error GoTo IntitializeError

  Set m_objManagedObject = New clsOrderDetail
```

```
    GetProxy

    m_eBOFAction = m_def_BOFAction
    m_eEOFAction = m_def_EOFAction
    m_strUserName = m_def_UserName
    m_strPassword = m_def_Password
    m_eEditMode = adEditNone

    Exit Sub

IntitializeError:

    MsgBox "Collection Managing Class can not be initialized"

End Sub
```

The `GetItem` method is dependent on the name of the Bottom Class, so we need to change this line of code:

```
Public Property Get Item() As clsOrderDetail

    Set Item = m_objManagedObject

End Property
```

We also need to change a call so that we return the relevant recordset:

```
Private Sub UpdateManagedObjects()

    On Error GoTo UpdateManagedObjectsError

    Set m_objManagedObject.ItemsRecordset = _
        m_objProxy.ReturnOrderDetailsRecordSet(UserName, Password, WhereClause)

    DataMemberChanged ItemsDataMember

    m_objManagedObject.RefreshDataMember

    Exit Sub

UpdateManagedObjectsError:

    MsgBox Err.Description & Err.Source

End Sub
```

OrderDetails: Middle Class - The Update Method

Updating the Order Details table is different from the Customer Update that we've seen so far.

When we created a new Customer, we created the Customer in the disconnected recordset, and then simply sent the information to the server object to be stored in the database.

When an Order is created, however, many rows may be added to the Order Details table. It makes more sense to wait until all the Order Details have been completed before we update the database. We only want save these rows to the disconnected recordset.

Therefore, we'll include a special Boolean, `v_blnSaveToDataBase`, in this `Update` sub to allow the sub to know whether the update is supposed to be sent to the server object (`v_blnSaveToDataBase = True`). If `v_blnSaveToDataBase` is `False`, the disconnected recordset will be updated and the recordset will hold multiple updates waiting to be saved to the database:

```
Public Sub Update(ByVal v_blnSaveToDataBase As Boolean)

   Dim lngPrimaryKeyValue As Long

   On Error GoTo UpdateError

   If m_objManagedObject.ItemsRecordset.State = adStateOpen And _
       m_objManagedObject.ItemsRecordset.EditMode <> adEditDelete Then

        If m_objManagedObject.ItemsRecordset.RecordCount <> 0 And (Not _
            IsNull(m_objManagedObject.ItemsRecordset.Fields(PrimaryKey))) Then
                lngPrimaryKeyValue = _
                        m_objManagedObject.ItemsRecordset.Fields(PrimaryKey)
        End If
   End If

   If EditMode <> adEditNone Then
```

First, check if we are performing a Batch update. If we are, just update the local recordset:

```
        If v_blnSaveToDataBase = False Then
            ItemsRecordset.Update
            RaiseEvent ChangeManagedObjects

            If lngPrimaryKeyValue <> 0 Then
                    m_objManagedObject.ItemsRecordset.Find PrimaryKey & "='" & _
                        lngPrimaryKeyValue & "'"
            End If

            EditMode = adEditNone
            Exit Sub

        Else
```

If we're not doing a Batch update, and we don't update the local recordset, the `EditMode` property will be set to `adEditAdd` or `adEditInProgress`. In this case, we can use the generic `Update` function:

```
        Set m_objManagedObject.ItemsRecordset = _
                m_objProxy.UpdateRecordset(UserName, Password, _
                m_objManagedObject.ItemsRecordset, m_eRecordsetName, _
                WhereClause)
        End If
        EditMode = adEditNone
        RaiseEvent ChangeManagedObjects

    End If
```

```
   If lngPrimaryKeyValue <> 0 Then
       m_objManagedObject.ItemsRecordset.Find PrimaryKey & "='" & _
           lngPrimaryKeyValue & "'"
   End If

   EditMode = adEditNone
   Exit Sub

UpdateError:

   Err.Raise Err.Number, "Update: " & Err.Source, Err.Description

End Sub
```

OrderDetails: Middle Class - The Scope of ItemsRecordset

As an `Order` and an `OrderDetails` object need to be able to be updated together, i.e. as a single transaction, we must have the ability to pass both the recordsets into the server component together. To do this, we will create a special method in the `Order` component that will retrieve the Order Details recordset from the OrderDetails component, and send this recordset and the Order recordset into the server component together. To make this possible, we'll have to make `ItemsRecordset`, the property that is used to retrieve the recordset, `Public`:

```
Public Property Get ItemsRecordset() As ADODB.Recordset

   Set ItemsRecordset = m_objManagedObject.ItemsRecordset

End Property
```

OrderDetails: Bottom Class - OrderDetail

Although there is some duplication of code from the `Customer` object, the majority of our `clsOrderDetail` Bottom Class will be different from the Customer equivalent (which was `clsCustomer`) because it will need different property procedures. I will therefore include the code for the whole component.

The declarations are practically the same except that we don't need `m_avarAcceptableValuesTitle` and `m_strManagedObjectDataMember`:

```
Option Explicit

Private m_blnIgnoreFieldChange As Boolean
Private m_blnInFieldChange As Boolean
Private m_strManagedObjectDataMember As String
Private m_blnValidatingFieldChange As Boolean
Private m_eEditMode As ADODB.EditModeEnum

Private WithEvents m_recManagedObjects As ADODB.Recordset

Public Event RefreshDataMember()
Public Event EditInProgress(ByVal v_eEditMode)
```

OrderDetails: Bottom Class - Properties that are the Same

These properties will not change from what was in the `Customer` component. What follows are the lines that belong in our `clsOrderDetail` Bottom Class that differ from those in the `clsCustomer` Customer Bottom Class:

```
Public Property Get EditMode() As ADODB.EditModeEnum

   EditMode = m_eEditMode

End Property

Friend Property Let EditMode(ByVal v_eNewEditMode As ADODB.EditModeEnum)

   m_eEditMode = v_eNewEditMode
   RaiseEvent EditInProgress(v_eNewEditMode)

End Property

Friend Property Get ItemsRecordset() As ADODB.Recordset

   Set ItemsRecordset = m_recManagedObjects

End Property

Friend Property Set ItemsRecordset(ByVal v_recNewRecordset As ADODB.Recordset)

   Set m_recManagedObjects = v_recNewRecordset

End Property

Friend Property Let ItemsDataMember(ByVal v_strNewOrderDataMember As String)

   m_strManagedObjectDataMember = v_strNewOrderDataMember

End Property

Friend Property Get ItemsDataMember() As String

   ItemsDataMember = m_strManagedObjectDataMember

End Property
```

OrderDetails: Bottom Class - Properties that are Different

The rest of the properties will need to be changed, since they are specific to our OrderDetails component.

OrderDetails:Bottom Class - OrderID Property

```
Public Property Get OrderID() As Long

   On Error Resume Next

   OrderID = ItemsRecordset.Fields(g_odFieldOrderID)

   If Err.Number <> 0 Then
```

```
        If Err.Number <> 3265 Then
          Err.Raise Err.Number, "OrderID Get" & Err.Source, Err.Description
        End If

    End If

End Property


Public Property Let OrderID(ByVal v_lngNewOrderID As Long)

  On Error GoTo OrderIDLetError

  If m_blnValidatingFieldChange = True Then
    Exit Property
  End If

  If m_eEditMode = adEditInProgress Or m_eEditMode = adEditAdd Then
      m_blnIgnoreFieldChange = True
      ItemsRecordset.Fields(g_odFieldOrderID) = v_lngNewOrderID

  ElseIf m_eEditMode = adEditNone Then
      Err.Raise 1001, "OrderID Let:", GetErrorText(errChangeFieldNoEdit)

  End If

  Exit Property

OrderIDLetError:

  Err.Raise Err.Number, "OrderID.Let " & Err.Source, _
    Err.Description

End Property
```

OrderDetails: Bottom Class - ProductID Property

```
Public Property Get ProductID() As Long

  On Error Resume Next

  If IsNull(ItemsRecordset.Fields(g_odFieldProductID)) Then
    ProductID = 0
  Else
    ProductID = ItemsRecordset.Fields(g_odFieldProductID)
  End If

  If Err.Number <> 0 Then

    If Err.Number <> 3265 Then
      Err.Raise Err.Number, "ProductID Get" & Err.Source, Err.Description
    End If

  End If

End Property


Public Property Let ProductID(ByVal v_lngNewProductID As Long)

  On Error GoTo ProductIDLetError
```

```
    If m_blnValidatingFieldChange = True Then
        Exit Property
    End If

    If m_eEditMode = adEditInProgress Or m_eEditMode = adEditAdd Then
        m_blnIgnoreFieldChange = True
        ItemsRecordset.Fields(g_odFieldProductID) = v_lngNewProductID

    ElseIf m_eEditMode = adEditNone Then
        Err.Raise 1001, "ProductID Let:", GetErrorText(errChangeFieldNoEdit)

    End If

    Exit Property

ProductIDLetError:

    Err.Raise Err.Number, "OrderDetails.ProductID.Let " & Err.Source, _
        Err.Description

End Property
```

OrderDetails: Bottom Class - UnitPrice Property

```
Public Property Get UnitPrice() As Currency

    On Error Resume Next

    If IsNull(ItemsRecordset.Fields(g_odFieldUnitPrice)) Then
        UnitPrice = 0
    Else
        UnitPrice = ItemsRecordset.Fields(g_odFieldUnitPrice)
    End If

    If Err.Number <> 0 Then

        If Err.Number <> 3265 Then
            Err.Raise Err.Number, "UnitPrice Get" & Err.Source, Err.Description
        End If

    End If

End Property
```

```
Public Property Let UnitPrice(ByVal v_curNewUnitPrice As Currency)

    On Error GoTo UnitPriceLetError

    If m_blnValidatingFieldChange = True Then
        Exit Property
    End If

    If m_eEditMode = adEditInProgress Or m_eEditMode = adEditAdd Then
        m_blnIgnoreFieldChange = True
        ItemsRecordset.Fields(g_odFieldUnitPrice) = v_curNewUnitPrice

    ElseIf m_eEditMode = adEditNone Then
        Err.Raise 1001, "UnitPrice Let:", GetErrorText(errChangeFieldNoEdit)
```

```
    End If

    Exit Property

UnitPriceLetError:

    Err.Raise Err.Number, "OrderDetails.UnitPrice.Let " & Err.Source, _
        Err.Description

End Property
```

OrderDetails:Bottom Class - Discount Property

```
Public Property Get Discount() As Long

    On Error Resume Next

    If IsNull(ItemsRecordset.Fields(g_odFieldDiscount)) Then
        Discount = 0
    Else
        Discount = ItemsRecordset.Fields(g_odFieldDiscount)
    End If

    If Err.Number <> 0 Then

        If Err.Number <> 3265 Then
            Err.Raise Err.Number, "Discount Get" & Err.Source, Err.Description
        End If

    End If

End Property
```

```
Public Property Let Discount(ByVal v_lngNewDiscount As Long)

    On Error GoTo DiscountLetError

    If m_blnValidatingFieldChange = True Then
        Exit Property
    End If

    If m_eEditMode = adEditInProgress Or m_eEditMode = adEditAdd Then
        m_blnIgnoreFieldChange = True
        ItemsRecordset.Fields(g_odFieldDiscount) = v_lngNewDiscount

    ElseIf m_eEditMode = adEditNone Then
        Err.Raise 1001, "Discount Let:", GetErrorText(errChangeFieldNoEdit)

    End If

    Exit Property

DiscountLetError:

    Err.Raise Err.Number, "OrderDetails.Discount.Let " & Err.Source, _
        Err.Description

End Property
```

OrderDetails:Bottom Class - Quantity Property

```
Public Property Get Quantity() As Long

   On Error Resume Next

   If IsNull(ItemsRecordset.Fields(g_odFieldQuantity)) Then
      Quantity = 1
   Else
      Quantity = ItemsRecordset.Fields(g_odFieldQuantity)
   End If

   If Err.Number <> 0 Then

      If Err.Number <> 3265 Then
         Err.Raise Err.Number, "Quantity Get" & Err.Source, Err.Description
      End If

   End If

End Property
```

```
Public Property Let Quantity(ByVal v_lngNewQuantity As Long)

   On Error GoTo QuantityLetError

   If m_blnValidatingFieldChange = True Then
      Exit Property
   End If

   If m_eEditMode = adEditInProgress Or m_eEditMode = adEditAdd Then
      m_blnIgnoreFieldChange = True
      ItemsRecordset.Fields(g_odFieldQuantity) = v_lngNewQuantity

   ElseIf m_eEditMode = adEditNone Then
      Err.Raise 1001, "Quantity Let:", GetErrorText(errChangeFieldNoEdit)

   End If

   Exit Property

QuantityLetError:

   Err.Raise Err.Number, "OrderDetails.Quantity.Let " & Err.Source, _
      Err.Description

End Property
```

OrderDetails:Bottom Class: ProductName Property

Although the code for the Product Name property isn't much different from the others, there is something worth mentioning.

The Product Name is not actually part of the Order Details record. We added this field onto the Order Details recordset by using the following query in the server component to build the Order Details recordset:

```
Private Const m_cstrOrderDetailsProductNameQuery As String = _
        "SELECT Products.ProductName, [Order Details].UnitPrice," & _
        "[Order Details].Quantity, [Order Details].Discount," & _
        "[Order Details].ProductID, [Order Details].OrderID " & _
        "FROM Products INNER JOIN [Order Details] ON " & _
        "Products.ProductID = [Order Details].ProductID "
```

This query is joining two tables: Order Details and Products. Order Details only has the ProductID, and it's unlikely this number, by itself, would be of much use to the Order Entry clerk. Instead, the clerk would probably use the Product Name. To get the Product Name, we'll have to do a join with the Products table and associate the appropriate Product Name with the ProductID in each Order Detail row. Since, the Product Name field does not really belong to the Order Details table, it can only be changed when updating Products.

We rebuild the Order Details recordset on the server when we are updating Order Detail recordsets. When we rebuild the recordset, we will just ignore the Product Name field. Thus, any changes made to the Product Name field on the client are completely ignored. The name is only there to make it easier for the user to read an order record.

The code will therefore look like this:

```
Public Property Get ProductName() As String

  On Error Resume Next

  ProductName = ItemsRecordset.Fields(g_odFieldProductName)

  If Err.Number <> 0 Then

     If Err.Number <> 3265 Then
        Err.Raise Err.Number, "ProductName.Get" & Err.Source, _
              Err.Description
     End If

  End If

End Property


Public Property Let ProductName(ByVal v_strNewProductName As String)

  On Error GoTo ProductNameLetError

  If m_blnValidatingFieldChange = True Then
     Exit Property
  End If

  If m_eEditMode = adEditInProgress Or m_eEditMode = adEditAdd Then
     m_blnIgnoreFieldChange = True
     m_recManagedObjects.Fields(g_odFieldProductName) = v_strNewProductName

  ElseIf m_eEditMode = adEditNone Then
     Err.Raise 1001, "ProductName Let: ", GetErrorText(errChangeFieldNoEdit)

  End If

  Exit Property
```

```
ProductNameLetError:

    Err.Raise Err.Number, "ProductName.Let " & Err.Source, _
        Err.Description

End Property
```

OrderDetails: Bottom Class - The Class Events

These are practically the same as for the Customer component. What follows are therefore the lines that belong in our clsOrderDetail that differ from those in the clsCustomer class:

```
Private Sub Class_Initialize()

    m_blnValidatingFieldChange = False
    m_blnIgnoreFieldChange = False
    m_blnInFieldChange = False
    m_eEditMode = adEditNone
    Set m_recManagedObjects = New ADODB.Recordset

End Sub

Private Sub Class_Terminate()

    If Not m_recManagedObjects Is Nothing Then

        With ItemsRecordset

            If .State = adStateOpen Then
                If Not .BOF And Not .EOF Then
                    If .EditMode <> adEditNone Then
                        .CancelUpdate
                    End If
                    .Close
                End If
            End If

        End With

        Set m_recManagedObjects = Nothing

    End If

End Sub

Private Sub Class_GetDataMember(DataMember As String, Data As Object)
    If ItemsDataMembers <> DataMember Then
    Exit Sub
    End If
    Set Data = m_recManagedObjects

End Sub
```

OrderDetails: Bottom Class - The ValidateFields Method

The ValidateFields has a Select Case statement dependent on the properties of a component, and will therefore have to be partially rewritten for OrderDetails:

```
Friend Function ValidateFields(ByVal v_vFields As Variant, ByVal _
    pRecordset As ADODB.Recordset) As Boolean

  On Error GoTo ValidateFieldsError

  m_blnValidatingFieldChange = True

    Select Case LCase(v_vFields(0).Name)

      Case g_odFieldOrderID
          OrderID = pRecordset.Fields(g_odFieldOrderID)

      Case g_odFieldProductID
          ProductID = pRecordset.Fields(g_odFieldProductID)

      Case g_odFieldUnitPrice
          UnitPrice = pRecordset.Fields(g_odFieldUnitPrice)

      Case g_odFieldQuantity
          Quantity = pRecordset.Fields(g_odFieldQuantity)

      Case g_odFieldDiscount
          Discount = pRecordset.Fields(g_odFieldDiscount)

      Case g_odFieldProductName
          ValidateFields = True

      Case Else
          ValidateFields = False

    End Select

  m_blnValidatingFieldChange = False

  ValidateFields = True

  Exit Function

ValidateFieldsError:

  ValidateFields = False
  m_blnValidatingFieldChange = False
  Err.Clear

End Function
```

You may notice that for the Product Name field we are simply returning True. This is because the Product Name field doesn't need to be validated here because this field will be ignored by the server component during the update of an Order Detail recordset.

OrderDetails: Bottom Class – Coding the Other Methods

The rest of the methods in the OrderDetails class will be identical to the methods in the Customer component:

```
    Friend Sub RefreshDataMember()

      DataMemberChanged ItemsDataMember

    End Sub


    Private Sub m_recManagedObjects_FieldChangeComplete(ByVal cFields As _
          Long, ByVal Fields As Variant, ByVal pError As ADODB.Error, adStatus _
          As ADODB.EventStatusEnum, ByVal pRecordset As ADODB.Recordset)

      If m_blnIgnoreFieldChange = True Then
         m_blnIgnoreFieldChange = False
         DataMemberChanged ItemsDataMember
         RaiseEvent RefreshDataMember
         Exit Sub
      End If

      If m_blnInFieldChange = True Then
         m_blnInFieldChange = False
         Exit Sub
      End If

      If ItemsRecordset.RecordCount =0 Or ItemsRecordset.EditMode _
         = adEditDelete Or ItemsRecordset.State <> adStateOpen Then
            Exit Sub
      End If

      If EditMode = adEditNone Then
         EditMode = adEditInProgress
         EditMode = EditMode
      End If

      If ValidateFields(Fields, pRecordset) = False Then
         m_blnInFieldChange = True
         ItemsRecordset.Fields(Fields(0).Name).Value = _
                 pRecordset.Fields(Fields(0).Name).UnderlyingValue
         DataMemberChanged ItemsDataMember
         RaiseEvent RefreshDataMember
         m_blnInFieldChange = False
      End If

    End Sub
```

OrderDetails: Top Class - cltOrderDetails

The Order Details control, `ctlOrderDetails`, will also require some changes, as we have different names for the Order Detail collections.

OrderDetails: Top Class - The Declarations Section

The code in the Declarations section of the `Customer` component Top Class (`ctlCustomers`) will need the following changes to work within the `OrderDetails` component Top Class, which is `ctlOrderDetails`:

```
    Public Enum ClientDataMember
        e_OrderIDOrderDetails = 1
    End Enum
```

```
Const m_clngOrderID As Long = 1
Const m_cstrFieldOrderDetailsID As String = "OrderID"
Const m_def_NumberOfOrderDetailsCollections = 1

Private WithEvents OrderDetailsCollectionOrder As clsOrderDetailManager
Private m_lngOrderIDEquals As Long
Private m_acolDataMembersArray() As clsOrderDetailManager
```

This does not need to be changed:

```
Private m_blnDataMembersInitialized() As Boolean
```

OrderDetails: Top Class - The UserControl Events

Change the code in these events as follows:

```
Private Sub UserControl_Initialize()

   m_lngOrderIDEquals = m_clngOrderID
   Set OrderDetailsCollectionOrder = New clsOrderDetailManager

   ReDim m_acolDataMembersArray(m_def_NumberOfOrderDetailsCollections)
   ReDim m_blnDataMembersInitialized(m_def_NumberOfOrderDetailsCollections)

   Set m_acolDataMembersArray(e_OrderIDOrderDetails) = OrderDetailsCollectionOrder

   m_blnDataMembersInitialized(e_OrderIDOrderDetails) = False

End Sub

Private Sub UserControl_Terminate()

   Set OrderDetailsCollectionOrder = Nothing

End Sub
```

OrderDetails: Top Class - The OrderIDEquals Property

Add this property so the user can change the value of m_lngOrderIDEquals, the value of the OrderID field to be used in the WHERE Clause of the g_oddmAllOrderDetails collection.

```
Public Property Get OrderIDEquals() As Long

   OrderIDEquals = m_lngOrderIDEquals

End Property

Public Property Let OrderIDEquals(ByVal v_lngNewOrderID As Long)

   m_lngOrderIDEquals = v_lngNewOrderID

End Property
```

OrderDetails: Top Class - The GetOrderDetailsCollection Method

This is different for the OrderDetails component than it is for the Customer component.

```
Public Function GetOrderDetailsCollection(ByVal v_eDataMember As _
    ClientDataMember) As clsOrderDetailManager

  If m_blnDataMembersInitialized(v_eDataMember) = False Then

    Select Case v_eDataMember

      Case e_OrderIDOrderDetails
          m_acolDataMembersArray(e_OrderIDOrderDetails).SetProxyInformation _
            e_OrderDetails, "WHERE OrderID =" & m_lngOrderIDEquals, _
            m_cstrFieldOrderDetailsID, g_oddmAllOrderDetails
    End Select

    m_acolDataMembersArray(v_eDataMember).Refresh
    m_blnDataMembersInitialized(v_eDataMember) = True

  End If

  Set GetOrderDetailsCollection = m_acolDataMembersArray(v_eDataMember)

End Function
```

OrderDetails: Top Class - The ChangeManagedObjects Method

This method will have to be rewritten to be specific for OrderDetails, but it is in the same format as the `ChangeManagedObjects` in the Customer component.

```
Private Sub ChangeManagedObjects(ByVal v_strDataMember As String)

  Dim lngOrderDetailsCollNumber As Long
  Dim lngIgnoreOrderDetailsNumber As Long

  Select Case v_strDataMember
    Case g_oddmAllOrderDetails
        lngIgnoreOrderDetailsNumber = 1
  End Select

  For lngOrderDetailsCollNumber = 1 To m_def_NumberOfOrderDetailsCollections

    If lngOrderDetailsCollNumber <> lngIgnoreOrderDetailsNumber Then
        If m_blnDataMembersInitialized(lngOrderDetailsCollNumber) = True Then
            m_acolDataMembersArray(lngOrderDetailsCollNumber).Refresh
        End If
    End If

  Next

End Sub
```

OrderDetails: Top Class - The ChangeManagedObjects Event

Code this event as follows in our OrderDetails component:

```
Private Sub OrderDetailsCollectionOrder_ChangeManagedObjects()

    ChangeManagedObjects g_oddmAllOrderDetails

End Sub
```

This completes our implementation of the OrderDetails component. Keep a note of how many elements were similar between the Customer and OrderDetails components – we're saving a lot of development time through these patterns.

Implementing the Order Component

Open the OrderEntry.vbp group. Add a new ActiveX Control project. Name the new project prjOrders.vbp. Call the control ctlOrders.

Add two regular classes to the project. Call them clsOrder and clsOrderManager.

Set the properties of the classes as follows:

DataSourceBehavior	1 - vbDataSource
DataBindingBehavior	0 - vbNone
Instancing	2 - Public Not Creatable
Persistable	0 - Not Persistable

Add the following references to your project:

❑ The Remote Data Service Library 2.0
❑ Microsoft ActiveX Data Objects 2.0 Library
❑ Microsoft Data Sources Library

Finally, we need to create a BAS module for constants and shared functions. Add a standard module to the project, and call it basOMain.

Here is how these Visual Basic elements map to our Order component class hierarchy:

❑ **Order Top Class**: ctlOrders control
❑ **Order Middle Class**: clsOrderManager class
❑ **Order Bottom Class**: clsOrder class

Order: basOMain

We will first need constants for all of the fields in the Order table:

```
Public Enum OrderErrors
    errChangeFieldNoEdit = 1001
    errEditPrimaryKey = 1002
    errPrimaryKeyLength = 1003
```

```
End Enum
Public Const g_oFieldOrderID As String = "OrderID"
Public Const g_oFieldCustomerID As String = "CustomerID"
Public Const g_oFieldEmployeeID As String = "EmployeeID"
Public Const g_oFieldOrderDate As String = "OrderDate"
Public Const g_oFieldRequiredDate As String = "RequiredDate"

Public Const g_oFieldShippedDate As String = "ShippedDate"
Public Const g_oFieldShipVia As String = "ShipVia"
Public Const g_oFieldFreight As String = "Freight"
Public Const g_oFieldShipName As String = "ShipName"
Public Const g_oFieldShipAddress As String = "ShipAddress"
Public Const g_oFieldShipCity As String = "ShipCity"
Public Const g_oFieldShipRegion As String = "ShipRegion"
Public Const g_oFieldShipPostalCode As String = "ShipPostalCode"
Public Const g_oFieldShipCountry As String = "ShipCountry"

Public Const g_odmOrderWhoseOrderID As String = "OrderWhoseOrderID"
Public Const g_odmAllOrders As String = "AllOrders"
```

Order: Coding the GetErrorText Method

Same as before:

```
Public Function GetErrorText(ByVal v_lngErrorNumber As Long)

  On Error GoTo GetErrorText_Error

  GetErrorText = LoadResString(v_lngErrorNumber)

  Exit Function

GetErrorText_Error:

  If Err.Number <> 0 Then
    GetErrorText = "An unknown error has occurred! "
  End If

End Function
```

Order: Middle Class - OrderManager

Copy all the code from the Customer component clsCustomerManager class into our clsOrderManager class.

This line of code must be changed in the declarations section of clsOrderManager:

```
Private WithEvents m_objManagedObject As clsOrder
```

This variable is initialized in the Class_Initialize event handler:

```
Private Sub Class_Initialize()

  On Error GoTo IntitializeError
```

```
    Set m_objManagedObject = New clsOrder

    GetProxy

    m_eBOFAction = m_def_BOFAction
    m_eEOFAction = m_def_EOFAction
    m_strUserName = m_def_UserName
    m_strPassword = m_def_Password
    m_eEditMode = adEditNone

    Exit Sub

IntitializeError:

    MsgBox "Collection Managing Class can not be initialized"

End Sub
```

The `GetItem` method will also depend on the name of the Bottom Class. We will need to change this line of code.

```
Public Property Get Item() As clsOrder

    Set Item = m_objManagedObject

End Property
```

Change the `UpdateManagedObjects` sub to return the correct recordset:

```
Private Sub UpdateManagedObjects()

    On Error GoTo UpdateManagedObjectsError

    Set m_objManagedObject.ItemsRecordset = _
        m_objProxy.ReturnOrdersRecordSet(UserName, Password, WhereClause)

    DataMemberChanged ItemsDataMember

    m_objManagedObject.RefreshDataMember
    Exit Sub

UpdateManagedObjectsError:

    MsgBox Err.Description & Err.Source

End Sub
```

Order: Middle Class - Changing the SetProxyInformation Method

This method took an extra parameter in the Customer component that we don't need in this component:

```
Friend Function SetProxyInformation(ByVal v_strWhereClause As String, _
    ByVal v_strPrimaryKey As String, ByVal v_eDataMember As String)
```

```
        m_strPrimaryKey = v_strPrimaryKey
        m_strWhereClause = v_strWhereClause
        m_strDataMember = v_eDataMember
        m_objManagedObject.ItemsDataMember = v_eDataMember

End Function
```

Order: Middle Class - The Update Method

The Update method is different again:

```
Public Sub Update()

   Dim lngPrimaryKeyValue As Long

   On Error GoTo UpdateError

   If ItemsRecordset.State = adStateOpen And ItemsRecordset.EditMode = _
        adEditInProgress Then
        If m_objManagedObject.ItemsRecordset.RecordCount <> 0 Then
            lngPrimaryKeyValue = _
                    m_objManagedObject.ItemsRecordset.Fields(PrimaryKey)
        End If
   End If

   If EditMode <> adEditNone Then

        Set m_objManagedObject.ItemsRecordset = _
            m_objProxy.UpdateRecordset(UserName, Password, _
            m_objManagedObject.ItemsRecordset, m_eRecordsetName, _
            WhereClause)

        m_objManagedObject.ItemsRecordset.Update
        EditMode = adEditNone
        RaiseEvent ChangeManagedObjects

   End If

   If lngPrimaryKeyValue <> 0 Then
        m_objManagedObject.ItemsRecordset.Find PrimaryKey & "=" & _
            lngPrimaryKeyValue & "'"
   End If

   If EditMode = adEditAdd Then
        m_objManagedObject.ItemsRecordset.MoveLast
   End If

   EditMode = adEditNone
   Exit Sub

UpdateError:

   Err.Raise Err.Number, "Update: " & Err.Source, Err.Description

End Sub
```

Order: Middle Class - The UpdateOrderOrderDetail Method

We need to add a special method to this Middle Class because Updating an `Order` requires both the Order and Order Details to be updated simultaneously:

```
Public Sub UpdateOrderOrderDetail(ByRef r_recOrderDetails As _
    ADODB.Recordset)

Dim lngPrimaryKeyValue As Long

On Error GoTo UpdateError

If ItemsRecordset.State = adStateOpen And ItemsRecordset.EditMode = _
        adEditInProgress Then

  If m_objManagedObject.ItemsRecordset.RecordCount <> 0 Then
        lngPrimaryKeyValue = _
              m_objManagedObject.ItemsRecordset.Fields(PrimaryKey)
  End If

End If

If EditMode <> adEditNone Then
    m_objManagedobject.ItemsRecordset.Fields(g_oFieldShipRegion)=""Then
    m_objManagedObject.ItemsRecordset.Fields(g_oFieldShipRegion)=Null
End If
  m_objProxy.SubmitNewOrder UserName, Password, _
          m_objManagedObject.ItemsRecordset, r_recOrderDetails

  m_objManagedObject.ItemsRecordset.Update
  EditMode = adEditNone
  RaiseEvent ChangeManagedObjects

Else

End If

If lngPrimaryKeyValue <> 0 Then
    m_objManagedObject.ItemsRecordset.Find PrimaryKey & "='" & _
          lngPrimaryKeyValue & "'"
End If

If EditMode = adEditAdd Then
    m_objManagedObject.ItemsRecordset.MoveLast
End If

EditMode = adEditNone
Exit Sub

UpdateError:

Resume Next
Err.Raise Err.Number, "Update: " & Err.Source, Err.Description

End Sub
```

Order: Bottom Class - Order

Again, there will be some similarity with the other Bottom Class components, but they will have different properties.

408

The declarations in `clsOrder` are the same as for `clsOrderDetail`:

```
Option Explicit
```

```
Private m_blnValidatingFieldChange As Boolean
Private m_eEditMode As ADODB.EditModeEnum
Private m_blnIgnoreFieldChange As Boolean
Private m_blnInFieldChange As Boolean
Private m_strManagedObjectDataMember As String

Private WithEvents m_recManagedObjects As ADODB.Recordset

Public Event RefreshDataMember()
Public Event EditInProgress(ByVal v_strEditMode)
```

Order: Bottom Class - Order Properties

These properties are specific to our Bottom `clsOrder` class:

Order: Bottom Class - OrderID Property

```
Public Property Get OrderID() As Long

  On Error Resume Next

  OrderID = ItemsRecordset.Fields(g_oFieldOrderID)

  If Err.Number <> 0 Then

    If Err.Number <> 3265 Then
      Err.Raise Err.Number, "clsOrder.OrderID.Get" & Err.Source, _
          Err.Description
    End If

  End If

End Property
```

We will exclude a `Let` property. When a new Order is added, an OrderID is assigned by the server component.

Order: Bottom Class – CustomerID Property

```
Public Property Get CustomerID() As String

  On Error Resume Next

  CustomerID = ItemsRecordset.Fields(g_oFieldCustomerID)

  If Err.Number <> 0 Then

    If Err.Number <> 3265 Then
      Err.Raise Err.Number, "Order.CustomerID Get" & Err.Source, _
          Err.Description
    End If

  End If

End Property
```

```
Public Property Let CustomerID(ByVal v_strNewCustomerID As String)

  On Error GoTo CustomerIDLetError

  If m_blnValidatingFieldChange = True Then
    Exit Property
  End If

  If m_eEditMode = adEditInProgress Or m_eEditMode = adEditAdd Then
    m_blnIgnoreFieldChange = True
    ItemsRecordset.Fields(g_oFieldCustomerID) = v_strNewCustomerID

  ElseIf m_eEditMode = adEditNone Then
    Err.Raise 1001, "CustomerID Let:", GetErrorText(errChangeFieldNoEdit)

  End If

  Exit Property

CustomerIDLetError:

  Err.Raise Err.Number, "Order.CustomerID.Let " & Err.Source, Err.Description

End Property
```

Order: Bottom Class – EmployeeID Property

```
Public Property Get EmployeeID() As Long

  On Error Resume Next

  EmployeeID = ItemsRecordset.Fields(g_oFieldEmployeeID)

  If Err.Number <> 0 Then

    If Err.Number <> 3265 Then
      Err.Raise Err.Number, "Order.EmployeeID.Get" & Err.Source, _
          Err.Description
    End If

  End If

End Property
```

```
Public Property Let EmployeeID(ByVal v_lngNewEmployeeID As Long)

  On Error GoTo EmployeeIDLetError

  If m_blnValidatingFieldChange = True Then
    Exit Property
  End If

  If m_eEditMode = adEditInProgress Or m_eEditMode = adEditAdd Then
    m_blnIgnoreFieldChange = True
    ItemsRecordset.Fields(g_oFieldEmployeeID) = v_lngNewEmployeeID

  ElseIf m_eEditMode = adEditNone Then
    Err.Raise 1001, "EmployeeID Let:", GetErrorText(errChangeFieldNoEdit)
```

```
      End If

      Exit Property

   EmployeeIDLetError:

      Err.Raise Err.Number, "Order.EmployeeID.Let " & Err.Source, Err.Description

   End Property
```

Order: Bottom Class – OrderDate Property

```
   Public Property Get OrderDate() As Date

      On Error Resume Next

      OrderDate = ItemsRecordset.Fields(g_oFieldOrderDate)

      If Err.Number <> 0 Then

        If Err.Number <> 3265 Then
           Err.Raise Err.Number, "Order.OrderDate.Get" & Err.Source, _
                     Err.Description
        End If

      End If

   End Property
```

```
   Public Property Let OrderDate(ByVal v_dtmNewOrderDate As Date)

      On Error GoTo OrderDateLetError

      If m_blnValidatingFieldChange = True Then
        Exit Property
      End If

      If m_eEditMode = adEditInProgress Or m_eEditMode = adEditAdd Then
        m_blnIgnoreFieldChange = True
        ItemsRecordset.Fields(g_oFieldOrderDate) = v_dtmNewOrderDate

      ElseIf m_eEditMode = adEditNone Then
        Err.Raise 1001, "OrderDate Let:", GetErrorText(errChangeFieldNoEdit)

      End If

      Exit Property

   OrderDateLetError:

      Err.Raise Err.Number, "Order.OrderDate.Let " & Err.Source, Err.Description

   End Property
```

Order: Bottom Class – RequiredDate Property

```
   Public Property Get RequiredDate() As Date

      On Error Resume Next
```

```
      RequiredDate = ItemsRecordset.Fields(g_oFieldRequiredDate)

   If Err.Number <> 0 Then

      If Err.Number <> 3265 Then
         Err.Raise Err.Number, "Order.RequiredDate.Get" & Err.Source, _
            Err.Description
      End If

   End If

End Property


Public Property Let RequiredDate(ByVal v_dtmNewRequiredDate As Date)

   On Error GoTo RequiredDateLetError

   If m_blnValidatingFieldChange = True Then
      Exit Property
   End If

   If m_eEditMode = adEditInProgress Or m_eEditMode = adEditAdd Then
      m_blnIgnoreFieldChange = True
      ItemsRecordset.Fields(g_oFieldRequiredDate) = v_dtmNewRequiredDate

   ElseIf m_eEditMode = adEditNone Then
      Err.Raise 1001, "RequiredDate Let:", GetErrorText(errChangeFieldNoEdit)

   End If

   Exit Property

RequiredDateLetError:

   Err.Raise Err.Number, "Order.RequiredDate.Let " & Err.Source, _
      Err.Description

End Property
```

Order: Bottom Class – ShippedDate Property

```
Public Property Get ShippedDate() As Date

   On Error Resume Next

   ShippedDate = ItemsRecordset.Fields(g_oFieldShippedDate)

   If Err.Number <> 0 Then

      If Err.Number <> 3265 Then
         Err.Raise Err.Number, "Order.ShippedDate.Get" & Err.Source, _
            Err.Description
      End If

   End If

End Property

Public Property Let ShippedDate(ByVal v_dtmNewShippedDate As Date)
```

```
    On Error GoTo ShippedDateLetError

  If m_blnValidatingFieldChange = True Then
    Exit Property
  End If

  If m_eEditMode = adEditInProgress Or m_eEditMode = adEditAdd Then
    m_blnIgnoreFieldChange = True
    ItemsRecordset.Fields(g_oFieldShippedDate) = v_dtmNewShippedDate

  ElseIf m_eEditMode = adEditNone Then
    Err.Raise 1001, "ShippedDate Let:", GetErrorText(errChangeFieldNoEdit)

  End If

  Exit Property

ShippedDateLetError:

  Err.Raise Err.Number, "Order.ShippedDate.Let " & Err.Source, _
    Err.Description

End Property
```

Order: Bottom Class – ShipVia Property

```
Public Property Get ShipVia() As Long

  On Error Resume Next

  ShipVia = ItemsRecordset.Fields(g_oFieldShipVia)

  If Err.Number <> 0 Then

    If Err.Number <> 3265 Then
      Err.Raise Err.Number, "Order.ShipVia.Get" & Err.Source, _
          Err.Description
    End If

  End If

End Property
```

```
Public Property Let ShipVia(ByVal v_lngNewShipVia As Long)

  On Error GoTo ShipviaLetError

  If m_blnValidatingFieldChange = True Then
    Exit Property
  End If

  If m_eEditMode = adEditInProgress Or m_eEditMode = adEditAdd Then
    m_blnIgnoreFieldChange = True
    ItemsRecordset.Fields(g_oFieldShipVia) = v_lngNewShipVia

  ElseIf m_eEditMode = adEditNone Then
    Err.Raise 1001, "ShipVia Let:", GetErrorText(errChangeFieldNoEdit)

  End If
```

```
    Exit Property

ShipviaLetError:

    Err.Raise Err.Number, "Order.ShipVia.Let " & Err.Source, Err.Description

End Property
```

Order: Bottom Class – Freight Property

```
Public Property Get Freight() As Currency

    On Error Resume Next

    Freight = ItemsRecordset.Fields(g_oFieldFreight)

    If Err.Number <> 0 Then

        If Err.Number <> 3265 Then
            Err.Raise Err.Number, "Order.Freight.Get" & Err.Source, _
                Err.Description
        End If

    End If

End Property
```

```
Public Property Let Freight(ByVal v_curNewFreight As Currency)

    On Error GoTo FreightLetError

    If m_blnValidatingFieldChange = True Then
        Exit Property
    End If

    If m_eEditMode = adEditInProgress Or m_eEditMode = adEditAdd Then
        m_blnIgnoreFieldChange = True
        ItemsRecordset.Fields(g_oFieldFreight) = v_curNewFreight

    ElseIf m_eEditMode = adEditNone Then
        Err.Raise 1001, "Freight Let:", GetErrorText(errChangeFieldNoEdit)

    End If

    Exit Property

FreightLetError:

    Err.Raise Err.Number, "Order.Freight.Let " & Err.Source, Err.Description

End Property
```

Order: Bottom Class – ShipName Property

```
Public Property Get ShipName() As String

    On Error Resume Next

    ShipName = ItemsRecordset.Fields(g_oFieldShipName)
```

```
      If Err.Number <> 0 Then

        If Err.Number <> 3265 Then
           Err.Raise Err.Number, "Order.ShipName.Get" & Err.Source, _
              Err.Description
        End If

      End If

End Property
```

```
Public Property Let ShipName(ByVal v_strNewShipName As String)

  On Error GoTo ShipNameLetError

  If m_blnValidatingFieldChange = True Then
    Exit Property
  End If

  If m_eEditMode = adEditInProgress Or m_eEditMode = adEditAdd Then
    m_blnIgnoreFieldChange = True
    ItemsRecordset.Fields(g_oFieldShipName) = v_strNewShipName

  ElseIf m_eEditMode = adEditNone Then
    Err.Raise 1001, "ShipName Let:", GetErrorText(errChangeFieldNoEdit)

  End If

  Exit Property

ShipNameLetError:

  Err.Raise Err.Number, "Order.ShipName.Let " & Err.Source, Err.Description

End Property
```

Order: Bottom Class – ShipAddress Property

```
Public Property Get ShipAddress() As String

  On Error Resume Next

  ShipAddress = ItemsRecordset.Fields(g_oFieldShipAddress)

  If Err.Number <> 0 Then

    If Err.Number <> 3265 Then
       Err.Raise Err.Number, "Order.ShipAddress.Get" & Err.Source, _
          Err.Description
    End If

  End If

End Property
```

```
Public Property Let ShipAddress(ByVal v_strNewShipAddress As String)

 On Error GoTo ShipAddressLetError
```

```
      If m_blnValidatingFieldChange = True Then
         Exit Property
      End If

      If m_eEditMode = adEditInProgress Or m_eEditMode = adEditAdd Then
         m_blnIgnoreFieldChange = True
         ItemsRecordset.Fields(g_oFieldShipAddress) = v_strNewShipAddress

      ElseIf m_eEditMode = adEditNone Then
         Err.Raise 1001, "ShipAddress Let:", GetErrorText(errChangeFieldNoEdit)

      End If

      Exit Property

   ShipAddressLetError:

      Err.Raise Err.Number, "Order.ShipAddress.Let " & Err.Source, _
         Err.Description

   End Property
```

Order: Bottom Class – ShipCity Property

```
   Public Property Get ShipCity() As String

      On Error Resume Next

      ShipCity = ItemsRecordset.Fields(g_oFieldShipCity)

      If Err.Number <> 0 Then

         If Err.Number <> 3265 Then
            Err.Raise Err.Number, "Order.ShipCity.Get" & Err.Source, _
               Err.Description
         End If

      End If

   End Property
```

```
   Public Property Let ShipCity(ByVal v_strNewShipCity As String)

      On Error GoTo ShipCityLetError

      If m_blnValidatingFieldChange = True Then
         Exit Property
      End If

      If m_eEditMode = adEditInProgress Or m_eEditMode = adEditAdd Then
         m_blnIgnoreFieldChange = True
         ItemsRecordset.Fields(g_oFieldShipCity) = v_strNewShipCity

      ElseIf m_eEditMode = adEditNone Then
         Err.Raise 1001, "ShipCity Let:", GetErrorText(errChangeFieldNoEdit)

      End If

      Exit Property
```

```
ShipCityLetError:

   Err.Raise Err.Number, "Order.ShipCity.Let " & Err.Source, Err.Description

End Property
```

Order: Bottom Class – ShipRegion Property

```
Public Property Get ShipRegion() As String

   On Error Resume Next

   ShipRegion = ItemsRecordset.Fields(g_oFieldShipRegion)

   If Err.Number <> 0 Then

      If Err.Number <> 3265 Then
         Err.Raise Err.Number, "Order.ShipRegion.Get" & Err.Source, _
            Err.Description
      End If

   End If

End Property
```

```
Public Property Let ShipRegion(ByVal v_strNewShipRegion As String)

   On Error GoTo ShipRegionLetError

   If m_blnValidatingFieldChange = True Then
      Exit Property
   End If

   If m_eEditMode = adEditInProgress Or m_eEditMode = adEditAdd Then
      m_blnIgnoreFieldChange = True
      ItemsRecordset.Fields(g_oFieldShipRegion) = v_strNewShipRegion

   ElseIf m_eEditMode = adEditNone Then
      Err.Raise 1001, "Ship Region Let:", GetErrorText(errChangeFieldNoEdit)

   End If

   Exit Property

ShipRegionLetError:

   Err.Raise Err.Number, "Order.ShipRegion.Let " & Err.Source, Err.Description

End Property
```

Order: Bottom Class – ShipPostalCode Property

```
Public Property Get ShipPostalCode() As String

   On Error Resume Next

   ShipPostalCode = ItemsRecordset.Fields(g_oFieldShipPostalCode)

   If Err.Number <> 0 Then
```

```
            If Err.Number <> 3265 Then
                Err.Raise Err.Number, "Order.ShipPostalCode.Get" & Err.Source, _
                    Err.Description
            End If

        End If

    End Property


    Public Property Let ShipPostalCode(ByVal v_sNewShipPostalCode As String)

        On Error GoTo ShipPostalCodeLetError

        If m_blnValidatingFieldChange = True Then
            Exit Property
        End If

        If m_eEditMode = adEditInProgress Or m_eEditMode = adEditAdd Then
            m_blnIgnoreFieldChange = True
            ItemsRecordset.Fields(g_oFieldShipPostalCode) = v_sNewShipPostalCode

        ElseIf m_eEditMode = adEditNone Then
            Err.Raise 1001, "ShipPostalCode Let:", GetErrorText(errChangeFieldNoEdit)

        End If

        Exit Property

    ShipPostalCodeLetError:

        Err.Raise Err.Number, "Order.ShipPostalCode.Let " & Err.Source, _
            Err.Description

    End Property
```

Order: Bottom Class – ShipCountry Property

```
    Public Property Get ShipCountry() As String

        On Error Resume Next

        ShipCountry = ItemsRecordset.Fields(g_oFieldShipCountry)

        If Err.Number <> 0 Then

            If Err.Number <> 3265 Then
                Err.Raise Err.Number, "Order.ShipCountry.Get" & Err.Source, _
                    Err.Description
            End If

        End If

    End Property

    Public Property Let ShipCountry(ByVal v_strNewShipCountry As String)

        On Error GoTo ShipCountryLetError
```

```
      If m_blnValidatingFieldChange = True Then
        Exit Property
      End If

      If m_eEditMode = adEditInProgress Or m_eEditMode = adEditAdd Then
        m_blnIgnoreFieldChange = True
        ItemsRecordset.Fields(g_oFieldShipCountry) = v_strNewShipCountry

      ElseIf m_eEditMode = adEditNone Then
        Err.Raise 1001, "ShipCountry Let:", GetErrorText(errChangeFieldNoEdit)

      End If

      Exit Property

  ShipCountryLetError:

      Err.Raise Err.Number, "Order.ShipCountry.Let " & Err.Source, _
        Err.Description

  End Property
```

Order: Bottom Class - Coding the ValidateFields Method

ValidateFields contains field information, so the Select Case statement for our clsOrder class will have to be rewritten. Since any changes to an OrderID field will be ignored by the server component during an update, we will just ignore changes to this field:

```
Friend Function ValidateFields(ByVal v_vFields As Variant, ByVal _
  pRecordset As ADODB.Recordset, Optional ByRef r_sErrorDetails) As Boolean

  On Error GoTo ValidateFieldsError

  m_blnValidatingFieldChange = True

  Select Case LCase(v_vFields(0).Name)

    Case g_oFieldCustomerID
      CustomerID = pRecordset.Fields(g_oFieldCustomerID)

    Case g_oFieldEmployeeID
      EmployeeID = pRecordset.Fields(g_oFieldEmployeeID)

    Case g_oFieldFreight
      Freight = pRecordset.Fields(g_oFieldFreight)

    Case g_oFieldOrderDate
      OrderDate = pRecordset.Fields(g_oFieldOrderDate)

    Case g_oFieldOrderID
      Exit Function

    Case g_oFieldRequiredDate
      RequiredDate = pRecordset.Fields(g_oFieldRequiredDate)

    Case g_oFieldShipAddress
      ShipAddress = pRecordset.Fields(g_oFieldShipAddress)
```

```
        Case g_oFieldShipCity
            ShipCity = pRecordset.Fields(g_oFieldShipCity)

        Case g_oFieldShipCountry
            ShipCountry = pRecordset.Fields(g_oFieldShipCountry)

        Case g_oFieldShippedDate
            ShippedDate = pRecordset.Fields(g_oFieldShippedDate)

        Case g_oFieldShipName
            ShipName = pRecordset.Fields(g_oFieldShipName)

        Case g_oFieldShippedDate
            ShippedDate = pRecordset.Fields(g_oFieldShippedDate)

        Case g_oFieldShipPostalCode
            ShipPostalCode = pRecordset.Fields(g_oFieldShipPostalCode)

        Case g_oFieldShipRegion
            If Not IsNull(pRecordset.Fields(g_oFieldShipRegion))Then
                ShipRegion = pRecordset.Fields(g_oFieldShipRegion)
            Else
                ShipRegion = ""
            End If

        Case g_oFieldShipVia
            ShipVia = pRecordset.Fields(g_oFieldShipVia)

        Case Else
            ValidateFields = False

    End Select

  m_blnValidatingFieldChange = False
  ValidateFields = True

  Exit Function

ValidateFieldsError:

  ValidateFields = False
  m_blnValidatingFieldChange = False
  Err.Clear

End Function
```

Order: Bottom Class - Routines that are the Same

These properties will not change in our `clsOrder` class from what we saw in the Customer component:

```
Public Property Get EditMode() As ADODB.EditModeEnum

  EditMode = m_eEditMode

End Property

Friend Property Let EditMode(ByVal v_eNewEditMode As ADODB.EditModeEnum)

  m_eEditMode = v_eNewEditMode
```

```
    RaiseEvent EditInProgress(v_eNewEditMode)

End Property

Friend Property Get ItemsRecordset() As ADODB.Recordset

   Set ItemsRecordset = m_recManagedObjects

End Property
```

```
Friend Property Set ItemsRecordset(ByVal v_recNewRecordset As ADODB.Recordset)

   Set m_recManagedObjects = v_recNewRecordset

End Property
```

```
Friend Property Let ItemsDataMember(ByVal v_strNewOrderDataMember As String)

   m_strManagedObjectDataMember = v_strNewOrderDataMember

End Property
```

```
Friend Property Get ItemsDataMember() As String

   ItemsDataMember = m_strManagedObjectDataMember

End Property
```

The class events are the same as they were in Order Details:

```
Private Sub Class_Initialize()
```

```
   m_blnValidatingFieldChange = False
   m_blnIgnoreFieldChange = False
   m_blnInFieldChange = False
   m_eEditMode = adEditNone
   Set m_recManagedObjects = New ADODB.Recordset
```

```
End Sub
```

```
Private Sub Class_Terminate()
```

```
   If Not m_recManagedObjects Is Nothing Then

     With ItemsRecordset

          If .State = adStateOpen Then
            If Not .BOF And Not .EOF Then
               If .EditMode <> adEditNone Then
                  .CancelUpdate
               End If
               .Close
            End If
          End If

     End With

     Set m_recManagedObjects = Nothing

   End If
```

```
    End Sub

    Private Sub Class_GetDataMember(DataMember As String, Data As Object)
      If Items.DataMember <> DataMember
        Exit Sub
      End If
      Set Data = m_recManagedObjects

    End Sub
```

The rest of the methods in this class will be identical to the methods in the Customer component:

```
    Friend Sub RefreshDataMember()

      DataMemberChanged ItemsDataMember

    End Sub
```

```
    Private Sub m_recManagedObjects_FieldChangeComplete(ByVal cFields As _
          Long, ByVal Fields As Variant, ByVal pError As ADODB.Error, adStatus _
          As ADODB.EventStatusEnum, ByVal pRecordset As ADODB.Recordset)

      If m_blnIgnoreFieldChange = True Then
        m_blnIgnoreFieldChange = False
        DataMemberChanged ItemsDataMember
        RaiseEvent RefreshDataMember
        Exit Sub
      End If

      If m_blnInFieldChange = True Then
        m_blnInFieldChange = False
        Exit Sub
      End If

      If ItemsRecordset.RecordCount = 0 Or ItemsRecordset.EditMode = _
          AdEditDelete Or ItemsRecordset.State <> adStateOpen Then
        Exit Sub
      End If

      If EditMode = adEditNone Then
        EditMode = adEditInProgress
        EditMode = EditMode
      End If

      If ItemsRecordset.Fields(Fields(0).Name).Value = _
        pRecordset.Fields(Fields(0).Name).UnderlyingValue Then
        Exit Sub
      End If

      If ValidateFields(Fields, pRecordset) = False Then
        m_blnInFieldChange = True
        ItemsRecordset.Fields(Fields(0).Name).Value = _
            pRecordset.Fields(Fields(0).Name).UnderlyingValue
        DataMemberChanged ItemsDataMember
        RaiseEvent RefreshDataMember
        m_blnInFieldChange = False
      End If

    End Sub
```

Order: Top Class - ctlOrders

The Top Class Order control, `ctlOrders`, will also require some changes, as we have different names for the Order collections.

Change this code in `ctlOrders`:

```
Public Enum ClientDataMember
  e_AllOrders = 1
  e_OrderWhoseOrderID = 2
End Enum

Const m_def_NumberOfOrderCollections = 2
Const m_def_OrderID As Long = 0

Private WithEvents OrderCollectionAll As clsOrderManager
Private WithEvents OrderCollectionOrderID As clsOrderManager
Private m_acolDataMembersArray() As clsOrderManager
Private m_lngOrderID As Long
```

This does not need to be changed:

```
Private m_blnDataMembersInitialized() As Boolean
```

Order: Top Class - The UserControl Methods

Change this code in the events for `ctlOrders` as follows:

```
Private Sub UserControl_Initialize()

    m_lngOrderID = m_def_OrderID

    Set OrderCollectionAll = New clsOrderManager
    Set OrderCollectionOrderID = New clsOrderManager

    ReDim m_acolDataMembersArray(m_def_NumberOfOrderCollections)
    ReDim m_blnDataMembersInitialized(m_def_NumberOfOrderCollections)

    Set m_acolDataMembersArray(e_AllOrders) = OrderCollectionAll
    Set m_acolDataMembersArray(e_OrderWhoseOrderID) = OrderCollectionAll

    m_blnDataMembersInitialized(e_AllOrders) = False
    m_blnDataMembersInitialized(e_OrderWhoseOrderID) = False

End Sub

Private Sub UserControl_Terminate()

    Set OrderCollectionAll = Nothing

End Sub
```

Order: Top Class - OrderIDEquals Property

Add this property so the user can change the value of `m_lngOrderID`, the value of the OrderID field to be used in the WHERE clause of the `g_odmAllOrders` collection.

```
Public Property Get OrderIDEquals()

  OrderIDEquals = m_lngOrderID

End Property
```

Order: Top Class - The ChangeManagedObjects Event

Code these events in `ctlOrders`:

```
Private Sub OrderCollectionOrderID_ChangeManagedObjects()

   ChangeManagedObjects g_odmOrderWhoseOrderID

End Sub

Private Sub orderCollectionAll_ChangeManagedObjects()

   ChangeManagedObjects g_odmAllOrders

End Sub
```

Order: Top Class - The ChangeManagedObjects Method

This method will have to be rewritten within `ctlOrders`, but it is in the same format as the other `ChangeManagedObjects`:

```
Private Sub ChangeManagedObjects(ByVal v_strDataMember As String)

  Dim lngOrderCollNumber As Long
  Dim lngIgnoreOrderNumber As Long

  Select Case v_strDataMember

    Case g_odmAllOrders
       lngIgnoreOrderNumber = 1

    Case g_odmOrderWhoseOrderID
       lngIgnoreOrderNumber = 2

  End Select

  For lngOrderCollNumber = 1 To m_def_NumberOfOrderCollections
    If lngOrderCollNumber <> lngIgnoreOrderNumber Then
        If m_blnDataMembersInitialized(lngOrderCollNumber) = True Then
            m_acolDataMembersArray(lngOrderCollNumber).Refresh
        End If
    End If
  Next

End Sub
```

Order: Top Class - The GetOrderCollection Method

Within `ctlOrders`, change the `Select Case` statement:

```
Public Function GetOrderCollection(ByVal v_eDataMember As ClientDataMember) As _
            clsOrderManager

   If m_blnDataMembersInitialized(v_eDataMember) = False Then

      Select Case v_eDataMember

        Case e_AllOrders
             m_acolDataMembersArray(e_AllOrders).SetProxyInformation "", _
                  g_oFieldOrderID, g_odmAllOrders

        Case e_OrderWhoseOrderID
             m_acolDataMembersArray(e_OrderWhoseOrderID).SetProxyInformation _
                  " WHERE " & g_oFieldOrderID & " = " & OrderIDEquals, _
                  g_oFieldOrderID, g_odmOrderWhoseOrderID

      End Select

      m_acolDataMembersArray(v_eDataMember).Refresh
      m_blnDataMembersInitialized(v_eDataMember) = True

   End If

   Set GetOrderCollection = m_acolDataMembersArray(v_eDataMember)

End Function
```

This completes our implementation of the Order component. As we saw, many of the Middle and Top Class details were extremely similar.

Implementing the Product Component

Open the OrderEntry.vbp group. Add a new ActiveX Control project. Name the new project prjProducts.vbp. Call the control ctlProducts.

Add two regular classes to the project. Call them clsProduct and clsProductManager.

Set the properties of the classes as follows:

DataSourceBehavior	1 - vbDataSource
DataBindingBehavior	0 - vbNone
Instancing	2 - Public Not Creatable
Persistable	0 - Not Persistable

Add the following references to your project:

❑ The Remote Data Service Library 2.0
❑ Microsoft ActiveX Data Objects 2.0 library
❑ Microsoft Data Sources Library

Finally, we need to create a BAS module for constants and shared functions. Add a standard module to the project, and call it basPMain.

Here is how these Visual Basic elements map to our Product component class hierarchy:

- ❑ **Product Top Class**: `ctlProducts` control
- ❑ **Product Middle Class**: `clsProductManager` class
- ❑ **Product Bottom Class**: `clsProduct` class

Product: basPMain

We will first need constants for all of the fields in the Products table.

```
Public Const g_pFieldProductID As String = "ProductID"
Public Const g_pFieldProductName As String = "ProductName"
Public Const g_pFieldSupplierID As String = "SupplierID"
Public Const g_pFieldCategoryID As String = "CategoryID"
Public Const g_pFieldQuantityPerUnit As String = "QuantityPerUnit"
Public Const g_pFieldUnitPrice As String = "UnitPrice"
Public Const g_pFieldUnitsInStock As String = "UnitsInStock"
Public Const g_pFieldUnitsOnOrder As String = "UnitsOnOrder"
Public Const g_pFieldReorderLevel As String = "ReorderLevel"
Public Const g_pFieldDiscontinued As String = "Discontinued"
Public Const g_cFieldProductName As String = "ProductName"

Public Enum ProductErrors
    errChangeFieldNoEdit = 1001
End Enum

Public Const g_pdmProductIDProducts As String = "ProductIDProducts"
```

Product: Coding the GetErrorText Method

This is the same as before:

```
Public Function GetErrorText(ByVal v_lngErrorNumber As Long)

  On Error GoTo GetErrorText_Error

  GetErrorText = LoadResString(v_lngErrorNumber)

  Exit Function

GetErrorText_Error:

  If Err.Number <> 0 Then
    GetErrorText = "An unknown error has occurred! "
  End If

End Function
```

Next we will code the Object Manager.

Product: Middle Class - ProductManager

Again copy and paste the code from the Customer component object manager.

This line of code must be changed in the declarations section:

```
      Private WithEvents m_objManagedObject As clsProduct
```

This variable is initialized in the `Class_Initialize` event handler:

```
    Private Sub Class_Initialize()

      On Error GoTo IntitializeError

      Set m_objManagedObject = New clsProduct

      GetProxy

      m_eBOFAction = m_def_BOFAction
      m_eEOFAction = m_def_EOFAction
      m_strUserName = m_def_UserName
      m_strPassword = m_def_Password
      m_eEditMode = adEditNone

      Exit Sub

    IntitializeError:

      MsgBox "Collection Managing Class can not be initialized"

    End Sub
```

The `GetItem` method will also depend on the name of the Bottom class. We will need to change this line of code.

```
    Public Property Get Item() As clsProduct

      Set Item = m_objManagedObject

    End Property
```

Change the `UpdateMangedObjects` sub to return the correct recordset:

```
    Private Sub UpdateManagedObjects()

      On Error GoTo UpdateManagedObjectsError

      Set m_objManagedObject.ItemsRecordset = _
          m_objProxy.ReturnProductsRecordSet(UserName, Password, WhereClause)

      DataMemberChanged ItemsDataMember

      m_objManagedObject.RefreshDataMember
      Exit Sub

    UpdateManagedObjectsError:

      MsgBox Err.Description & Err.Source

    End Sub
```

Product: Middle Class - The Update Method

Once again the Update method needs tweaking, so we'll need to change some code in our clsProductManager class. Like with the OrderDetails Update method, we want to wait until an order is complete before updating the database:

```
Public Sub Update(ByVal v_blnSaveToDataBase As Boolean) 'CAB

   Dim lngPrimaryKeyValue As Long

   On Error GoTo UpdateError

   If ItemsRecordset.State = adStateOpen And ItemsRecordset.EditMode = _
         adEditInProgress Then

      If m_objManagedObject.ItemsRecordset.RecordCount <> 0 Then
            lngPrimaryKeyValue = _
               m_objManagedObject.ItemsRecordset.Fields(PrimaryKey)
      End If

   End If

   If EditMode <> adEditNone Then

      If v_blnSaveToDataBase = False Then
         ItemsRecordset.Update
         RaiseEvent ChangeManagedObjects

         If lngPrimaryKeyValue <> 0 Then
            m_objManagedObject.ItemsRecordset.Find PrimaryKey & "='" & _
               lngPrimaryKeyValue & "'"
         End If

         EditMode = adEditNone
         Exit Sub

      Else

            m_objProxy.UpdateRecordset UserName, Password, _
               m_objManagedObject.ItemsRecordset, m_eRecordsetName, WhereClause
            EditMode = adEditNone
            RaiseEvent ChangeManagedObjects

      End If

   Else

   End If

   If lngPrimaryKeyValue <> 0 Then
      m_objManagedObject.ItemsRecordset.Find PrimaryKey & "='" & _
         lngPrimaryKeyValue & "'"
   End If

   If EditMode = adEditAdd Then
      m_objManagedObject.ItemsRecordset.MoveLast
   End If

   EditMode = adEditNone
   Exit Sub
```

```
   UpdateError:

     Err.Raise Err.Number, "Update: " & Err.Source, Err.Description

 End Sub
```

Product: Middle Class - The Find Method

We're going to add a `Find` method for Products. It's very similar to that for Customers:

```
Public Function Find(ByVal v_strProductName As String)

  Dim strProductName As String

  If v_strProductName = "" Then
     Exit Function
  End If

  If InStr(v_strProductName, "'") > 0 Then
        strProductName=Mid(v_strProductName, 1, InStr(v_strProductName, "'") - 1)
  Else
        strProductName = v_strProductName
  End If

  ItemsRecordset.Find g_pFieldProductName & "= '" & strProductName & _
     "'", 0, adSearchForward, adBookmarkFirst
  Refresh

End Function
```

Also note that this time we didn't have to change to the `SetProxyInformation` *method.*

Product: Bottom Class - Product

Again there will be some similarity with the other Bottom Classes, but our `clsProduct` class for the Product component will have different properties.

The declarations are the same as the others in this chapter:

```
Option Explicit

Public Event RefreshDataMember()
Public Event EditInProgress(ByVal v_sEditMode)

Private WithEvents m_recManagedObjects As ADODB.Recordset

Private m_blnIgnoreFieldChange As Boolean
Private m_blnInFieldChange As Boolean
Private m_strManagedObjectDataMember As String
Private m_blnValidatingFieldChange As Boolean
Private m_eEditMode As ADODB.EditModeEnum
```

429

Product: Bottom Class - Product Properties

These properties are specific to this class:

Product: Bottom Class – SupplierID Property

```
Public Property Get SupplierID() As Long

  On Error Resume Next

  SupplierID = m_recManagedObjects.Fields(g_pFieldSupplierID)

  If Err.Number <> 0 Then

    If Err.Number <> 3265 Then
       Err.Raise Err.Number, "Product.SupplierID.Get" & Err.Source, _
          Err.Description
    End If

  End If

End Property
```

```
Public Property Let SupplierID(ByVal v_lngNewSupplierID As Long)

  On Error GoTo SupplierIDLetError

  If m_blnValidatingFieldChange = True Then
     Exit Property
  End If

  If m_eEditMode = adEditInProgress Or m_eEditMode = adEditAdd Then
     m_blnIgnoreFieldChange = True
     m_recManagedObjects.Fields(g_pFieldSupplierID) = v_lngNewSupplierID

  ElseIf m_eEditMode = adEditNone Then
     Err.Raise 1001, "SupplierIDLet:", GetErrorText(errChangeFieldNoEdit)

  End If

  Exit Property

SupplierIDLetError:

  Err.Raise Err.Number, "Product.SupplierID.Let " & Err.Source, _
    Err.Description

End Property
```

Product: Bottom Class - QuantityPerUnit Property

```
Public Property Get QuantityPerUnit() As String

  On Error Resume Next

  QuantityPerUnit = m_recManagedObjects.Fields(g_pFieldQuantityPerUnit)

  If Err.Number <> 0 Then
```

```
            If Err.Number <> 3265 Then
                Err.Raise Err.Number, "Product.QuantityPerUnit.Get" & _
                    Err.Source, Err.Description
            End If

        End If

    End Property

    Public Property Let QuantityPerUnit(ByVal v_strNewQuantityPerUnit As String)

        On Error GoTo QuantityPerUnitLetError

        If m_blnValidatingFieldChange = True Then
            Exit Property
        End If

        If m_eEditMode = adEditInProgress Or m_eEditMode = adEditAdd Then
            m_blnIgnoreFieldChange = True
            m_recManagedObjects.Fields(g_pFieldQuantityPerUnit) = v_strNewQuantityPerUnit

        ElseIf m_eEditMode = adEditNone Then
            Err.Raise 1001, "QuantityPerUnit Let:", GetErrorText(errChangeFieldNoEdit)

        End If

        Exit Property

    QuantityPerUnitLetError:

        Err.Raise Err.Number, "Product.QuantityPerUnit.Let " & Err.Source, _
            Err.Description

    End Property
```

Product: Bottom Class - UnitPrice Property

```
    Public Property Get UnitPrice() As Currency

        On Error Resume Next

        UnitPrice = m_recManagedObjects.Fields(g_pFieldUnitPrice)

        If Err.Number <> 0 Then

            If Err.Number <> 3265 Then
                Err.Raise Err.Number, "Product.UnitPrice.Get" & Err.Source, _
                    Err.Description
            End If

        End If

    End Property

    Public Property Let UnitPrice(ByVal v_curNewUnitPrice As Currency)

        On Error GoTo UnitPriceLetError
```

```
      If m_blnValidatingFieldChange = True Then
         Exit Property
      End If

      If m_eEditMode = adEditInProgress Or m_eEditMode = adEditAdd Then
         m_blnIgnoreFieldChange = True
         m_recManagedObjects.Fields(g_pFieldUnitPrice) = v_curNewUnitPrice

      ElseIf m_eEditMode = adEditNone Then
         Err.Raise 1001, "UnitPrice Let:", GetErrorText(errChangeFieldNoEdit)

      End If

      Exit Property

UnitPriceLetError:

      Err.Raise Err.Number, "Product.UnitPrice.Let " & Err.Source, _
         Err.Description

End Property
```

Product: Bottom Class - UnitsInStock Property

```
Public Property Get UnitsInStock() As Long

   On Error Resume Next

   UnitsInStock = m_recManagedObjects.Fields(g_pFieldUnitsInStock)

   If Err.Number <> 0 Then

      If Err.Number <> 3265 Then
         Err.Raise Err.Number, "Product.UnitsInStock.Get" & _
            Err.Source, Err.Description
      End If

   End If

End Property
```

```
Public Property Let UnitsInStock(ByVal v_lngNewUnitsInStock As Long)

   On Error GoTo UnitsInStockLetError

   If m_blnValidatingFieldChange = True Then
      Exit Property
   End If

   If m_eEditMode = adEditInProgress Or m_eEditMode = adEditAdd Then
      m_blnIgnoreFieldChange = True
      m_recManagedObjects.Fields(g_pFieldUnitsInStock) = v_lngNewUnitsInStock

   ElseIf m_eEditMode = adEditNone Then
      Err.Raise 1001, "UnitsInStock Let:", GetErrorText(errChangeFieldNoEdit)

   End If

   Exit Property
```

```
UnitsInStockLetError:

   Err.Raise Err.Number, "Product.UnitsInStock.Let " & Err.Source, _
      Err.Description

End Property
```

Product: Bottom Class - UnitsOnOrder Property

```
Public Property Get UnitsOnOrder() As Long

   On Error Resume Next

   UnitsOnOrder = m_recManagedObjects.Fields(g_pFieldUnitsOnOrder)

   If Err.Number <> 0 Then

      If Err.Number <> 3265 Then
         Err.Raise Err.Number, "Product.UnitsOnOrder.Get" & Err.Source, _
            Err.Description
      End If

   End If

End Property
```

```
Public Property Let UnitsOnOrder(ByVal v_lngNewUnitsOnOrder As Long)

   On Error GoTo UnitsOnOrderLetError

   If m_blnValidatingFieldChange = True Then
      Exit Property
   End If

   If m_eEditMode = adEditInProgress Or m_eEditMode = adEditAdd Then
      m_blnIgnoreFieldChange = True
      m_recManagedObjects.Fields(g_pFieldUnitsOnOrder) = v_lngNewUnitsOnOrder

   ElseIf m_eEditMode = adEditNone Then
      Err.Raise 1001, "UnitOnOrder Let:", GetErrorText(errChangeFieldNoEdit)

   End If

   Exit Property

UnitsOnOrderLetError:

   Err.Raise Err.Number, "Product.UnitsOnOrder.Let " & Err.Source, Err.Description

End Property
```

Product: Bottom Class - ReorderLevel Property

```
Public Property Get ReorderLevel() As Long

   On Error Resume Next

   ReorderLevel = m_recManagedObjects.Fields(g_pFieldReorderLevel)
```

```
    If Err.Number <> 0 Then

        If Err.Number <> 3265 Then
            Err.Raise Err.Number, "Product.ReorderLevel.Get" & _
                Err.Source, Err.Description
        End If

    End If

End Property

Public Property Let ReorderLevel(ByVal v_lngNewReorderLevel As Long)

    On Error GoTo ReorderLevelLetError

    If m_blnValidatingFieldChange = True Then
        Exit Property
    End If

    If m_eEditMode = adEditInProgress Or m_eEditMode = adEditAdd Then
        m_blnIgnoreFieldChange = True
        m_recManagedObjects.Fields(g_pFieldReorderLevel) = v_lngNewReorderLevel

    ElseIf m_eEditMode = adEditNone Then
        Err.Raise 1001, "ReorderLevel Let:", GetErrorText(errChangeFieldNoEdit)

    End If

    Exit Property

ReorderLevelLetError:

    Err.Raise Err.Number, "Product.ReorderLevel.Let " & Err.Source, _
        Err.Description

End Property
```

Product: Bottom Class - Discontinued Property

```
Public Property Get Discontinued() As Boolean

    On Error Resume Next

    Discontinued = m_recManagedObjects.Fields(g_pFieldDiscontinued)

    If Err.Number <> 0 Then

        If Err.Number <> 3265 Then
            Err.Raise Err.Number, "Product.Discontinued.Get" & _
                Err.Source, Err.Description
        End If

    End If

End Property

Public Property Let Discontinued(ByVal v_blnNewDiscontinued As Boolean)

    On Error GoTo DiscontinuedLetError
```

```
   If m_blnValidatingFieldChange = True Then
      Exit Property
   End If

   If m_eEditMode = adEditInProgress Or m_eEditMode = adEditAdd Then
      m_blnIgnoreFieldChange = True
      m_recManagedObjects.Fields(g_pFieldDiscontinued) = v_blnNewDiscontinued

   ElseIf m_eEditMode = adEditNone Then
      Err.Raise 1001, "Discontinued Let:", GetErrorText(errChangeFieldNoEdit)

   End If

   Exit Property

DiscontinuedLetError:

   Err.Raise Err.Number, "Product.Discontinued.Let " & Err.Source, _
      Err.Description

End Property
```

Product: Bottom Class - ProductID Property

```
Public Property Get ProductID() As Long

   On Error Resume Next

   ProductID = m_recManagedObjects.Fields(g_pFieldProductID)

   If Err.Number <> 0 Then

      If Err.Number <> 3265 Then
         Err.Raise Err.Number, "Product.ProductID.Get" & _
            Err.Source, Err.Description
      End If

   End If

End Property
```

Once again, we will ignore the Let property.

Product: Bottom Class - ProductName Property

```
Public Property Get ProductName() As String

   On Error Resume Next

   ProductName = m_recManagedObjects.Fields(g_pFieldProductName)

   If Err.Number <> 0 Then

      If Err.Number <> 3265 Then
         Err.Raise Err.Number, "Products.ProductName.Get", Err.Description
      End If

   End If
```

```
    End Property

    Public Property Let ProductName(ByVal v_strNewProductName As String)

      On Error GoTo ProductNameLetError

      If m_blnValidatingFieldChange = True Then
        Exit Property
      End If

      If m_eEditMode = adEditInProgress Or m_eEditMode = adEditAdd Then
        m_blnIgnoreFieldChange = True
        m_recManagedObjects.Fields(g_pFieldProductName) = v_strNewProductName

      ElseIf m_eEditMode = adEditNone Then
        Err.Raise 1001, "ProductName Let:", GetErrorText(errChangeFieldNoEdit)

      End If

      Exit Property

    ProductNameLetError:

      Err.Raise Err.Number, "ProductName Let " & Err.Source, Err.Description

    End Property
```

Product: Bottom Class - The ValidateFields Method

ValidateFields contains field information and so the Select Case statement will have to be rewritten. Since any changes to an ProductID field will be ignored by the server component during an update, we will just ignore changes to this field. Therefore change the code in our clsProduct class to this:

```
    Friend Function ValidateFields(ByVal v_vFields As Variant, ByVal _
      pRecordset As ADODB.Recordset, Optional ByRef r_sErrorDetails) As Boolean

      On Error GoTo ValidateFieldsError

      m_blnValidatingFieldChange = True

      Select Case LCase(v_vFields(0).Name)

        Case g_pFieldProductName
            ProductName = pRecordset.Fields(g_pFieldProductName)

        Case g_pFieldProductID
            ValidateFields = True

        Case g_pFieldUnitPrice
            UnitPrice = pRecordset.Fields(UnitPrice)

        Case g_pFieldDiscontinued
            Discontinued = pRecordset.Fields(g_pFieldDiscontinued)

        Case g_pFieldSupplierID
            SupplierID = pRecordset.Fields(g_pFieldSupplierID)
```

```
      Case g_pFieldSupplierID
          SupplierID = pRecordset.Fields(g_pFieldSupplierID)

  End Select

  m_blnValidatingFieldChange = False
  ValidateFields = True

  Exit Function

ValidateFieldsError:

  m_blnValidatingFieldChange = False
  ValidateFields = False
  Err.Clear

End Function
```

Product: Bottom Class - Routines that are the Same

These properties in our `clsProduct` class will not change from those we saw in the Customer component:

```
Public Property Get EditMode() As ADODB.EditModeEnum

   EditMode = m_eEditMode

End Property
```

```
Friend Property Let EditMode(ByVal v_eNewEditMode As ADODB.EditModeEnum)

   m_eEditMode = v_eNewEditMode

   RaiseEvent EditInProgress(v_eNewEditMode)

End Property
```

```
Friend Property Get ItemsRecordset() As ADODB.Recordset

   Set ItemsRecordset = m_recManagedObjects

End Property
```

```
Friend Property Set ItemsRecordset(ByVal v_recNewRecordset As ADODB.Recordset)

   Set m_recManagedObjects = v_recNewRecordset

End Property
```

```
Friend Property Let ItemsDataMember(ByVal v_strNewOrderDataMember As String)

   m_strManagedObjectDataMember = v_strNewOrderDataMember

End Property
```

```
Friend Property Get ItemsDataMember() As String
```

```
      ItemsDataMember = m_strManagedObjectDataMember

   End Property
```

The Class events in `clsProduct` are almost the same as we've previously seen in the other Bottom Classes:

```
Private Sub Class_GetDataMember(DataMember As String, Data As Object)
   If ItemsDataMember <> DataMember Then
   Exit Sub
   End If
   Set Data = m_recManagedObjects

End Sub

Private Sub Class_Initialize()

   m_blnValidatingFieldChange = False
   m_blnIgnoreFieldChange = False
   m_blnInFieldChange = False
   m_eEditMode = adEditNone
   Set m_recManagedObjects = New ADODB.Recordset

End Sub

Private Sub Class_Terminate()

   If Not m_recManagedObjects Is Nothing Then

      If ItemsRecordset.State = adStateOpen Then

        If ItemsRecordset.EditMode <> adEditNone Then
           ItemsRecordset.CancelUpdate
        End If

        ItemsRecordset.Close

      End If

      Set m_recManagedObjects = Nothing

   End If

End Sub
```

The rest of the methods in our `clsProduct` class will be identical to the methods in the Customer component:

```
Friend Sub RefreshDataMember()

   DataMemberChanged ItemsDataMember

End Sub


Private Sub m_recManagedObjects_FieldChangeComplete(ByVal cFields As _
   Long, ByVal Fields As Variant, ByVal pError As ADODB.Error, adStatus _
   As ADODB.EventStatusEnum, ByVal pRecordset As ADODB.Recordset)
```

```
        If m_blnIgnoreFieldChange = True Then
            m_blnIgnoreFieldChange = False
            DataMemberChanged ItemsDataMember
            RaiseEvent RefreshDataMember
            Exit Sub
        End If

        If m_blnInFieldChange = True Then
            m_blnInFieldChange = False
            Exit Sub
        End If

        If m_recManagedObjects.RecordCount = 0 Or m_recManagedObjects.EditMode _
            = adEditDelete Or m_recManagedObjects.State <> adStateOpen Then
            Exit Sub
        End If

        If EditMode = adEditNone Then
            EditMode = adEditInProgress
            EditMode = EditMode
        End If

        If ValidateFields(Fields, pRecordset) = False Then
            m_blnInFieldChange = True
            m_recManagedObjects.Fields(Fields(0).Name).Value = _
                pRecordset.Fields(Fields(0).Name).UnderlyingValue
            DataMemberChanged ItemsDataMember
            RaiseEvent RefreshDataMember
            m_blnInFieldChange = False
        End If

End Sub
```

Product: Top Class - cltProducts

The Products Top Class control, `ctlProducts`, will also require some changes from the other Top
Classes, as we have different names for the Products collections.

Copy the code from one of the other Top Class components (such as Order) into our `ctlProducts`
control and change this code:

```
Option Explicit
```

```
Public Enum ClientDataMember
    e_ProductsCategoryID = 1
End Enum

Const m_def_NumberOfProductCollections = 1
Const m_def_CategoryIDEquals As Long = 0

Private WithEvents ProductCollectionCatalogID As clsProductManager

Private m_acolDataMembersArray() As clsProductManager
Private m_blnDataMembersInitialized() As Boolean
Private m_lngCategoryIDEquals As Long
```

Product: Top Class - The UserControl Events

Change this code in these events as follows:

```
Private Sub UserControl_Initialize()

    Set ProductCollectionCatalogID = New clsProductManager

    m_lngCategoryIDEquals = m_def_CategoryIDEquals

    ReDim m_acolDataMembersArray(m_def_NumberOfProductCollections)
    ReDim m_blnDataMembersInitialized(m_def_NumberOfProductCollections)

    Set m_acolDataMembersArray(e_ProductsCategoryID) = ProductCollectionCatalogID

    m_blnDataMembersInitialized(e_ProductsCategoryID) = False

End Sub

Private Sub UserControl_Terminate()
    Set ProductCollectionCatalogID = Nothing
End Sub
```

Product: Top Class -The ChangeManagedObjects Event

```
Private Sub ProductCollectionCatalogID_ChangeManagedObjects()

    ChangeManagedObjects g_pdmProductIDProducts

End Sub
```

Product: Top Class - The ChangeManagedObjects Method

This method will have to be rewritten, but it is in the same format as the `ChangeManagedObjects` in the Customer component.

```
Private Sub ChangeManagedObjects(ByVal v_strDataMember As String)

    Dim lngProductCollNumber As Long
    Dim lngIgnoreProductNumber As Long

    Select Case v_strDataMember

        Case g_pdmProductIDProducts
            lngIgnoreProductNumber = 1

    End Select

    For lngProductCollNumber = 1 To m_def_NumberOfProductCollections

        If LngProductCollNumber <> lngIgnoreProductNumber Then

            If m_blnDataMembersInitialized(lngProductCollNumber) = True Then
                m_acolDataMembersArray(lngProductCollNumber).Refresh
            End If

        End If
    Next

End Sub
```

Product: Top Class - The GetProductCollection Method

Change the `Select Case` statement:

```
Public Function GetProductCollection(ByVal v_eDataMember As _
    ClientDataMember) As clsProductManager

  If m_blnDataMembersInitialized(v_eDataMember) = False Then

    Select Case v_eDataMember

        Case e_ProductsCategoryID
            m_acolDataMembersArray(e_ProductsCategoryID).SetProxyInformation _
                e_Products, " Where " & g_pFieldCategoryID & " = " & _
                CategoryIDEquals, g_pFieldProductID, g_pdmProductIDProducts
    End Select

    m_acolDataMembersArray(v_eDataMember).Refresh
    m_blnDataMembersInitialized(v_eDataMember) = True

  End If

  Set GetProductCollection = m_acolDataMembersArray(v_eDataMember)

End Function
```

Product: Top Class - The CategoryIDEquals Property

Add this property to the `ctlProducts` control so that the user can change the value of
`m_lngCategoryIDEquals`, the value of the CategoryID field to be used in the `WHERE` Clause of the
`g_pdmProductIDProducts` collection.

```
Public Property Get CategoryIDEquals() As Long

  CategoryIDEquals = m_lngCategoryIDEquals

End Property
```

```
Public Property Let CategoryIDEquals(ByVal v_strNewCategoryIDEquals As Long)

  m_lngCategoryIDEquals = v_strNewCategoryIDEquals
  m_acolDataMembersArray(e_ProductsCategoryID).SetProxyInformation e_Products, _
      "Where " & g_pFieldCategoryID & " = " & CategoryIDEquals, _
      g_pFieldProductID, g_pdmProductIDProducts

End Property
```

Summary

Congratulations! We have now coded the vast majority of the Northwind system. As you can see,
once we had coded one of the Client components, the rest fell into place in no time. In fact we could
continue to extend the implementation to include the Shipper and Employee components without
much trouble, since our design is taking advantage of the patterns we identified throughout the UML
design process.

In order to see the project running, we're going to build a fairly simple Win32 GUI in the next
chapter, which will allow us to Add and Edit Customers - and place an order.

Get ADO connection

[Successful]

Set Recordset cursor location

Set Recordset source

Set Recordset connection

14

Creating the GUI Order Form

Now that we've created four of the client components, we can build our Order Form. Since our components will be doing most of the work for our Form, such as retrieving, updating, moving through the information, and so on, our forms will have very little to do. As we know, we now have the ability to build data provider classes, which means we also will not have to write special modules to handle populating each control on our form.

In Visual Basic 5, writing an application like this resulted in fifty to one hundred pages of code to populate text boxes, grid controls, perform updates on these controls, etc. These days are gone.

Building the GUI Form

In Chapter 6, we prototyped the basic design of our GUI. Now let's build it. We're going to build it in three basic stages, for each of the three main frames on the form. I'm going to assume that you can add the controls and set them up to look like the screenshots provided. All I'm going to provide is the non-apparent properties such as Name and Tag.

Add a Standard EXE project to the OrderEntry.vbg group and set it as StartUp. Name the project prjClient and the form frmClient.

Add references to the following in the Components dialog:

- ❑ Microsoft DataGrid Control 6.0 (OLEDB)
- ❑ Microsoft Tabbed Dialog Control 6.0
- ❑ Microsoft Windows Common Controls-2 6.0

The Customers Frame

Add a frame for Customer Information and set it up to look like this:

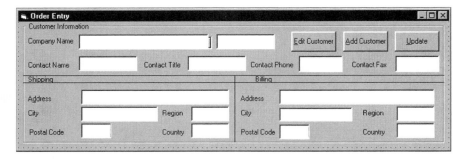

One thing we can't really see here is that behind the Company Name and Contact Title text boxes there are two combo boxes. We can see more clearly in the figure below, where they should be:

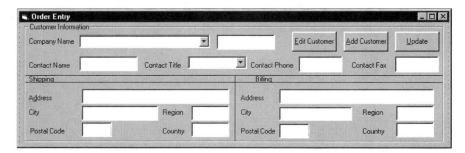

Apart from the five text boxes found in the Shipping section, the rest of the text boxes are a control array called `txtCustomer()`, each of which has its Tag property set to the Field it relates to:

Name	Tag
txtCustomer(0)	CompanyName
txtCustomer(1)	ContactTitle
txtCustomer(2)	ContactName
txtCustomer(3)	CustomerID
txtCustomer(4)	Phone
txtCustomer(5)	Fax
txtCustomer(6)	Address
txtCustomer(7)	City
txtCustomer(8)	PostalCode
txtCustomer(9)	Region
txtCustomer(10)	Country

> We'll be iterating through the text box Tags to find particular fields.
> Therefore, it makes sense that the fields that we will be searching the most
> for should have lower indexes. This way the iteration will never go beyond
> a few text boxes.

Set the Visible property for `txtCustomer(0)` to `False`, as it's only going to be used for editing or adding a Customer.

The Shipping section text boxes are also a control array, but this time called `txtOrder()`:

Name	Tag
txtOrder(0)	ShipAddress
txtOrder(1)	ShipCity
txtOrder(2)	ShipPostalCode
txtOrder(3)	ShipRegion
txtOrder(4)	ShipCountry

The three command buttons are called:

- ❑ cmdCustomerEdit
- ❑ cmdCustomerAdd
- ❑ cmdCustomerUpdate

Set the Enabled property for `cmdCustomerUpdate` to `False` - we'll enable it when appropriate in the code.

The two combo boxes are set up as follows:

Name	Tag	Sorted
cboCustomer	CompanyName	True
cboContact	ContactTitle	False

Also set the Visible property of `cboContact` to `False`, as it's only going to be used for editing or adding a Customer.

The Products and Categories Frame

Extend the form and add another frame for Categories and Products:

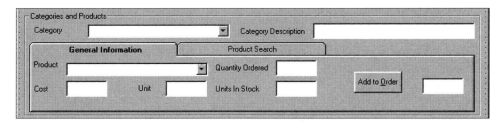

The things to note about this form are that the text box in the bottom right (we'll call it 'Unlabelled") should have its Visible property set to False. Also I'm not going to use the Product Search tab, but I've put it in for completeness.

Finally, the Category Description text box requires the Categories component that we haven't coded together yet. Therefore, it won't display the relevant description unless you've coded the Categories component yourself.

The Categories controls are set up like this:

Control	Property	Setting
Combo box	Name	CboCategory
	Tag	Category
Text box	Name	txtCategoryDescription

The Products controls on the General Information tag again include a text box control array, txtProduct():

Text box	Name	Tag
Cost	txtProduct(0)	UnitPrice
Unlabelled	txtProduct(1)	QuantityPerUnit
Units In Stock	txtProduct(2)	UnitsInStock
Unit	txtProduct(3)	ProductID

Three more things to do here:

- ❑ The Quantity Ordered text box is not part of the control array but is called txtQuantity.
- ❑ The Combo box is called cboProduct with its Tag property set to Product.
- ❑ The Command button is called cmdOrderAdd.

The Order Details Frame

Extend the form again and add the final frame to record the Order Details (note that the date combo boxes in the bottom-left are actually DateTimePicker controls):

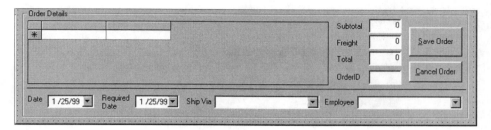

The grid is an OLEDB DataGrid control, called grdOrderDetails.

The two DateTimePicker controls are set up like this:

Name	Tag	Format
DtpDate	OrderDate	1- dtpShortDate
dtpRequired	RequiredDate	1- dtpShortDate

Two of the text boxes (Subtotal and Total) are part of the txtOrder() control array:

Name	Tag
txtOrder(5)	Freight
txtOrder(6)	OrderID

The other two are simply called cmdOrderSubtotal and cmdOrderTotal.

The command buttons are called cmdOrderSave and cmdOrderCancel.

Finally, the remaining two combo boxes are:

Name	Tag
cboOrderShipVia	ShipVia
cboOrderEmployee	Employee

Adding the Client Components

Finally, because we created our client components as ActiveX controls we need to add an instance of each component to the form. You can add them wherever you like, if you set the visible property to False.

You'll need to close all the code windows for the client components in order to enable their icon on the toolbar.

By default, Visual Basic will rename each instance of your components by adding a 1 to the end of each name:

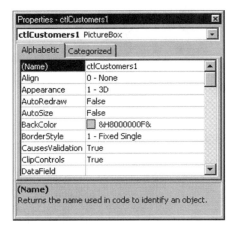

Rename your component instance to remove the extra 1.

The Completed Form

Your completed form should look something like this:

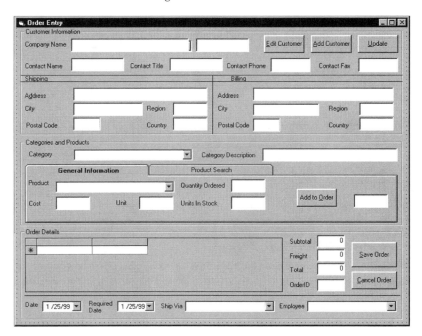

We're now ready to examine the code behind these controls.

The Code Behind the Form

As we chose to make our client components data provider classes, the code in the form only needs to deal with setting the properties of the controls. There will be almost no code actually manipulating the information in the form; our data provider classes will do all this.

For this form, we'll simply write one long initialization subroutine that sets all of the properties of the form's controls. The rest of the code deals with filling combo boxes and performing the updates.

It would be very simple to add a function into our components that takes a list box or combo box as a parameter (the name of a property associated with that component) and fill the combo box with all of the records associated with that field. If we had done that, our code probably would have been virtually halved. Considering what this application is doing, I would say that is pretty good going.

The Initialize Routine

The `Initialize` method will be responsible for binding our data consumer controls to our data provider classes.

Looking back, we can see that our data provider classes consisted of the Bottom and Middle Classes. In order to get at these classes we'll need to go through the Top Class. This is because the Bottom and Middle Classes are not publicly creatable; they can only be accessed through the hierarchy we built. This guarantees that the components will have control over how the component is used and accessed. We will see how this works in a moment.

We have built this form with a text box array to make the form run more efficiently. Therefore, we'll create a long counter to iterate through the text box arrays. The `Tag` property of the text boxes will be used to identify which field each of the text boxes is associated with.

> *To keep things simple and clear, I have not placed constants in this form for field names, nor made enumerated types for the possible data member names, or set the text box tags equal to an appropriate constant for the name of each field. Realize that to make this form complete we would have to make these final changes.*

We will use a variable called `lngTxtBoxIndex` to iterate through the text boxes, and two long counters to iterate through the values of the Product and Customer records to fill the combo boxes:

```
Private Sub Initialize

    Dim lngTxtBoxIndex As Long
    Dim lngCustomerRecordCounter As Long
    Dim lngProductRecordCounter As Long
```

The first thing we will do is fill-in the Customer drop-down combo box. Hiding under this combo box is a text box. The combo box will be used when selecting a customer for an Order, the text box will be used to enter a new Customer or edit an existing Customer. When we are in edit or review mode, the text box will be visible, otherwise the combo box will be visible.

First, we will iterate through all of the Customers and add their Company Names to the combo box. We'll use `ctlCustomers` to get access to the Customer component. To access the Middle and Bottom objects we can use the `GetCustomerCollection` method. This method has a parameter that allows us to specify the Customer collection we want. In this case, we want to retrieve all Customers:

```
With ctlCustomers.GetCustomerCollection(e_AllCustomers)
```

We will call the `MoveFirst` method of the Middle object to move to the first customer:

```
.MoveFirst
```

Now we'll iterate through all of the Customers using the `RecordCount` property of our Middle object to determine the number of customers:

```
For lngCustomerRecordCounter = 1 To .RecordCount
```

The `Item` property of the Middle object will return the Bottom objects, which will have information on the current Customer:

```
        cboCustomer.AddItem .Item.CompanyName
          .MoveNext
    Next
    .MoveFirst
```

Now we will iterate through all of the Customer text boxes to set their `DataField` equal to their Tag, set their data member to the appropriate value, `AllCustomers`, and set their `DataSource` equal to `Item`, which is the Bottom object. Doing this will now bind all of our Customer text boxes to the Customer object. We will also lock these text boxes, as we don't want the user to change information in them unless they are editing or adding information:

```
    For lngTxtBoxIndex = 0 To txtCustomer.Count - 1
        txtCustomer(lngTxtBoxIndex).DataField = _
                    txtCustomer(lngTxtBoxIndex).Tag
        txtCustomer(lngTxtBoxIndex).DataMember = "AllCustomers"
        Set TxtCustomer(lngTxtBoxIndex).DataSource = .Item
        txtCustomer(lngTxtBoxIndex).Locked = True
    Next

End With
```

We'll do almost the same thing with the Order text boxes using the Order control to bind the text boxes to the Bottom objects of the Order object, except that we won't lock them:

```
With ctlOrders.GetOrderCollection(e_OrderWhoseOrderID)

    For lngTxtBoxIndex = 0 To txtOrder.Count - 1
        txtOrder(lngTxtBoxIndex).DataField = _
                txtOrder(lngTxtBoxIndex).Tag
        txtOrder(lngTxtBoxIndex).DataMember = "OrderWhoseOrderID"
        Set txtOrder(lngTxtBoxIndex).DataSource = .Item
    Next
```

Once the binding is complete, we need to start adding a new order because this form can only perform an Add New on the Order component.

> *Remember, our Sales Representative role is only responsible for entering the Orders, so this is the only possibility. If you later expanded this form to be used by a person in the Manager role, you would have to allow for the possibilities of editing and deleting an Order.*

```
    .AddNew
```

We'll initialize the cost of the freight to be zero:

```
    .Item.Freight = 0

End With
```

We'll set the caption so the user knows what the form is doing:

```
frmOrders.Caption = "Order Entry: ADD NEW"
```

We've not written any code in our components for the ShipVia field. It's likely that we would not want an entire component for something that has less than five entries. Realistically, ShipVia could become part of the Order component. Since there are only three values, we'll just hard code the values in, but of course, these values should come from the database through one of the components:

```
cboOrderShipVia.AddItem "Speedy Express"
cboOrderShipVia.AddItem "United Package"
cboOrderShipVia.AddItem "Federal Shipping"
```

Move the combo to the first value:

```
cboOrderShipVia.ListIndex = 0
```

We did not create an Employee component so we will just hard code an employee into Employee combo box:

```
cboOrderEmployee.AddItem "Davolio"
cboOrderEmployee.ListIndex = 0
```

We'll now bind all of the Order Details text boxes to the Order Details object using `ctlOrderDetails`. In this case, we'll be using a grid control, so we want to bind to all of the Order Detail records in the collection. To do this we bind the grid box to the Middle object:

```
With ctlOrderDetails
    grdOrderDetails.DataMember = "OrderDetails"
    Set grdOrderDetails.DataSource = _
                .GetOrderDetailsCollection(e_OrderIDOrderDetails)
End With
```

Set the columns, hiding the ones with ID fields:

```
grdOrderDetails.Columns.Item(2).Width = 950
grdOrderDetails.Columns.Item(1).Width = 950
grdOrderDetails.Columns.Item(4).Width = 0
grdOrderDetails.Columns.Item(5).Width = 0
```

Fill in the possible Contact Titles. We could add a method to our Customer component to take a list box and fill it with the possible titles, too. This would eliminate the need for this code being in the form:

```
cboContact.AddItem "Contact Title"
cboContact.AddItem "Sales Representative"
cboContact.AddItem "Order Administrator"
cboContact.AddItem "Marketing Manager"
cboContact.AddItem "Accounting Manager"
cboContact.AddItem "Sales Associate"
cboContact.AddItem "Sales Agent"
cboContact.AddItem "Owner"
cboContact.ListIndex = 0
```

As we have not built a Categories component, we'll also have to hard code in the possible categories. The CategoryID will be one less than the List Index we are assigning each product:

```
cboCategory.AddItem "Beverages", 0
cboCategory.AddItem "Condiments", 1
cboCategory.AddItem "Confections", 2
cboCategory.AddItem "Dairy Products", 3
cboCategory.AddItem "Grains/Cereals", 4
cboCategory.AddItem "Meat/Poultry", 5
cboCategory.AddItem "Produce", 6
cboCategory.AddItem "Seafood", 7

cboCategory.ListIndex = 0
```

We will use `ctlProducts` to get Product information, and fill in the Product combo box as we did before for the Customer combo box. We will also bind the text boxes to `ctlProducts` in the same way we did for the other objects:

```
With ctlProducts
    .CategoryIDEquals = 1
    With .GetProductCollection(e_ProductsCategoryID)
        .MoveFirst
```

```
            For lngProductRecordCounter = 1 To .RecordCount
                cboProduct.AddItem .Item.ProductName, _
                    lngProductRecordCounter - 1
                .MoveNext
            Next

            .MoveFirst

            For lngTxtBoxIndex = 0 To txtProduct.Count - 1
                txtProduct(lngTxtBoxIndex).DataField = _
                        txtProduct(lngTxtBoxIndex).Tag
                txtProduct(lngTxtBoxIndex).DataMember = "ProductIDProducts"
                Set txtProduct(lngTxtBoxIndex).DataSource = .Item
                txtProduct(lngTxtBoxIndex).Locked = True
            Next

        End With

        cboProduct.ListIndex = 0
        cboCustomer.ListIndex = 0
    End With
```

Finally we will set our date pickers to an appropriate date and call a function that will place all of the Customer Address information into the Ship To Field:

```
    DTPRequired.Value = DateAdd("d", 10, Now)
    DTPDate = Now

    CustomerAddressToShipperAddress

End Sub
```

Last, we must call this sub in the `Form_Load` event:

```
Private Sub Form_Load()

    Initialize

End Sub
```

Finally, we will have the function to put the values into the Shipper fields:

```
Private Sub CustomerAddressToShipperAddress()

    Dim lngAddressTxtCounter As Long
    Dim lngOrderTxtCounter As Long
```

First, iterate through all of the Customer text boxes:

```
    For lngAddressTxtCounter = 0 To txtCustomer.Count - 1
```

For each Customer text box, iterate through the Order text boxes (which contain the Ship Address information).

```
With ctlOrders.GetOrderCollection(e_OrderWhoseOrderID).Item

        Select Case txtCustomer(lngAddressTxtCounter).Tag

            Case "Address"
                .ShipAddress = txtCustomer(lngAddressTxtCounter).Text

            Case "PostalCode"
                .ShipPostalCode = txtCustomer(lngAddressTxtCounter).Text

            Case "City"
                .ShipCity = txtCustomer(lngAddressTxtCounter).Text

            Case "Region"
                .ShipRegion = txtCustomer(lngAddressTxtCounter).Text

            Case "Country"
                .ShipCountry = txtCustomer(lngAddressTxtCounter).Text

        End Select
    End With
Next

End Sub
```

The Click Events

Now that our form is intialized, the only remaining code is to handle the `Click` events.

The Combo Boxes

When the user click on either the Customer, Category or Product combo boxes we need to update some of the other controls on the form.

The cboCategory Click Event

When a Category is selected, we must update the Products in the Products combo box as well as updating the Products component itself:

Begin by declaring a variable and clearing the combo box:

```
Private Sub cboCategory_Click()

    Dim lngProductCounter As Long

    cboProduct.Clear
```

Before we do this, we want to make sure that the product information has been initialized, if it has not, there will be no value for the `DataMember` property of the Product text boxes:

```
    If txtProduct(0).DataMember = "" Then
        Exit Sub
    End If
```

We will now reset the CategoryID to equal the new CategoryID that was selected, which will be the `ListIndex +1`. Once we do this, we must refresh the Product control:

```
With ctlProducts
    .CategoryIDEquals = cboCategory.ListIndex + 1
    .GetProductCollection(e_ProductsCategoryID).Refresh
End With
```

We will now refill the Product combo with the new information:

```
With ctlProducts.GetProductCollection(e_ProductsCategoryID)

    For lngProductCounter = 0 To .RecordCount
        cboProduct.AddItem .Item.ProductName
        .MoveNext
    Next

End With

cboProduct.ListIndex = 0

End Sub
```

The cboCustomer Click Event

When we click the Customer combo box, we must set the Customer Name property of the Customer control equal to this new Customer. We will use the `Find` method to do this:

```
Private Sub cboCustomer_Click()
```

```
ctlCustomers.GetCustomerCollection(e_AllCustomers).Find cboCustomer.Text
```

Next, we want to call the function to set the Shipper Address to the Customer Address:

```
CustomerAddressToShipperAddress
```

```
End Sub
```

The cboProduct Click Event

Selecting a Product from the Product combo box will require you to use the `Find` method of the Product control to find the appropriate Product:

```
Private Sub cboProduct_Click()
```

```
With ctlProducts.GetProductCollection(e_ProductsCategoryID)
    .Find cboProduct.Text
End With
```

```
End Sub
```

The Command Buttons

It is in the various command buttons' `Click` events that most of the work goes on.

The cmdCustomerAdd Click Event

Adding a Customer requires unlocking the text boxes, and calling the `AddNew` method on the Middle Customer object. We will also have to do a little extra work here. We want to hide the text box that shows the Contact Title, and show the combo box that has a list of all allowable titles. Equally, we'll also want to hide the combo box of all Company Names and show the text box that will allow the user to enter a new Customer. As we iterate through the Customer text boxes, we'll check if the `Tag` is from one of these fields, and if so, take the appropriate action:

```
Private Sub cmdCustomerAdd_Click()

Dim lngTxtBoxIndex As Long

For lngTxtBoxIndex = 0 To txtCustomer.Count - 1
    txtCustomer(lngTxtBoxIndex).Locked = False

    Select Case txtCustomer(lngTxtBoxIndex).Tag

        Case "ContactTitle"
            txtCustomer(lngTxtBoxIndex).Visible = False
            cboContact.Text = txtCustomer(lngTxtBoxIndex).Text

        Case "CompanyName"
            txtCustomer(lngTxtBoxIndex).Visible = True
            cboCustomer.Text = txtCustomer(lngTxtBoxIndex).Text

    End Select

Next
```

We next want the update button enabled, and to disable the Add and Edit buttons:

```
cmdCustomerUpdate.Enabled = True
cmdCustomerAdd.Enabled = False
cmdCustomerEdit.Enabled = False
```

We now want to call the `AddNew` method:

```
ctlCustomers.GetCustomerCollection(e_AllCustomers).AddNew
```

Next, we want to make the combo box for Contacts visible, and combo box for Customer Companies to be invisible:

```
cboContact.Visible = True
cboCustomer.Visible = False
```

Finally, we change the caption of the form so the user can know they are doing a Customer Add New:

```
        frmOrders.Caption = "Order Entry: Add ADDING CUSTOMER"

    End Sub
```

The cmdCustomerEdit Click Event

This will work just like the **Add New** button, except we will be calling the `Edit` method of the Middle object of the Customer control:

```
    Private Sub cmdCustomerEdit_Click()

      Dim lngTxtBoxIndex As Long

      For lngTxtBoxIndex = 0 To txtCustomer.Count - 1
          txtCustomer(lngTxtBoxIndex).Locked = False

          Select Case txtCustomer(lngTxtBoxIndex).Tag

              Case "ContactTitle"
                  txtCustomer(lngTxtBoxIndex).Visible = False
                  cboContact.Text = txtCustomer(lngTxtBoxIndex).Text

              Case "CompanyName"
                  txtCustomer(lngTxtBoxIndex).Visible = True
                  cboCustomer.Text = txtCustomer(lngTxtBoxIndex).Text

          End Select

      Next

      cmdCustomerUpdate.Enabled = True
      cmdCustomerAdd.Enabled = False
      cmdCustomerEdit.Enabled = False

      ctlCustomers.GetCustomerCollection(e_AllCustomers).Edit

      cboContact.Visible = True
      cboCustomer.Visible = False

      frmOrders.Caption = "Order Entry: Add EDITING CUSTOMER"

    End Sub
```

The cmdCustomerUpdate Click Event

The **Update** button will require a little extra work, as we don't have our Titles combo box bound to our control. We will have to set the Title property to this value:

```
    Private Sub cmdCustomerUpdate_Click()

      Dim lngTxtBoxIndex As Long

      On Error GoTo cmdCustomerUpdateError
```

First, get a reference to the Middle Customer object:

```
      With ctlCustomers.GetCustomerCollection(e_AllCustomers)
```

Set the `ContactTitle` property:

```
.Item.ContactTitle = cboContact.Text
```

When we are adding a new Customer, we'll need to create a new `CustomerID`. In this case, we are doing this in the form, but it could easily be another responsibility of the Customer component.

To create a new 5 character CustomerID, we're using the following algorithm:

- ❏ Iterate through the text boxes, finding the text box with the `Tag = CompanyName`, and get the first three letters of company's name
- ❏ Take the first letter, and throw it into a Randomize function to get a random letter for the fourth letter
- ❏ Repeat the last step to generate the fifth letter

This should prevent us from having to any identical IDs.

> *Of course, it's theoretically possible that we could still end up with two identical IDs. To allow for this possibility, the server component should have the ability to test if an `AddNew` fails because of an already existing ID We didn't add this functionality to our server component to keep the component as simple as possible.*

The formula for our randomizing equation is:

```
Int((UpperBound - LowerBound + 1) * Rnd(Seed) + LowerBound)
```

In our case:

- ❏ UpperBound is 90 for Z
- ❏ LowerBound is 65 for A
- ❏ The seed will be the first letter in the Customer Company Name
  `(Mid(txtCustomer(lngTxtBoxIndex).Text, 1, 1)`

We will use the Visual Basic function `Asc` to convert the resulting letter to its ASCII number, and the `Chr` function to convert numbers to characters. Thus:

```
(UpperBound - LowerBound + 1) = (90 - 65 +1)

Rnd(seed) = Rnd(Asc(Mid(txtCustomer(lngTxtBoxIndex).Text, 1, 1)))
```

Therefore, putting them together we get this:

```
If .EditMode = adEditAdd Then

    For lngTxtBoxIndex = 0 To TxtCustomer.Count - 1

        If txtCustomer(lngTxtBoxIndex).Tag = "CompanyName" Then
            .Item.CustomerID = _
```

```
                            UCase(Mid(TxtCustomer(lngTxtBoxIndex).Text, 1, 3)) & _
                            Chr(Int((90 - 65 + 1) * _
                            Rnd(Asc(Mid(TxtCustomer(lngTxtBoxIndex).Text, 1, 1))) + 65)) _
                            & Chr(Int((90 - 65 + 1) * _
                            Rnd(Asc(Mid(TxtCustomer(lngTxtBoxIndex).Text, 2, 1))) + 65))
                    Exit For
                End If

            Next

        End If
```

Some of you may be thinking that the code would be much more compact if I just added things together, like 90 - 65 +1. *The code would be more compact but someone reading your code would have no idea where* 26 *came from. Someone reading this code can figure out that* 90 *is Z and* 65 *is A, and determine what the code is doing. Better a few extra lines of code that can be read than very condensed code that no one can read.*

If there is an edit, we already have a CustomerID assigned, so we can now just do an update, and add the new customer to the combo box:

```
        .Update
        cboCustomer.AddItem .Item.CompanyNam
        cboCustomer.ListIndex = cboCustomer.NewIndex
    End With
```

We want to once again hide text boxes or combo boxes and reset the command buttons:

```
    For lngTxtBoxIndex = 0 To txtCustomer.Count - 1

        txtCustomer(lngTxtBoxIndex).Locked = True

        Select Case txtCustomer(lngTxtBoxIndex).Tag

            Case "ContactTitle"
                    txtCustomer(lngTxtBoxIndex).Visible = True

            Case "CompanyName"
                    txtCustomer(lngTxtBoxIndex).Visible = False

        End Select

    Next

    cmdCustomerUpdate.Enabled = False
    cmdCustomerAdd.Enabled = True
    cmdCustomerEdit.Enabled = True

    cboCustomer.Visible = True
    cboContact.Visible = False
    frmOrders.Caption = "Order Entry: Add"

    Exit Sub

cmdCustomerUpdateError:
```

```
        MsgBox "The following error has occured:" & vbCrLf & _
               "Error Number: " & Err.Number & vbCrLf & _
               "Error Description: " & Err.Description & vbCrLf & _
               "Error Source: " & Err.Source, "Error"

    End Sub
```

The cmdOrderAdd Click Event

This event will simply add Order Detail information into the Order Detail object. We will exit out if there is no Quantity entered:

```
    Private Sub cmdOrderAdd_Click()

        Dim lngIndexCounter As Long

        On Error GoTo cmdOrderAddError
```

The `GetOrderDetailsCollection` method of the Order Details control can return the Middle object of the Order Details collection that has its ID equal to some `OrderID`. Right now, the collection is set on the `OrderID` =0 (the default we put in the Order Details component), so there are no records. This is the `OrderID` we want for doing an `AddNew`:

```
        With ctlOrderDetails.GetOrderDetailsCollection(e_OrderIDOrderDetails)
```

Start an `AddNew`:

```
            .AddNew

            If txtQuantity.Text = "" Then
                Exit Sub
            End If
```

Use the `Item` method to return the lower class that has the new Order Detail record:

```
            .Item.Quantity = txtQuantity.Text
```

Iterate through the Product text boxes and set the appropriate fields:

```
            For lngIndexCounter = 0 To txtProduct.Count - 1

                Select Case txtProduct(lngIndexCounter).Tag

                    Case "ProductID"
                        .Item.ProductID = txtProduct(lngIndexCounter)

                    Case "UnitPrice"
                        .Item.UnitPrice = txtProduct(lngIndexCounter)

                End Select

            Next
```

We're just going to hard code the discount to a value:

```
.Item.Discount = 0.1
```

Get the Product Name out of the combo box:

```
.Item.ProductName = cboProduct.Text
```

Update the Order Details record. We want to pass in a parameter of False so that we only perform a Batch update that will not go to the recordset. This allows us to add other items to the Order without having to update the database each time:

```
.Update (False)
```

Recalculate the Order amount:

```
txtOrderSubtotal.Text = CCur(txtOrderSubtotal.Text) + _
    CCur(.Item.UnitPrice * .Item.Quantity)
```

Find the Freight field and use it to calculate the total:

```
For lngIndexCounter = 0 To txtOrder.Count - 1

    If txtOrder(lngIndexCounter).Tag = "Freight" Then
        txtOrderTotal = CCur(txtOrderSubtotal.Text) + _
            CCur(txtOrder(lngIndexCounter).Text)
        Exit For
    End If

Next

End With
```

Finally, calculate the new Units In Stock and reset the Quantity:

```
With ctlProducts.GetProductCollection(e_ProductsCategoryID)
    .Edit

    With .Item
        .UnitsInStock = .UnitsInStock - CLng(txtQuantity.Text)
    End With

    .Update (False)

End With

txtQuantity.Text = ""

Exit Sub

cmdOrderAddError:
```

```
      MsgBox "The following error has occured:" & vbCrLf & _
             "Error Number: " & Err.Number & vbCrLf & _
             "Error Description: " & Err.Description & vbCrLf & _
             "Error Source: " & Err.Source, "Error"

   End Sub
```

The cmdOrderSave Click Event

The `cmdOrderSave Click` event will work in the same manner as the `cmdCustomerAdd Click` event, except that we don't need to create an OrderID (it's an auto-incrementing field):

```
   Private Sub cmdOrderSave_Click(Index As Integer)

      Dim lngCustomerIndexCounter As Long

      On Error GoTo cmdOrderSaveClickError
```

Get a reference to the Middle object:

```
      With ctlOrders.GetorderCollection(e_OrderWhoseOrderID)
```

Get a reference to the Bottom object:

```
         With .Item
```

Set the properties:

```
            .RequiredDate = DTPRequired.Value
            .OrderDate = DTPDate
            .EmployeeID = cboOrderEmployee.ListIndex + 1
            .ShipVia = cboOrderShipVia.ListIndex + 1
```

Find the CustomerID text box:

```
            For lngCustomerIndexCounter = 0 To txtCustomer.Count - 1

               Select Case txtCustomer(lngCustomerIndexCounter).Tag
                  Case "CustomerID
                    .CustomerID.txtCustomer(lngCustomerIndexCounter)
                  Case "ContactName"
                    .ShipName = txtCustomer(lngCustomerIndexCounter
               End Select
            Next

         End With
```

Call the special `UpdateOrderDetail` method of the Middle object, passing in the Order Details recordset:

```
         .UpdateOrderOrderDetail ctlOrderDetails. _
             GetOrderDetailsCollection(e_OrderIDOrderDetails).ItemsRecordset

      End With
```

Then we need to refresh the collections and reset the controls:

```
    ctlOrderDetails.GetOrderDetailsCollection(e_OrderIDOrderDetails).Refresh
    ctlOrders.GetOrderCollection(e_OrderWhoseOrderID).Refresh

    ctlProducts.GetProductCollection(e_ProductsCategoryID).Refresh

    ctlOrders.GetOrderCollection(e_OrderWhoseOrderID).AddNew
    ctlOrders.GetOrderCollection(e_OrderWhoseOrderID).Item.Freight = 0

    CustomerAddressToShipperAddress

    txtOrderSubtotal.Text = 0
    txtOrderTotal.Text = 0

    Exit Sub

cmdOrderSaveClickError:

    Err.Raise Err.Number, Err.Source, Err.Description

End Sub
```

The cmdOrderCancel Click Event

When an Order is canceled, all changes must be undone. We could have done this by using a transaction, but we can also do this by simply calling the `Cancel` method and refreshing all of the client objects that may have been changed. We need to start by canceling the Order Detail changes:

```
Private Sub cmdOrderCancel_Click(Index As Integer)
```

```
    ctlOrderDetails.GetOrderDetailsCollection(e_OrderIDOrderDetails).Cancel
```

Next we will refresh the order detail object to get a fresh copy:

```
    ctlOrderDetails.GetOrderDetailsCollection(e_OrderIDOrderDetails).Refresh
```

We will repeat this for orders:

```
    ctlOrders.GetOrderCollection(e_OrderWhoseOrderID).Cancel
    ctlOrders.GetOrderCollection(e_OrderWhoseOrderID).Refresh
```

Start the add new and set the freight:

```
    ctlOrders.GetOrderCollection(e_OrderWhoseOrderID).AddNew
    ctlOrders.GetOrderCollection(e_OrderWhoseOrderID).Item.Freight = 0
```

Finally we will refresh the Products (items may have been removed from the Units In Stock), and clear the text fields:

```
    ctlProducts.GetProductCollection(e_ProductsCategoryID).Refresh

    CustomerAddressToShipperAddress
```

```
        txtOrderSubtotal.Text = 0
        txtOrderTotal.Text = 0

    End Sub
```

The project, as far as we're concerned, is now complete. We are now able to run the application, then add and edit Customers, and place a new Order.

Summary

The code in this form was relatively brief. I did leave out some of the error checking, such as checking if all the Order or Customer information had been entered before doing a Save, as I wanted to focus on binding the components to the form. With a few extra additions to our components, such as the ability to fill combo boxes, we could even reduce the code in our form to only a few pages!

Going back to our original idea of DNA, building components that can easily be reused in a multitude of places, we begin to see how our data binding classes help us fulfil this goal. Making the user interface that's using these components, even for the most complicated task such as Order Entry, boils down to simply setting properties and calling a few methods.

We could build a multitude of applications from these components, and all of them would require only a small amount of coding to function properly. To me, this is incredible.

```
              ┌─────────────────┐
              │    Get ADO      │
              │   connection    │
              └─────────────────┘
                       │
                       ▼
                     ◇◇◇◇◇
                   ◇       ◇
                   ◇       ◇
                     ◇◇◇◇◇
                       │
                [Successful]
                       │
                       ▼
              ┌─────────────────┐
              │  Set Recordset  │
              │ cursor location │
              └─────────────────┘
                       │
                       ▼
              ┌─────────────────┐
              │  Set Recordset  │
              │     source      │
              └─────────────────┘
                       │
                       ▼
              ┌─────────────────┐
              │  Set Recordset  │
              │   connection    │
              └─────────────────┘
                       │
                       ▼
```

15

Testing and Quality Control

While good design may be the most important ingredient in a successful Visual Basic project, **Quality Control** is nearly as important. Unfortunately, both Quality Control and Project Design are often completely ignored by Visual Basic programmers.

Since this book is about UML design and development, rather than Visual Basic Quality Control, we're not going to discuss it in much detail. What this chapter should give you is some helpful ideas on debugging classes. I would therefore urge you to consider this an important topic – even if I am only able to introduce you to it here.

What we'll cover in this chapter:

- ❑ The levels of testing
- ❑ Unit Testing
- ❑ How to test our components

Different Levels of Testing

Quality control can be performed on many levels. For example, we've already coded a small application to test RDS. This was a standard test application made during the design phase but there are many other levels of testing, such as:

- ❑ Unit Testing
- ❑ Integration Testing

Unit Testing

This level of testing involves a separate test of each individual component by itself to see if it works properly. Every method, property and Business Rule should be tested. We should also attempt to follow every alternative flow in our use cases and make sure that proper error handling is in place.

Integration Testing

This level builds upon unit testing, where several components are put together and tested. The results can be quite unexpected.

When to Use Each Level of Testing

Clearly, unit testing should be carried out before integration testing. With our Customer component, for example, we have three classes. We would want to build the Bottom Class first, write a test function, and thoroughly test that class by itself. Then we would build the Middle Class, thoroughly test it by itself, and then together with Bottom Class. Finally, we would build the Top Class, test it by itself, and then test it together with the other classes.

In this chapter, we're going to combine the unit testing with the integration testing. We can do this because the only thing the Top Class does is retrieve a Middle Class. Therefore, the only thing to test in the Top Class is its ability to retrieve a Middle Class and make sure that the Middle Class and the Top Class communicate correctly.

> *It therefore follows that as the Top Class also communicates to the Bottom Class through the Middle class, we are also able to test accessing the Bottom Class from the Top Class via the Middle Class.*

If we perform a series of tests for every method and property, we'll probably find many dormant bugs. By this process, we can usually eliminate all major bugs, and all but a very few, harder-to-find minor bugs.

> *These last stubborn bugs will probably be found during the last stages of beta testing.*

Quality Control

Testing should be based upon a careful plan. Our UML diagrams can help us make such a plan. We're going to see a simple way to develop a plan and test our project that anyone can do.

This plan involves making a chart for every method and property of our class. This chart should have the following columns:

- ❑ The maximum values for the parameters
- ❑ The minimum values for the parameter
- ❑ The parts of the system the method or property affects
- ❑ Invalid values for the parameters
- ❑ The expected return values (if a function)
- ❑ The expected outcomes

There should also be a section for alternative flows. It should show how the system would respond to alternative flows, which use case the alternative flow comes from, and the Business Rule associated with the alternative flow.

Once all of these sections have been mapped out, we need to write code that will test each of the conditions.

For example, we could have the following chart for the `CustomerID Property Let` methods:

Maximum Value	Minimum Value	System Components Affected by Property	How Affected	Valid Values	Invalid Values
5 characters	5 characters	Local disconnected recordset	Recordset Field value changed to new value	Unique value not in recordset	Non-unique Value

Alternative Flows:

Flow	Business Rule	Use Case	Outcome
Change during Edit	Modify Customer	CustomerEdit	Raise Error 1002

From this information we can see that we should test the following:

- ❑ Setting the CustomerID to a unique value that is less than or greater than five characters, see if an error is raised.
- ❑ Setting the CustomerID to a non-unique value that is less than or greater than five characters, see if an error is raised.
- ❑ Setting the CustomerID to a valid value and see if the disconnected recordset is updated.
- ❑ Setting the CustomerID to an invalid value to ensure the disconnected recordset is not updated.
- ❑ Setting the CustomerID to a new value during an Edit to see if an error is raised.

When we perform these tests on our Customer component, we discover that we don't actually check if a new value is unique. Trying to add a non-unique value for the primary key would cause an error to be raised from the server component when the database rejected the new CustomerID value. It would be better if the error were handled by creating a new ID at the server component, and using the new ID to complete the update.

> **This is why we undertake quality control: to find the missing steps.**

The focus of this chapter is creating a test function that will test a component. This method of testing could be used to test all of the above possibilities.

Creating Component Test Modules

As we concentrated so hard on building our Customer component, we'll create a module within the component to test the component. Similar modules can be built to test each of the three classes separately, as well as together.

To keep it simple, we'll write the debug information to the Immediate window, but in a real test it would be better to write it to a file or database. Getting the hang of this is quite easy - so we won't test every function, or any of the alternative flows.

This will avoid us having to write too much more code in this book... but I hope you will recognize the benefit of more thorough testing in your own mission-critical projects.

Building a Test Module for the Customer Component

Open up clsCustomers. We are going to use conditional compiling again, just as we did when we were debugging MTS components (see Appendix C). Go to your Project Properties window, click on the Make tab and add this line to the Conditional Compilation Arguments box:

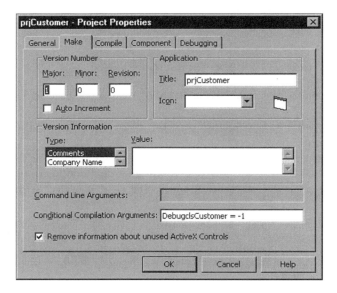

This line allows us to create conditional code, denoted with # marks, which is only run when the above line is in Project Properties. To turn off this debugging, set DebugclsCustomer = 0.

Now go back to the General tab and set the StartUp Object as Sub Main:

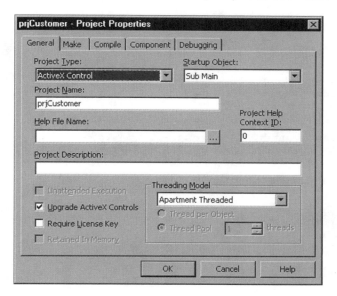

Now add the following code to basCMain. It creates an instance of our Customer object and calls a conditional debugging routine that we'll create in a minute:

```
Sub Main()

  #If DebugclsCustomer Then

    Dim objCustomers As New clsCustomer

    objCustomers.DebugCheckCustomers

    Set objCustomer = Nothing

  #End If

End Sub
```

Now go to the code window for the clsCustomers class and add the following:

```
#If DebugClsCustomers Then

Public Sub DebugCheckCustomers()
```

This creates a function that is visible only when we have the DebugClsCutomers = -1 set in the Project Properties.

For now we will ignore errors:

```
On Error Resume Next
```

We will first test if the `GetCustomerCollection` has successfully retrieved the `e_AllCustomer` collection:

```
With GetCustomerCollection(e_AllCustomers)
    Debug.Print "Test if customer recordset has been retrieved"
```

We'll first of all try to retrieve the `RecordCount`. We can check this against the real Record Count in the database. If the RecordCount is correct, the `AllCustomers` Collection was initialized properly:

```
Debug.Print "Record Count after initialization: " & _
            GetCustomerCollection(e_AllCustomers).RecordCount
```

Next we will test the `Move` methods of the Middle object:

```
    Debug.Print "Current record: " & .ItemsRecordset.Fields("CustomerID")
    Debug.Print "Test MoveNext"
    .MoveNext
    Debug.Print "Current record: " & .ItemsRecordset.Fields("CustomerID")
    Debug.Print "Test MoveLast"
    .MoveLast
    Debug.Print "Current record: " & .ItemsRecordset.Fields("CustomerID")
    Debug.Print "Test MoveFirst"
    .MoveFirst
    Debug.Print "Current record: " & .ItemsRecordset.Fields("CustomerID")
End With
```

We will next try to edit a Customer record. We want to simulate a bound control changing the values of the fields. We'll do this by getting the recordset through the `ItemsRecordset` property, and then change the fields.

We start by checking the Edit Mode property in both the Customer Middle and Top Classes:

```
With GetCustomerCollection(e_AllCustomers)
    Debug.Print "Customer EditMode:" & .Item.EditMode
    Debug.Print "Customer Managing EditMode:" & .EditMode
```

An edit can be started by calling the `Edit` method:

```
    .Edit
```

We now need to check if the `EditMode` property has been properly changed:

```
    Debug.Print "Customer EditMode:" & .Item.EditMode
    Debug.Print "Customer Managing EditMode:" & .EditMode
```

First, let's print out the current values by using the properties in the Bottom object:

```
    Debug.Print "Test Customers Edit"

    With .Item
```

```
        Debug.Print "Item Object Values: " & vbCrLf & _
            "CompanyName: " & .CompanyName & vbCrLf & _
            "ContactName: " & .ContactName & vbCrLf & _
            "ContactTitle: " & .ContactTitle & vbCrLf & _
            "Country: " & .Country & vbCrLf & _
            "CustomerID: " & .CustomerID & vbCrLf & _
            "Fax: " & .Fax & vbCrLf & _
            "Phone: " & .Phone & vbCrLf & _
            "PostalCode: " & .PostalCode & vbCrLf & _
            "Region: " & .Region & vbCrLf
    End With
```

Now we'll check the values from the recordset. These are the values a Data Consumer control bound to the Bottom object would have. These values should be the same as those above:

```
    With .ItemsRecordset
        Debug.Print "Customers Object Values: " & vbCrLf & _
            "CompanyName: " & .Fields("CompanyName: ") & _
            vbCrLf & "ContactName: " & .Fields("ContactName") & _
            vbCrLf & "ContactTitle: " & .Fields("ContactTitle:") & _
            vbCrLf & "Country: " & .Fields("Country") & vbCrLf & _
            "CustomerID: " & .Fields("CustomerID:") & vbCrLf & _
            "Fax: " & .Fields("Fax") & vbCrLf & _
            "Phone: " & .Fields("Phone") & vbCrLf & _
            "PostalCode: " & .Fields("PostalCode") & vbCrLf & _
            "Region: " & .Fields("Region") & vbCrLf
```

Now we'll try to directly change the records in the recordset (an alternative flow would be to try to change the Primary Key):

```
        .Fields("CompanyName") = "TestCompanyName"
        .Fields("ContactName") = "TestContactName"
        .Fields("ContactTitle") = "TestContactTitle"
        .Fields("Country") = "TestCountry"
        .Fields("Fax") = "TestFax"
        .Fields("Phone") = "TestPhone"
        .Fields("PostalCode") = "TestP"
        .Fields("Region") = "TestRegion"
        Debug.Print "CUSTOMERS editmode: " & .EditMode
    End With
```

Now call the Update method:

```
    .Update
```

Next, we'll see if both the properties and the Fields collection return the new values. First check the properties:

```
    Debug.Print "Edit complete"

    With .Item
        Debug.Print "Item Object Values: " & vbCrLf & _
            "CompanyName: " & .CompanyName & vbCrLf & _
```

```
        "ContactName: " & .ContactName & vbCrLf & _
        "ContactTitle: " & .ContactTitle & vbCrLf & _
        "Country: " & .Country & vbCrLf & _
        "CustomerID: " & .CustomerID & vbCrLf & _
        "Fax: " & .Fax & vbCrLf & _
        "Phone: " & .Phone & vbCrLf & _
        "PostalCode: " & .PostalCode & vbCrLf & _
        "Region: " & .Region & vbCrLf
    End With
```

Next check the recordset values:

```
    With .ItemsRecordset
        Debug.Print "Customers Object Values: " & vbCrLf & _
            "CompanyName: " & .Fields("CompanyName: ") & _
            vbCrLf & "ContactName: " & .Fields("ContactName") & _
            vbCrLf & "ContactTitle: " & .Fields("ContactTitle:") & _
            vbCrLf & "Country: " & .Fields("Country") & vbCrLf & _
            "CustomerID: " & .Fields("CustomerID:") & vbCrLf & _
            "Fax: " & .Fields("Fax") & vbCrLf & _
            "Phone: " & .Fields("Phone") & vbCrLf & _
            "PostalCode: " & .Fields("PostalCode") & vbCrLf & _
            "Region: " & .Fields("region") & vbCrLf
    End With
```

Now we're going to try to Edit the same record by changing the properties in the Bottom object. We know the current values (they were just printed) so we can immediately try to change the values:

```
    .Edit

    With .Item
        .CompanyName = "TestCompanyName3"
        .ContactName = "TestContactName3"
        .ContactTitle = "TestContactTitle3"
        .Country = "TestCountry3"
        .Fax = "TestFax3"
        .Phone = "TestPhone3"
        .PostalCode = "Test3"
        .Region = "Test3"
    End With
```

Let us also make sure the EditMode is being properly set back when we do the update:

```
    Debug.Print "Customers editmode" & .ItemsRecordset.EditMode
    .Update
    Debug.Print "Edit complete"
    Debug.Print "EditMode CUSTOMERS:" & .ItemsRecordset.EditMode
    Debug.Print "EditMode customer:" & .Item.EditMode
    Debug.Print "Edit complete"
```

Next check the new values:

```
    With .Item
        Debug.Print "Item Object Values: " & vbCrLf & _
            "CompanyName: " & .CompanyName & vbCrLf & _
```

```
            "ContactName: " & .ContactName & vbCrLf & _
            "ContactTitle: " & .ContactTitle & vbCrLf & _
            "Country: " & .Country & vbCrLf & _
            "CustomerID: " & .CustomerID & vbCrLf & _
            "Fax: " & .Fax & vbCrLf & _
            "Phone: " & .Phone & vbCrLf & _
            "PostalCode: " & .PostalCode & vbCrLf & _
            "Region: " & .Region & vbCrLf
    End With

    With .ItemsRecordset
        Debug.Print "Customers Object Values: " & vbCrLf & _
            "CompanyName: " & .Fields("CompanyName: ") & _
            vbCrLf & "ContactName: " & .Fields("ContactName") & _
            vbCrLf & "ContactTitle: " & .Fields("ContactTitle:")& _
            vbCrLf & "Country: " & .Fields("Country") & vbCrLf & _
            "CustomerID: " & .Fields("CustomerID:") & vbCrLf & _
            "Fax: " & .Fields("Fax") & vbCrLf & _
            "Phone: " & .Fields("Phone") & vbCrLf & _
            "PostalCode: " & .Fields("PostalCode") & vbCrLf & _
            "Region: " & .Fields("Region") & vbCrLf
    End With
```

Now we'd like to test `AddNew`:

```
    .AddNew
```

Make sure the `EditMode` has been properly changed:

```
    Debug.Print "Customer EditMode" & .Item.EditMode
    Debug.Print "Customer Managing EditMode" & .EditMode
    Debug.Print "Test Customers AddNew"
```

Print out the values to make sure a new record has been returned:

```
    With .Item
        Debug.Print "Item Object Values: " & vbCrLf & _
            "CompanyName: " & .CompanyName & vbCrLf & _
            "ContactName: " & .ContactName & vbCrLf & _
            "ContactTitle: " & .ContactTitle & vbCrLf & _
            "Country: " & .Country & vbCrLf & _
            "CustomerID: " & .CustomerID & vbCrLf & _
            "Fax: " & .Fax & vbCrLf & _
            "Phone: " & .Phone & vbCrLf & _
            "PostalCode: " & .PostalCode & vbCrLf & _
            "Region: " & .Region & vbCrLf
    End With

    With .ItemsRecordset
        Debug.Print "Customers Object Values: " & vbCrLf & _
            "CompanyName: " & .Fields("CompanyName: ") & _
            vbCrLf & "ContactName: " & .Fields("ContactName") & _
            vbCrLf & "ContactTitle: " & .Fields("ContactTitle:") & _
            vbCrLf & "Country: " & .Fields("Country") & vbCrLf & _
            "CustomerID: " & .Fields("CustomerID:") & vbCrLf & _
```

```
                    "Fax: " & .Fields("Fax") & vbCrLf & _
                    "Phone: " & .Fields("Phone") & vbCrLf & _
                    "PostalCode: " & .Fields("PostalCode") & vbCrLf & _
                    "Region: " & .Fields("region") & vbCrLf
```

Then enter new values directly into the fields:

```
            .Fields("CompanyName") = "TestCompanyName4"
            .Fields("ContactName") = "TestContactName4"
            .Fields("ContactTitle") = "TestContactTitle4"
            .Fields("Country") = "TestCountry4"
            .Fields("CustomerID") = "TsID4"
            .Fields("Fax") = "TestFax4"
            .Fields("Phone") = "TestPhone4"
            .Fields("PostalCode") = "Test4"
            .Fields("region") = "TestR"
            Debug.Print "Customers EditMode" & .EditMode
        End With
```

Update it and check the values:

```
        .Update
        Debug.Print "AddNew complete"

        With .Item
            Debug.Print "Item Object Values: " & vbCrLf & _
                "CompanyName: " & .CompanyName & vbCrLf & _
                "ContactName: " & .ContactName & vbCrLf & _
                "ContactTitle: " & .ContactTitle & vbCrLf & _
                "Country: " & .Country & vbCrLf & _
                "CustomerID: " & .CustomerID & vbCrLf & _
                "Fax: " & .Fax & vbCrLf & _
                "Phone: " & .Phone & vbCrLf & _
                "PostalCode: " & .PostalCode & vbCrLf & _
                "Region: " & .Region & vbCrLf
        End With

        With .ItemsRecordset
            Debug.Print "Customers Object Values: " & vbCrLf & _
                "CompanyName: " & .Fields("CompanyName: ") & _
                vbCrLf & "ContactName: " & .Fields("ContactName") & _
                vbCrLf & "ContactTitle: " & .Fields("ContactTitle:") & _
                vbCrLf & "Country: " & .Fields("Country") & vbCrLf & _
                "CustomerID: " & .Fields("CustomerID:") & vbCrLf & _
                "Fax: " & .Fields("Fax") & vbCrLf & _
                "Phone: " & .Fields("Phone") & vbCrLf & _
                "PostalCode: " & .Fields("PostalCode") & vbCrLf & _
                "Region: " & .Fields("region") & vbCrLf
        End With

    End With

#End If
```

We could have improved this code by creating a function to print out the current values using the properties and using the recordset, but I wanted to keep the code as simple and clear as possible.

This is all the code we're going to include for this test, as I'm sure you've got the hang of it by now. We could have gone on to test the following:

- ❑   Placing values into the recordset through from the Bottom to simulate a bound Data Consumer
- ❑   Deleting records
- ❑   All of the alternative flows in our use cases
- ❑   Business rules
- ❑   And more...

You can now run your project and debug the Customer component.

Testing the Bottom Customer Object

Testing the Bottom object would have required us to pass in a recordset through the `ItemsRecordset` property. We would place a testing function in `clsCustomer`. The testing function would start as follows:

```
#If DebugClsCustomer Then

Public Sub TestClsCustomer

  Dim objProxy as New prjServer.clsServer

  Set ItemsRecordset = objProxy.ReturnCustomerRecordSet _
      (UserName, Password, WhereClause)
```

This would give us a reference to a valid recordset that we could use for testing `clsCustomer`.

Summary

This small chapter should give you a few good ideas on how to debug your classes.

Every time I made a change to the project, I would run these test functions. I could detect an error in a class immediately. It was then just a matter of putting break points in, tracing the code and finding the source. While it's true a few errors took me some time to find, most of them were tracked down in a few minutes. These little test functions were a lifesaver. Without them, I would never have made my deadline, and you would not be reading this chapter.

It's not so much about the method we actually use to test our classes; what is important is that we do test them in a thorough, consistent manner. Making charts for our properties and methods is a simple, thorough way to test our components. We can make the charts, then go through our Business Rules and use cases to fill in the appropriate sections. From this we can make a list of what needs to be tested.

In this way, we can be sure that every rule, alternative flow and use case will be tested. Finally, we can make a test function, just as we did above. The end result should be a component that is completely bug-free and ready to be plugged into our project.

16

What Comes Next?

Overview

We have finally reached the end of the road. In reality, this is only the beginning of course. These chapters have only laid out the basic framework that you can use to make powerful Visual Basic Enterprise applications.

When I was given the task of writing this book, I not only wanted to write it to teach you about UML, but also to give you plenty of useful information about design and development in Visual Basic with UML... information that you might not be able to find elsewhere. As I did my research for this book, I found some rather interesting things. To begin with, there were very few books on UML and Visual Basic. I suppose this is because most Visual Basic programmers still have not realized the value of UML when they're creating a Visual Basic project. I would consider proper design as the most critical element in making all projects. You simply cannot produce good Visual Basic code without good design, and one of the best tools for object-oriented design is UML.

Since UML is for modeling object-oriented projects, and Visual Basic is still not fully accepted as an OOP language, it is likely that this attitude has also played a role in the lack of Visual Basic UML books. I hope, once and for all, that this book will lay to rest the question of Visual Basic's ability to build object-oriented programs. We have not only built VB objects and components in this book, but we did it with UML patterns and Visual Basic code templates.

Some UML books are very intense and theoretical. These are great books for universities, hardcore C++ programmers, and those who like deep theory. For those who were expecting an intense theoretical discussion of UML and the models, I apologize if I disappointed you. There are many great books that can give you the entire history of object-oriented modeling. In this book, I was more interested in teaching you how to make the diagrams than who invented a particular diagram, its entire lineage through the history of time, and the impact each diagram has had on modern civilization.

By far the most difficult problem I found, while researching UML, was finding a book that really told me how to apply UML to making my applications. Sure, there were books with samples, but these samples were simplistic and had absolutely nothing to do with the Visual Basic programs that you and I are going to be making for the Enterprise applications. Most books do not even explain why we should bother going to all of the trouble of making these diagrams.

It is my hope that this book has provided you with an insight into how and why Visual Basic programmers should make UML diagrams, and how we can use these diagrams to build real-world Visual Basic projects.

Using UML

UML diagrams make our lives easier. They shorten the time it takes to make our project, they clearly define how we're going to build our project, and they provide us with a tool to experiment with the design of our project in an easy, clear way. I could not imagine programming without them.

There is a small learning curve when you first explore how to make UML diagrams, but once you figure it all out, they become easy. You can use sophisticated tools like HOW, or scribble little diagrams on the back of napkins. It doesn't matter. UML works everywhere, even on paper scraps.

The DNA Framework

There was another thing that I felt was very important when writing this book. If you are going to invest a lot of time and effort to read my book, you should be rewarded for your effort. I felt a fair reward would be to give you a Visual Basic 6 DNA framework that you could use in your current projects. The problem with using a real-world example is its complexity. I hope this example was not too difficult to follow. For those of you who have worked through it, you will walk away with:

- ❑ An in-depth understanding of Microsoft's Alphabet Soup (MTS, ADO, RDS, DNA...)
- ❑ An understanding of three-tier Visual Basic projects
- ❑ Visual Basic Hierarchies
- ❑ Visual Basic Data Providers

It was my hope that those of you who had some basic understanding of all of these concepts would gain a deeper understanding of them, and how they fit together, by working out a real-world example. I have tried at every turn to avoid complicated code. I realize that the end result was still some pretty heavy code samples, but I believe they are worth your time to understand.

This book was not only about UML: it was also about Microsoft's DNA framework. DNA can be explained in many ways, but in its simplest form DNA boils down to this:

> *Build reusable components that can be used in many different applications. These applications will do different things and may work under different conditions.*

Thus, we can build a Product component that works in:

- ❑ A Visual Basic Order Entry application, providing a list of products for creating an order
- ❑ An ASP page providing data for HTML pages for customers to order products through the Internet
- ❑ A Visual Basic ActiveX document that generates a sales report for each product for management running over an intranet

This is what DNA is all about. Building components like this should reduce production time, and enable developers to make a multitude of projects with little effort. Yet, for this to work, there is one hidden requirement: the components must not require a great deal of code to work.

Consider this: if I need one hundred pages of code to bind a component to my form's objects, then what have I gained? If this is required, I will end up writing nearly as much code to reuse my components than I would have if I had just built several applications without them.

The key to DNA is not just building reusable components, but to build reusable components that can be used with a minimum amount of work and code. What we've built in this book is just this type of component. In the end, we found ourselves making Client components in a cookie cutter fashion. Based on the Customer component template, we were able to quickly build the rest of our components. Once the components were done, it took less than six pages of code to make our order entry application functional. By adding a few more features onto our components, we could have probably reduced the code to two or three pages. This is what DNA is about, and this is what good design, using UML and project management, can achieve.

Components like these can only come out of a thorough design phase. Once they are completed, they become a powerful tool that can reshape the way you wish to develop your programs.

I would like to finish this book by discussing where we would take our project from the point we have currently reached.

The Next Steps

Our Northwind project was built in iterative steps. The point we've reached at the end of this book would certainly be considered a good stage at which to sit down and discuss the design of the rest of the project - based on what we've just built.

> *It's likely that if Northwind really existed, and we were actually making this project, the next step would be completing the Client components.*

Using the pattern that we made for the Customer component, we could now create a complete set of UML diagrams for all of our components. Our Order component would be the most complex, and I suggest you sit down and try to draw the sequence diagrams for this component.

Improving the System

I have already made some suggestions on how to improve the Order component; for instance, we could make a special combined component that contained the Order and OrderDetails Bottom and Middle Classes. We could add to this component the ability to return a string array with the possible values of the ShipVia - so we wouldn't need an extra component here. We could also give the component a method to add or remove a ShipVia. The best choice will be found by mapping out all of the possibilities in UML diagrams and finding which is the best solution for the system we are building.

If we had tried to jump into the code for the Order component, without a thorough design phase, we would probably have found ourselves one month into coding before we suddenly realizing that we were not making this component in the best way possible. If this had happened, we would have been left with a choice of either continuing down a bad path, reworking the component, or throwing away a month of work. Even in the best situation, where we chose the right technique, we would be coding a component without any guidance or direction. Why would we want to do something so frustrating when we can map everything out with UML?

Testing the System

Once the Client components are designed, coded, integration and unit tested, and the Server component is completed, IES Inc. would begin a thorough testing of the components as a single unit. While quality control was being performed, other IES programmers could be completing the rest of the user interfaces for the project. Once the Order Entry forms were complete, they could begin testing the completed application. When the application passes these tests, they can make the initial release of the Order Entry application to Northwind. Northwind can then begin testing the application.

More than One Release?

It's quite possible that the first release may only address Order Entry. Some of the more complicated tasks such as Deleting Employees could be left for the next release. Based on the first release, we would begin designing the second portion of the application.

The second portion of the application could include essential reports and any additional key functionality such as deleting Employees. When this part of the project is complete, the final stage may be additional non-essential reports and perhaps some additional features on the user interface. The last phase of the project may be to use these components to build an Internet application. The various components could be used to pass information to an ASP page that will build HTML code for an Internet e-commerce site running under Microsoft Commerce server.

> How a project is divided can depend on many factors such as the client's needs, the project deadlines, critical features, etc. It is not important how the project is divided, only that the project is built with components and it uses a staged delivery of functioning components.

Visual Basic is a powerful language that is capable of building powerful Enterprise applications. Hopefully, this book has given you some tools to build your own Enterprise Visual Basic solutions. Thank you for taking the time to read 'Visual Basic 6 UML Design and Development'. I hope it has provided you with useful information.

UML to VB Mapping

Purpose of the VB Mapping

UML is a wonderful thing - it allows us to 'see' the design of a system. However the diagrams we take trouble to create are only useful if they directly contribute to our final system. Developers who are new to modeling can understandably wonder whether all the extra effort is worth it. Therefore the point of this mapping is simple: to help the VB developer understand how to map the UML constructs into VB code.

UML Version Covered

The current version of UML as supported by most tools is 1.1.

As of writing, version 1.3 was in draft, although there are no major changes to this version that VB developers need to be aware to.

The current UML documentation can be found on `http://www.rational.com/uml/`

It is recommended that VB Developers visit this site and review the official documents before trying to understand the mapping in detail.

How the Mapping is Structured

The official UML specification is very detailed and precise but is also very abstract! Most VB developers will find a great deal of the detail unimportant in getting up to speed with mapping the UML.

Therefore, the mapping that follows concentrates on the concrete elements from the UML that have notation and appear on diagrams. These are also the artifacts that the VB Developer will have the most contact with. These include *class*, *attribute*, *operation*, *interface*, etc. Each of these elements will be discussed in turn and references will be made to the more abstract elements in the UML semantics document that they derive from, so that the developer can choose to cross-reference with the official specification.

So to reiterate, the mapping focuses essentially on how the diagrams you draw and communicate with relate to the code you write.

> *Please refer to the Mapping Guide at the beginning of the mapping itself for a breakdown of the sections therein.*

How Well Does the UML Map to VB?

The UML allows you to capture both the static knowledge about your application (packages, classes, associations, etc.) and also the dynamic behavior (operation calls, events, etc.). We will see that most diagrams have a very close mapping to VB but a few are more vague. Class diagrams for instance, are key diagrams to us and it will be quite straightforward to see how these map to VB. The coincidence between 'class' in the UML and 'class' in VB is not a coincidence! These are essentially the same things.

Statechart diagrams, on the other hand, are not so clear. This is because the standard VB language does not come with a 'standard' statechart implementation (often called a 'finite state machine'). This is also partly because of the many different ways we can write them. Nonetheless, some guidelines are provided to help get you started.

UML and Components

It is rather ironic that although the UML is rich and powerful for modeling classes, their relationships and the logical packaging of such things, it is not so good at modeling components, as VB developers know them. This is something that hopefully later revisions of the UML might cover more clearly.

Fortunately for us, we can come up with conventions that developers can follow to help us define components. A further discussion of this can be found in the mapping.

Concrete Or By Convention?

Some mappings from the UML to VB are plain and concrete - there is no debate as to its correctness. Some mappings, on the other hand, are purely by convention because VB simply doesn't support the construct. When convention is used, developers should use their judgment as to whether they follow the convention or invent their own. Remember, though, that the suggestions given are tried and tested.

Upgrade to at Least VB5

If you are currently using a version of VB prior to version 5, I suggest you upgrade immediately! There were some significant features added to VB5 that are key to writing solid components in VB. These include the ability to 'implement' an interface and also the support for 'events' from classes. The features added in VB6 are not so important but there are better storage mapping facilities provided (ADO support).

The mapping assumes that you are using VB5 or later.

Styles Used in the Mapping

Concepts that refer to UML will be stated in *Italics*.

VB Code fragments that are presented in this style:

```
Public m_Car As Car
```

While sections of VB code that are provided as context, but are not directly relevant to the topic under discussion are presented like this:

```
Public m_Car As Car
```

How to Use this Mapping

The mapping is a reference rather than something you would read end-to-end, however it might be worth giving it the 'once over' just to get a feeling for things.

As you become more familiar with the UML, you will soon only need to refer to this Appendix periodically, as the core mappings are very intuitive and easy to remember.

Building Your Diagrams

To help you design your diagrams, it is recommended that you enlist the help of a tool.

There are many choices here from general symbol tools like Visio (UML templates are available for this on the web) to a full-blown repository-based CASE tool that will also ensure your diagrams are in-sync' with each other. Of course never underestimate the power of a whiteboard and marker!

So, without further ado, let's start to look at the VB to UML mapping.

Mapping Guide

These are the sections that are included in this mapping.

1.0 General Extension Mechanisms

1.1 Constraints and Comments

A UML constraint generally maps to a fragment of code in VB that checks the constraint. The location and style of such code depends on the type of constraint. For instance, a UML constraint might suggest that an object be only associated with one object at a time - not two.

In VB, this would translate into validation code inside the procedures of the VB class, such as an `Order` class:

```
'Set the customer related to the order
'Constraints:
'A customer is not already associated

Public Sub SetCustomer(ByVal aCustomer As Customer)

    'we can only be associated with one customer
    'it is an error to set a customer twice
    Debug.Assert m_myCustomer Is Nothing

    Set m_myCustomer = aCustomer
End Sub
```

With this example, an order can only be associated with one customer. It is a constraint that only one customer can be associated at a time. (Assume a separate routine is available to disassociate the customer.)

One useful feature of VB is to make copious use of `Debug.Assert`. This build-in library feature allows us to make assertions in our code that must always be satisfied. If you are running in design mode and an assertion fails, then VB will take you straight to the place where the assertion failed. This is very effective way of catching logic bugs in your code, early.

Sometimes it is not always possible to translate a constraint to code. In these situations, the best you can do is place an appropriate comment into the code to remind yourself and your colleagues that the constraint exists.

1.2 Element Properties

The UML defines *element properties* as values that can be tagged on to arbitrary model elements. In VB, these simply become comments against the related item. A typical property might be the name of the author who created the model. If this property was tagged to a particular diagram, then we would include a author comment inside the definition of each class on the diagram:

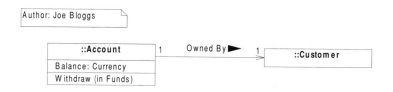

Corresponding Code in `Account.cls`:

```
'Account - defines a single account in the accountancy system
'
'Author: Joe Bloggs

Private m_theBalance As Currency

Public Sub Withdraw(ByVal theFunds As Currency)
    '....
End Sub
```

1.3 Stereotypes

Most UML elements come with a set of standard stereotypes. Some CASE Tools also extend the range of stereotypes to match the languages targeted. Here are examples of two class stereotypes:

Stereotypes have a big impact on how we map UML to VB. In some cases, they affect only the properties of the target VB item and sometimes it will completely change the mapping.

When we discuss each UML construct, the standard stereotypes of that item will also be covered.

2.0 Model Management

UML Notation	VB	Notes
Package 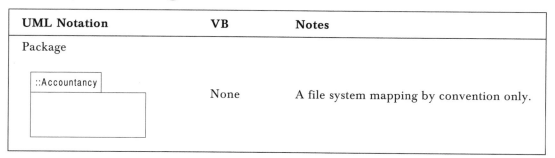	None	A file system mapping by convention only.

2.1 Packages

Packages in the UML are a logical grouping of related items such as *classes*. A *Package* has no direct mapping to VB so conventions are used instead.

A convention typically used is to include the *package* name in the name of contained elements. For instance, an Accountancy Package may contain a class called `Account`. Therefore, the class will have a name in VB of `Accountancy_Account`. This will ensure that classes with similar names in different packages will not collide. This activity is usually called *Name Mangling*.

The corresponding class names in VB would look like this:

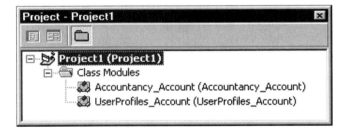

2.1.1 External Libraries as Packages

During modeling, it is also useful to model popular VB libraries as packages. For instance, we can model popular services like RDO as a package:

2.1.2 Nested Packages

Packages can be nested. If you choose to map packages to a naming convention, you will need to define 'short' names for the packages so that the class names don't get too long!

2.1.3 Packages and the File System

When deciding how to structure your source code it is a good idea to choose a directory in your file-system that acts as the root for your source code. Each logical package defined can be created as a sub-directory underneath this root. Classes in a particular package are placed in the corresponding directory:

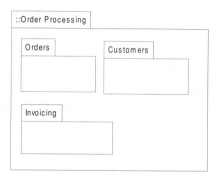

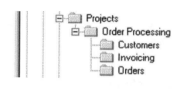

The Nested Packages   **The Nested Folder Structure**

This technique will not only keep the source code files manageable, but and also help partition the work up between developers. For instance, one developer may be working on an Accountancy package, whilst another is working on a User interface package.

2.1.4 Package Stereotypes

The *<<system>> package stereotype* denotes the complete system that is being built in VB. Usually the *<<system>> package* maps to a VB Project group, i.e. the VB project group contains all packages and the elements that define the whole VB application.

A *<<façade>> package* indicates that the *package* is present to provide a façade on to other packages in the system. In VB terms, this could represent a set of related classes that are providing a simple, more high-level interface onto another set of more detailed classes. Again, because *package* is a logical grouping or items, there is no explicit language feature in VB that you can use. It is all defined by convention.

A *<<framework>> package* indicates that the package contains a framework of items. In VB terms, we might design a set of related classes that perform a certain framework service, e.g. generic database access. The *<<framework>>* constraint simply implies that the package would be used as part of a complete system, together with the extra classes that complement the framework and make it complete.

2.1.5 Package Dependencies

A *package* can have *dependencies* to others. A *dependency* of *stereotype* <<*import*>> maps to a reference in a VB project's references list.

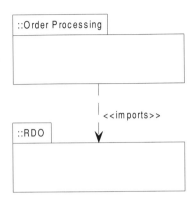

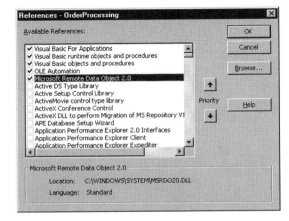

| A Package Reference | A VB Reference |

3.0 Static Structure Diagrams

The static structure diagrams like the Class Diagram are a fundamental tool in the UML toolbox and are used more in practice than any other diagram.

UML Notation	VB	Notes
Association $\underset{\text{Transport}}{\overset{1}{\rule{2cm}{0.4pt}}}$ ::Car	Class	Mapping varies. See Association notes.
Attribute - Balance : Currency	Variable	

UML Notation	VB	Notes
Class `::Car`	Class, Module or Form	Derived from Classifier
Classifier (no notation)	Class	Abstract class of Class, DataType and Interface
Constraint { ordered }	Assert statement, comment or validation code.	
Interface ○———— IPersistent or – «interface» ::IPersistent	Class	A specialization of Classifier. For an ActiveX component, `Instancing = PublicNotCreatable`
Operation `Withdraw()`	Procedure without body	Typically on a VB interface

4.0 Classifiers

4.1 General

A UML *Classifier* is the abstract definition of a *Class, DataType or Interface* in the UML. All of these elements map to a VB Class, Standard Module or Form.

(*Classifiers* are defined in the UML to simply capture the similarities between *Classes, DataTypes* and *Interfaces*. They are abstract however and don't appear directly on diagrams. Consult the UML semantics document for further details about them.)

UML *classes* are the most used of all the *Classifier* types and these map straight to VB Classes or Forms as shown:

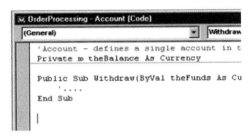

A Class In UML   A Class In Visual Basic

4.1.1 Name

The name of the UML *classifier* becomes the name of the VB item.

4.1.2 Features

All UML *classifiers* have *features*, which are further defined as *attributes* and *operations* and these map to VB Member *Variables* and *Procedures*, respectively. These are discussed later.

4.1.3 Inheritance and Stereotypes

Most VB developers know that VB doesn't support full inheritance. However, VB does support the ability to 'implement' an interface. This is an extremely useful facility that makes regular inheritance 'not so important'.

The first thing we must do is distinguish between two types of inheritance:

- ❑ Inheritance of interface (sub-typing)
- ❑ Inheritance of implementation (class extension or code reuse)

If we consider these two forms of inheritance, it is important to realize that the first form is more important for building components that exhibit good qualities of design like low coupling. (A component with low coupling means that the component has few dependencies on other parts of a system. This means that the component could be used easily in *other* systems without too much work). The details of this are beyond the scope of this book and I suggest you read the 'VB Books On-line' for a background on interfaces and the `Implements` construct.

In UML terminology, a *class* can *realize* many *interfaces*. This directly maps to the meaning of `Implements`, in VB.

4.1.4 Implementation Inheritance

Implementation inheritance or code reuse, as it is often called, is a very useful feature and time saver. However it is not so essential in providing the system your users want. Also code reuse can be achieved by 'aggregating' or 'composing' the object that contains the services (methods) you want to reuse instead.

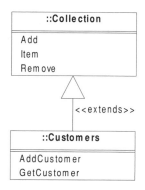

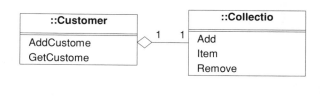

Code reuse via Inheritance   **Code reuse via composition (the VB way)**

In this situation, any operations you want to reuse, involves writing delegation code to delegate to the reused object. Here is an example 'customers' collection:

```
'this is my hidden implementation of the collection
Private m_myCollection As New Collection

Public Sub AddCustomer(ByVal theCustomer As Customers)
    'delegate to my collection
    m_myCollection.Add theCustomer
End Sub

Public Sub RemoveCustomer(ByVal theCustomer As Customers)
    'delegate to my collection
    m_myCollection.Remove theCustomer
End Sub
```

Of course this can be very tedious when there are many services involved. This is where CASE tools are useful for doing the 'grunge work'. VB Developers may wish to develop their own VB 'add-in' that performs this task.

So to recap, if you are turning an *<<extends>>* inheritance relationship into containment, do the following:

- ❑ Add an `Implements` statement for the class being reused.
- ❑ Add a `Private` variable that holds a reference to the reused object (the aggregation)
- ❑ Add the set of methods (procedures) that delegate to their counterparts on the aggregated object.

497

If the stereotype is <<*implements*>> then this maps simply to the VB construct 'implements':

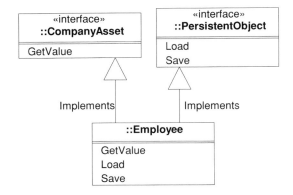

The VB code for the above model could look like this: -

```
'Employee Class

Implements CompanyAsset
Implements PersistentObject

'my implementation of GetValue
Private Property Get CompanyAsset_GetValue() As Variant
    'return asset value of this employee
End Property

'my implementation of load
Private Sub PersistentObject_Load()
    'load employee details from disk
End Sub

Private Sub PersistentObject_Save()
    'save employee details to disk
End Sub
```

4.1.5 Static Members

The UML allows *features* to be either part of each class instance or part of the class itself. This means that the *feature*, whether it is an *attribute* or an *operation* is part of the *class* and not each *instance* of the *class*. These are often called 'static' in VB. VB does not support *features* that are only part of the *class* so, if we wish to model them, we need to define a convention to support them.

One convention we can use is to create a standard (.bas) module for each class that has static members. All static operations and attributes can then be added as members of this module. When naming the module, try to pick a name that relates the module to the VB class. For instance, if we have a class called `Account`, we may choose to name the module `AccountClass`.

Account
Balance: Currency
OverdraftRate: double {static}
Withdraw (in Funds)

The Overdraft attribute would be placed in `AccountClass.bas`:

```
'AccountClass - the Account class object
'holds all static features

'the percentage that all overdafts are charged at
'applies to *all* overdrawn accounts
Public OverdraftRate As Double
```

4.1.6 Parameterized Classes (Templates)

VB does not support parameterized classes. This is a tradeoff that VB developers must accept in return for a simpler programming model.

If you include parameterized classes in your design then this is OK but remember that you will have to manually write the specific versions yourself. It may be better to avoid modeling with them to start with.

4.1.7 Class Mapping Advice

If you are using the package to name mapping convention, then the class name will also include the names of its containing packages.

It is good practice to choose a filename for the class that is similar to the class name.

4.2 Interfaces

An *interface*, which is a specialized *Classifier* in the UML maps directly to a class in VB.

This mapping is not explicitly stated and checked in VB - it is only apparent that a VB class is an interface by the way it is used by other classes and the fact that the VB class contains empty procedures.

```
'IPersistent - responsibilities that must be provided by persistent objects

Public Sub Save()
    'abstract operation
End Sub

Public Sub Load()
    'abstract operation
End Sub
```

Interfaces are crucial when building components in VB. To expose an interface from a VB ActiveX Component, the Instancing property of the VB class should be set to PublicNotCreatable.

In all other respects, an *interface* has a similar mapping to a UML *class* in that is also has *features* that can be *operations, attributes, associations,* etc.

Note: Developers should not confuse *interface* with user-interface or user-interface class. Refer to the UML documentation for a precise definition of *interface*.

4.3 Attributes

An *attribute* of a UML *classifier* maps to a VB variable.

Account
- Balance: Currency
+ Withdraw (in Funds)

A UML Attribute on Account

```
'Account class
'
Private Balance As Currency
```

A Variable definition in a VB Class

A UML attribute has the following form: -

visibility name : type = { initial-value }

4.3.1 Visibility

The *visibility* of the attribute has a partial mapping to the *access* of the VB attribute as captured in this table:

UML Visibility	UML Notation	VB Access	Notes
Public	+	Public	Same meaning
Protected	#	None	Due to VB not supporting implementation inheritance.
Private	-	Private	Same meaning.

4.3.2 Name

The *name* of the attribute simply maps to the name of the VB variable.

4.3.3 Type

The type specified for the attribute will be the name of either a built-in VB type such as an Integer or a Long, a user-defined type or a VB object type such as a Class or Form.

4.3.4 Initial Value

An attribute in the UML can be given an *initial-value*. In VB, we achieve this by adding initial assignments inside the `Initialize` routine of the class:

Account
- Balance: Currency = 10
+ Withdraw (in Funds)

```
'Account class
'
Private m_theBalance As Currency

Private Sub Class_Initialize()
    'this generous bank gives you a tenner to
    'start!
    m_theBalance = 10
End Sub
```

An initialized UML Attribute   **Variable initialized inside the class initializer**

If the attribute is tagged as *{frozen}* then this implies that the attribute is constant. Constant attributes are easily represented in VB as Const variables. For example:

```
Private Const PI As Double = 3.1412
```

Note: VB does not allow classes to declare public constants. This is more of a nuisance rather that a logical restriction. It is recommended that constants that relate to a class be placed in module that is closely related to either the class or the package containing the class. For instance, if you have a package called `Accountancy` that contains the related classes, `Account` and `Ledger`, then you might want to place your constants in a bas module that is related to the package called, say, `Accountancy (Accountancy.bas)`.

4.4 Operations

An *operation* on a UML *class* maps to a VB Procedure.

A UML *operation* has the following form:

visibility name (parameters) : return-type { property string }

4.4.1 Visibility

The *visibility* of the operation has a partial mapping to the access of the VB procedure as captured in this table:

UML Visibility	UML Notation	VB Access	Notes
Public	+	Public	Same meaning
Protected	#	Friend	See notes
Private	-	Private	Same meaning

The actual meaning of public, protected and private really comes down to the language you are using to implement your models in. In C++ for instance, public, protected and private all have quite distinct meanings that are different to VB.

In VB, the visibility options provided in the UML will map to different things in VB. When we are building VB components, we are interested in three levels of access:

- ❏ Things that are visible only to the inside of a class (Private)
- ❏ Things that are visible only to the inside of a the component (Friend)
- ❏ Things that are visible to all other components and classes (Public)

So when using the UML we should choose the mapping as shown in the table.

4.4.2 Name

The *name* of the operation simply maps to the name of the procedure in VB.

4.4.3 Parameters

(see below)

4.4.4 Return Type

The *return-type* specified for the operation will be the name of either a built-in VB type such as an `Integer` or a `Long`, a user-defined type or a VB object type such as a Class or Form.

If a *return type* is present then we map the item to a VB Function, otherwise we map it to a Subroutine:

Account
- Balance: Currency = 10
+ Withdraw (in Funds)
+ IsOverdrawn: Boolean

```
'Account class
Private m_theBalance As Currency

Public Sub Withdraw(ByVal theFunds As Currency)
    m_theBalance = m_theBalance - theFunds
End Sub

Public Function IsOverdrawn() As Boolean
    IsOverdrawn = (m_theBalanced < 0)
End Function
```

4.4.5 The Operation and Method Distinction

The UML often refers to both *operations* and *methods*, which many VB developers may consider to be the same thing. The UML offers a distinction whereby *operations* define a service, and the *method* is the implementation of that *operation*. In VB terms, the distinction is very subtle as both concepts are implemented with the same language constructs, i.e. as functions or subroutines.

If we really want to make a distinction in VB, then we can say that the empty procedures defined in a VB interface are the *operations* and the *methods* are the actual implementations in each of the VB classes that implement the interface.

4.4.6 Parameters

Each parameter in UML has the following form:

kind name : type = default value

Kind

The kind of the operation is either *in*, *out* or *inout*, and indicates how the parameter is passed to the operation's body. VB has an approximate mapping for these:

UML kind	VB	Notes
in	ByVal	
out	ByRef	Not really supported but a compatible mapping
inout	ByRef	

Type

The type specified for the parameter will be the name of either a built-in VB type such as an `Integer` or a `Long`, a user-defined type or a VB object type such as a Class or Form.

Default Value

If a parameter is given a default value then this can be implemented in VB too. For a VB parameter to have a default value, the **Optional** keyword must be present:

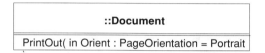

```
Public Sub PrintOut(Optional ByVal Orient As PageOrientation = Portrait)
    'print out
End Sub
```

4.4.7 Polymorphic Operations

If a UML *Operation* is marked as polymorphic (*isPolymorphic = True*), then this signifies that the *operation* can be overridden in subclasses and thus has many implementations. In VB, this property only applies to operations (procedures) defined on a VB interface. (All operations defined on a VB interface are automatically polymorphic because the operation will have many implementations in the classes that implement the interface.)

4.4.8 Stereotypes

A *<<get>> or <<set>> operation stereotype* is an operation whose role is to provide access to a value on the object. In VB terms, Property procedures are good examples of these types of operations.

4.5 Utilities

A *UML utility class* represents just a cohesive group of global procedures or variables. These are usually mapped to standard (bas) modules in VB because they don't have multiple instances like a regular class does. Examples of utility classes are the standard procedure libraries that come with VB. It is convenient to show them in this way to make a model easier to understand. These are shown as a stereotype of class:

```
        «utility»
        ::WINAPI

 SendMessage
 PostMessage
 GetDlgItem
 CreateWindow
```

The Windows API as a <<utility>>

4.6 Associations

4.6.1 Multiplicity

The multiplicity of an association determines how we implement the association. If the multiplicity is **1**, then we may choose to implement the association using an object reference. If the multiplicity is a fixed number then we might employ the use of VB arrays. If the multiplicity is unbounded, e.g. **1+** then a collection may be used instead. See the implementation section for examples of this.

4.6.2 Qualifiers

A UML qualifier in is effectively a key for navigating to the object at the other end of an association. For instance, we may initially model that a Person owns many Cars. However in later design revisions, we may state that a Person owns a single Car when qualified by a particular registration plate. See the following examples for more about this.

4.6.3 N-ary Associations

Most associations involve just two objects - one at each end. However there are occasions when three or more classes are involved in the association. When considering how to map these, look at the example of how we implement link classes. These effectively represent an association of three objects.

4.6.4 Aggregation and Composition

Aggregation and composition are implemented in the same way in VB. This is because unlike some languages such as C++, you cannot physically contain one VB object within another. However VB does allow you to achieve a similar effect by ensuring your composed objects are created at the same time. We achieve this by adding the 'new' keyword to the Private variable that holds the sub-object:

```
'Class Car
'My engine - this will be created when I get created
Dim m_theEngine As New Engine

'code for class..
```

4.6.5 Implementing Associations

Because *associations* are not part of the Visual Basic Language it can be hard for Developers to know how to map them. The follow section provides some techniques and examples for implementing associations in VB.

Let's first look at how we might implement simple associations in VB.

4.6.6 Basic 1-to-1 Unidirectional Associations

The most common way to implement a unidirectional association is to use an object reference embedded in the source class. In the following example, a Person owns a single Car:

Here is the code for a simple unidirectional association (note that the example actually holds a link from Car to Person).

First, let's create a simple definition of the Car (Car.cls):

```
'our private implementation
Private m_Make As String      'make of car

'our hidden link implementation to person
Private m_theOwner As Person
```

```
'get the car owner
Public Property Get Owner() As Person
    Set Owner = m_theOwner
End Property
```

```
'set the car owner
'note: this makes the owner changeable during
'the car's lifetime
Public Property Set Owner(ByVal theOwner As Person)
    Set m_theOwner = theOwner
End Property
```

```
'get the make of the car
Public Property Get Make() As String
    Make = m_Make
End Property
```

```
'set the make of the car
Public Property Let Make(ByVal newMake As String)
    m_Make = newMake
End Property
```

505

Now let's create a simple `Person` class:

```
'private implementation of person
Private m_myName As String

'return person's name
Public Property Get Name() As String
    Name = m_myName
End Property

'set person's name
Public Property Let Name(ByVal newName As String)
    m_myName = newName
End Property
```

To test the association, we will place some code in the main routine of the application:

```
Sub Main()
    'simple 1 to 1 unidirectional association

    '1. create some objects to connect
    Dim aPerson As New Person
    aPerson.Name = "Russell"

    Dim aCar As New Car
    aCar.Make = "Ferrari"

    '2. set the person as the owner of the car
    Set aCar.Owner = aPerson

    '3. print the owner's name via the car
    Debug.Print aCar.Owner.Name + " is driving a " + aCar.Make
End Sub
```

4.6.7 Basic 1-to-Many Unidirectional Associations

If the Person gets rich then we might want to model the person owning many cars, as shown:

A basic implementation of this is to embed a collection of `Cars` into `Persons` and then allow client code to add `Cars` to `Person` at will.

Here is some rudimentary code from `Person`:

```
'private implementation of person
Private m_myName As String

Private m_myTransport As New Cars

'return person's name
Public Property Get Name() As String
    Name = m_myName
End Property
```

```vb
'set person's name
Public Property Let Name(ByVal newName As String)
    m_myName = newName
End Property
```

```vb
Public Property Get Transport() As Cars
    Set Transport = m_myTransport
End Property
```

Note the embedded, hidden Cars collection in Person. This holds the references to the associated Car objects. The code for Car follows. (This was generated by the class builder add-in.)

The Cars collection code:

```vb
Option Explicit

'local variable to hold collection
Private mCol As Collection
```

```vb
Public Function Add(Make As String, Owner As Person, Optional sKey As String) _
                                                              As Car
    'create a new object
    Dim objNewMember As Car
    Set objNewMember = New Car

    'set the properties passed into the method
    objNewMember.Make = Make
    If IsObject(Owner) Then
        Set objNewMember.Owner = Owner
    Else
        objNewMember.Owner = Owner
    End If
    If Len(sKey) = 0 Then
        mCol.Add objNewMember
    Else
        mCol.Add objNewMember, sKey
    End If

    'return the object created
    Set Add = objNewMember
    Set objNewMember = Nothing

End Function
```

```vb
Public Property Get Item(vntIndexKey As Variant) As Car
    'used when referencing an element in the collection
    'vntIndexKey contains either the Index or Key to the collection,
    'this is why it is declared as a Variant
    'Syntax: Set foo = x.Item(xyz) or Set foo = x.Item(5)
    Set Item = mCol(vntIndexKey)
End Property
```

```vb
Public Property Get Count() As Long
    'used when retrieving the number of elements in the
    'collection. Syntax: Debug.Print x.Count
    Count = mCol.Count
End Property
```

```
Public Sub Remove(vntIndexKey As Variant)
    'used when removing an element from the collection
    'vntIndexKey contains either the Index or Key, which is why
    'it is declared as a Variant
    'Syntax: x.Remove(xyz)

    mCol.Remove vntIndexKey
End Sub
```

```
Public Property Get NewEnum() As IUnknown
    'this property allows you to enumerate
    'this collection with the For...Each syntax
    Set NewEnum = mCol.[_NewEnum]
End Property
```

```
Private Sub Class_Initialize()
    'creates the collection when this class is created
    Set mCol = New Collection
End Sub
```

```
Private Sub Class_Terminate()
    'destroys collection when this class is terminated
    Set mCol = Nothing
End Sub
```

To test the collection, we can write some code for the main application routine like this:

```
Sub Main()
    'simple 1 to many unidirectional association

    '1. create some objects to connect
    Dim aPerson As New Person
    aPerson.Name = "Russell"

    Dim aFastCar As New Car
    aFastCar.Make = "Ferrari"

    Dim aSlowCar As New Car
    aSlowCar.Make = "Reliant"

    '2. associate the cars with the person
    aPerson.Transport.Add "Ferrari", aPerson, "R999 ICH"
    aPerson.Transport.Add "Reliant", aPerson, "S111 LOW"

    '3. print the makes of car the person owns
    Debug.Print aPerson.Name + " owns the following car makes: - "
    Dim aCar As Car
    For Each aCar In aPerson.Transport
        Debug.Print "A " + aCar.Make
    Next
End Sub
```

The example code assumes that the collection is not ordered in any way.

Building collection classes can be tedious so it is recommended that developers take a look at the Class Builder add-in, which provides collection-building features.

4.6.8 Implementing Qualifiers

As we elaborate our design model, associations that start off as 1-to-many, often turn out to be 1-to1 when qualified by some index. If we take our Person-to-Car example, we could refine the model to get the following:

As mentioned in the mapping, a qualifier becomes an index when traversing the association. If we are using property procedures, then the qualifier will become a parameter of that procedure. So, to access a single `Car` that the `Person` owns, we must provide a registration number. Clients wishing to access an individual car would supply the registration number of the car of interest:

```
Dim aCar As Car
Set aCar = aPerson.Transport("R999 ICH") 'get a particular car
```

4.6.9 Bi-directional Associations and Referential Integrity

Implementing unidirectional associations with just pointers is just about workable and is quite common. However, in business models, we often need to traverse in both directions. Now we could just implement the above techniques on both ends, i.e. each object has a reference to the other:

First, here is the `Car` with an `Owner` link:

```
'our private implementation
Private m_Make As String      'make of car

'our hidden link implementation to person
Private m_theOwner As Person

'get the car owner
Public Property Get Owner() As Person
    Set Owner = m_theOwner
End Property

'set the car owner
'note: this makes the owner changeable during
'the car's lifetime
Public Property Set Owner(ByVal theOwner As Person)
    Set m_theOwner = theOwner
End Property
```

```
'get the make of the car
Public Property Get Make() As String
    Make = m_Make
End Property

'set the make of the car
Public Property Let Make(ByVal newMake As String)
    m_Make = newMake
End Property
```

Here is the code for `Person` also with a link back to `Car`:

```
'private implementation of person
Private m_myName As String

'our hidden link implementation to the car
Private m_Transport As Car

'get the person's sole transport
Public Property Get Transport() As Car
    Set Transport = m_Transport
End Property

'set the person's transport
Public Property Set Transport(ByVal someTransport As Car)
    Set m_Transport = someTransport
End Property

'return person's name
Public Property Get Name() As String
    Name = m_myName
End Property

'set person's name
Public Property Let Name(ByVal newName As String)
    m_myName = newName
End Property
```

Here is some simple client code to associate the respective objects:

```
Option Explicit

Sub Main()
    '1 to 1 bidirectional association
    'with *no* referential integrity

    '1. create some objects to connect
    Dim aPerson As New Person
    aPerson.Name = "Russell"

    Dim aCar As New Car
    aCar.Make = "Ferrari"

    '2. set the person as the owner of the car
    Set aCar.Owner = aPerson
```

```
            '3. set the person's means of transport
            Set aPerson.Transport = aCar

            '4. print the car owner's name
            Debug.Print aCar.Owner.Name + " is driving a ";

            '5. print the owner's transport
            Debug.Print aPerson.Transport.Make
    End Sub
```

4.6.10 Problems with Simple Associations

Now, it is very difficult to ensure the integrity of these models so far. It would be very easy to accidentally set one end of the association and not the other at run-time. This will ultimately lead to the infamous 'error 91 – object variable or with block not set', when we later try to traverse the association.

If we want to build more robust bi-directional associations, we must build referential integrity into our models. We can do this in a number of ways.

4.6.11 Link Management Routines

These routines are separate routines often placed in standard (.bas) modules and are responsible for attaching both ends of an association at the same time. They are also responsible for disconnecting an association. By performing the connection at the same time, at the same place, we have a better chance of maintaining referential integrity.

So let's revisit our original 1-to-1 bi-directional association between Person and Car but this time, we will add some association link management.

The code for Person and Car is almost the same as before but we have a new module to add which contains the link management:

The code for the PersonOwnsCar_Manager module:

```
    'associate a person and car
    Public Sub LinkPersonAndCar(ByVal aPerson As Person, ByVal aCar As Car)
        'ensure we are not breaking an existing association
        Debug.Assert aPerson.Transport Is Nothing
        Debug.Assert aCar.Owner Is Nothing

        'link up in both directions
        Set aPerson.Transport = aCar
        Set aCar.Owner = aPerson
    End Sub
```

```
    'cater for removal of person from model
    Public Sub UnlinkPerson(ByVal aPerson As Person)
        'ensure we have a valid person to begin with
        Debug.Assert Not aPerson Is Nothing

        Set aPerson.Transport.Owner = Nothing
        Set aPerson.Transport = Nothing
    End Sub
```

```
'cater for removal of car from model
Public Sub UnlinkCar(ByVal aCar As Car)
    'ensure we have a valid car to begin with
    Debug.Assert Not aCar Is Nothing

    Set aCar.Owner.Transport = Nothing
    Set aCar.Owner = Nothing
End Sub
```

We also have one new procedure to add to `Car`:

```
'Destroy the car from the model
Public Sub Destroy()
    'get link manager to sort out the integrity
    PersonOwnsCar_Manager.UnlinkCar Me
End Sub
```

Finally, let's look at some code that tests the association:

```
Option Explicit

Sub Main()
    '1 to 1 bidirectional association
    'with referential integrity

    '1. create some objects to link
    Dim aPerson As New Person
    aPerson.Name = "Russell"

    Dim aCar As New Car
    aCar.Make = "Ferrari"

    '2. Link up the two
    PersonOwnsCar_Manager.LinkPersonAndCar aPerson, aCar

    '3. Test: print the car owner's name
    Debug.Print aCar.Owner.Name + " is driving a ";

    '4. Test: print the owner's transport
    Debug.Print aPerson.Transport.Make

    '5. now write off the car
    '(this will disassociate the person too)
    aCar.Destroy

    '6. check the association no longer exists in both directions
    If aCar.Owner Is Nothing Then
        Debug.Print aPerson.Name + " no longer owns the car."
    End If

    If aPerson.Transport Is Nothing Then
        Debug.Print aPerson.Name + " no longer has transport!"
    End If
End Sub
```

4.6.12 Association Classes and Link Management

If we have a design that incorporates an association class, then we have an alternative home for the link management that Developers may find is more cohesive.

Let's assume that association between Person and Car is supplemented with a 'Log Book' that records the Car's history:

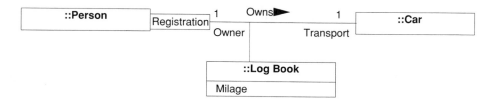

We will now want to ensure that when a Person is associated to a Car, a LogBook is also associated. We will assume that the LogBook already exists. If we do this, we can end up with the following implementation.

(Note that some properties in the code have been omitted from the model to make it easier to read. In fact, we can see that the LogBook in the code actually has a number of {derived} attributes that get their information from the Car.)

Firstly, here is the LogBook association class, which also contains the link management code:

```
'LogBook Association Class
'My associations
Private m_theLoggedCar As Car
Private m_theOwner As Person

Private m_myIssueDate As Date
```

```
'to check we have entered an 'initialized state'
Private m_blnInitialized As Boolean
```

```
'attributes  -----------------------------------

'When was I issued?
Public Property Get IssueDate() As Date
    IssueDate = m_myIssueDate
End Property
```

```
'set issue date
Public Property Let IssueDate(ByVal aDate As Date)
    m_myIssueDate = aDate
End Property
```

```
'you can only get the milage - you can't set it
'that would be illegal!
Public Property Get Milage() As Long
    Debug.Assert m_blnInitialized = True
```

```
        'derived property - get from the car
        Milage = m_theLoggedCar.Milage
End Property

'who owns the car?
Public Property Get RegisteredOwner() As String
        Debug.Assert m_blnInitialized = True

        'derived property - get from the person
        RegisteredOwner = m_theOwner.Name
End Property

'operations --------------------------------
'Register the log book for use
Public Sub Register(ByVal aPerson As Person, ByVal aCar As Car)
        'delegate to link
        Link aPerson, aCar
End Sub

'Unregister the log book from use
Public Sub UnRegister()
        'destroy the asociation
        'just delegate to unlink
        UnLink
End Sub

Private Sub Link(ByVal aPerson As Person, ByVal aCar As Car)
        Debug.Assert Not aPerson Is Nothing
        Debug.Assert Not aCar Is Nothing

        'link up in both directions
        Set aPerson.Transport = aCar
        Set aCar.Owner = aPerson

        'set my links too
        Set m_theLoggedCar = aCar
        Set m_theOwner = aPerson

        m_blnInitialized = True
End Sub

Private Sub UnLink()
        'destroy the asociation

        'deal with person first
        Set m_theOwner.Transport = Nothing      'person looses transport
        Set m_theOwner = Nothing                'log book looses person

        'unlink car now
        Set m_theLoggedCar.Owner = Nothing      'car looses owner
        Set m_theLoggedCar = Nothing            'log book looses car
End Sub
```

Here is the Car source code now (some extra attributes have been added to spice things up):

```
'Car Class
'our private implementation
Private m_Make As String           'make of car
Private m_myRoadMilage As Long     'My Milage
```

```
'our hidden link implementation to person
Private m_theOwner As Person

'attributes --------------------------

'get the car owner
Public Property Get Owner() As Person
    Set Owner = m_theOwner
End Property

'set the car owner
'note: this makes the owner changeable during
'the car's lifetime
Public Property Set Owner(ByVal theOwner As Person)
    Set m_theOwner = theOwner
End Property

'get the make of the car
Public Property Get Make() As String
    Make = m_Make
End Property

'set the make of the car
Public Property Let Make(ByVal newMake As String)
    m_Make = newMake
End Property

'get the car's milage so far
Public Property Get Milage() As Long
    Milage = m_myRoadMilage
End Property

'operations --------------------------
'Bump up the car milage
Public Sub BumpMilageBy(ByVal someMiles As Long)
    m_myRoadMilage = m_myRoadMilage + someMiles
End Sub
```

When we now want to associate `Person` and `Car`, we first create a `LogBook` and then get the `LogBook` to associate all three objects together. In the example client code we first associate the objects and then iterate over the assocation and list the information:

(Code in `App.bas`)

```
Option Explicit

Sub Main()
    '1 to 1 bidirectional association with association class

    '1. create some objects to link
    Dim aPerson As New Person
    aPerson.Name = "Russell"

    Dim aCar As New Car
    aCar.Make = "Ferrari"
    aCar.BumpMilageBy 50
```

```
        Dim aLogBook As New LogBook
        aLogBook.IssueDate = Now

        '2. Link everything up
        aLogBook.Register aPerson, aCar

        '3. Print out the ownership details
        'We can do this soley via the LogBook
        Debug.Print "Car Registration Details:"
        Debug.Print "Registration Date : " + CStr(aLogBook.IssueDate)
        Debug.Print "Owned By : " + aLogBook.RegisteredOwner
        Debug.Print "Milage on Clock : " + CStr(aLogBook.Milage)

        '4. Lets give the car to someone else
        '(I must be mad!)
        'lets take it out for the weekend first!
        aCar.BumpMilageBy 200

        'a new owner gets lucky
        Dim aLuckyPerson As New Person
        aLuckyPerson.Name = "Dave"

        aLogBook.Register aLuckyPerson, aCar

        '5. Print out the new ownership details
        'car should now be registered to Dave:
        Debug.Print "Car Registration Details:"
        Debug.Print "Registration Date : " + CStr(aLogBook.IssueDate)
        Debug.Print "Owned By : " + aLogBook.RegisteredOwner
        Debug.Print "Milage on Clock : " + CStr(aLogBook.Milage)

        '6. finally, write off the car
        'Unregistering the log book is as good as writing off the car
        'so let's do that instead
        aLogBook.UnRegister
End Sub
```

4.6.13 A Final Example: Bi-directional 1-to-Many Association with Link Management and Qualifier

As a final example, here is an implementation of a bi-directional 1-to-many *association* with *association class* and *qualifier,* which is built upon our earlier example. The design model of the implementation looks like this:

The code in `LogBook`, which now deals with multiple `Cars`:

```
'LogBook association class
'
'My associations
Private m_theLoggedCar As Car
Private m_theOwner As Person

Private m_myIssueDate As Date

'to check we have entered an 'initialized state'
Private m_blnInitialized As Boolean
```

```
    'attributes  -----------------------------------

'When was I issued?
Public Property Get IssueDate() As Date
    IssueDate = m_myIssueDate
End Property

'set issue date
Public Property Let IssueDate(ByVal aDate As Date)
    m_myIssueDate = aDate
End Property

'you can only get the milage - you can't set it
'that would be illegal!
Public Property Get Milage() As Long
    Debug.Assert m_blnInitialized = True

    'derived property - get from the car
    Milage = m_theLoggedCar.Milage
End Property

'who owns the car?
Public Property Get RegisteredOwner() As String
    Debug.Assert m_blnInitialised = True

    'derived property - get from the person
    RegisteredOwner = m_theOwner.Name
End Property

'operations -------------------------------------
'Register the log book for use
Public Sub Register(ByVal aPerson As Person, ByVal aCar As Car)
    'delegate to link
    Link aPerson, aCar
End Sub

'Unregister the log book from use
Public Sub UnRegister()
    'destroy the asociation
    'just delegate to unlink
    UnLink
End Sub

Private Sub Link(ByVal aPerson As Person, ByVal aCar As Car)
    Debug.Assert Not aPerson Is Nothing
    Debug.Assert Not aCar Is Nothing

    'link up in both directions
    Set aPerson.Transport(aCar.Registration) = aCar
    Set aCar.Owner = aPerson
    Set aCar.LogBook = Me

    'set my links too
    Set m_theLoggedCar = aCar
    Set m_theOwner = aPerson

    m_blnInitialised = True
End Sub
```

```
    Private Sub UnLink()
        'destroy the asociation

        'deal with owner first
        Set m_theOwner.Transport(m_theLoggedCar.Registration) = Nothing
        'person looses transport
        Set m_theOwner = Nothing                'log book looses person

        'now loose the car
        Set m_theLoggedCar.Owner = Nothing  'car looses owner
        Set m_theLoggedCar.LogBook = Nothing  'car looses log book (me!)
        Set m_theLoggedCar = Nothing            'log book looses car
    End Sub
```

Here is the revised `Person` class. Note that the `Transport` property is now qualified with a registration plate:

```
'Person Class with qualified Transport()
'private implementation of person
Private m_myName As String

'our hidden link implementation to the cars
Private m_Transport As Cars

'attributes  -----------------------------

'get the person's transport qualified by registration plate
Public Property Get Transport(ByVal theReg As String) As Car
    Set Transport = m_Transport.Item(theReg)
End Property

'set the person's transport
'note we could have got the registration from the car
'but it makes it easier to understand the client code
'
'If the car passed is nothing then this means we want to drop the
'associated car
Public Property Set Transport(ByVal theReg As String, ByVal someTransport As Car)
    If someTransport Is Nothing Then
        m_Transport.Remove thReg
    Else
        m_Transport.Add someTransport
    End If
End Property

'return person's name
Public Property Get Name() As String
    Name = m_myName
End Property

'set person's name
Public Property Let Name(ByVal newName As String)
    m_myName = newName
End Property
```

```
Public Property Get Cars() As Cars
    Set Cars = m_Transport
End Property

'operations -------------------------------
Private Sub Class_Initialize()
    Set m_Transport = New Cars
End Sub
```

We also have a slightly revised implementation of the `Cars` collection. This is the same as the previous version except that it has been changed to accept an existing object rather than creating it itself. Here is the revised `Add` operation.

```
'add a car
Public Function Add(ByVal aCar As Car) As Car
    mCol.Add aCar, aCar.Registration

    'return the car for convenience
    Set Add = aCar
End Function
```

Finally, here is the client code to test the whole association:

```
Option Explicit

Sub Main()
    '1 to many, bidirectional association with association class

    '1. create some objects to link

    'an owner
    Dim aPerson As New Person
    aPerson.Name = "Russell"

    'the cars
    Dim aFastCar As New Car
    aFastCar.Make = "Ferrari"
    aFastCar.Registration = "R999 ICH"
    aFastCar.BumpMilageBy 50

    Dim anEconomicCar As New Car
    anEconomicCar.Make = "Ford"
    anEconomicCar.Registration = "E123 ECO"
    anEconomicCar.BumpMilageBy 10

    'the log books
    Dim theFerrariLogBook As New LogBook
    theFerrariLogBook.IssueDate = Now

    Dim theFordLogBook As New LogBook
    theFordLogBook.IssueDate = Now

    '2. Link everything up
    theFerrariLogBook.Register aPerson, aFastCar
    theFordLogBook.Register aPerson, anEconomicCar
```

```
        '3. Print out the car details
        'We can do this via the person's cars
        Debug.Print "Car Registration Details for " + aPerson.Name; " : "
        Dim aCar As Car
        For Each aCar In aPerson.Cars
            Debug.Print "Registration Date : " + CStr(aCar.LogBook.IssueDate)
            Debug.Print "Make of Car : " + CStr(aCar.Make)
            Debug.Print "Milage on Clock : " + CStr(aCar.Milage)
        Next
    End Sub
```

Points to note:

❏   Car objects can now navigate to their associated LogBooks. This was because I wanted to report
    the issue date of the log book via the car.

❏   This is also a good example of how the UML can help you understand quite a complex code
    structure. Consider redrawing the model with the extra operations and attributes added and then
    review the design visually.

❏   I have used the Registration Plate of the Car as the qualifier from Person to Car. This makes sense
    because the Registration Plate will always identify a single Car.

❏   I have chosen in this example to continue to give the LogBook class the link management
    responsibilities. In practice this responsibility will vary depending on your model. The objective is
    usually to produce a simpler model that other developers can pick up easier later.

4.6.14 Miscellaneous Advice

There are many ways to implement associations. Here are some tips on writing good associations.

Associations Advice: Always Hide Your Implementation

Make sure you always hide the implementation of your association behind a Property 'Get'
procedure. If you do this, you will benefit in many ways:

❏   It allows you to vary the way you store the reference to the associated object. This hidden
    reference may change over the lifetime of the system.
❏   It allows you to provide an association that is created "on-demand", to improve performance. For
    instance, you might have an association to a large collection of objects. By hiding the association
    behind a property procedure, you could build the collection when the property is first called
    (which of course may never happen for the object's lifetime).
❏   It allows you to provide a "Derived" association. Because your implementation of the association
    is hidden, it may never actually take up any fixed storage at all. In other words, you have an
    algorithm behind the property procedure that calculates the associated object by traversing many
    other objects.

Associations Advice: Avoid Cyclic Dependencies

Try to avoid cyclic dependencies. Whenever you implement a bi-directional association, you are
effectively introducing a cyclic dependency between the two related objects.

For example, given two classes, `Person` and `Car`, `Person` has a reference to `Car`, and `Car` has a reference to `Person`. If you introduce such a cycle, the VB run-times are often unable to clean up the objects, even after you released the objects:

How should you avoid this? There are a number of solutions to this. The first suggestion is to allow cyclic references but make sure you explicitly break the cycles when releasing a model. The technique is to add explicit `Destroy()` routines to classes which are called when the object is ready to be released.

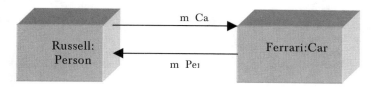

Here is the `Destroy` operation on `Car`:

```
'Car Class
Private m_Engine As Engine
Private m_Alarm As Alarm

'other operations.......

Public Sub Destroy()
    'Destroy all my aggregate objects
    Set m_Engine = Nothing
    Set m_Alarm = Nothing
End Sub
```

Associations Advice: "Keyed" References

Another solution is to avoid cycles to begin with. The technique here is to hold a reference on one object only and an 'object id' on the other (a kind of 'Keyed' pointer, if you like).

So, given the Person-Owns-Car example, we might choose to hold a reference from the `Person` to the `Car`, but on the `Car` we place an ID that uniquely identifies the `Person`. To support this implementation, we will need to introduce a 'registry object' that keeps a track of `Persons` and their associated ID. When the `Car` wants to traverse to its owner, it now consults the registry.

Both techniques have their merits and different performance tradeoffs. It is a judgment call as to which technique is better for a particular situation.

Associations Advice: Use Property Procedures to Provide Read-Only Associations

It is often useful to provide associations that can be traversed but not changed. You can do this by just providing only a property 'Get', without a 'Let' or 'Set'. This will further ensure that your model stays intact for its lifetime.

Associations Advice: Build Type-Safe Collections

As previously mentioned, it is now possible in VB to build fully type-safe collections. Prior to VB5, it was only possible to create collections based on the standard 'Collection' object that comes in the standard VB library. When you build collections of an object, feel free to use `Collection` as your implementation but ensure you wrap up the collection inside your own abstraction. For instance, here's the final version of the type-safe `Cars` collection:

```vb
'local variable to hold collection
Private mCol As Collection

'add a car
Public Function Add(ByVal aCar As Car) As Car
    mCol.Add aCar, aCar.Registration

    'return the car for convenience
    Set Add = aCar
End Function

Public Property Get Item(vntIndexKey As Variant) As Car
    'used when referencing an element in the collection
    'vntIndexKey contains either the Index or Key to the collection,
    'this is why it is declared as a Variant
    'Syntax: Set foo = x.Item(xyz) or Set foo = x.Item(5)
  Set Item = mCol(vntIndexKey)
End Property

Public Property Get Count() As Long
    'used when retrieving the number of elements in the
    'collection. Syntax: Debug.Print x.Count
    Count = mCol.Count
End Property

Public Sub Remove(vntIndexKey As Variant)
    'used when removing an element from the collection
    'vntIndexKey contains either the Index or Key, which is why
    'it is declared as a Variant
    'Syntax: x.Remove(xyz)

    mCol.Remove vntIndexKey
End Sub

Public Property Get NewEnum() As IUnknown
    'this property allows you to enumerate
    'this collection with the For...Each syntax
    Set NewEnum = mCol.[_NewEnum]
End Property

Private Sub Class_Initialize()
    'creates the collection when this class is created
    Set mCol = New Collection
End Sub

Private Sub Class_Terminate()
    'destroys collection when this class is terminated
    Set mCol = Nothing
End Sub
```

Associations Advice: Use "Debug.Assert" to Firm up the "Contract" of Your Operations

By using `Debug.Assert`, we can ensure that the objects passed are always valid before you try to build the association. By inserting these assertions, we are doing just that - asserting that the client code *must* provide a valid object to create a valid association.

Associations Advice: Consider Using Events to Trigger Link Management

Consider using custom class events to trigger link management routines. For instance, if the Car was destroyed, it could fire an event to say 'Hey, I'm a going' without caring who handles it. The LogBook could respond by cleaning up the association. The Car would never need to explicitly tell the LogBook. If the Car never needs to know about the LogBook, then this is one dependency you could drop, which is also a good thing.

5.0 Use Case Diagrams

UML Notation	VB	Notes
Actor 	None	See below
 <name> Use Case	Class	By Convention only. (See below.)

Use case diagrams are basically an analysis tool - they are created to help all parties involved in a development understand *what* is being delivered rather than *how* it is to be built. Therefore it is not usual to map the artifacts from these diagrams to actual source code.

5.1 A Word of Warning

In fact we are actually touching on an area of use cases that is often misunderstood. Often, Developers from a non-object-oriented background will view *use cases* as just a wordy representation of what the system should do in code. As the development cycle moves into the first design phase, the developer then turns the use cases into separate procedures, where the *<<uses>>* relationship between two *use cases* ends up as a procedure call between the two respective procedures. This is wrong and should be avoided!

This is wrong because the *use cases* are there to help the potential users of the system understand what the system will do for them – not how the system should be written.

5.2 Use Cases and Transactions

With the previous comments accepted and understood, there are times when turning use cases into code *is* beneficial and as long as we know what we are doing and trying to achieve.

The useful thing about *use cases* is that they clearly define the boundaries of candidate transactions, (where a transaction is defined as a distinct, logical unit of work that our system might perform). 'Create Order' is a good example of a transaction. In other words, the use case 'Create Order' must run to completion or not at all. If we 'half' created an Order, that simply wouldn't do and could leave our system is a nasty state. Therefore it would be useful if we could help ensure that transactions are cleanly defined and applied in our system.

5.3 Use Cases and Controllers

In considering how we might map *use cases* to VB, one useful way is to map them to *<<controller>>* *class stereotypes* that are responsible for 'controlling' the overall use case and also responsible for the transaction as a whole.

(A *<<controller>>* *class stereotype* is a class that is mainly responsible for controlling and coordinating the implementation of a use case but doesn't actually perform any of the use case-specific detail, itself.)

Let's start by looking at a use case model of the example use case:

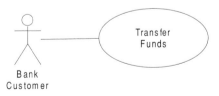

The use case will be performed by the following classes. Note the presence of the use case controller:

This is a high-level model. The two accounts will be the source and target accounts.

As previously stated, the controller is just acting as a coordinator but also knows about the whole transaction. Therefore the lifetime of the controller is synonymous to the lifetime of the transaction and use case. When we discuss collaboration diagrams, we will show how the controller performs the use case.

6.0 Behavioral Diagrams

In contrast to the *static diagram* mapping that is dealing with the static aspects of your design, the *behavioral diagram* mappings deal with how to translate the *dynamic* aspects of your design into VB code.

The UML offers four different diagrams for capturing your design dynamics and these are detailed in two parts: The first part looks at how we map *sequence* and *collaboration diagrams*. They are focused on *object instances* and the *messages* and *events* that travel between them.

In the second part we look at *statechart and activity diagrams*. These are closely tied in with *Collaboration Diagrams* but are focused more on *states* that an item such as an *object* can be in and how external and internal *events* change that *state*.

7.0 Sequence & Collaboration Diagrams

Here is a typical sequence diagram showing some object instances connected by the messages they pass to each other. This is the 'Transfer Funds' use case that was previous discussed:

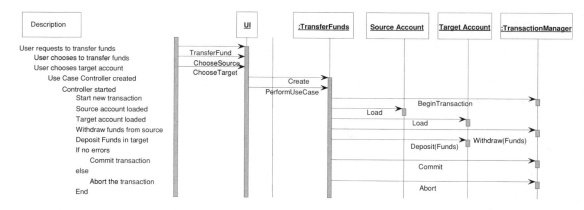

The first thing to note about sequence diagrams (and collaboration diagrams, for that matter) is that they are usually drawn with a context in mind. The first time we use these diagrams is when we are designing how our use cases will be handled. In this case the context is just the system as a whole. Later in the design we will use sequence diagrams to understand how a particular object method behaves. In this case the context is the method.

7.1 Object Instances and Context

This context is important because the object instances we place on the diagram (the columns) are usually named relative to the context. If we are doing the former kind of diagrams, then the objects will usually be given their full names in the system. In the latter case, the object names may relate to local variable names within the method.

Here is an example of a sequence diagram scoped to a method together with the resultant code:

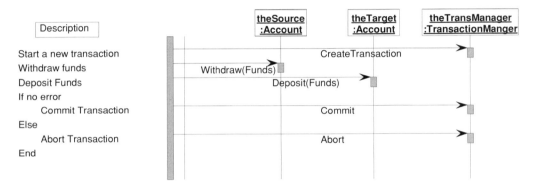

Here is the VB code on the use case controller TransferFunds:

```vb
Public Sub PerformUseCase(ByVal theSource As Account, ByVal theTarget _
                          As Account, ByVal theFunds As Currency)
    On Error GoTo TransferError:

    Dim theTransManager As New TransactionManager

    'Start a new transaction
    theTransManager.CreateTransaction

    'Withdraw funds
    theSource.WithdrawFunds theFunds

    'Deposit Funds
    theTarget.DepositFunds theFunds

    'commit
    theTransManager.Commit

    Exit Sub

TransferError:
```

```
        'Abort Transaction
        theTransManager.Abort
    End Sub
```

Notice that we have slightly changed the logic so that we can make use of VB's built in error system. This is OK as long as we don't impact the core interaction design.

7.2 Interactions

The horizontal interactions connecting the object instances tell us what operations on the objects need to be called (they also tell us what extra operations we need to add to our static model). The order of these interactions is crucial– this is the main point behind (*message*) *sequence* diagrams. Each horizontal line represents a single message and this represents an actual operation *call*. So we need to map this *call* into an actual VB operation *call*. The next question is 'which VB method makes the call?'

By studying the diagram it is usually easy to see which previous operation is making the call.

7.3 Pseudo-Code

The left-hand side of a sequence diagram usually contains pseudo-code that provides more clues about how the *operations* used on the diagram are actually behaving. This code is usually stated in three basic control constructs: sequence, selection and iteration. The Developer can use these constructs to write the skeleton of the related method's logic. So the mapping here is quite straightforward. Once the Diagram has matured somewhat, the Developer will use the pseudo-code as the basis for the body of the related VB method.

7.4 Collaboration Diagrams

In terms of mapping, collaboration diagrams have a lot in common with sequence diagrams. They differ of course, because they are in network form but we are still mapping the interactions between object instances.

Collaboration diagrams do however allow us to show which associations between two objects are being used to perform the interaction. This will be reflected in the names of the objects being manipulated in the procedure, i.e. if the objects have a 'm_' naming prefix, then it implies that the objects are defined at class scope – not the procedure scope.

8.0 Statechart Diagrams

UML Notation	VB	Notes
state	Depends on implementation	Abstract – see notes
Transition	Depends on implementation	Abstract – see notes

State modeling is one of the more specialized areas of the UML. Although all objects in your system have state, many applications such as client-server applications *don't* contain objects with very much state so the need to model *state* is less important.

If you *are* using VB in a real-time systems environment, then understanding how to map statecharts to VB will be very useful to you.

As was suggested in the introduction, *statecharts* have no straight mapping to VB. The main use behind *statecharts* is to understand clearly how objects with complex state behave. Looking at the source code of a complex object isn't very intuitive. So, once you've created your *statechart* and you are happy with it, what comes next?

8.1 Mapping States and Transitions

Although it is possible to explain where *states* and *transitions* are in a VB program, it can be almost impossible to point them out in code. This is because they are usually implicit in the design of a class and how visible they are depends on how you implement your object's state.

8.2 Implementing State

There are generally two ways of implementing *statecharts* in VB (or any other language for that matter). The first way is just to code the object's *state* just like any other. In other words, the member variables of the class *implicitly* define the state of the object. To understand what state the object is at any particular time involves inspecting the member's variables. This could be termed an *implicit* implementation of *state*.

Alternatively, if the object in question is going to have a particularly complex state, then it is sometimes worthwhile implementing an explicit 'Finite State Machine' inside the object. What we do here is create a machine that is driven from a table loaded with information about what to do for a particular combination of *state* and *event*. It is also possible with this technique to change this data at run-time thus altering the dynamic behavior of the object. (This technique is akin to *data-driven* programming, where the data is partially controlling the program flow.)

8.3 An Example

As always, the best way to understand the difference in implementation is to see some examples.

Let's start by defining a simple statechart for a car's security system. Here is the Car's static class model, showing the objects involved in the state machine activities:

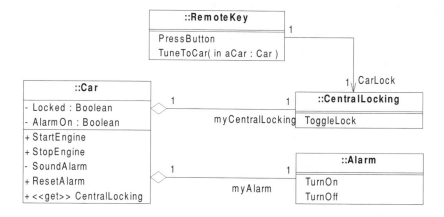

Now, the part we are interested in is the state of the Car object as shown:

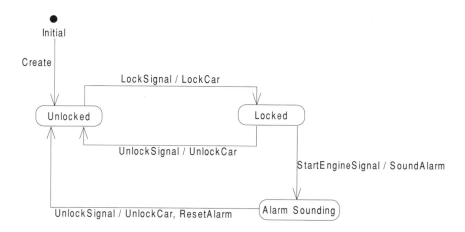

8.4 Implicit Implementation

Let's first take a look at an implicit implementation, where the member variables of the Car define the Car's state:

Firstly, here is the Car implementation:

```
Private m_Locked As Boolean
Private m_AlarmOn As Boolean

Private m_myAlarm As Alarm
Private WithEvents m_myCentralLocking As CentralLocking
'an artifical way to get the car's central locking objects
'this is just to simlate the radio connection between
'the central locking and the remote key
Public Property Get CentralLocking() As CentralLocking
    Set CentralLocking = m_myCentralLocking
End Property
```

```
'initialise self
Private Sub Class_Initialize()
    'create my composite objects
    Set m_myAlarm = New Alarm
    Set m_myCentralLocking = New CentralLocking

    'set initial state
    m_Locked = False      'initially unlocked
    m_AlarmOn = False     'alarm is off
End Sub
```

```
'start the car
'you can't do this unless you're inside!!
Public Sub StartEngine()
    If m_Locked Then
        'uh oh - break in!
        SoundAlarm
    Else
        Debug.Print "Engine started. Brmmmm"
    End If
End Sub
```

```
'here for completeness
Public Sub StopEngine()
    Debug.Print "Engine Stopped"
End Sub
```

```
'I have been locked
Private Sub m_myCentralLocking_Locked()
    m_Locked = True
    Debug.Print "Car locked"
End Sub
```

```
'I have been unlocked
Private Sub m_myCentralLocking_Unlocked()
    m_Locked = False
    If m_AlarmOn Then
        ResetAlarm
    End If
    Debug.Print "Car unlocked, alarm reset"
End Sub
```

```vb
Private Sub SoundAlarm()
    m_myAlarm.TurnOn
    m_AlarmOn = True
    Debug.Print "alarm sounding..."
End Sub
```

```vb
Private Sub ResetAlarm()
    m_myAlarm.TurnOff
    m_AlarmOn = False
    Debug.Print "alarm cancelled"
End Sub
```

Next, let's look at the code for the Alarm (quite simple):

```vb
'The Car Alarm
Public Sub TurnOn()
    Debug.Print "BEEP! BEEP! BEEP! BEEP! BEEP!"
End Sub
```

```vb
Public Sub TurnOff()
End Sub
```

Next, we have the code for the CentralLocking object:

```vb
'Central Locking Class
Private m_Locked As Boolean
Public Event Unlocked()
Public Event Locked()
```

```vb
'this is called by the receiver hardware
'when the driver sends the unlock signal
Public Sub ToggleLock()
    If m_Locked Then
        'locked - now unlock
        Debug.Print "Click"
        m_Locked = False 'set locked state

        RaiseEvent Unlocked
    Else
        'unlocked - now lock
        Debug.Print "Click"
        m_Locked = True 'set unlocked state

        RaiseEvent Locked
    End If
End Sub
```

Finally, we have the code for the Remote Key fob:

```vb
'Remote Key class
'this is our artificial way of communicating with the
'car. In reality this would be achieved by a radio link
Public CarLock As CentralLocking
```

```
Public Sub TuneToCar(ByVal aCar As Car)
    Set CarLock = aCar.CentralLocking
End Sub
```

```
Public Sub PressButton()
    CarLock.ToggleLock
End Sub
```

Here is some client code to test the state machine:

```
Public Sub Main()
    Dim aCar As New Car
    Dim aKey As New RemoteKey    'to open the car

    '1. (artificially) connect key to car for the demo
    aKey.TuneToCar aCar

    '2. lock car
    aKey.PressButton 'lock

    '3. first use the car legally :)
    aKey.PressButton 'unlock
    aCar.StartEngine
    aCar.StopEngine
    aKey.PressButton 'locked

    '4.someone doesn't have the key....
    aCar.StartEngine 'uh oh!

    '5.owner resets the alarm
    aKey.PressButton 'Unlocked
End Sub
```

Considering the complexity of the statechart (low!) the example is quite easy to follow. If the Car had more states and events (which it could be if we considered the whole Car), then an explicit version might be preferable.

8.5 Explicit Implementation: A Finite State Machine

To contrast the implicit implementation, here is the code for the explicit version where we build an explicit state machine to manage the state of the Car object, starting with the Car class again:

```
'Car Class - external state machine version
Option Explicit

Private m_myAlarm As Alarm
Private WithEvents m_myCentralLocking As CentralLocking
Private m_MyFSM As CarFSM

Private m_CurrentState As CarState

'an artifical way to get the car's central locking objects
'this is just to simlate the radio connection between
'the central locking and the remote key
Public Property Get CentralLocking() As CentralLocking
```

```
        Set CentralLocking = m_myCentralLocking
    End Property

    'initialise self
    Private Sub Class_Initialize()
        'create my composite objects
        Set m_myAlarm = New Alarm
        Set m_myCentralLocking = New CentralLocking
        Set m_MyFSM = New CarFSM
        m_MyFSM.LinkCar Me

        'set initial state
        m_CurrentState = Unlocked
    End Sub

    'start the car (requested by client)
    'remember you can't do this unless you're inside!!
    Public Sub StartEngine()
        m_CurrentState = m_MyFSM.ProcessEvent(m_CurrentState, EngineStarted)
    End Sub

    'here for completeness
    Public Sub StopEngine()
        Debug.Print "Engine Stopped"
    End Sub

    'I have been locked
    Private Sub m_myCentralLocking_Locked()
        m_CurrentState = m_MyFSM.ProcessEvent(m_CurrentState, LockSignal)
    End Sub

    'I have been unlocked
    Private Sub m_myCentralLocking_Unlocked()
        m_CurrentState = m_MyFSM.ProcessEvent(m_CurrentState, UnlockSignal)
    End Sub

    'actions -------------------------------------------------------

    'actually start the engine
    Friend Sub InternalStartEngine()
        Debug.Print "Engine started. Brmmmm"
    End Sub

    Friend Sub LockCar()
        Debug.Print "Car locked"
    End Sub

    Friend Sub UnlockCar()
        Debug.Print "Car unlocked"
    End Sub

    Friend Sub SoundAlarm()
        m_myAlarm.TurnOn
        Debug.Print "alarm started"
    End Sub

    Friend Sub ResetAlarm()
        m_myAlarm.TurnOff
        Debug.Print "alarm reset"
    End Sub
```

The `CentralLocking`, `Alarm`, and `RemoteKey` classes are the same but we have now introduced a separate state machine that will drive the `Car` object:

```
'The Car FSM
Option Explicit

Private m_myActionTable(MAX_STATE, MAX_EVENT) As ActionEntry

Private m_theCar As Car

Public Sub LinkCar(ByVal aCar As Car)
    Debug.Assert Not aCar Is Nothing
    Set m_theCar = aCar
End Sub


'build up state table
Private Sub Class_Initialize()
    '               (in state, on event) = do actions and then go to [NextState]

    'lock and car is unlocked - just lock car
    m_myActionTable(Unlocked, LockSignal).ActionsToPerform(0) = LockCar
    m_myActionTable(Unlocked, LockSignal).ActionsToPerform(1) = NoAction
    m_myActionTable(Unlocked, LockSignal).NextState = LockedAndIdle

    'unlock and car is already unlock - do nothing
    m_myActionTable(Unlocked, UnlockSignal).ActionsToPerform(0) = NoAction
    m_myActionTable(Unlocked, UnlockSignal).NextState = Unlocked

    m_myActionTable(Unlocked, EngineStarted).ActionsToPerform(0) = _
                                        InternalStartEngine
    m_myActionTable(Unlocked, EngineStarted).ActionsToPerform(1) = NoAction
    m_myActionTable(Unlocked, EngineStarted).NextState = Unlocked

    'lock signal and car's already locked - do nothing
    m_myActionTable(LockedAndIdle, LockSignal).ActionsToPerform(0) = NoAction
    m_myActionTable(LockedAndIdle, LockSignal).NextState = LockedAndIdle

    'unlock signal and car is locked - unlock and reset alarm
    m_myActionTable(LockedAndIdle, UnlockSignal).ActionsToPerform(0) = UnlockCar
    m_myActionTable(LockedAndIdle, UnlockSignal).ActionsToPerform(1) = ResetAlarm
    m_myActionTable(LockedAndIdle, UnlockSignal).ActionsToPerform(2) = NoAction
    m_myActionTable(LockedAndIdle, UnlockSignal).NextState = Unlocked

    'car is locked but engine started!
    m_myActionTable(LockedAndIdle, EngineStarted).ActionsToPerform(0) = SoundAlarm
    m_myActionTable(LockedAndIdle, EngineStarted).ActionsToPerform(1) = NoAction
    m_myActionTable(LockedAndIdle, EngineStarted).NextState = AlarmSounding

    'unlock and alarm is sounding
    m_myActionTable(AlarmSounding, UnlockSignal).ActionsToPerform(0) = UnlockCar
    m_myActionTable(AlarmSounding, UnlockSignal).ActionsToPerform(1) = ResetAlarm
    m_myActionTable(AlarmSounding, UnlockSignal).ActionsToPerform(2) = NoAction
    m_myActionTable(AlarmSounding, UnlockSignal).NextState = Unlocked
End Sub


Public Function ProcessEvent(ByVal currentState As CarState, ByVal anEvent _
                                        As CarEvent) As CarState
    'first perform all actions for the current state and event combination
    Dim iActionIndex As Integer
    Dim iActionID  As Integer
```

```
            'get first action to perform
            'stop on first "NoAction"
            iActionID = m_myActionTable(currentState _
                                    nEvent).ActionsToPerform(iActionIndex)
        Do While NoAction <> iActionID
            'translate action ID into the actual action call
            Select Case iActionID
                Case Is = LockCar
                    m_theCar.LockCar
                Case Is = UnlockCar
                    m_theCar.UnlockCar
                Case Is = SoundAlarm
                    m_theCar.SoundAlarm
                Case Is = ResetAlarm
                    m_theCar.ResetAlarm
                Case Is = InternalStartEngine
                    m_theCar.InternalStartEngine
            End Select

            'get next action ID
            iActionIndex = iActionIndex + 1
            iActionID = m_myActionTable(currentState, _
                anEvent).ActionsToPerform(iActionIndex)
        Loop

        'move to next state (might be the same)
        ProcessEvent = m_myActionTable(currentState, anEvent).NextState
End Function
```

The State Machine data structures are held in a separate module:

```
'data for Car FSM

Public Type ActionEntry
    ActionsToPerform(2) As CarAction    'currently allow max 3 actions per event
processed
    NextState As CarState               'state to transition to
End Type

'things the car can do in response to state/event combinations
Public Enum CarAction
    NoAction            'used as a placeholder to mark end of actions for an entry
    LockCar
    UnlockCar
    SoundAlarm
    ResetAlarm
    InternalStartEngine
End Enum

'events that a car can receive
'these will be either be sourced from the client or sub components of car
Public Enum CarEvent
    LockSignal
    UnlockSignal
    EngineStarted
    MAX_EVENT
End Enum
```

```
'states that a car can be in
Public Enum CarState
    none        'intial state
    Unlocked
    LockedAndIdle
    AlarmSounding
    MAX_STATE
End Enum
```

The *state/event/action* information has been stored in a two-dimensional table. To find out what *actions* need to be performed on a given *event*, the state machine just indexes into this table using the current *state* and *event* just received.

Each entry in the table contains a list of *actions* to perform in sequence, terminated by the special *action* "NoAction". Each entry also contains "Next State", which is the *state* that the Car to enter after performing the *actions*.

Note that the finite state machine (FSM) is part of the Car's implementation. The client code has remained the same in both the examples. Clients shouldn't be aware of how you have implemented the state of the object. (This is the power of object encapsulation.)

In the example it was decided that the state machine should be a separate abstraction. By doing this we have made the Car class simpler to understand. However this decision has introduced some compromises. For instance, the actions that Car can perform can no longer be private as the state machine (CarFSM class) needs to call these procedures. These procedures now have 'Friend' access to at least ensure that they are not visible outside of the component - only inside.

9.0 Activity Diagrams

These diagrams have a lot in common with Statechart diagrams in terms of the symbols used and their underlying meaning. However, instead of concentrating on the state of an *object*, they generally focus on the dynamic behavior of individual methods and the flow of *actions* within.

In VB terms, a single activity diagram usually maps to a single VB method. You should use activity diagrams *only* when dealing with *complex operations* that are easier to understand visually than in code.

The interesting items on activity diagrams are *action* and *transitions*. An *action* usually maps to either a single VB statement or a cohesive group of statements. We can see how this relates to our previous example. The procedure *call* to SoundAlarm can be treated as a single *action* in an *activity diagram*. *Transitions* are simply the invisible transition from one VB statement to the next so they don't have any concrete mapping to deal with.

The text associated with an *action*, can also be conveniently mapped to a comment near to the statements, particularly when the statements themselves aren't self-explanatory.

For completeness, here is an example activity diagram. This is the `PerformUseCase` operation on the *<<controller>> class* `TransferFunds` we looked at earlier:

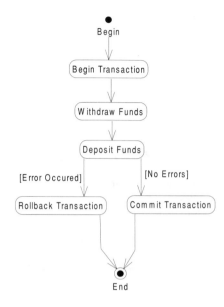

Note that the code mapped from this is identical to that produced from the sequence diagram for the same operation, so we won't repeat it.

10.0 Implementation Diagrams: Component & Deployment Diagrams

UML Notation	VB	Notes
Component	Project	The stereotype of the component determines the type of VB project.
Interface	'PublicNotCreatable' Class	

Table Continued on Following Page

UML Notation	VB	Notes
Node	None	Outside the scope of the language. Relates to a process such as a machine or a process inside that machine that is capable of running a program binary.

10.1 UML Components and Visual Basic

Components are hot stuff at the moment. However, the terminology of *components* can get very confusing at times. A *component* could be defined as any software artifact that is reusable. This could be a *class*, a user control or even a design document.

Still, when developers talk about components, we are usually referring to either *physical components*, i.e. Active X components, DLLs, etc. or *logical components*, i.e. Business Objects, such as Account, Sale, etc., contained and exposed from these *physical components*.

It's important to make a distinction here.

- ❑ Logical components expose services that applications can use, e.g. Account exposes the service Withdraw Cash.
- ❑ Physical components, on the other hand, are the *packaging* and *deployment* of these logical *components* and their partitioning is influenced by the technical requirements of the target system.

This is what Component Diagrams help us visualize.

10.2 Logical components

A **logical component** is simply a class in UML terms that expose a number of **interfaces**.

For mapping purposes, it is probably easier to look at an alternative but more familiar representation:

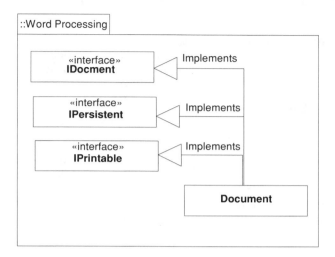

Components also have a private implementation, which typically involves one or more private *classes* that carry out the work for the *component*. The client code using the *component* via *interfaces* is completely unaware of how the services requested are being handled internally. This is the key strength of component development.

Any VB class in a Project that has an instancing property that is *not* private can be treated as a logical component. The classes in the project that have an instancing property of 'Private' are usually there to provide the implementation of the exposed components.

If we consider the Car example introduced in the Statechart mapping, the Car could be exposed as a logical component and the CarFSM would be part of the private implementation.

10.3 Physical Components

A physical *component* in UML is mapped to a VB Project, i.e. the project builds the *component*.

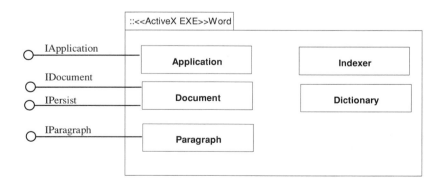

The UML can show a *component* offering many *interfaces* to its prospective users. Here is an example physical component together with exposed logical components and two hidden implementation classes:

However VB Developers should note that it isn't really the UML *component* that is offering *interface* - rather the *classes* within the *component* (project) that are marked as public. This is something that the UML is not clear about. It is likely that the distinction will be clarified in later drafts.

10.4 Stereotypes

The UML comes with a standard set of *stereotypes* for *components*:

An *<<executable>>* stereotype of component simply states that the item represents an executable file, such as 'program.exe', and can be individually deployed onto a node on a network.

A *<<file>>* component stereotype is nothing more than a physical file. However, this notation gives us the opportunity to model files and more importantly, show where files live on a network of *nodes* in the system we are building.

Most CASE tools extend the range of *stereotypes* available for *components* to cover those supported by target programming languages. Visual Basic, for instance, is capable of creating the following *component stereotypes*:

Stereotype	Meaning
<<ActiveX DLL>>	An ActiveX server packaged as a dynamic link library.
<<ActiveX EXE>>	An ActiveX server packaged as an executable program.
<<EXE>>	A regular Win32 executable (without COM).
<<DLL>	A regular Win32 dynamic link library.

Get ADO
connection

[Successful]

Set Recordset
cursor location

Set Recordset
source

Set Recordset
connection

Adding Keys to the Registry

We saw, in Chapter 10, that we could write some VBScript that allowed us to register objects. Let's take a look at how to do this manually.

To add the key to the registry, we must first use `Regsvr32`, and then `RegEdit`. Go to the Windows Start menu, select <u>R</u>un and type **Regsvr32 path\nameofmy.dll** as follows:

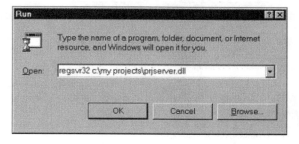

If you've built your Visual Basic DLL on the server and compiled it, the DLL will already be registered and you can skip the step above.

> *I would recommend that you have a machine on which you do the bulk of your designing and building that is separate from the clients and servers which your application will ultimately be deployed on.*

Next, you must manually add a registry entry using `RegEdit.exe`. On the Windows **Start** menu, click <u>R</u>un. Type `RegEdit` into the **Run** box, and then click **OK**. Find the following key in the registry:

```
HKEY_LOCAL_MACHINE
     \SYSTEM
          \CurrentControlSet
                \Services
                     \W3SVC
                          \Parameters
                               \ADCLaunch
```

To find this key, click the HKEY_LOCAL_MACHINE folder, then SYSTEM, then CurrentControlSet, then Services. This should look as follows:

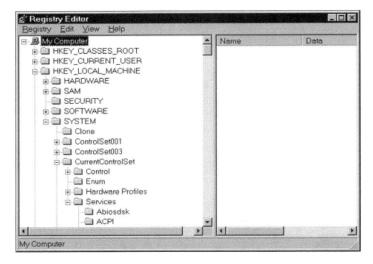

Scroll down through the services until you get to the W3SVC folder and click on it; then click on the Parameters folder, and finally click on ADCLaunch.

> **If ADCLaunch is missing from your system, you probably haven't installed Remote Data Services (RDS) on to your computer.**

When you add a new key, name it with the programmatic ID of the server object you created. The format of the key will be ProjectName.ClassName. For example, if you named your project prjServerTest and the class clsServerTest the programmatic ID would look as follows:

```
prjServerTest.clsServerTest
```

Now right mouse click on `ADCLaunch`, select **Add New Key** from the drop-down list and type in the programmatic ID:

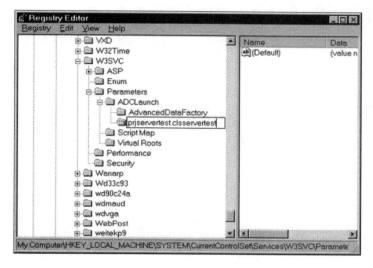

Once you've done this, you can now access this object with RDS through HTTP. As only the name of the project and class are used, a change to the GUID will not affect this registry entry.

```
          ▼
┌───────────────────┐
│     Get ADO       │
│    connection     │
└───────────────────┘
          │
          ▼
         ◇
        ◇ ◇
       ◇   ◇─────────────
        ◇ ◇
         ◇
          │
    [Successful]
          │
          ▼
┌───────────────────┐
│   Set Recordset   │
│  cursor location  │
└───────────────────┘
          │
          ▼
┌───────────────────┐
│   Set Recordset   │
│      source       │
└───────────────────┘
          │
          ▼
┌───────────────────┐
│   Set Recordset   │
│    connection     │
└───────────────────┘
          │
          ▼
```

C

Using MTS

We covered the basic theory of MTS in Chapter 11, but I didn't have time there to explain how you use it. In this Appendix, I will give you a brief run through of the steps involved in placing our DLLs in MTS.

Hosting a DLL in MTS

Once we have a DLL all set up to run under MTS, we need to get MTS to recognize its existence. We can do this by installing our objects into a **package**.

> A package is one or more components that have been grouped together so that they can be easily set up and managed as a collective group.

With packages, it's a lot easier to distribute, administer, and use multiple components. We may have a project with multiple classes that will need MTS services. Instead of working with each one on an individual basis, we can create packages that can be distributed to other MTS servers or clients through a single install process.

A package can be configured to host objects in their own process space when set and run as a server package, or to create components in the process space of the calling base client when configured as a library package.

Installing a New Package

Installing a component in MTS permanently changes the way that the component is referenced within Windows - or at least until you remove it from within MTS. This gives MTS complete control over the object creation process, and enables MTS to return an instance of a Context Wrapper object to clients, rather than your object.

In this section, we'll see how to get our objects running under MTS on a local machine. Once we've done this, we'll see in the next section how we can export our objects so they can be used from a remote client.

Open the Transaction Server Explorer and browse to the Packages Installed node:

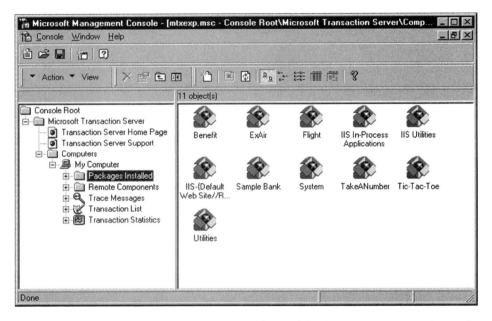

We need to add a new package, so choose the Action | New | Package option from the toolbar.

MTS will bring up a wizard to guide us through the process of adding a package. The first page asks whether we're creating a new empty package or importing an existing one. Since we haven't placed our DLL into MTS we need to Create an empty package:

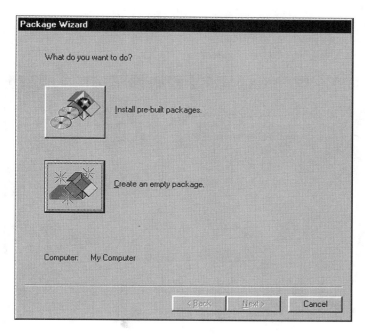

Next, we need to supply a name for our new package. Let's call our package `prjServer`, jut like the DLL:

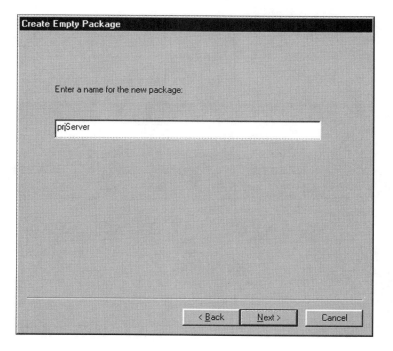

Finally, we need to provide MTS with information about the user under which the component will be running (this page doesn't appear under the 9x version). We can either supply a specific user account or use the currently logged-on user. Typically, you'd want to use a specific account but for simplicity we'll just use the Administrator account:

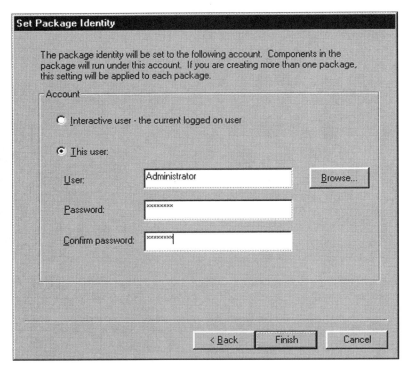

Now when we click Finish, MTS will add our new packages to the list of installed packages:

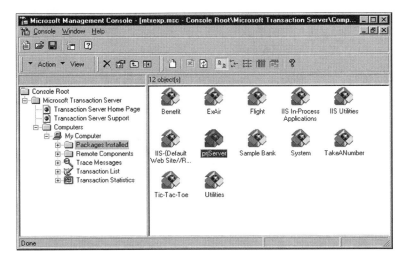

So far, we've only created an empty package. We also need to get our objects from our DLL into the package. This is simpler than even creating the package. It's merely a matter of dragging and dropping. Expand our package until you can see the empty Components folder:

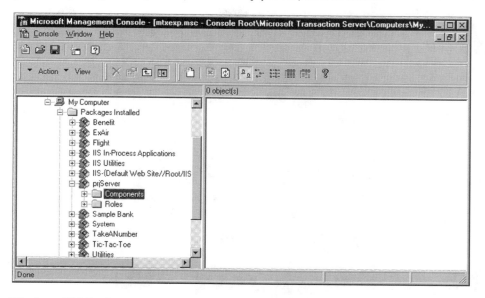

Then, using Windows NT Explorer, simply drag and drop the `prjServer.dll` file into the empty Components folder. The result will be a listing of all the classes contained in the DLL shown as components of this package:

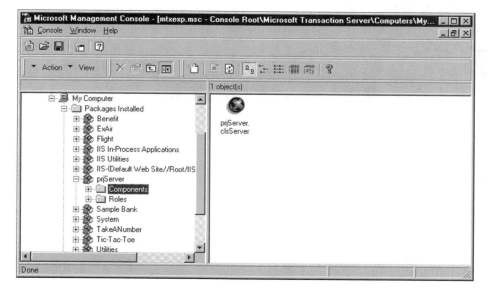

If you then right-click on a component and select Properties you will bring up the properties windows for that component. If you then go to the Transaction tab you will see the setting that we specified in the class Properties window:

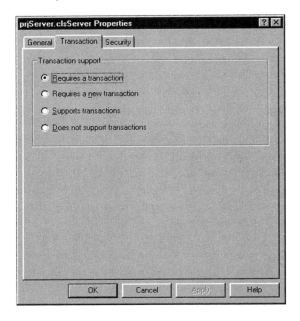

The actual terminology doesn't exactly match those in the Properties window but the mapping is clear enough.

Exporting a Package

Running a component in MTS on a local machine is all very well, but what MTS is really designed for is scaling components to be used by multiple clients. We therefore need an easy method of exporting a package to its clients. Using the MTS Explorer this is easily achieved.

Select the package that you want to create a client set up for (in our case this is the prjServer package) in the MTS Explorer:

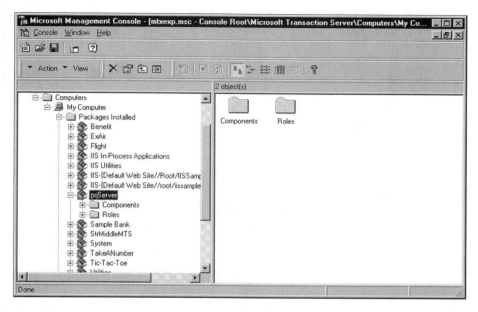

Use the Action | Export option on the tool bar. This will bring up a dialog asking where we want to create the .PAK file. The PAK file can be used to export out a package to other installations of MTS:

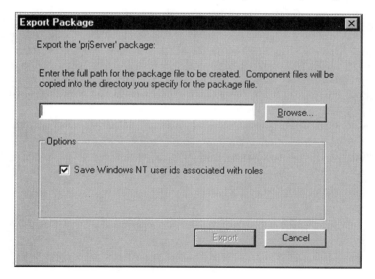

Click the **Export** button and MTS will create the PAK file at the location we specified. MTS will also create a `Clients` subdirectory beneath this, where you will find the client install program:

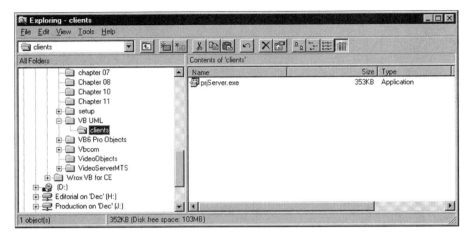

The Windows 9x version cannot generate executables and so you will only be able to create the PAK file.

The client install program has everything it needs to install and register your components on a client. All you need to do is run the executable on the client.

Debugging an MTS DLL With Visual Basic

To debug a Visual Basic 6 ActiveX DLL running under MTS, you need the following:

❑ Service Pack 4 for Windows NT 4.0 on both the server and the client machine. You can get Service Pack 4 from the Microsoft site. It may take a few hours to download unless you have a T1 connection, but it is the only way to make it work.

❑ Debugging only works for a single-client accessing one copy of the MTS server component at a time.

❑ Debugging requires that the DLL is hosted in a Library Package:

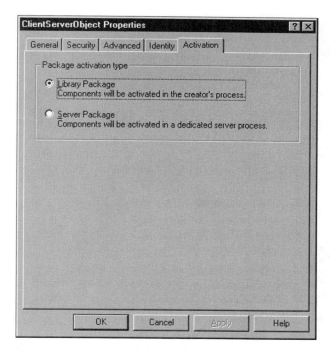

Now if you run the DLL project, you may see the following exciting message box:

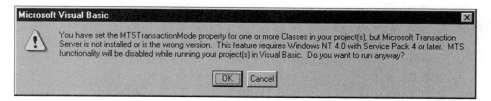

You will get this even with NT Service Pack 4 and the correct version of MTS. This is a bug (documented in the Microsoft Knowledge Base). If you get this message, you need to install Service Pack 1 or later for Visual Studio. This will get rid of the message box, but you still will not get the object context when debugging.

Setting Up a Database

Because debugging any component is important, I would make the following recommendation.

In order to keep track of the errors, make a database called `Debug` with one table called `DebugTable`. Do not allow Access to make a primary key for the table. Make one table with an auto-incrementing field and a field called `DebugValue`:

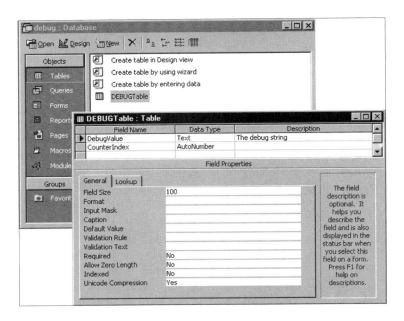

Coding For Debugging

Add the following line of code to the declarations section of the class you will run under MTS:

```
Option Explicit

#If debugging Then
   Private m_objDebugADOConnection As ADODB.Connection
#End If
```

The # creates a conditional statement. I will show you how to turn it on in a moment.

Add the following method that will open our debugging database and write string information to it:

```
#If debugging Then
Public Sub DebugPrint(ByVal strError As String)

  Dim recRecordset As ADODB.Recordset

  If strError = "" Then Exit Sub

  Set m_objDebugADOConnection = CreateInstance("ADODB.Connection")

    With m_objDebugADOConnection
        .CursorLocation = adUseClient
        .ConnectionString=" "Provider=Microsoft.Jet.OLEDB.3.51;" _
                "Persist Security Info=False;Data Source=C:\Wrox\UML\Debug.mdb"
        .Open
        Set recRecordset = New ADODB.Recordset
        recRecordset.CursorLocation = adUseClient
        recRecordset.Open "Select * From DebugTable", _
```

```
                        m_objDebugADOConnection, adOpenStatic, adLockOptimistic
            recRecordset.AddNew "DebugValue", strError
        End With

    CloseADOConnection
    Set recRecordset = Nothing

End Sub
#End If
```

You will need to set the ConnectionString *to wherever you saved your Debug database.*

So, if we wanted to add debugging to our ReturnCustomerRecordset function we could change it as follows:

```
Public Function ReturnCustomerRecordSet(ByVal v_strUserID As String, ByVal _
    v_strPassword As String, Optional ByVal v_strParameter As String) As _
    ADODB.Recordset

    Dim recCustomers As ADODB.Recordset

    On Error GoTo ReturnCustomerRecordSetError

    SetADOConnection v_strUserID, v_strPassword

    #If debugging Then
        Call DebugPrint(v_strParameter)
    #End If

    GetRecordSet recCustomers, m_cstrCustomersQuery & v_strParameter

    #If debugging Then
        Call DebugPrint(v_strParameter)
    #End If

    Set recCustomers.ActiveConnection = Nothing
    Set ReturnCustomerRecordSet = recCustomers

    #If debugging Then
        If m_objContext Is Nothing Then
            Call DebugPrint("Context Is Not Available")
        Else
            Call DebugPrint("Context Available")
        End If
    #End If

    SetComplete
    CloseADOConnection
    Set recCustomers = Nothing

    Exit Function

ReturnCustomerRecordSetError:

    CloseADOConnection
    SetAbort
```

```
Err.Raise Err.Number, "ReturnCustomers" & Err.Source, _
    Err.Description

End Function
```

Switching Debugging On

However, in order for the conditional statements to work we need to set the debugging function to −1, otherwise Visual Basic will simply ignore everything enclosed in the conditional compile # statements.

To set the debugging function, go to Project Properties dialog and then select the Make tab. Under the Conditional Compilation Arguments section add debugging = -1:

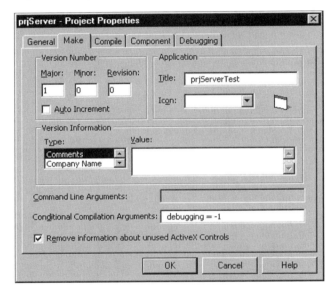

This now turns on all of the sections inside the conditional arguments. To turn off the conditional components, we could set debugging = 0.

Is this an ugly hack? Yes, but it does allow you to get information from your DLL while it is running under MTS. The other solution is to debug using the C++ debugger, but I will leave it up to the hardcore VB programmers to explore that route. Using the C++ debugger will provide the same information found in the Visual Basic debugger, plus additional low-level information Visual Basic Programmers do not usually see.

```
            ┌─────────────────────┐
            │     Get ADO         │
            │   connection        │
            └─────────────────────┘
                      │
                      ▼
                    ◇─────────
                   ◇   ◇
                    ◇─────────

          [Successful]
                      │
                      ▼
            ┌─────────────────────┐
            │   Set Recordset     │
            │   cursor location   │
            └─────────────────────┘
                      │
                      ▼
            ┌─────────────────────┐
            │   Set Recordset     │
            │      source         │
            └─────────────────────┘
                      │
                      ▼
            ┌─────────────────────┐
            │   Set Recordset     │
            │    connection       │
            └─────────────────────┘
                      │
                      ▼
```

Fine Tuning Visual Basic Components Running Under MTS

We learned, in this book, that there are some special rules that have to be taken into consideration when we're working with MTS. Our MTS Visual Basic components will need to call either `SetComplete` or `SetAbort`, depending on whether the component has successfully completed its task, of if the component has failed its task. The last `SetComplete` or `SetAbort` called will determine the outcome. Are there any other special considerations? Yes, there are – and we will look at these in this Appendix.

We will consider, here:

- ❑ MTS Performance Issues for open connections
- ❑ Code That Works With And Without MTS
- ❑ Debugging an MTS Visual Basic Component
- ❑ MTS Transaction Statistics

MTS Performance Issues for Open Connections

When we program with a continuous connection to the database using the ADO, we could write code in the following sort of way:

```
Get ADO Connection object
Begin Transaction
Do something with the ADO Connection object
Either Commit or Rollback transaction
```

In this case, we must keep a reference to the Connection object from the beginning to the end, as our transaction is based on this particular Connection object. Thus, programming with continuous connections requires us to hold on to our Connection object. Every time we make a connection to the database, the ADO must initialize a new Connection object and communicate to the database. This takes time, so it is not uncommon in this type of programming to have a global Connection object that is connected to the database for long periods of time.

By programming under MTS, we now have a completely different situation, because our Connection objects are pooled, and our transaction is running under MTS. When our components are built to run under transactions, MTS will manage the transaction. Therefore, we will not use the ADO Connection object for managing transactions for components set to use transactions running under MTS. This means that we can perform all of the following steps within a single transaction, even though we're closing the connection object between steps in this transaction:

```
Create a Connection object
Bind the Connection object to an Order recordset
Update the Order records to the database
Close the Connection object
Perform some tasks
Reopen the Connection object
Bind the Order Details recordset to the Connection object
Update the Order Details records
Close the Recordset object
Do a series of calculations on the Products
Reopen the Connection object
Bind and update the Products information
Close the Connection object
SetComplete or SetAbort
```

Even though we haven't kept the Connection object open throughout all of these steps, MTS will still manage this as one complete transaction. If we call Get all the way to the Product update, and then call SetAbort before leaving the component, all the changes made to Order and Order Details will still be rolled back. This will happen even though you do not still have a connection to the database with these recordsets.

Some of you may be wondering: Why we would go through all of this work opening and closing connections? After all, database connections are pooled when running under MTS. Well, there are only so many connections lying around. If our application is required to scale to be able to service tens of thousand of possible clients, we will have the potential to use up all of our Connection objects. If we only use a Connection object for the split second that we need it, and then get rid of it while we're doing other work, we will allow other components to use this Connection object.

As for that other question some of you may be thinking: no, it does *not* take time to keep reopening the Connection object. The Connection objects are not only pooled, but they are kept hanging around for a while in case they are needed again. As long as we are using the same data provider and the same data source, MTS will not need to recreate the Connection object. Once it is created, as long as you keep using it, it will be there waiting for us when we need this. Therefore, there is no extra cost for opening an closing the Connection object. The only cost is when we first create the Connection object, and from that point on we will have a connection to the database waiting for us.

To make our code work both ways (with and without MTS) we would probably write a routine as follows...

VB Code That Works With And Without MTS

We would create the SetADOConnection as we did before, except this time we will not call the Open method of the Connection object. Next, we make a routine to close the connection object if we're running under MTS:

```
Private Sub CloseADOUnderMTS ()

    If Not m_objContext Is Nothing Then
         m_objADOConnection.Close
    End If
End Sub
```

```
Private Sub OpenADOUnderMTS ()
    If Not m_objContext Is Nothing Then
         m_objADOConnection.Open
    End If
End Sub
```

Now, in our code we would need to write the following:

```
If m_objContext IsNothing Then
     m_objADOConnection.BeginTrans
       m_objADOConnection.Open
End If

'Do some work

OpenADOUnderMTS
'Do some work with the database

CloseADOUnderMTS

'Do some work

OpenADOUnderMTS
'Do some work with the database

CloseADOUnderMTS

If m_objContext IsNothing Then
     m_objADOConnection.CommitTrans
       m_objADOConnection.Close
End If

m_objContext.SetComplete
```

Because we only want to open the object connection right before we use it, we will not open the connection when the Activate event is raised. Instead, we will wait until we need the connection.

Debugging an MTS Visual Basic Component

With the current service packs, we can debug an MTS Visual Basic component in Visual Basic. The trick is to have the server component and the client component running in two different instances of Visual Basic. If we put them together as a group, we will not get the Context object during debugging.

MTS Transaction Statistics

As a final comment on MTS and Visual Basic, there is a very useful tool in the MTS Management Console. If we open the console, and open the tree, we will find the Transaction Statistics. It will look something as follows:

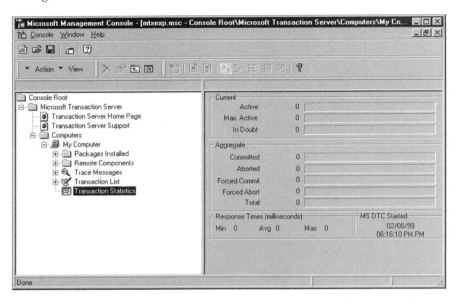

The transaction statistics will show how many transactions are currently running, how many have been committed, aborted, etc. If we stop our server component in the middle of a transaction, we can actually see the transaction in the statistics. I have stopped our server component in the middle of a transaction, and my statistics now looks as follows:

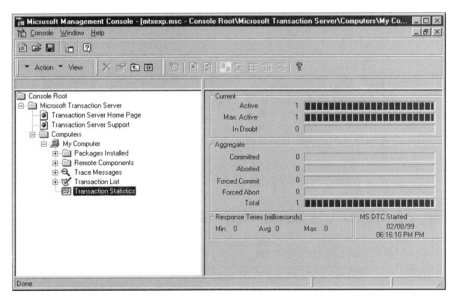

This shows that there is one active transaction, as I have stopped the server component in the middle of SetADOConnection.

A few seconds later, the transaction timed out, so it aborted; my statistics now look as follows:

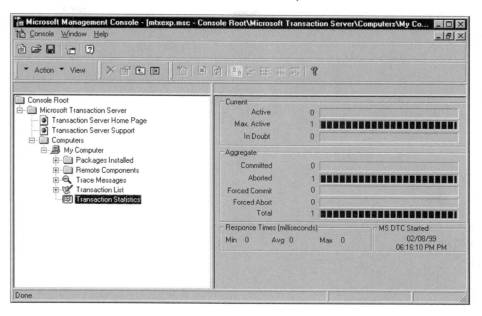

If we right mouse click on My Computer, select Properties, we can set the time out value:

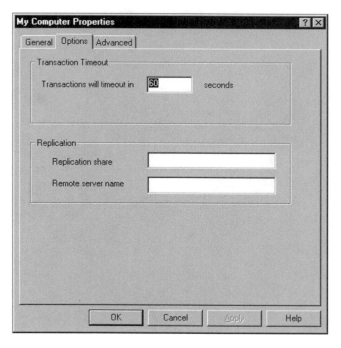

We can increase this value for debugging, but we should remember to put it back when we're done.

Using these statistics, we can watch how our components are performing, and see if everything is working as we'd expected.

Index

```
       Get ADO
      connection
           │
           ▼
          ◇──────────────
           │
    [Successful]
           │
           ▼
     Set Recordset
    cursor location
           │
           ▼
     Set Recordset
        source
           │
           ▼
     Set Recordset
      connection
           │
           ▼
```

Wrox writes books for you. Any suggestions, or ideas about how you want information given in your ideal book will be studied by our team. Your comments are always valued at Wrox.

Free phone in USA 800-USE-WROX
Fax (312) 397 8990

UK Tel. (0121) 687 4100   Fax (0121) 687 4101

VB6 UML Design and Development

Name _____

Address _____

_____

_____

City_____ State/Region _____

Country_____ Postcode/Zip _____

E-mail _____

Occupation _____

How did you hear about this book?_____

☐ Book review (name) _____

☐ Advertisement (name) _____

☐ Recommendation _____

☐ Catalog _____

☐ Other _____

Where did you buy this book?_____

☐ Bookstore (name)_____ City _____

☐ Computer Store (name)_____

☐ Mail Order _____

☐ Other_____

What influenced you in the purchase of this book?

☐ Cover Design

☐ Contents

☐ Other (please specify) _____

How did you rate the overall contents of this book?

☐ Excellent   ☐ Good

☐ Average   ☐ Poor

_____

What did you find most useful about this book? _____

_____

What did you find least useful about this book? _____

_____

Please add any additional comments. _____

_____

What other subjects will you buy a computer book on soon? _____

_____

What is the best computer book you have used this year?

_____

Note: This information will only be used to keep you updated about new Wrox Press titles and will not be used for any other purpose or passed to any other third party.

wrox

NB. If you post the bounce back card below in the UK, please send it to:

Wrox Press Ltd., Arden House, 1102 Warwick Road,
Acocks Green, Birmingham. B27 6BH. UK.

Computer Book Publishers

NO POSTAGE
NECESSARY
IF MAILED
IN THE
UNITED STATES

BUSINESS REPLY MAIL
FIRST CLASS MAIL   PERMIT#64   CHICAGO, IL

POSTAGE WILL BE PAID BY ADDRESSEE

**WROX PRESS
1512 NORTH FREMONT
SUITE 103
CHICAGO IL 60622-2567**